P9-BXZ-598

THE TOOL BOOK

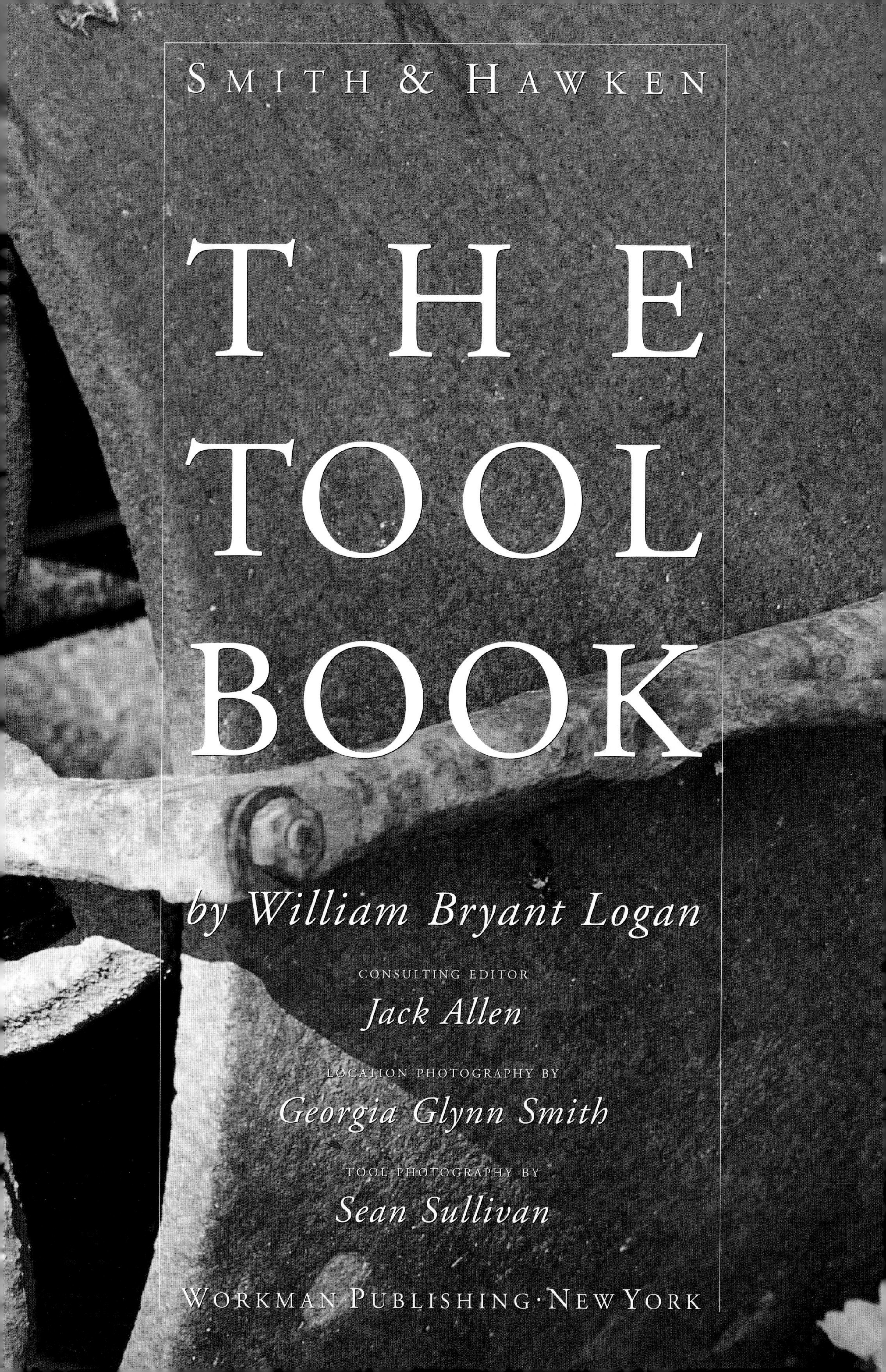

SMITH & HAWKEN

THE
TOOL
BOOK

by William Bryant Logan

CONSULTING EDITOR

Jack Allen

LOCATION PHOTOGRAPHY BY

Georgia Glynn Smith

TOOL PHOTOGRAPHY BY

Sean Sullivan

WORKMAN PUBLISHING·NEW YORK

Text copyright © 1997 by Smith & Hawken

Location photographs copyright © 1997
by Georgia Glynn Smith

Illustrations and tool photographs copyright © 1997
by Smith & Hawken and Workman Publishing Company, Inc.

All rights reserved. No portion of this book may be reproduced—
mechanically, electronically, or by any other means, including photocopying—
without written permission of the publisher. Published simultaneously in
Canada by Thomas Allen & Son Limited.

Smith & Hawken is a registered trademark
of Smith & Hawken Ltd., a CML Company.
All other trademarks found in this book are
the property of their respective owners.

Library of Congress Cataloging-in-Publication

Logan, William Bryant.
Smith & Hawken The Tool Book / by William Bryant Logan.
p. cm.
Includes index.
ISBN 0-7611-0855-6
1. Garden tools. I. Smith & Hawken. II. Title.
SB454.8.L64 1997
635.9' 134—dc21   97–21835 CIP

Workman Publishing Company, Inc.
708 Broadway
New York, NY 10003-9555

Printed in Italy
by Arnoldo Mondadori
Editore, Verona

First printing October 1997

10 9 8 7 6 5 4 3 2 1

For my father, who taught me to dig,
and my mother, who taught me to weed.

A WORD *of* THANKS

A full acknowledgment of everyone who helped me write this book would take a chapter. Representatives of tool companies—not only in the United States but from as far away as Japan, England, and Ireland—provided huge amounts of data. Jack Allen, the tool maven at Smith & Hawken, always sent me in the right direction and corrected me more than once. Genevieve Anderson Morgan, who wrote the tool captions, deserves special thanks. And Jim Anderson's line drawings never failed to bring the text descriptions to life. Lynn Strong's text editing and Mary Wilkinson's wonderful tool caption editing immensely strengthened the book. Paul Hanson's unrivaled book design and Elizabeth Johnsboen's art direction and craftsmanship are evident on every page. Bonnie Dahan and Sally Kovalchick saw the book through rough seas and never lost faith. Countless thanks to all the folks at Workman and Smith & Hawken who are not acknowledged here, but who helped make this book possible. Above all, thanks are due to my editor, John Meils, who got it done with spirit and great goodwill.

W. B. L.

PREFACE

SMITH & HAWKEN's roots are in tools. We were founded more than twenty years ago when John Jeavons, a member of Ecology Action, had a need for British Bulldog tools that were critical for double digging and biointensive gardening. He asked some friends to import them from England, and Smith & Hawken, a company of gardeners, was started.

It has been observed (by Will and Ariel Durant) that gardening is the most ephemeral of all the arts. To be sure, a garden is a composition in constant flux not only from season to season, but also from moment to moment—subject to whims of weather, soil conditions, and serendipity.

By contrast, a gardening tool is anything but ephemeral. Like a good friend, it grows more helpful, stalwart, and dependable with time. As such a tool ages, it becomes more beautiful and acquires a personality all its own. Perhaps Gertrude Jekyll has the last word here: "No carpenter likes a new plane; no house-painter likes a new brush. It is the same with tools as with clothes; the familiar ease can only come of use and better acquaintance."

Tools put plan into action. They are the conduit from the mental image of a potager to the deliciously fresh summer salad or pesto, and the route from the virtual rose garden to a real, fragrant mass of heady, nodding antique roses.

This book is a jubilant examination of good and honest gardening tools. Like all products that arise from genuine utility, they are beautiful to behold and satisfying to use. Consider the ergonomics of a well-balanced English watering can, the clean lines of a nursery spade, the forge marks on a finely crafted ax head. Later, they will gain the patina of years and the polish born of good labor, meeting their mettle after making intimate and sustained contact with dirt and rock and hardscrabble.

A dream book, a wish list, a reference, this is a celebration of the tools that have served gardeners for centuries. They come unencumbered by power cords or complicated mechanics. And they will continue to serve as long as people have the interest, need, and desire to work the soil.

JACK ALLEN
Smith & Hawken

CONTENTS

CHAPTER THREE

CULTIVATING · 59

CHAPTER FOUR

PROPAGATING · 83

CHAPTER FIVE

PLANTING · 115

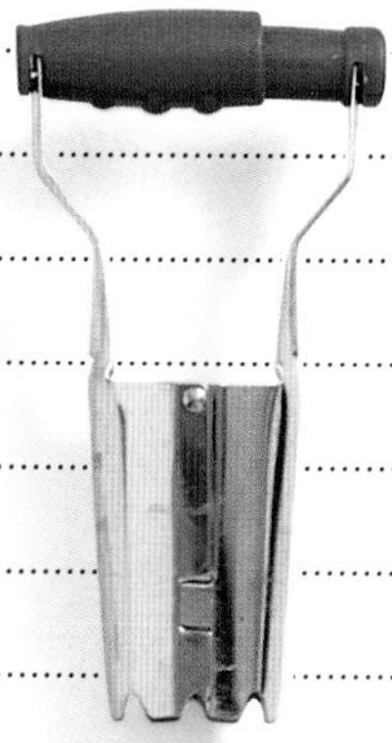

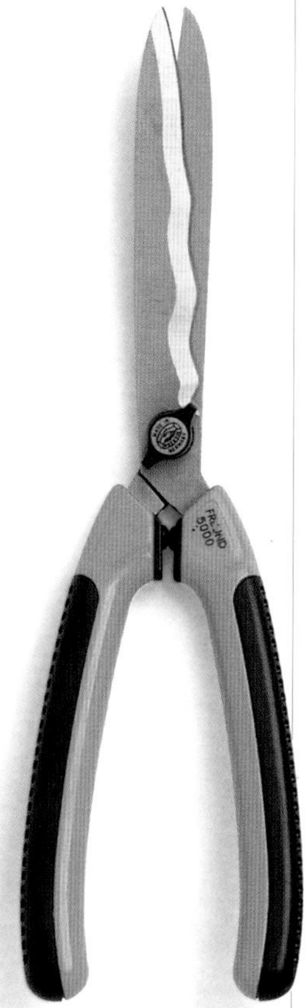

CHAPTER SIX

CUTTING · 137

CHAPTER SEVEN

WATERING · 179

CHAPTER EIGHT

COMPOSTING · 207

THE LOVE *of* TOOLS

In the Mojave Desert, when I was a boy, we had a vegetable garden. It was a little rectangle of green in the front courtyard of one of the ranch houses that were built by the thousands after World War II. The hot sun beat on the garden, but when you gave water to the sandy soil, the plants practically jumped out of it. One warm afternoon, when the shadows seemed as solid as what cast them, my dad and I were working in the garden. I was four years old. For the first time, he let me clip ripe tomatoes from the vine. I can still smell the acrid odor of tomato stems on my hands. Taking the tomatoes from me, he handed them through the open kitchen window to my mother.

Ever after, I have known that this is how life should be lived. But that memory is no more vivid to me than the feel of the tools that made our small harvest possible. My parents never gave in to power tools, even when we moved first to a larger ranch house with a lawn and trees and finally to a wonderful old house nested among conifers and surrounded with gardens. The shovel, the hoe, the rake, the watering can, and the flower shears all came with us from the desert and remained with us always. They never broke. The wood of the long-handled tools went smooth and gray-brown from use, the plastic wore off the shears handles, and the blades were sharpened again and again until they were perceptibly smaller.

Bigger gardens called for new tools. We got a reel mower and hedge clippers, hand pruners, and lengths of hose. In those days, I often wished for electric hedge clippers or a power mower, but in retrospect I'm glad to have done without them.

Through hand tools, I became intimate with the sight, smell, sound, and feel of the garden. The whir of the mower stopped when I stopped, as did the "snick-snick" of the edging shears and the deeper "tock-tock" of the hedge shears. The pruners made virtually no noise, and if you used them correctly, you got a clean cut that showed the living interior of the stem. The cut might also release the sweet odor of birch or the pungent stench of willow. The hose put water in on the top surface of a potted plant, and a little trickle came out below. Where had the rest gone? The shovel exposed worlds beneath the ground, while the rake combed them back into order.

My parents always had good tools. I didn't know there were any other kind. It wasn't until I was older and began to buy my own tools that I came to admire the craftsmanship of the tools themselves. The sharp head of a forged spade head is lovely in itself, not only for its shape and its taper, but also for the way it hefts when you lift it.

A cheap spade with a stamped metal head and plastic hilt looks and feels tinny and thin by comparison. A 5-ply hose is supple and bends without kinking. It seems almost a different species from its cheap 2-ply brother—stiff, kinky, and unruly—though on the shelf they look almost alike. And what a pleasure it is to load and roll a good garden cart, as opposed to a shallow, stamped steel wheelbarrow.

In this book, you will learn to distinguish fine garden tools from poor ones, and to choose what is right for your needs. Often you can find what you need to know by closely reading the product label, and if you cannot, then insist that the sales staff provide you with the information. (If they are unable or unwilling to do so, it's probably a good idea to shop elsewhere.)

Garden tools are more various than other tools, since gardens themselves are so various. One part of the garden may have wet, heavy soil, another part sandy or loamy. One moment we may be pruning a tall oak, the next planting a tiny geranium, the next making a row for the broccoli. One summer's day we are coping with drought, breaking the soil's crust, and on a spring morning we are trying to wade through the mud.

In using this book, keep in mind all the different parts and states of your garden, and think how you work in it. Choose the tools according to your needs. I have always used Felco pruners because they are so well made and so beautiful, but since I began to work as an arborist, climbing and pruning trees, my needs have changed. Recently, I tried a pair of Sandvik shears, with their light graphite handles. Though they may have borrowed the basic design from Felco, the lightweight Sandviks are just as serviceable and easier to carry up a tree.

I can teach you to choose tools that are well made and appropriate for their purposes, but only you can choose the ones that actually fit you. A tool that you will use for the rest of your life, or even for a few years, must fit your hand, your body, and your intentions as well as does a favorite sweater.

There are no objective criteria for this fitness; it's primarily a psychological choice. For example, I have used a long-handled round-point shovel since I was a kid. I admire and use fine spades for double digging, but my body craves a good shovel that is big enough for me to get on the back with both feet and ride. I love the feel of a shovel handle, slender in the middle and slightly bulging at the end, so that you keep hold of it almost effortlessly.

Because tool selection is a completely subjective practice, some friends of mine disagree with my choices vehemently. One woman loves a scaled-down shovel called the floral shovel. It's small and light enough to serve her as both spade and trowel. And while standing, she can dig her perennial beds. She says the tool is so light that she never tires. Kneeling, she takes it in one hand and uses it for fine planting and cultivating work.

Heft, swing, balance, power, grace, suppleness, feel against the skin, fit in the hand—all these are intimate choices that only you can make because they represent the marriage between you and the tool. Everyone has seen a few such happy marrriages: the man who seems to dance across the field with his scythe, or the woman whose light shears seek the spent blooms with astonishing speed and accuracy.

Once, I had the privilege of watching a young Korean woman graft Japanese maples. I have no idea what brand of knife she used, but she cut rootstock and scion in two swift motions, opening angled slices in each stem. Every time, the two cuts fit perfectly together. She would wind a rubber band around them to seal the union, then quickly proceed to the next. This kind of know-how is hard-won and precious. She patiently showed me what to do, but it took half a dozen experiments and a little loss of blood before I got a pair to fit even approximately.

To use any garden tool well takes time, practice, and often as not, a few blisters, bruises, or cuts. But it is well worth the effort because in this collaboration with nature, we produce a rare kind of beauty. Other people have to find their beauty in a picture gallery or on a shelf. Ours grows all around us. We walk through it, kneel in it, sit in its shade.

Perhaps the best thing about garden tools is how quickly their work becomes invisible. The graft makes a new tress with red-brown lacy leaves; the watering brings up a crop of rhubarb; the compost worked in the bed makes the peonies bloom as they never have before; and a timely pruning saves the junipers from cedar apple rust.

Nothing in the garden is ever finished. To our nongardening friends, it may seem as though the whole thing were seamless and effortless. But we know how much digging, cultivating, propagating, planting, cutting, watering, composting, carting, and raking have gone into making this picture whole. And we know that if we do not keep it up, the picture will quickly dissolve.

"What a lot of work!" exclaim the nongardeners when they hear of it. They don't know what they're missing. More than half the pleasure of gardening is the work itself.

WILLIAM BRYANT LOGAN
May 1997

CHAPTER ONE

THE WELL-TEMPERED TOOL

In literature, the earliest gardeners are gods, demigods, or progenitors of races. A woodcut from the thirteenth century shows Deucalion, son of Prometheus, working with a mattock, while his wife Pyrrha stands by with a long-handled shovel. It was a key moment in the history of humanity: the great flood had just receded and a messenger from Mt. Olympus came down to tell the couple that they should throw the bones of their mother over their shoulders. Deucalion guessed the meaning of this strange instruction. The earth is our mother, he reasoned, and all these stones are her bones. The couple pried up the stones with the mattock, and with the shovel lifted them and threw them over their shoulders. Behind them, a whole new race of men and women rose to rebuild the world.

> "My hoe as it bites the ground revenges my wrongs. . . . In smoothing the rough hillocks, I soothe my temper."
>
> —RALPH WALDO EMERSON

In this recension, garden tools were midwives at the birth of our kind, holding a place of honor among all tools. And myth or not, it is certain that fine tools can be passed down as heirlooms from generation to generation. Tools carry the signature of the work of someone we have loved: in the uneven pattern of wear along the edge of the spade; in the slight bend of the rake shaft; in the reflexed fork tine that struck a rock back in Illinois during the 1920s.

Committed gardeners want the finest tools, not only because they last longer but also because they feel right to the touch and swing smoothly with grace. On the other hand, there will always be faddish materials or tools—stainless steel spades or supposedly preternatural weeders—that seduce because of their beauty or promised usefulness.

The trick is to choose solid, serviceable tools at the best price—not always an easy task.

"Profusion" is a paltry word when it comes to discussing garden tools. In 1930s Germany, for example, there were more than 12,000 kinds of spades alone. And even today, when there are far fewer actual choices, the different languages of various promotional schemes seem to imply that each and every tool is better than the last. Fortunately, behind the cacophony of high-sounding claims are fewer than a dozen standards. Garden tools are designed to turn the soil, cultivate and weed, propagate and plant, prune, compost, fertilize, water, harvest, and move material. And beyond choosing the right tool for each job, the gardener has only to learn a few principles of structure and material.

ANATOMY OF A TOOL

Some garden tools are unique in shape. A planting box has no handle. A hose has no sharp end. The majority of common tools, however, have two basic parts: a handle and a head. The former may be a simple cylinder or a contoured rod that is long, short, or even curved, according to how the tool is meant to be used. Some handles are divided into a shaft and a grip; a few, like the scythe handle, have two grips. Pruners and shears are examples of tools that have a pair of handles joined at a fulcrum.

The heads of fine garden tools vary in material, shape, and orientation, according to their use. Solid-headed tools make space in chunks. The head of a spade is rectilinear and sharp to make straight cuts into the soil. The shovel and its smaller cousin the trowel usually have rounded points, enabling them to break into stiff soil, but their heads are also slightly dished to form shallow bowls for lifting and throwing loose material. Scoops have broad, deeply dished heads, made of the lightest possible material, so they can lift large quantities of gravel or snow. Dibbers have solid, thumblike heads for poking holes to plant.

Tined heads rake over the soil or the lawn, drawing along a portion of material and leaving the rest. A garden fork or a steel rake loosens the soil deeply or superficially, either with a few long tines or with many short ones. Lawn rakes are made with heads composed of long, flexible teeth arranged in a broad fan shape; their flexibility helps them ride gently over rough spots, holding on to fallen leaves, without scratching the soil or the lawn beneath. Hayforks and manure forks—according to the number of tines and their spacing—will lift quantities of straw, compost, or other soil amendments.

The heads of some garden tools, whether solid or tined, are angled on the shaft to slice or undermine the soil, facilitating weeding and

Square-edge spade head

Round-point shovel head

Wide-mouth scoop head

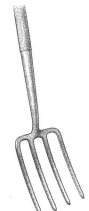

All-purpose digging fork head

Collinear hoe

Four-prong cultivator head

harvesting. Hoes are the best example of this type among the solid-headed tools. Hooks and drags for cultivating, weeding, and potato harvesting are the primary examples among tined tools. Of course, smaller versions of these two concepts grace the ends of countless styles of handheld weeders.

The last group of garden-tool heads belong to the cutters: knives, pruners, loppers, axes, and saws. Here, the beveled edge is key, and, according to the size and orientation of the blade, the head may neatly cut anything from a slender twig to a trunk 4' in diameter.

WEIGHT AND MEASURE

All-purpose pick head

In *The Ergonomic of Shovelling and Shovel Design*, Professor A. Freivalds writes: "The length of the shovel is adjusted to the operator's xiphoid process of the sternum." Indeed. But however arcane the good professor makes the matter sound, the way a tool fits the user is as important as how well the tool is made. Anyone who is about to purchase a particular tool should have the chance to lift and swing it first. Generally speaking, the lighter the tool, the more rapidly the job can be completed. The very obvious reason for the popularity of scaled-down versions of common tools—like the border fork, which is almost a third smaller than the average fork—is that their lighter weight makes them easier and more efficient to wield.

In most cases, longer-handled tools are also easier to use because they increase the leverage that can be brought to bear and thus reduce strain on the user. Parrot-billed pruners are comical icons of this principle: all handle and almost no blade, these tools are even more powerful than the best hand pruners. The same leverage principle holds true for the shovel, spade, and fork. If it's too short, it will hurt—right in the chest. According to one study, a long-handled shovel is 25% more efficient than a shorter one. Shovels usually have hiltless handles at least 48" long, but spades and forks come in standard lengths, 28"–32". For many people, even 32" is just barely long enough.

TAKING HISTORIC EXCEPTION

Writing indignantly to the Royal Horticultural Society, one P. Felgett suggested that standard tool lengths were created in the Victorian era, when people were smaller, and that manufacturers maintained the lengths to save on materials. "The best length for good leverage and control," he wrote, "seems to be that which brings the top of the handle to the user's elbow when the blade or tines rest lightly on the ground."

Mr. Felgett was precisely correct. He custom-made his own long-handled fork, but it is not impossible to find 36" handles in the trade today.

As for children's tools, it's usually best to buy the shortest versions of adult implements. If a handle is too long, they can always choke up on it as if it were a baseball bat.

CONSTRUCTION

From a distance, a cheap garden tool looks almost exactly like a fine one. Much of the unquestionable difference lies in the materials and methods involved in their manufacture. Once you develop an eye for these things, you'll recognize the difference at a glance. The best tool has a smooth handle, and the wood's grain flows steady and straight along its length. The head is contoured properly for its task; it is reinforced where stress is high, and flexible or sharp where it meets the ground or the twig. The material is as light as possible, yet the tool itself has an indescribable "heft" that makes you want to hold and wield it.

Pocketknife blade

The best tools for digging, planting, cutting, and weeding are made with heads of high-carbon steel, an alloy formed by mixing iron with a small amount of carbon at high temperatures. Afterward, the alloy is reheated to a lower temperature in a process called "tempering," which allows the carbon and iron grains to mix thoroughly. Tempering makes the steel both stronger and more malleable. At the right temperature, carbon steel can be stretched to a thousand times its original length without breaking. When cooled, however, it becomes very hard and able to hold a fine edge. (The famous Damascus swords—so sharp they can cut a skein of wool in midair— were made of carbon steel mixed with iron.)

Hand pruner blades

Stainless steel is carbon steel with 18% chromium and 8% nickel added. Neither strength nor flexibility is appreciably affected by these two elements, but the chromium makes the tool rustproof. Still, given the dramatically higher cost of stainless steel tools, you're better off sticking to ordinary carbon steel. In a way, stainless steel is an invitation to forget about taking proper care of the tools.

Lopper blades

FORGED OR STAMPED?

Sharpness is not an abstraction. The ability to penetrate any object is determined by the pressure applied, and pressure is determined by the force exerted per unit area. In short, it doesn't matter how hard you push if you haven't got a slender edge. If the edge bends when it runs smack against an underground stone, the tool is ruined. This is why any implement used for digging, cultivating, or cutting should be made of quality steel. The word "tempered," "heat-treated," "forged," or "drop-forged" should appear somewhere on the tool. In forging, a piece of bar steel is heated and rolled over dies (blocks that help shape the metal), achieving thickness where maximum stress occurs and thinness where a sharp edge is needed.

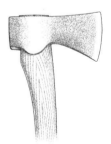

Ax head

Straight-edged saw blade

Cheaper tools are stamped rather than forged. In this process, a machine cuts a uniform section called a blank from a sheet of steel, then bends it into the form of a shovel, trowel, hoe, or whatever it may be. Stamped tools, though serviceable for light or medium duty, are intrinsically weaker because the metal is of a single thickness and therefore not shaped to the particular stresses of the task. Moreover, the socket that fits over the shaft is frequently made by further bending the blank to form an open-backed tube called a "frog." When fitted to the shaft, this kind of socket attracts dirt along its back edge and can cause rotting to occur.

Worse still are those economy-grade tools on which the socket or tines are welded together. Bad welds, visible as a kind of rough scar where the two points have been joined, are a failure waiting to happen. A good tool—even a big five-tine fork—is forged from a single piece.

A forged tool (the lower of each pair above) is heated and cast in dies to give added strength where pressure on the head is greatest. Stamped tools (top of each pair), cut from sheets of metal and bent into the desired shape, are considerably weaker than forged models.

THE TOOL HEAD

A solid head should never bend, but a tine that can withstand all bending forces has yet to be made. The best tined tools, therefore, are designed to bend without breaking. Each tine, or prong, of a garden fork is slender enough to give if it comes up against an embedded boulder. (Even the big 12-lb. forks intended for breaking blacktop can bend under the load.) Top-quality tines are made of carbon steel high in manganese, a metal whose presence in the alloy makes the steel bendable even when cold. All you need is a vise and a cheater pipe to haul the bent tine of a fine garden fork back into line; because of the quality of the steel, the tool is not thereby weakened.

For heavy-duty digging forks, four tines shaped in a square or oblong cross section give the most strength. A fifth tine with a lighter-duty rounded or pyramidal cross section is better for manure or beet forks that will be used to lift compost, manure, or other comparatively light materials. (The five prongs are set closer together, making it easier to pick up crumbly material, though serious potato forks may have up to ten tines.)

The tines of a lawn rake or light weeder often require even greater flexibility to contour its shape to the ground as you draw it toward you. Among the best lawn rakes are the bamboo versions made for more than half a century by a New Jersey company, whose founder got the idea by watching a Zen priest rake the Ryoanji temple grounds in Kyoto. Another excellent choice—one that, unlike bamboo, will not wear down over time—is spring steel.

Most spade and fork heads for digging are inserted straight into the shaft so the gardener can drive the whole tool vertically into the soil; when pulled back by the hilt, the tool breaks up and lifts the soil with maximum mechanical advantage. Long-handled shovels are usually constructed so that they meet the soil at a shallow angle. If you lay the shovel down flat, there will be a 20°–30° angle between the head and the ground. This angle is called the lift, or cant, and is most useful in a dished shovel intended for catching and holding material. And as anyone who has ever slung gravel or earth knows, the lift angle helps to launch the soft stuff into various receptacles.

The "cant" of a digging tool is the angle between the head and the ground. A wider angle (top) is more suitable for lifting and throwing, while less of an angle (bottom) is better for digging and holding soil.

THE HANDLE

One of the great inventions of history, the handle offered new possibilities that resulted in all kinds of tools, from wheelbarrow to saw to mattock. Fundamentally, a handle allows you to stand instead of squat. Its length increases the arc and velocity of a swing, multiplying the force of a blow. A long handle also serves as a lever when you wish to move earth, or a stone, or to sever a stubborn stem.

Every handle is composed of at least a shaft, but many also have a grip or hilt. Consider, for example, the classic English spade, which has a shaft of straight-grained ash wood split at the end and fitted with a wood-and-metal transverse bar to form a YD-shaped grip.

THE SHAFT: A tool's shaft is almost always straight. It has to be; any flaw or bend in the wood is a weak point liable to break under stress. Ash is the preferred wood for shafts since it is very strong but not brittle. (Maple, by comparison, is a harder wood, but it's heavy and breaks in unpredictable ways.) Hickory is the second choice for shafts; though heavier than ash, it has the same combination of flexibility and great strength. When a tool says "solid hardwood handle," the reference is not necessarily to ash or hickory. If you're seeking an heirloom tool, check to see that the kind of wood is specified.

Be sure to examine the whole handle of a tool before you buy it. Almost always, knots or other imperfections in the grain will prove to be weak points that end up causing cracks. For this reason, it's also best to avoid wooden shafts that have been painted. That pretty coat of red may conceal a fatal flaw.

SCYTHE HANDLES

The only tool whose shaft is intentionally made of a soft wood is the scythe. The long, curved shaft of a scythe is called the snath, and it works almost like a whip to propel the scythe blade through the grass.

The scythe is not an easy tool to handle, but those who get past the first round of blisters never want to put it down.

A wood shaft (left) should be made of ash or an equally resilient hardwood. Plastic-capped fiberglass (center) is extremely durable, but can transfer vibrations directly to the hands. A tubular steel shaft with a wood cap (right) is strongest but feels cold to the touch.

T-handle

D-handle

YD-handle

Many garden tools, particularly spades and forks, are now manufactured with fiberglass, steel, or aluminum shafts for lighter weight and greater durability. (Fiberglass, for instance, is 20% to 30% stronger than wood.) One drawback to a metal or fiberglass shaft becomes evident when the tool is used to thrust or strike—the vibrations transmitted through the shaft can tire the user's arms and even numb the fingers. Second, metal shafts feel icy and uncomfortable if you use them outdoors in winter. Third, while a broken wooden handle can be fixed in under an hour, a broken metal or fiberglass handle may necessitate ordering a whole new part.

Metal handles demonstrate real superiority, however, in small tools like pruners and trowels. Single-piece alloy or aluminum construction makes a light and virtually indestructible tool. Furthermore, when it comes to the precise shape needed to make pruners with replaceable blades, a well-made pair of metal handles is definitely a better choice.

THE GRIP: On tools such as spades and forks, a grip greatly increases the leverage, but even the best shaft in the world won't do much good if the grip is ill fit. There should be no proud edges or even slightly protruding rivets at the connection point. And each grip must be the right shape and material for the task.

Spades and forks are usually made with a handle grip in the shape of a D, T, or hybrid YD. All grips (except the wooden T) are attached to the end of the shaft by rivets. The T is the most comfortable to push against, but it can be weakened when the tool must be twisted to loosen the soil. (Good T-handles are mortise-and-tenoned to make the joint between shaft and grip as strong as possible.) Historically, the best use of the T-handle has been for a shallow-angled spade pushed from waist level with both hands in order to pare off a layer of turf or topsoil.

A D-handle is far easier to hold during twisting motions. It has a sporting feel to it—like the handles on ski poles—particularly when constructed of strong, light plastic. The rivet is a weak link; this single metal post takes all the stress of bending and twisting, but long exposure to sunlight can degrade the structure of the plastic so that ultimately it cracks and breaks.

Though wooden YD-handles may be the most sensuous, metal YD-handles are the sturdiest. The former are through-riveted onto the shaft, just like a D-handle, but the two sides of the handle converge in a Y that is finished with a crosspiece made of metal-reinforced wood. Here, too, the rivet is the weak point, but the incurved parts of the handle capture and translate twisting forces, dissipating them harmlessly down the shaft. Again, be aware that any plastic part—or indeed the whole assembly—

is subject to slow degradation by sunlight and therefore less durable.

The wooden YD springs from the end of the shaft itself. The Y is created by splitting the shaft end and steam-bending it. A steel-reinforced metal crosspiece closes the Y across the top, creating the YD. The construction is as strong as a tree root—more so when the Y is partly filled with a wooden plug that prevents the shaft from further splitting. (This is sometimes called an FD-handle.)

Though a good wooden YD-handle makes the sort of tool you could proudly pass on to your grandchild, it must be noted that one prominent English manufacturer has to reject 40% of the timber used for such tools. Either it shows signs of weakness or it actually fails in the manufacturing process, most often by splitting along the grain.

THE TIE THAT BINDS

The most important stress point in any handled tool is the place where the handle joins the head. Forged-solid sockets or long steel straps riveted through the shaft with two or three rivets make strong attachment points. Sockets and straps cause the softer wood to bend up against the harder steel. Good carbon steel flexes but will not hollow out, and the rivets hold the whole arrangement in place.

The tang-and-ferrule style is generally weaker. In this construction, a tapered metal bar, or tang, is driven into the end of the hilt, which is protected from splitting by a small ring of steel called a ferrule. Tang-and-ferrule joints are commonly found on cheaper, small tools like trowels and hand forks. Though serviceable for a time, they suffer from a problem in practical physics. If the tool continually bends, as almost anything inserted into the soil is bound to do, the hard tang will constantly be brought up against the softer wood of the shaft until it hollows the shaft enough to fall out. Nothing is more discouraging than a row of these dead heads (hoes are particularly prone to this fate) lining a wall of the garden shed. The gardener promises to fix them but almost never does.

A forged socket (top) or steel-strapped head (middle) provides the strongest connection between blade and handle. The weakest construction is the tang-and-ferrule joint (bottom); the metal tang driven into the shaft tends to hollow it out, loosening the connection.

CHAPTER TWO

DIGGING

For an ordinary man or woman who has a little piece of ground—as little as an urban tree pit or perhaps a window box—the garden affords the best chance to get to know the world and one's place upon (and within) it. By driving a spade right to the treads deep into the earth, turning up clods, and smelling the unique and indescribable odor, the gardener already learns something that no amount of thinking, reading, arguing, or feeling could reveal: this work is satisfying and the soil is alive.

The garden also teaches true modesty. After all, the gardener does little more than create the conditions for the primordial principals of light, water, air, and earth to work together in the matrix of the soil— to sprout the seed, nurture the plant, and yield the flower or fruit. The forces belong to nature, and it is the gardener's responsibility to prepare the ground, or the seedbed, so that they can work efficiently. True enough, farmers no longer till the ground as deeply as once they did. Stubble is left on the field, and winter weather is counted on to break up clods. And because the work is large-scale, the soil must be helped to care for itself.

> The cure for this ill
> is not to sit still
> Or frowst with a book by
> the fire;
> But to take a large hoe
> and a shovel also,
> And dig till you gently
> perspire.
>
> —RUDYARD KIPLING

The goal is good tilth, a condition in which the soil both holds on tightly and lets go lightly. Such a soil has the texture of a corn cake, with thousands of microscopic channels through which air and water can pass freely. At the same time, the sinuous bends and eddies of these channels catch and hold particles of humus and charged mineral elements that work together with a teeming microscopic world of flora and fauna to feed the growing plants. It takes good tools to make good tilth, because the tool is what connects you to the surface of the earth and to the processes that mellow the soil.

GETTING TO THE DIRT

Three tasks are required to make a fine, friable soil. First, the ground has to be cleared; second, the soil needs amending; and third, the mixture must be stirred. The first task takes a good back and the right tools. Though it is the indispensable foundation of any garden, the work of clearing weeds, brambles, stones, and debris from a future garden plot can seem menial and thankless. Clearing is heavy work even in long-used soils, and one wonders if the job will ever get done. In the Northeast, for example, boulders appear mysteriously to rise through the soil, and every spring the spade hits new ones. Some are small enough to pry out with the spade itself, though more than one tool has lost its head for this reason. The better choices for prying out rocks are picks and long steel crowbars.

A pick weighs 7 lbs. or more. One end is chisel-shaped; the other comes to a point. Properly swung, a pick will cut hardpan like butter and wrap a curved point right around a recalcitrant rock. By pushing on the handle of the embedded tool, the gardener gets tremendous leverage to budge the stone.

If this is still not enough, a crowbar will give even greater leverage. A long, slender rod of steel with a wedge-shaped end, the crowbar is lifted with two hands and then plunged into the ground. Once the bar is under a rock, it's usually necessary to enlist a smaller rock or a piece of wood to make a fulcrum against which the tool must be pressed to loosen the heavy stone.

It takes a good heavy mattock to dispose of roots, whether they are the thick roots of trees or matted, fibrous clumps of grass. A pick lacks the width and the sharpness for this job. However, the two tools closely resemble one another: both are "eye" implements with the shaft fitted over an oval steel hole in the head; both are two-sided and heavy with honed edges; and both are best wielded broadsword style. The real difference is that the mattock's double head has one hoe-shaped end and one ax-shaped end.

No matter how often forests are cleared or thick sod peeled back, they will return if a field or a garden is left fallow for only a few years. The countryside in New England is littered with old stone fences—

MATTOCK'S REVENGE

The most trying moments in the digger's day come when the pick gets stuck beneath a root. When you try to raise the handle, the only result is a wrenched back because the pick end catches on the root. The mattock is the best revenge. Properly sharpened and swung with fervor, either end can cut a root up to 4" thick. It is a pleasure when a stubborn root at last yields and the tool's edge hisses into the soil beneath.

once the boundary markers of farmers' fields—that now snake their way through forests of second-growth maple. When a garden is let go in northern California, the golden grasses quickly grow tall in the vacated ground. And almost anywhere, a stiff clay soil needs the lateral hoelike blade of the mattock to lift and break the big lumps.

FROM DIRT TO SOIL

Without the right tools, a pleasantly tiring task can become back-breaking labor.

Once the garden has been tolerably cleared, the second task in creating friable soil is to spread well-aged compost, lime, and peat, or other soil amendments. Nature accomplishes this task through the transformations that ensue from floods, fires, erosion, the death of passing animals and staying plants, and the fall of bark and leaves. But because we take from the soil, it is our responsibility to replenish its forces. Ancient gardeners did this by letting rivers flood the land or burning off the covering plants—a practice still observed today. On most ground, however, it becomes our job to amend the soil.

Compost is best, because it most closely imitates the cycle of life and death in the garden—returning in digested form the very husks, stems, and half-eaten seeds and skins that originated there. Other organic supplements, such as bone, kelp, and blood meals, imitate the death and decay of animals on land or the flood tide that brings kelp onto the polder or lowlands. Lime and other mineral amendments help to balance the soil's forces, replacing the elements that are leached out of the soil by water on its way to the subterranean aquifers.

Of course, all these materials have to be carted about and spooned onto the soil. This is the step that most people forget to figure into the work. It seems simple, but it takes time and effort. (When you're laying drainage pipes, for example, the least considered and most time-consuming step is bringing the fill gravel from the spot where the truck dumped it to the edge of the trench.) Without the right tools, a pleasantly tiring task can become backbreaking labor. But even with the right tools, a poorly planned job will take longer than expected.

For most lift-carry-and-throw jobs, the best tool is a shovel. When the materials are light and leggy, like salt hay or autumn leaves, a scooping fork is better. Whether long- or short-handled, scooped or dished, round- or square-point, five- or ten-tined, every shovel and fork works on a single principle. Since the blade or prongs are set at a shallow angle with the back upright, you can very easily push the bottom of the head parallel to the ground. This principle is the chief difference between shovels and spades, and between scooping forks and garden forks.

TURNING THE SOIL

The third task in creating good soil is to break and stir it, mixing the amendments into the mineral earth and turning rough, raw dirt into yeasty, fine-textured tilth. A good round-point shovel can be used effectively for this purpose, but the best tools for the task are the spade and the garden fork.

The spade is meant to lift and break the soil mass into clods so the compost, lime, or meal can slip down among the crevices. Then, by turning the soil to break the clods smaller, the foods become thoroughly mixed. In long-worked soils in rainy climates, where the mineral nutrients have sunk deep into the subsoil, you may reach down to a second spade depth (24" beneath the soil surface); this will stir up and raise the iron and other elements that have lain there uselessly, creating a very hard layer of hardpan.

The garden fork is a relative latecomer to the repertoire of digging tools, since reliable ones required the development of tough but bendable carbon steel. This fork takes the spade one step further, allowing you to stir soil simply by shaking the tool. For this reason, "double diggers" prefer using a fork to loosen the subsoil deep down in the second layer of the trench.

A soil that has enjoyed all three attentions—clearing, amending, and stirring—is ready to receive the seed. There is a definite plumpness to a well-made garden bed. It stands up from the level of the surrounding, unworked soil as if it had swollen to make room within itself. Indeed, its structure literally differs from that of its surroundings. Falling water will not puddle in it, nor will the water that percolates up from its depths evaporate too quickly; a thumb can gently punch a hole to plant a seed, and the cupped hand can smooth soil back over it.

Such a soil is a pleasure to hold. You can take a palmful of it and mold it into a rough shape. But when you drop the clods, it breaks into bits, as though eager to return to its nurturing work.

THE DOUBLE DIG

The technique called "double digging," developed by Alan Chadwick and John Jeavons during the 1970s in California and based on nineteenth-century French intensive methods, creates a fine, porous soil at least 24" deep. To begin a double dig, first remove all stones and roots from the digging area. Next, mark the extent and width of the bed. Then, beginning at one end, dig out a swath of ground as deep and wide as the blade. Carry this material to the other end of the bed, where it will be integrated into the mass, and return to your work site. With a strong garden fork, loosen the subsoil and break it up by lifting it and letting it drop back into the hole. Take a good panful of compost or another amendment and drop it into the hole. Finally, dig out an equal-size chunk of topsoil adjacent to the first, drop this soil onto the compost, and thoroughly mix the two. Repeat this process down the full length of the bed, until that first scoop of topsoil is woven into the last compost-filled hole.

Those who practice double digging faithfully become quite attached to their tools, as Chadwick did. He was said to carry his bright yellow garden fork everywhere, even to lectures and dinner parties.

HISTORY OF DIGGING

However hard it may be, digging is not drudgery. It is a way to help nature be fruitful, and to help yourself be fed—not only with peas and beans, but with flowers, shade trees, cool grass, and useful work. The first humans probably dug with their hands, as children delight in doing today. In fact, virtually every shovel, spade, fork, and rake has been loosely modeled on the incredibly supple capabilities of the human hand. To delve, to lift, to throw, to smooth, to mix, to squeeze, to break—all these talents belong to the hand.

But the hand itself has two problems as a digging tool: it is not very durable, and with age it seems to get farther and farther away from the soil, until at last it is painful to cover all that distance. Thus, the history of gardening consists in large part of the effort to find an efficient substitute. Nothing so versatile as the hand has ever been found, but much has been invented that, according to Wendell Berry's definition of a good tool, "makes the work both faster and better."

RISE AND FALL OF THE ROMAN INFLUENCE

The growth of civilization paralleled the evolution of the spade and the shovel. The Chinese had a bronze spade—closely resembling the modern one in shape—as early as 1100 B.C. But it was the Romans who set the pattern for all the spades and shovels that we use today.

The Romans were the first people of Western culture to study and defend the soil. They were also the first to insist upon attaching a garden to each private house. Their garden writers—Cato, Varro, Virgil, Columella—defined husbandry as an art. But as the Empire grew, so did the scale of farming. By the third century, the whole Empire was fed by vast, slave-run farms located on its margins. Columella and his fellow villa gardeners railed against the loss of respect for the soil. They begged for a return to the modest garden and the small farm that was personally worked and watched over by the owner.

When Rome fell, the technology of the forge—that indispensable structure for heating iron to its malleable point—went into a decline. (The secrets of saw making, for example, were lost in the West for almost 500 years.) At this time, inherited tools became as precious as jewels. A spade might be lovingly cleaned, polished, oiled, and kept in an honored place by the fire, until at last its blade had worn almost to nothing.

As the cities of Europe rose, the garden came to symbolize intimacy and right relationship to nature. With the new moldboard

Virtually every shovel, spade, fork, and rake has been loosely modeled on the incredibly supple capabilities of the human hand.

plow, which broke and turned over even heavy clay soils, it became possible to cultivate extensive lands once thought beyond the reach of the farmer. On the home ground, though, the hand tool was supreme because it related the gardener and the soil directly. Indeed, the seventeenth-century garden writer John Evelyn equated the garden with Elysium, the Greek name for paradise and filled the pages of his *Elysium Britanicum* with sketches of everything from cloches, sickles and billhooks, ironshod shovels, and dibbers to a lawn roller and a large moving platform mounted by means of a ladder.

Pride in a small garden plot was experienced by rich and poor alike. And the love of fine tools was an intimate part of this shared experience. When a poor Welshman, driven from his land by the social policy of enclosures, went over the sea to the Colonies, he might take with him nothing but his boots, his clothes, and his precious shovel or spade.

TOOL IMPROVEMENTS

During the centuries between the fall of Rome and the rise of the machine, garden tools kept their form but improved in construction. A medieval spade had been a rough, heavy thing, often made entirely of wood, with only the working edge shod in iron. Beginning in the middle of the fourteenth century, the technology of iron smelting allowed blades that were lighter and more precisely shaped. When the industrial revolution brought high-temperature processes by which steel and other alloys could be created, tools began to be made finer, lighter, and more durable than any yet seen.

The garden fork, for example, was transformed. It had been a heavy and unwieldly monstrosity whose tines had to be quite fat, quite broad, or both, to resist bending. Sometimes the tines would be joined across the front edge to add support, creating a kind of cut-out spade. When Sir Henry Bessemer invented the blast furnace in 1856, however, it became possible to cheaply create carbon steel that was very hard and moderately flexible.

The medieval tradition of the dooryard garden had grown with the middle class, and the yard garden had as much pretension to beauty

SECRET GARDENS

Based on the principle of enclosure, the medieval gardens of castle keeps, monastery precincts, and householders' wattle-hedged yards were maintained behind fences or walls. These enclosures were quite literally sacred, and laws often gave sanctuary to anyone within the precincts of his garden. A man guilty of a capital crime might escape punishment by ceremonially vaulting over his hedge and leaving the territory forever. (This was not an occasional practice; even the length of the vaulting pole was prescribed.)

Whether it was a formal herb garden, the lord's orchard, or a family's front yard, the enclosure had to be tended intensively. To exhaust the soil was to destroy the source of medicines, food, preservatives, perfumes, and colors for dyeing. In fact, thoughtful gardening was a specific requirement of the Benedictine Rule, the founding document of Western monasticism. To shovel manure onto the soil and to work it in with shovel and spade was deemed a religious act.

and order as the finest estate garden. Plants both useful and beautiful had been imported from around the globe: rhododendrons from India, tomatoes from Peru, camellias from Mexico, euphorbia from South Africa, peonies from China. The lawn, once the exclusive symbol of wealth, was becoming a fixture on every quarter-acre. For the first time, a whole family might garden together, not because they had to but because they wanted to.

BRITAIN'S CONTRIBUTIONS

Nowhere have digging tools reached a higher degree of elaboration than in the British Isles, whose fine, mild climate encouraged gardening and where an abundance of turf and peat ground cover required a tremendous amount of digging. There are more sorts of spades, forks, and hoes in Britain than anywhere else. Each different type seems to have been formed by the genius of its place, and was so named. "His face is as long as a Lurgan spade," goes one saying, referring to a narrow draining spade with a blade as long as a forearm.

At one time, every county in Britain had a digging tool particular to its own needs and wants. It might have been one-sided with a footrest or two-sided with a square end and bent at a 45° angle. Some spades were triangular or sharpened on one side only. There were paring spades that were pushed ahead of the user at a low angle to take off the top layer of turf. (These were the descendants of the breast spade, a large spade pushed by a man with his hips and used to remove turf topping.) Then there was everything from underfoot spades, flauchters, and Cornish spades to ditching spades, border spades, and drain ladles.

TECHNOLOGY SPAWNS DIVERSITY

In the late nineteenth century, tools of every gauge and size, for every gardener and for each purpose, were made. A light strapped ladies' fork—weighing almost 3 lbs.—might be so well wrought and fit that you could hold it without difficulty balanced on the edge of your first finger. There might be a choice of three different long, narrow blades for tree planting, all manufactured by the same firm.

Controversies often developed in which one's manhood might be judged by the kind of spade he used. The northern English, for example, favored the T-handle, which was big enough for their large mitts to close around. The effete dandies of the south, they felt, were the only ones who could use the dainty little D-handles.

By the middle of the nineteenth century, the spade was considered so British an instrument that even the troubles between Catholics and Protestants could be stated in terms of its use. "He digs with the wrong foot," went a common saying, since the English tended to use two-sided modern spades worked with the left foot pressing down, and the old-time Catholic peasants of Ireland tended to use a one-sided spade, worked with the right foot.

AMERICAN PREFERENCES

Americans didn't have the slightest use for the spade. They loved the dish-bladed, round-point, long-handled tool that we call a shovel, although they might concede that it wasn't quite as useful when it came to pure digging.

In fact, the immigrants had a whole continent to dig up—one that had never felt the press of anything heavier than a Native American's clamshell adze. A witness to the early need for shovels is one of the oldest continuously operating corporations in the nation: the Ames Lawn & Garden Tool company, founded in 1774 and now turning out about 50,000 shovels per day.

The irony is that the American preference for the shovel probably dates to the Pilgrim fathers, many of whom were West Country men, or Cornish dissenters. The favorite "spade" of the Cornwall gardener was and still is what they call the Cornish spade. If you look at the tool, however, you'll see that it is none other than the American shovel with an even longer shaft. So the great American shovel—the tool that dug its way across a continent, garden by garden, canal by canal, rail by rail—is probably none other than the old Cornish spade.

THE SHOVEL

The standard American round-point shovel is the most versatile of garden tools, and the one that you can't do without. There are specialized shovels, meant only to lift and move material, but the common shovel is present for almost every garden task.

It's easy to break stiff ground with a shovel because the "round point" of the blade, or pan, focuses the thrust of the tool on a single point. The pan, described as "dished" because it's shaped like a shallow bowl in cross section, holds dirt that has been broken without spilling, making it easy to carry or throw a load. The angle between shaft and blade makes it possible to push the shovel into a pile without bending your back. The long handle of the common shovel will let either a tall or a short person grasp it firmly when driving the blade into the soil. It also lets you adjust your hands for the best leverage when you're lifting a full pan.

With a good round-point shovel, there is little you can't do in the garden. You can mix cement to fix the walk or move soil, compost, or gravel for a drainage ditch. Its long handle focuses the energy of your

The great American shovel is probably none other than the old Cornish spade.

thrust, making it a good posthole digger. It can even cut medium-size roots and pry up large stones. It won't dig as neatly as a square-point spade, but for most plant beds in American gardens a straight line hardly matters. And the curved edge is actually more convenient when it comes to digging around perennials or shrubs for transplanting. Because the blade is set at an angle to the shaft, you can even use a shovel as a scuffle hoe in a pinch—to cut off weeds at the soil surface.

The all-purpose round-point shovel led to the evolution of dozens of specialized versions, from the short-handled, broad-bladed contractor's shovel to the light, deeply dished floral shovel. Each version has been designed to take advantage of one special capability of the shovel form.

CHOOSING A SHOVEL

Shovels can be bought almost anywhere. The trouble is, some models are no more long-lasting than the pair of chopsticks that come with takeout. On the cheaper ones, the shaft snaps, the socket parts from the blade, or the point bends the first time it strikes a stone.

To buy a long-lasting shovel, you must know about its construction and the manufacturers' system for grading the quality of different lines of tools.

To buy a long-lasting shovel, you must know about its construction and the manufacturers' system for grading the quality of different lines of tools. For light duty, a "homeowner's" grade may do, but if you're a serious gardener you'll definitely want to buy the top-of-the-line contractor's grade.

An open-back shovel is usually the cheapest and least durable. Turn it over, and you'll see a hollow depression in the back of the blade where the shaft is fit. This type is usually made by rolling out a piece of metal flat for the head, then stamping out the pattern and folding it into shape. The stamped steel is of uniform thickness, and on cheaper shovels it may be of a gauge too light to resist bending on a stone. (When considering metal thickness, or gauge, a lower number means greater thickness. The strongest gauge of steel available in a shovel is 14. A gauge of 15 is fine, and for most uses 16 is adequate, but an 18-gauge shovel head is not worth owning.)

The folding procedure mentioned above produces a dished blade with a hollow-backed protrusion called the "frog." Folding makes the blade stronger (just as you make a piece of paper stronger at the edge by gathering the paper near the opposite edge), but it also creates a zone of weakness at the front edge of the frog, where the stresses of digging are focused. Not only will an open-back shovel usually either break at the frog or bend at the front edge, but it also has a problem owing to the back itself. The open dimple collects dirt that, if not thoroughly cleaned out after use, can eventually corrode the metal and rot away the wood of the shaft. A closed-back shovel solves one of these problems. Though the back is often merely welded on, it still keeps dirt out. But this style does little to strengthen the edge or the front of the frog.

By far the best and strongest shovels have heads made of a single forged and tempered piece of steel. The socket is closed, so there is no hollow frog to contend with, and it is an integral part of the head. Furthermore, the process of forging allows the smith to taper the blade for better penetration and to thicken the metal where bending stresses are high. Such shovels are more expensive because more work and care are required to make them, but for long-term value and heavy-duty use, they're unquestionably the best choice.

Knowing something about materials and construction will help you choose the right shovel. Keep in mind that the three big companies use a grading system to distinguish their lines of tools. In general, the best lines are solid-socket shovels, while the cheapest, or promotional, lines are open-back models constructed with light-gauge steel.

Lightweight scoops are another matter. The heads of these tools are usually twice as large as standard shovel blades. Often, the blades are made of lightweight steel or aluminum alloy or of plastic. The handle is inserted into the blade socket but usually less deeply than an all-purpose shovel.

The last variable in shovel design is the tread—the slender, flattened area on the back edge of some shovel blades. Many good shovels have a rolled tread, in which metal has been rolled backward from the face of the shovel to make a small step on either side of the shaft. A forward-turned shovel tread is best; not only is it more comfortable to step on, but it will also help to hold material in the shovel's pan.

ANATOMY OF A ROUND-POINT SHOVEL

The double-tapered handle is made of straight, tight-grained ash or fiberglass with a solid core. At its narrowest point (approximately 6" from the top of the shovel), the shaft should fit loosely in a circled hand.

Features a closed-back, or solid-forged, solid-shank construction.

Wide forward-rolled tread is comfortable and safe.

A strong "dish" to the blade makes it more stiff and able to hold dirt better.

The round point allows easy penetration of a variety of materials.

USING THE SHOVEL

For digging or scooping, wear a good pair of hard-soled boots. Many shovels, even some of high quality, have no tread to protect the soles of your feet from the back edge of the tool. And even if the shovel has a tread, it's better to wear boots that will resist the bruising pressure of repeatedly applying your full weight to the tool. Never jump on the tread; it isn't healthy for the shovel or your ankles. To dig down, apply firm pressure with the whole weight of your body. Then, standing straight, pull back on the handle to loosen a panful of soil.

To scoop loose matter, bend at the knees and thrust the tool into the mass, holding it parallel to the ground. If you bend properly and move your hips to throw, it can feel like getting a massage. (Even aged adepts of the practice of tai chi perform a movement called "squatting single whip," which is essentially the same movement as the correct use of a shovel.)

There is only one additional catch to the shovel motion. At its low point, you must pick up the material in question. The trick is not to take too much at a time. The greatest temptation is to carry too much with a single scoop. Instead of digging deep into a mound of soil, take slices from the edge. A century's worth of studies conducted in coal mines and among road crews have demonstrated that a faster rhythm with lighter loads is far more efficient and less likely to cause injury.

ROUND-POINT SHOVELS: The standard round-point shovel has a blade about 8" wide and 12" deep. (In the old parlance of shovel sizes, this is a #2 head.) The best shovel shafts are made of straight-grain ash. Though some shovels come with short D-handles, most have long shafts contoured with a slender waist and bulbous end, like an elongated Coke bottle. A shaped shaft is easier to grip than a shaft like a broom-handle. For heavy-duty use, there are fiberglass- and steel-shaft shovels. Though fiberglass is 30% to 50% stronger than wood, it's harder to attach to the head. Steel, of course, is also much harder to break than wood, but like fiberglass it's not as good as wood in absorbing the shock of striking a rock or a root.

Since the round-point shovel is designed for digging, lifting, and throwing, its head has low to moderate lift. (To figure the lift, measure the elevation of the end of the blade above the ground when the tool is lying flat, face side up. A 6" lift is common in general-purpose shovels.)

Border and Floral Shovels. Among the most popular shovels today are the lightweight, small-bladed ones called border and/or floral shovels. (There are even gardeners who look for old World War I shovels because they're about this size.) This class of shovel is made like the large round-point shovel, except that the blade is typically one-half to two-thirds the size of the standard type, the handle is correspondingly shorter, and sometimes the blade is more deeply dished. The border shovel can be operated easily while you're on your knees transplanting a perennial, for instance. With the rootball in one hand, you can take the shovel in the other and adjust the planting hole to the proper width and depth.

Correct shovel use begins with driving the shovel straight down into the soil (or parallel to the ground when shoveling a pile). Stand straight up as you pull back on the shaft to loosen dirt. When scooping, bend at the knees and use your hips to throw the pile to the side or into the wheelbarrow.

The dishing of the blade seems to be particularly useful for transplanting container-grown plants.

SQUARE-POINT SHOVELS: This shovel, meant only for moving material, is flat-bottomed, unsharpened, and shaped like a long-handled scoop. (Its Irish ancestor has the picturesque name "frying pan shovel.") The blade lift is higher than that of the general-purpose shovel, making it useful for digging but much more adept at lifting and moving; with a slight flex of the knees, never bending the back, you can thrust such a shovel into a pile and withdraw it with ease.

The square-point shovel is the standard for mixing concrete. Its steep sides hold the sloppy mix, and the square end deposits it accurately where wanted. This shovel can be found with a long shaft or a shorter, YD-handled one.

SCOOPS: The scoop shovel has a much larger head, easily twice the size of the standard square-end type. If it were made of steel, it would take Paul Bunyan to lift it. Plastic and aluminum are now the usual materials used for scoops. As a result, they have little mass to help you thrust them into soil or gravel. For handling snow, grain, or light mulch, however, they are unsurpassed.

There are two patterns of scoop: the Western and the Eastern. No one seems to know why they were thus distinguished. The two models have different patterns of ribbing worked into the pan of the tool, but there appears to be no difference at all in function.

The numbering system frequently used for scoops goes in even numbers from 8 to 12. The number refers simply to the width (in inches) of the blade.

TRENCHING SHOVELS: These shovels are among the most beautiful, so it's ironic that they're intended for the yeoman labor of digging drainage trenches and irrigation channels. The heads are typically twice as long as they are wide, and they may have square, pointed, or rounded edges. The most curious-looking one—the high-lift trenching shovel—is bent almost 90° at the angle and has an extra-long handle. The idea is to reach to the bottom of a trench and make it smooth while scarcely bending your back.

Round-Point Shovels

1. OPEN-BACK BORDER SHOVEL

2. TREADED GENERAL-SERVICE SHOVEL

3. POWERFLEX FIBERGLASS-HANDLED SHOVEL

4. FLORAL SHOVEL

5. OPEN-BACK SHOVEL

6. RAZORBACK CLOSED-BACK SHOVEL

7. FIBERGLASS-HANDLED SHOVEL

1. **OPEN-BACK BORDER SHOVEL:** This tool features a small head, ideal for all-purpose work in flower beds and for digging holes for transplants. Graceful and lightweight, it is a good-quality shovel for smaller hands and sensitive backs. The handle is tapered at the top to fit snugly in the palm without chafing. A reinforced, riveted socket allows the user to scoop up large loads without breaking or bending the blade, which is made from open-back, stamped steel. The forward-rolled tread grips the foot. LENGTH 52½", WEIGHT 2.5 LBS., HEAD 6" × 8".

2. **TREADED GENERAL-SERVICE SHOVEL:** A professional-quality shovel designed in England and built to withstand even the most serious shoveling. It boasts a deeply canted, solid-forged, high-carbon steel head, solid-strap construction, and a hardwood handle ending in a T-grip. Ideal for moving heavy loads such as gravel from one spot to another, the deep cant lets the user dig deeply into a pile without having to bend over too far. LENGTH 37", WEIGHT 4.7 LBS., HEAD 7¾" × 9¾".

3. **POWERFLEX FIBERGLASS-HANDLED SHOVEL:** This large shovel is essentially the same tool as the Razorback Closed-Back Shovel, only it's equipped with a patent-pending lightweight fiberglass handle (no splinters!) strengthened by a northern white ash core. The high-carbon stamped-steel head is connected by a joint that is reinforced with two rivets. A large tool with a wide head, intended for hard work in unrestricted areas. LENGTH 58", WEIGHT 5 LBS., HEAD 8½" × 11¾".

4. **FLORAL SHOVEL:** A top-quality tool designed for use in flower beds and other tight working spaces. It's easy to maneuver and, with a smaller head, accomplishes many of the same tasks as the Open-Back Border Shovel, but due to the YD-grip, it may be preferred by those who must work in heavy or clay soil. The solid-forged (not stamped) steel head gives this particular version by Bulldog added durability, as do the solid-socket construction and ash handle. LENGTH 36¾", WEIGHT 4.2 LBS., HEAD 7" × 9½".

8. SOLID-FORGED SHOVEL

9. CONTRACTOR'S SHOVEL

11. FORGED IRRIGATION SHOVEL

10. LI'L PAL SHOVEL

5. OPEN-BACK SHOVEL:

A good-quality example of a standard, medium-size shovel designed for all-purpose work. The open-back, epoxy-coated, stamped steel head is connected to the handle by a double-bolted, solid-socket joint. Attractive and easy to care for, this is a good choice for the home gardener, without a huge investment. LENGTH 56½", WEIGHT 3.4 LBS., HEAD 4½" × 11".

6. RAZORBACK CLOSED-BACK SHOVEL:

This heavy-duty, large-headed tool will stand up to hard use in home gardens without a big financial invest-ment. Good-quality construction features a 14-gauge, heat-treated, closed-back steel head for added strength; a forward-rolled tread with reinforced riveted socket; and a pol-ished hardwood han-dle. LENGTH 60", WEIGHT 6 LBS., HEAD 9¾" × 11½".

7. FIBERGLASS-HANDLED SHOVEL:

The long-lasting fiberglass handle and steel collar distin-guish this light-weight, all-purpose shovel. Polypropy-lene YD-grip and large head allow the user to dig in deep and transfer a large load of soil or other material. The open-back, heat-tempered steel head with for-ward-rolled tread lends added stability. Shorter length and lighter materials may be preferred by smaller users who don't want to sacri-fice load capacity for heft. LENGTH 37", WEIGHT 3.7 LBS., HEAD 8½" × 11½".

8. SOLID-FORGED SHOVEL:

This long-handled, solid-shank shovel has been used for a century. The solid-forged steel blade with forward-rolled tread is the best shovel head money can buy. Hardwood ash han-dle and solid-socket construction are designed to with-stand years of hard use by both profes-sional gardeners and home users. A time-less silhouette and fine craftsmanship make this tool by Bulldog a joy to work with. LENGTH 60", WEIGHT 6 LBS., HEAD 8½" × 11½".

9. CONTRACTOR'S SHOVEL:

A top-quality shovel, used primarily by profes-sional contractors due to superior con-struction. Extra-wide, solid-shank forged steel head is flatter than that of an all-purpose shovel. A great tool for trans-ferring heavy bulk materials like stones or gravel from one place to another, this is also an opti-mal digging imple-ment. Solid-shank construction and ash handle with YD-grip allow user to thrust the shovel deeply into a pile and lift out a large load. This tool is a good choice for gardeners who plan to do extremely heavy-duty tasks. LENGTH 39", WEIGHT 6.2 LBS., HEAD 10½" × 12½".

10. LI'L PAL SHOVEL:

This is a handy, practical shovel, ideal for use in small areas, patios, beds, borders, and roof gardens. The very small head and plastic handle yield an extremely light-weight, maneuver-able tool that does not sacrifice crafts-manship. Open-back, heat-tempered steel head is connect-ed to the handle by a solid shaft extending three-quarters of the way up the handle. YD-grip is rot-resis-tant polypropylene. Shorter length makes this a good tool for kids or when working on knees; also a good choice for setting out transplants and other lighter tasks. LENGTH 26½", WEIGHT 1.7 LBS., HEAD 6" × 8½".

11. FORGED IRRIGATION SHOVEL:

Another variation of a very small-headed shovel, originally designed to dig small trenches for irrigation and sprinkler pipes. This example fea-tures a solid-shank steel head, solid-forged construction, and a varnished hardwood handle. Good for digging around existing plants or in restrict-ed areas. The long handle makes it less agile, but it may be preferred by users who like to dig standing up. LENGTH 56", WEIGHT 4 LBS., HEAD 7" × 9½".

Square-Point Shovels

1. OPEN-SOCKET SHOVEL:
This good-quality, all-purpose shovel is distinguished by its T-shaped handle, which makes it a good tool for inserting deeply into a pile of loose material. Large, splayed, open-back, tempered steel head is attached by rolled-socket construction to a hardwood handle, and reinforced with a metal collar. Deep cant allows the user to scoop up a large load without having to bend over too far. Shorter handle makes the shovel easier to control.
LENGTH 39",
WEIGHT 4.7 LBS.,
HEAD 9¾" × 12½".

2. FIBERGLASS-HANDLED SHOVEL WITH STEEL COLLAR:
A sturdy, affordable, all-purpose shovel for heavy-duty lifting and moving. The long fiberglass handle attaches to an open-back, 14-gauge steel head by a socket strengthened with a solid-steel collar. Fiberglass handle is rot-resistant and light, while the reinforced collar guards against breakage by transferring the weight evenly up the shaft. The head scoops a large load.
LENGTH 58",
WEIGHT 4.1 LBS.,
HEAD 9" × 11".

3. MEDIUM SQUARE SHOVEL:
This hard-to-find shovel is useful for many light tasks that demand more control. Superior manufacturing features a forged steel head, solid-socket construction, and an ash handle with a steel-and-wood YD-grip. A top-quality tool for smaller users who may appreciate its scaled-down size but who demand long-lasting craftsmanship. This is an ideal shovel for carrying and spreading loose material, like sifted compost or mulch, around garden beds.
LENGTH 37",
WEIGHT 5.1 LBS.,
HEAD 8" × 10½".

4. STEEL-SHAFTED SHOVEL:
A classic, all-purpose shovel. This particular version, however, is crafted almost entirely from metal. The large head is solid-forged steel, the handle is heavy-duty tubular steel, and the YD-grip is made from steel with a hand-saving wood grip. Extremely tough, it is a superior choice for moving large, bulky materials and for spreading concrete, and is preferred by professional contractors and road crews. May be more suited to strong users who want a lot of heft.
LENGTH 38½",
WEIGHT 6.8 LBS.,
HEAD 10" × 12½".

1. OPEN-SOCKET SHOVEL

3. MEDIUM SQUARE SHOVEL

2. FIBERGLASS-HANDLED SHOVEL WITH STEEL COLLAR

4. STEEL-SHAFTED SHOVEL

5. CHUCKED-SOCKET SHOVEL

6. LARGE SQUARE SHOVEL

5. CHUCKED-SOCKET SHOVEL: This example features a long handle and a unique chucked socket. The heat-treated, 14-gauge steel head is stamped and connected to a traditional ash handle, strengthened by a single rivet.
LENGTH 59",
WEIGHT 4.1 LBS.,
HEAD 9½" × 11".

6. LARGE SQUARE SHOVEL: A top-quality, solid-forged steel head and weldless solid-socket construction make up the backbone of this classic YD-grip square-point shovel. This large tool is a great option for loading, lifting, and transferring bulk materials, spreading concrete and gravel, and other heavy-duty tasks.
LENGTH 38¾",
WEIGHT 6.2 LBS.,
HEAD 10" × 12¼".

Scoops

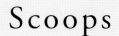

1. STEEL EASTERN SCOOP

2. ALUMINUM SCOOP

3. STEEL WESTERN SCOOP

4. PLASTIC GRAIN SCOOP

1. **STEEL EASTERN SCOOP:** This style scoop has a splayed, epoxy-coated steel head. Lightweight and durable, it is a good-quality mid-size choice for lifting and transferring airy, loose materials like grain and mulch. Slightly squatter shape identifies the head as Eastern. This example boasts a wide mouth and a deeply canted, high-carbon steel head with a 21" lift. The YD-handle allows the user to insert the scoop deeply into a pile and lift with a minimum of effort. A deep dish keeps material inside the head. LENGTH 43", WEIGHT 6.4 LBS., HEAD 14" × 17".

2. **ALUMINUM SCOOP:** Intended for hefting the lightest of loads, this scoop has a head fashioned from extremely lightweight aluminum. The square shape is good for pushing, and the unusual hardwood T-handle makes it easy to toss a load to the side or over the shoulder. Sparkling aluminum alloy is easy to find in a grain pile. A small, useful, portable option. LENGTH 40", WEIGHT 3.5 LBS., HEAD 11¾" × 13¾".

3. **STEEL WESTERN SCOOP:** Note the slight variation between this Western scoop and its Eastern cousin. A slightly larger size lifts more goods per shovelful, but both styles are used for virtually the same general cleanup tasks. It is merely a matter of personal preference. Features a high-carbon steel head bolstered by ribbed welts, and a long hardwood handle. LENGTH 63¾", WEIGHT 7.3 LBS., HEAD 15" × 18½".

4. **PLASTIC GRAIN SCOOP:** A rust-, rot-, and vermin-resistant scoop. This tool takes advantage of new technology and is made entirely of lightweight plastic. It is primarily meant to lift grain but is strong enough to shovel snow. It also features molded ribs for extra strength. LENGTH 44", WEIGHT 3 LBS., HEAD 14½" × 17¾".

Trenching Shovels

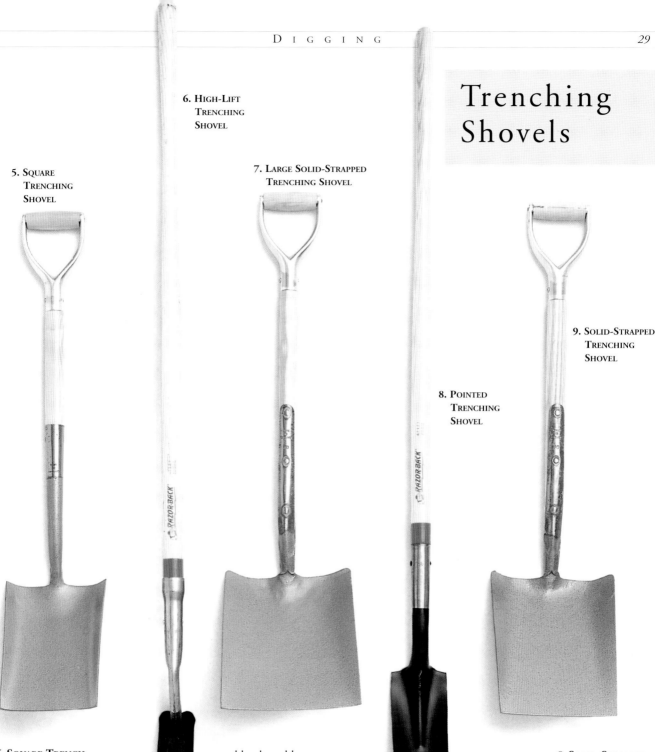

5. Square Trenching Shovel

6. High-Lift Trenching Shovel

7. Large Solid-Strapped Trenching Shovel

8. Pointed Trenching Shovel

9. Solid-Strapped Trenching Shovel

5. **Square Trenching Shovel:** A good, mid-size choice when a decision can't be made between a spade and a shovel, this tool will do everything in a pinch. It features a YD-handle and more cant than a spade, however, and is therefore more suited to digging and lifting, rather than breaking dense, untouched ground. Hardwood handle, solid-socket construction, and a forged steel head make this a superior tool. LENGTH 37½", WEIGHT 6 LBS., HEAD 7" × 11".

6. **High-Lift Trenching Shovel:** Ideal for scooping up narrow columns, or slugs, of soil (for irrigation, for example), this trenching shovel was intended to be wielded without bending over. A very deep cant (almost 90°) means the head rides almost parallel to the ground before insertion. Features a tempered-steel head, rolled-socket joint, and hardwood handle. Not suitable for heavy loads. LENGTH 61½", WEIGHT 3.6 LBS., HEAD 2¾" × 9½".

7. **Large Solid-Strapped Trenching Shovel:** The solid-forged steel head with steel straps extends halfway up the hardwood handle to transfer stress evenly. A very durable tool, it should not bend or break, even with the heaviest loads. LENGTH 39½", WEIGHT 6 LBS., HEAD 10" × 12½".

8. **Pointed Trenching Shovel:** Similar to the High-Lift Trenching Shovel, this tool has a wider and taller head with a pointed edge. A better choice for wet or clay soil, it penetrates unbroken ground more easily and can withstand greater weight. It also has less of a cant, which makes it a better digging tool. This example is equipped with a heat-treated, tempered steel head with an open back, a hardwood handle, and solid-socket construction—all reinforced by a rivet. LENGTH 58½", WEIGHT 3.6 LBS., HEAD 4" × 11½".

9. **Solid-Strapped Trenching Shovel:** Solid-strap construction makes this an unusually strong option for both digging and the traditional tasks of a square-point shovel, lifting and moving. The tapered head is forged steel and should withstand the hardest use. YD-grip lends added control when lifting large loads. LENGTH 39½", WEIGHT 6.1 LBS., HEAD 8½" × 12¼".

THE SPADE

The shovel may be known for its versatility, but the spade is a serious digging tool. Hanging face up in the garden shed, with its long square-edge blade staring straight at you, it appears to look on with a certain disapproval. "Well?" it seems to ask. "When are you going to begin?"

Consider a top-of-the-line spade—one that's strapped, for example, with a YD-handle. A spade like this is sleek and looks almost dangerous. In contrast to a shovel, the blade is almost flat, not dished. The edge is straight and beveled sharp on one side. The shoulders are generously treaded, so they look almost like epaulets. The steel straps are riveted to the ash handle in three places, making the connection virtually unbreakable. The shaft and the head meet at a very slight angle or no angle at all, permitting the user to drive the blade straight into the ground at full force. The handle springs from the shaft directly, having been formed by parting the shaft, steam-bending it into the shape of a Y, and riveting a steel-capped wooden crosspiece over the end.

Perhaps this spit-and-polish British posture of the spade is partially responsible for the fact that Americans historically have preferred the shovel. Nonetheless, once you've taken it down off its pegs, the spade becomes a garden companion second only to the shovel in its capacity to tackle a wide range of jobs.

The spade is incredibly handy: it cuts fine straight edges for a bed at the edge of a lawn and loosens the soil, prying out rocks and reducing clods to pea-size. It digs a long straight trench for a row of apple trees, mounding soil where the plantings will be set. Its flat pan can spoon material gently around transplants, never touching them. And it can take off spits of turf when you're setting bulbs to naturalize beneath them.

In the vegetable garden, the spade is excellent for beginning a double dig—use the back of the tool to smash the heavy clods. And where the onions are already up and growing, use the spade's edge like a scuffle hoe, cutting off weeds with a short, jabbing motion. Its versatility is practically limitless in the garden, where improvisation is often necessary.

THE VERSATILE SPADE

A smart manufacturer could probably hold a contest to find new uses for the spade. If a spade is well sharpened, it will break open a fertilizer bag or cut cord for edging the vegetable bed. The back of a spade can be used as a hammer to pound in stakes for the pea fence. Spades have been used to split kindling, and ice fishermen have been known to take them out on the pond.

Some gardeners carry their spades with them every day, ready for anything. The only thing this tool is not good for is what the shovel is most surely meant for: to hold and throw the soil.

CHOOSING A SPADE

There were once many more kinds of spades than there are today. The biggest ones were heavier than a shot-putter's shot, and some had hollow heads or blades angled like a swallowtail. Still, there are more than twenty different models in commerce, most with square-end blades. Usually, the shafts are shorter than shovel shafts—28"–36" long—and there are grips on the ends.

Because a spade is used for heavy-duty digging, buying a cheap one is counterproductive. Like inferior, stamped-metal shovels, bargain-basement spades are quite liable to bend in the head or break at the shaft.

Most spades worth the investment are forged out of rolled carbon steel using specially made shaping dies. The most expensive ones are made out of stainless steel (a steel alloyed to chromium as well as carbon), which never rusts and shines like the bumper of a mint Corvette. At the price, however, you might as well use them for serving Christmas dinner. Plain carbon steel is equally strong, if not absolutely rustproof, and a much less expensive option.

A fine spade is attached to its ash shaft either by a socket or by straps. The socket version costs less and is a little heavier. It's also a very durable tool, and even if it breaks, the weakness is precisely at the juncture of socket and wood, so replacing the shaft is easy. Straps that extend halfway or more up the shaft are stronger than sockets because they distribute the stresses of digging along their whole length.

Sockets do have one advantage: should the shaft break, a socketed tool is easier to repair. Standard replacement shafts are easy to trim to fit a socket. Conversely, it is no simple matter to align the two sides of a strapped tool, to re-rivet the shaft and head together.

Fiberglass and metal shafts are somewhat stronger, but they absorb less shock when you hit a hidden boulder. The fiberglass shafts, moreover, are harder to fit to the head. (Wood fibers are more compressible and the wood itself can be sculpted to fit, whereas fiberglass is a stiffer material and more difficult to sculpt.) Still, fiberglass shafts are often lighter, making the tool easier to wield. Also, the shafts

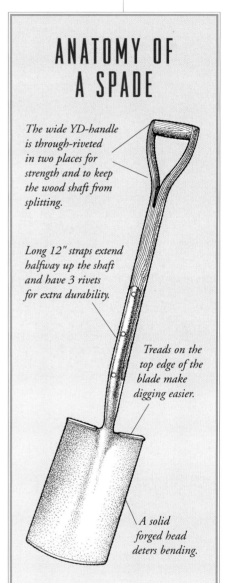

ANATOMY OF A SPADE

The wide YD-handle is through-riveted in two places for strength and to keep the wood shaft from splitting.

Long 12" straps extend halfway up the shaft and have 3 rivets for extra durability.

Treads on the top edge of the blade make digging easier.

A solid forged head deters bending.

are frequently colored bright yellow or orange, which makes it hard to forget the tool in the garden.

Almost all spades, except for Irish spades, have some kind of grip at the end of the shaft. The cheapest of these have plastic D-handles, affixed with a single rivet. They offer the advantage of being lightweight, but they're unpleasant to hold and can fail at the rivet. Metal D-handles, though heavier, tend to be found on the better-grade tools. These are more sturdily affixed to the shaft with a socket-and-rivet construction like that of the tool's head.

YD-handles are certainly the most elegant-looking. Made by splitting the shaft end, steam-bending it, and finishing it off with a steel-reinforced ash crosspiece, the YD-handle is perhaps the best handle available. The process of splitting the wood and steam-bending it does make this type of handle vulnerable and occasionally one may break, but most reputable companies will promptly replace it. These companies regularly reject 30% of their ash handles in the process of manufacture, so they will not be alarmed if a problem occurs.

T-handles are attached to the shaft by mortise and tenon. Large hands can envelop the handle and are not limited by the width of any opening. In theory, the T-handle should be vulnerable to twisting forces, but the gardeners who love this kind of handle won't have any other.

In Ireland, the T-handle is well-loved, but the favorite Irish spades have long shafts—like those usually reserved for shovels—with no handles at all.

USING THE SPADE

To dig properly with a spade, insert the blade straight down into the soil. Stepping on the tread, drive it all the way into the ground. Then, standing straight, pull back against the handle to loosen the soil. To lift out the crumbling clods, bend your knees and straighten them, bringing your arms up as you go.

Especially for Americans, who are so accustomed to long-handled tools, it's important to remember to bend at the knees, not in the back. For both spades and shovels, the hand lower on the shaft is used as a fulcrum in loosening the soil, but the trailing hand and arm exercise different sets of muscles for each tool. The spade calls for pulling on the handle, whereas the shovel requires a movement more like pushing down a rod. The two movements are efficient but distinct. The gardener's frequent mistake is to treat a shovel like a spade and vice versa. With this in mind, remember that a spade might well be too short for your stature. Spades and forks come in standard 28"–32" lengths, and for many people even 32" is barely long enough.

The first two motions of using a spade are identical to that of a shovel (see page 22). The third motion, which involves lifting and throwing material, is slightly different. When lifting soil, bend your knees low to the ground and allow your arms to extend as you pull up the load.

Quality strapped spades are available with longer shafts from British manufacturers. A few American nursery spades, including the draining and rootball spades, also come with long shafts. And if these are still too short, the Irish garden spade has a handle 48"–54" long. Even though the heads of Irish spades are typically narrower than those of the English garden spade, these tools are good diggers and may be preferred by tall gardeners.

THE ENGLISH GARDEN SPADE: The classic English garden spade is a miracle of balance and craft. It is the preferred tool for double digging and for spading up ground. Either socketed or strapped, it is made with forged and heat-treated carbon steel. A full-size English garden spade weighs 4–5 lbs., and you can balance it on the edge of your hand. Size and weight vary with the maker and the model, but the blade will generally have a length-to-width ratio of 4 to 3. The largest models with the longest socket or straps are best for rough, raw ground; the smaller models are better for previously worked soil. The head of a standard English garden spade is roughly 12" long and 9" wide.

THE NURSERY SPADE: Various high-quality forged and strapped spades are made in America chiefly for the commercial trade. In the garden, these tools are used to dig around shrubs and small trees, breaking the smaller roots and preparing the plant to be balled-and-burlapped. They must be very strong so that they can cut, dig, and pry.

For this reason, nursery spades are tough as nails, often with straps that extend almost all the way up the ash handle. (Sometimes the handle is made of fiberglass or steel, for extra strength.) They are quite heavy as a rule, some weighing more than 6 lbs. The blade is often tapered to make it easier to break the ground.

A lighter-weight version that is nonetheless excellent for transplanting is the Iowa pattern nursery spade. Its blade is slightly curved for even better penetration, and at 4.8 lbs. it's a superior choice for the home garden.

SPADES VS. SHOVELS

Functionally speaking, it is not so hard to make the distinction between spade and shovel. The word "spade" comes from Latin *spada*, meaning "blade," while "shovel" comes from Old English *scofl* or *scofan*, "to thrust away." The spade cuts down into the soil like a sword. The shovel pushes away into piles of loose gravel, compost, soil, or sand.

The spade is designed to dig. Its blade is almost always flat in cross section and set in the same plane as the shaft, so it strikes straight down into the soil. Usually, it has treads at the blunt end of the blade to step on the head and drive it all the way in. A spade is thrust down, then levered back using the handle to lift soil.

The shovel can dig, but it is meant to lift and throw. The blade is frequently dished so loose material will remain on it. Alternatively, it may be flat with raised edges at the side and back. Often, the blade is set at an angle to the shaft to allow the scooped blade to be pushed into a pile of loose soil or gravel, without bending the back.

Almost every basic digging tool is available in a smaller size, suitable for use in cramped quarters or by those who need a lighter tool.

Before buying an American spade, check to see how it has been made. The best are formed out of forged carbon steel; cheaper models are stamped, most with closed backs but a few with open backs. Keep in mind that the stamped models are adequate for light work but will prove less durable when used for heavy jobs.

THE BORDER SPADE AND THE RABBITING SPADE: Almost every basic digging tool is available in a smaller size, suitable for use in cramped quarters or by those who need a lighter tool. The border spade is precisely like its larger cousin, the English garden spade, but it usually weighs less than 4 lbs. and its blade is about 9" long. (This is why it's sometimes called the ladies' spade.)

Rabbiting or poacher's spades are likewise small and lightweight. The heads are long and narrow, with a rounded tip. As the name suggests, these tools were once used by groundskeepers and poachers for digging rabbits and other varmints out of their burrows. Nowadays, they make very fine transplanting tools; the small, narrow blade is perfectly configured to dig the smooth-walled holes for the usual nursery sizes of perennial plants. You can even use them while down on your knees to divide clumps of old perennials, to work in a narrow flower bed beside a wall, or to transplant shrubs.

THE IRISH GARDEN SPADE: The Irish garden spade has approximately the same weight and heft as the English variety, but it's somewhat longer and narrower. There are gents' and ladies' models—larger and smaller, respectively. Once there was at least one kind of spade for every one of the twenty-six counties of Ireland. Those that survive as "Irish spades" in the trade are from County Slingo and from Leenane in Connemara, where a narrow spade was more appropriate for working in stony soils.

Unlike other spades, most Irish spades have long contoured shafts without handles. This is simply the Irish preference. It's also the choice in some places on the Continent, where the Dutch spade is essentially similar to the Irish spade.

For taller gardeners, Irish spades are an alternative to the short-shafted English or American spades. Though the blade is not quite so large, it will still take a good full pan of soil and is fine for general digging and spading. On narrow borders and in stony soils, it is also the best choice.

THE DRAINING SPADE AND THE ROOTBALL SPADE: Among specialty spades, the most frequently used are the long, narrow ones that are meant for digging deep holes. These spades may be as slender as 3" across and as long as 18". Usually, they are short-shafted with D- or YD-handles.

The lift varies according to the purpose of the tool. A post or ditch spade is intended for cleaning up the edges or bottoms of holes or trenches that have already been roughed out with a "ditchwitch" or a posthole digger. It is not meant to do the actual digging and removal of the bulk of the material, so it has no treads.

The draining spade, on the other hand, has higher lift and is treaded. Designed for digging a drainage ditch by hand, this tool is long and narrow to fit the desired dimensions of the channel. Models are available at 3", 4", 5", and 6" widths, and in some lines the spades are color-coded by width.

The rootball spade is the most useful specialty spade on home ground. It's treaded and has a low lift, so you can use it for digging out channels and postholes, but this is also an especially good tool for making holes to plant seedling and "containerized" trees and shrubs. Rootball spades are usually round-ended, so they penetrate the ground with greater ease than a square-end spade.

UNUSUAL SPADES: There were once spades that looked like hearts and others that looked like rakish sets of prison bars. As the tool-making industry continues on its homogenizing course, however, many of these wonderful oddities have unfortunately fallen by the wayside.

Still, a few unusual models do hang on. The diamond-point spade is a case in point. This spade is meant to penetrate anything; and it's made to be practically indestructible, its sharp triangular blade capable of slicing the hardest red iron hardpan or caliche. To render it even more formidable, the tool is often made with a steel shaft and handle.

The serrated garden spade exists simply because some people swear by it, convinced that the serrated edge cuts easier and better. The only undisputed claim on behalf of this spade is that its serrated edge does not need to be sharpened frequently.

TIME OUT

In addition to choosing the right tools for the job, there are two or three steps you can take to keep digging from becoming a tiresome task. Take along enough drinking water so you can sprinkle some on your face and the back of your neck. Take frequent breaks, and use the time for stretching exercises. Above all, don't overdo it—especially if it's your first or second day at the site.

Spades

1. PRESSED STEEL GARDEN SPADE

2. SOLID-STRAPPED GARDEN SPADE

3. JUNIOR SPADE

1. **PRESSED STEEL GARDEN SPADE:** Light in weight, this relatively inexpensive tool features a pressed or stamped steel blade, an ash shaft, and a molded polypropylene grip. Manufactured with the same precision as the traditional tool, it is intended for light- or medium-duty tasks. LENGTH 39", WEIGHT 3.8. LBS., HEAD 7" × 11".

2. **SOLID-STRAPPED GARDEN SPADE:** Similar to the Standard Full-Strapped Nursery Spade (see page 41), this tool is fashioned in the best British style. It boasts solid-forged construction with a carbon steel blade. With a longer handle and shorter straps, it is designed more for use in the home garden than is the nursery spade. This is an excellent, heavy-duty tool for soil preparation. LENGTH 42½", WEIGHT 4.8. LBS., HEAD 7⅜" × 11¼".

3. **JUNIOR SPADE:** Top-quality craftsmanship should not be sacrificed when buying a junior or kid-size tool. This example features the same attention to detail found in recommended adult tools: a solid-forged carbon steel head, solid-socket construction with reinforced collar, and a polished ash handle. The T-grip is easy for small hands to grasp and the green epoxy coating mimics grown-up versions. Smaller adults, as well as those who garden in restricted areas or pots, may prefer to work with a tool of this size. LENGTH 32", WEIGHT 3.8 LBS., HEAD 5" × 7".

4. **FIBERGLASS GARDEN SPADE:** Taking advantage of new advances in technology, this spade has a handle and grip that are molded entirely from fiberglass resin. The same size and height as the traditional garden spade, it was originally designed for use by public utility crews and is specifically suited to perpetually damp or tropical environments (fiberglass is rustproof). The handle is replaceable and is connected to the solid-forged steel head by socket construction halfway down the shaft. A high-quality choice for those who prefer a lighter spade. LENGTH 39½", WEIGHT 5 LBS., HEAD 7½" × 11½".

5. **SOLID-FORGED BORDER SPADE:** A smaller but equally tough rendition of the English Garden Spade, this tool is ideal for setting out small plants, digging up bulbs, and working around existing plants in beds and borders. A solid ash

4. FIBERGLASS GARDEN SPADE

5. SOLID-FORGED BORDER SPADE

6. ENGLISH GARDEN SPADE

handle and carbon steel head feature a solid-socket connection that won't bend, even when digging a deep hole to transplant a shrub or small tree. Green epoxy coats upper half of blade for corrosion-resistance. Reinforced YD-grip

may be preferable to the grip of the T-handled Junior Spade. Treadless. LENGTH 37", WEIGHT 3.75 LBS., HEAD 5½" × 9".

6. **ENGLISH GARDEN SPADE:** This ultimate garden spade features top-notch construction: solid-

forged steel blade, 12" weldless solid-socket joint, foot-gripping tread, and a blisterproof ash handle with a YD-grip. One small step beneath the Solid-Strapped Garden Spade in terms of durability (solid-strapped tools have

an added layer of support), it will more than surpass the needs of most gardeners, including the professionals. An essential tool for intensive digging, preparing beds, and prying up stones and rocks from soil, it will last a lifetime

with proper care. This particular example is suited to tall gardeners. LENGTH 43", WEIGHT 4.75 LBS., HEAD 7½" × 11".

Long-Handled Spades

1. LONG-HANDLED TAPERED SPADE

2. IRISH GARDEN SPADE

3. LONG-HANDLED SLINGO SPADE

4. LONG-HANDLED IRISH GENT'S SPADE

1. **LONG-HANDLED TAPERED SPADE:** The longer, slender blade and deeper cant make this a great tool for working in climates with wet soil. In fact, the narrow tapered blade shape is found in most classic Irish spades. A stamped-steel head attached by open-socket connection to a varnished ash handle guarantees that with proper care, it will last a lifetime. A long handle gives more leverage when lifting and transferring heavy, wet soil but is less efficient when used to strike the ground. The slightly wider tread ensures a good foothold, even with a narrow blade. LENGTH 60", WEIGHT 4.3 LBS., HEAD 4½" × 13".

2. **IRISH GARDEN SPADE:** Having a slightly shorter T-handle and more tapered blade than its longer-handled cousins, the Irish Garden Spade is perfect for trenching, for double digging, and deep plantings. Solid-forged blade and straps are triple riveted to the ash shaft. The treaded, narrow blade easily penetrates hard soils. LENGTH 51", WEIGHT 5.5 LBS., HEAD 6½" × 13".

3. **LONG-HANDLED SLINGO SPADE:** This stamped-steel spade boasts a specialty-shaped head (the narrow blade ends in a flared bottom edge) that originated with the Dutch. Used in Holland to open drains and dig channels, it is a top-of-the-line tool for working in heavy, wet soil. The carbon steel blade will not bend or break, and the forward-rolled tread enables the user to get a solid foot on the blade, even when digging in standing water. This spade digs a marginally wider trench due to its shape. LENGTH 60", WEIGHT 4.4 LBS., HEAD 6" × 13".

4. **LONG-HANDLED IRISH GENT'S SPADE:** Of all the spades pictured here, this tool most resembles the classic spade used for centuries throughout Europe. It features a slightly narrower blade than the British or American standards, with a square edge and a shallow dish that pierces the soil easily. Solid-socket construction with a reinforced, solid-forged, carbon-coated steel head means this tool will not bend or break, even when used to pry stones or roots from the soil. A polished ash handle adds to its durability and usability. Crafted from superior materials and priced accordingly, it is ideal for a variety of tasks and may be the only spade a gardener need purchase. LENGTH 58", WEIGHT 5 LBS., HEAD 5½" × 13".

Specialty Spades

5. **DYKING AND IRRIGATION SPADE:** This solid-forged tool is used for digging for drainage and irrigation ditches. The pointed end penetrates wet soil, while the shallow head scoops up a large load of dirt. Solid-strapped construction with a polished ash handle offers exceptional strength (another bonus when digging in heavy, wet soil). The unusual combination of a T-grip and no tread indicates that although this spade digs deeply into the ground, it is more efficient in loose or sandy soil. A specialty tool developed for professional use that has been adapted to specific home use. LENGTH 41¼", WEIGHT 5.4 LBS., HEAD 9" × 12½".

6. **NEWCASTLE DRAINING TOOL:** This specialty spade originated in Staffordshire, England, where seasonal rains make a tool of this length and durability a necessity. The extra-long head with blunt edge is used to open up draining channels in saturated soil, while the deep but narrow dish lifts the appropriate amount of soil without back strain. A forged steel head is connected by solid socket to an ash handle with a reinforced steel YD-grip. The top of the treadless blade features a unique T-shape that not only identifies this tool as the Newcastle variety, but also gives the user a broader base on which to place the foot. LENGTH 43½", WEIGHT 6.1 LBS., HEAD 4¼" × 16".

7. **RABBITING SPADE:** Originally developed in England by landowners troubled by rabbits, this blunt spade with a slightly dished head was used to slice into rabbit warrens, breaking them up and scaring off their inhabitants. Hot-dipped green epoxy coats a solid-forged steel head that is connected by a weldless solid-socket joint to a polished hickory handle. This attractive, small, light spade is rarely used nowadays to eliminate rabbits, but it will still come in handy when setting out plants, digging up bulbs, or filling in the occasional gopher hole. LENGTH 36", WEIGHT 4.2 LBS., HEAD 5" × 10½".

8. **IRISH BOY'S SPADE:** This is a junior-size take on the Irish Garden Spade, featuring a carbon steel blade, solid-socket construction, and a sturdy ash handle with T-grip. Suited for most of the same tasks, it may be preferred by smaller gardeners due to its abbreviated size. LENGTH 43", WEIGHT 4.5 LBS., HEAD 5¼" × 11".

5. **DYKING AND IRRIGATION SPADE**

6. **NEWCASTLE DRAINING TOOL**

7. **RABBITING SPADE**

8. **IRISH BOY'S SPADE**

Digging Spades

1. **DRAINING SPADE:** The tall, narrow head creates a perfectly shaped ditch for open or tiled drains. The forged steel head with solid shank ends in a lipped socket for extra strength. A stiff ash shaft with YD-handle and forward-rolled tread allow maximum weight to be used on each stroke, while the deep-dished blade scoops up plenty of soil. This spade is perfect for digging deep planting holes. LENGTH 44", WEIGHT 4.75 LBS., HEAD 5¼" × 14".

2. **EVERGREEN GARDEN SPADE:** An affordable, good-quality tool that lends the user all the strength of a standard garden spade with a much lighter heft. The traditional broad, solid-forged head is connected to a lightweight polypropylene handle with a reinforced plastic YD-grip. This tool is useful for general garden digging in average soil, but it is not a spade for heavy-duty tasks. Its weight makes it ideal for smaller gardeners or for those who find working with a heavier spade to be unwieldy and hard on the joints. LENGTH 39", WEIGHT 4.6 LBS., HEAD 7" × 11¼".

3. **ROOTBALL SPADE:** Also known as a tree transplanting tool, this spade digs deep, wide holes with ease. The long, flared head scoops a large amount of soil with each pass, making this a good choice for any gardener who frequently transplants large items or for those who simply want to dig deeper holes in less time. Similar in construction to the Draining Spade, the solid-shank forged blade stands up to years of heavy digging. An ash handle with a reinforced aluminum YD-grip rounds out this reasonably priced, durable option. LENGTH 39", WEIGHT 4.75 LBS., HEAD 6¼" × 14".

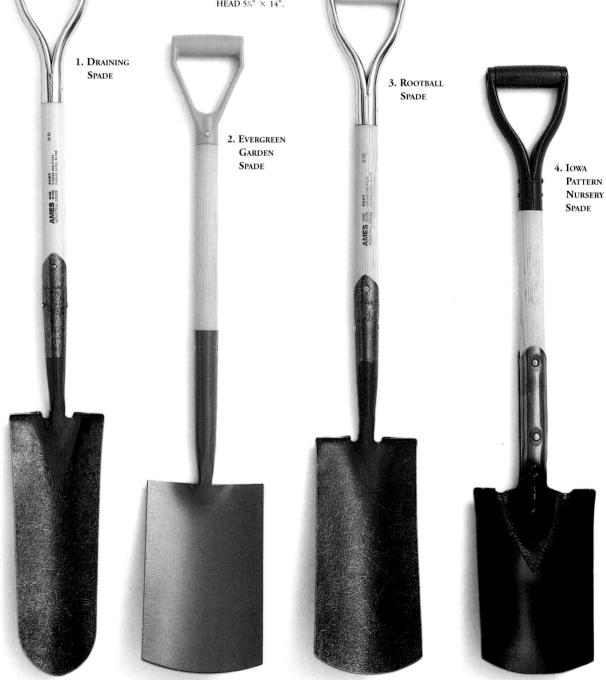

1. DRAINING SPADE

2. EVERGREEN GARDEN SPADE

3. ROOTBALL SPADE

4. IOWA PATTERN NURSERY SPADE

4. **IOWA PATTERN NURSERY SPADE:** This stocky spade with its shorter, curved blade is a uniquely American shape. A forged steel head with solid-strap connection makes this tool a tough number, designed for serious digging, but in a slightly smaller form than the English standard. The broad head carries a load of soil, while the slight taper and curved edge pierce the ground with a minimum of effort. Short ash handle with metal YD-grip. LENGTH 37", WEIGHT 4.8 LBS., HEAD 7" × 11".

5. **SERRATED GARDEN SPADE:** This basic stamped-steel American spade has straight sides for general digging and a unique serrated edge that is especially good for cutting through rocky or dense soil, tough underground roots, and even hardpan. The handle is fashioned from durable, smooth ash that won't splinter or split. The blade is reinforced in the back to resist bending. LENGTH 59", WEIGHT 4 LBS., HEAD 7" × 11".

6. **ALL-STEEL DIAMOND-POINT SPADE:** A radically designed all-purpose spade for daily use, combining aspects of both a spade and a shovel. Constructed of oval tubular steel welded to a carbon steel blade, this spade comes as close to being unbreakable as a spade can be. The weighty shaft and wide D-grip make it a good option for stronger gardeners. The heavier gauge head with zinc finish ends in a pointed, or "diamond," edge that pierces clay soil easily, and the deeper cant makes it useful as a shovel. The absence of rivets on the shaft provides for a smooth, rust-resistant presentation. LENGTH 40", WEIGHT 5.6 LBS., HEAD 7⅓" × 13".

Heavy-Duty Specialty Spades

7. **STANDARD FULL-STRAPPED NURSERY SPADE:** A heavy-duty nursery spade for serious gardeners that's built to last even under duress, this tool is strapped and riveted all the way up the hardwood handle. The reinforced wood-and-metal YD-grip won't rust or deteriorate with age and is suited to heavy digging in tough soil. A typically American spade designed for every kind of soil, the closed-back, two-piece, stamped-steel head begins wide and tapers. The deeply scooped dish allows more soil to be lifted than does the flatter English-style spade. Forward-rolled tread enables the user to put more weight into each thrust. LENGTH 39", WEIGHT 6.3 LBS., HEAD 6" × 13".

5. SERRATED GARDEN SPADE

6. ALL-STEEL DIAMOND-POINT SPADE

7. STANDARD FULL-STRAPPED NURSERY SPADE

THE FORK

A fork operates much the same way as your fingers do. If you spread your fingers and cup them slightly, you can get them to dig deep into a tub of barley. The stronger your fingers, the more they can do. You can use them for scooping up loose-lying objects, and you can spread them to certain widths in order to capture only some of the objects while letting others fall through.

Forks are basically designed to fulfill either of these two functions. Some forks are used for digging, while others are intended to scoop and carry materials like hay or compost. (Hand forks are for cultivating or scratching; see page 71.) The fork is characterized by the fact that it carries its load on a set of tines, or prongs, numbering from two to ten or even more.

The garden fork (a term that is sometimes used interchangably with digging or spading forks, which are actually more adept at heavy-duty tasks as opposed to turning the soil) can penetrate ground that a spade will scarcely dent because each pointed or chisel-ended tine exerts effective pressure at its slender end. These forks are particularly good for converting subsoil hardpans into crumbly clods. Scooping forks (including bedding, manure, hay, and compost forks) are made from lighter-weight steel, and the tines are angled into an arc resembling that of the fingers when used for the same purpose. This arrangement allows materials to be moved from one place in the garden to another.

Though the Basques have dug since time immemorial with a two-tined fork called the *laya*, the common garden fork is a largely modern invention. Until the advent of strong and flexible steels, iron forks had to be prodigiously heavy, just so each tine might be able to resist the bending forces generated by digging. The first all-steel digging fork was introduced by Alexander Parkes at the Great Exhibition in London in 1851. The story goes that Parkes, a well-known inventor, had been in direct conversation with Henry Bessemer (soon to invent the blast furnace, which made it possible to create many different grades of steel cheaply) about a steel that would demonstrate a triumvirate of qualities: lightness, stiffness, and suppleness. Reasoning that it would be impossible to make a slender tine that would never bend under stress, Parkes concluded that the best thing was to make the prongs so that in case they did bend, they could easily be restraightened with no loss of strength.

Parkes proved correct in his analysis. The carbon-manganese steel upon which he finally settled had just these qualities, and it is still used in fine English garden forks today.

CHOOSING A FORK

Watching the process of forging a steel fork is like witnessing the miracle of birth. From a single bar of high-carbon steel, the smith first bends out a thick piece that will become the socket or the straps. Then, one by one, he rolls out and stretches the four fingers of the fork.

Though such a fork is very strong, it can still bend against a stubborn rock. This is where the superior properties of high-carbon and high-manganese steels become evident, allowing the tool to be bent right back into shape without losing any strength.

The best garden forks are made of forged steel and finished with either a long socket or straps through-riveted to the handle. Stamped garden forks, usually distinguished by the comparatively flat cross section of their tines, can be serviceable—depending upon the gauge of steel used in their making—but they will never become heirlooms. Not only are they more liable to bend, but once bent they cannot be straightened again without loss of strength.

Scooping forks are made with steel prongs that are typically arched with round or oval cross sections. These would never do for digging in the soil, but should they bend or break in the course of their daily work scooping manure or compost, all is not lost. Whatever remains of a given tine can be resharpened, and the tool can still be used. Old scooping forks often look gap-toothed since some tines may have broken off.

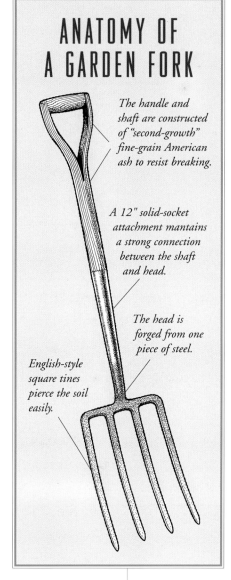

ANATOMY OF A GARDEN FORK

The handle and shaft are constructed of "second-growth" fine-grain American ash to resist breaking.

A 12" solid-socket attachment mantains a strong connection between the shaft and head.

The head is forged from one piece of steel.

English-style square tines pierce the soil easily.

USING THE FORK

As a spade is to a shovel, so is a digging fork to a pitchfork. The gardener stands down on the step of the digging fork and drives it full into the ground, then pulls back on the handle to break and loosen the soil. To operate a pitchfork or a manure fork, the motion is more supple and continuous. Bending at the knees, not in the back, the gardener drives the prongs into the pile of material, lifting up to extract a forkful and finally pitching the load. With a scooping fork, there is often an intermediate step where the gardener shakes the tool, releasing straw or other unwanted material through the space between the prongs.

Again, it's better to take a moderate load than too much at one time, which strains the tool as well as the user's knees, shoulders, and back.

THE ENGLISH GARDEN FORK: The English garden fork is a serious tool, capable of breaking up the stiffest clay soils. It is a heavy instrument—some versions weigh 6 lbs.—with long, riveted straps to permit twisting and bending under heavy loads. Each of the four tines has a square cross section for maximum strength, and the points are chiseled. Where clay would stick to the surface of a spade, it has little chance to do so with the fork.

This is the fork to choose if you have a substantial vegetable garden that needs annual double digging. It is also useful for digging up potatoes, carrots, and other root crops.

SPADING AND DIGGING FORKS: Lighter in weight than a digging fork, the spading fork has four tines, each with an oblong or triangular cross section; the prongs taper to a diamond point. Like any garden fork, it's useful in clay but excels in sandy or more friable soil.

Spading forks are usually stamped, not forged. They are not as strong as digging forks, though the tines are often slightly incurved in order to increase their resistance to bending. They are best used for stirring subsoil in a double-digging operation or for spading over existing beds in the spring.

THE BORDER FORK: Only two-thirds the size of a standard fork, this tool is a delight to hold. A big gardener can use one practically like a dinner utensil, working with one hand to loosen soil around fruit trees or raspberry canes. A small gardener finds—at last—a tool that is not overbearing or exhausting. Both forged and stamped forks are found in this size.

THE BROADFORK: To look at this big ungainly contraption, with its two handles and wide-spaced tines, you'd think it had been invented by medieval monks as a form of penance. But in fact it's a twentieth-century invention, developed from the work of Alan Chadwick and John Jeavons in California for the purpose of double digging.

This is the best fork for reworking beds in which the ground has already been broken. With a rolling motion of its curved tines, it gently breaks up compressed soil, lifting and crumbling it without inversion.

HAYFORKS: All scooping forks ultimately derive from the lovely and sinuous wooden two-tine hayforks that were essentially "found" tools, created by cutting out and smoothing a naturally crotched branch. Sometimes a third tine would be joined to the tool with a mortise-and-tenon joint.

Steel versions of these forks imitate the gentle curve of the wooden tool, up to and including the long, slender prongs. Neither type is meant to withstand the stress of digging. Originally, these forks were meant to lift stalks of wheat and throw them into the wind to winnow grain from the chaff. Today, they are chiefly used to move hay and straw mulches, leaf mold, and light compost.

Where the straw is uniform and long, a two-tine fork is sufficient—indeed preferable—because it is slightly lighter. For most situations, however, where long and short lengths of straw are mixed, a three-tine fork is better because it will drop less.

MANURE FORKS: The more tines a fork has and the closer they are spaced, the less material falls through the cracks. Standard manure forks have five or six prongs, making them useful for cleaning up a cow barn, moving compost, scooping up a litter of fallen twigs, or lifting moderately bulky root crops like beets.

Ten- and twelve-tine forks were invented for horse stables, where the manure is small enough in size that it would fall through the cracks of a wider fork. As you might expect, such a tool is most useful in the garden for lifting smallish root crops such as new potatoes. In fact, a blunt-end ten-tine fork is actually made for the exclusive purpose of potato harvesting.

BEDDING FORKS: These forks are essentially variations of manure forks and traditional hayforks. Primarily, they are used for spreading various mulches and composts. They often look like a sturdy, tightly strung rake, but they're used for mixing soil that has already been dug and loosened. A typical ten-tine variety combines the attributes of a manure and a scooping fork—the tines are spaced closely together and allow for easy transporting of materials from a cart or wheelbarrow to the garden bed.

HOOKS AND DRAGS

Though their names sound vaguely sinister, these tools represent the distillation of centuries of agricultural wisdom. Potato hooks, manure hooks, refuse drags, and corn drags all are made strong and wide with solid, deep tines. Up to twice as wide and half again as deep as ordinary four-tine cultivators, these tools can bite deep into the soil or drag along its surface. In either case, they will resolutely pull along whatever they meet, be it potatoes, stones, stubble, weeds, or stall bedding.

Some gardeners fear these tools. Though most appreciate their width and strength, they find the tines too long for safe weeding and cultivating in the garden. If that is the case, however, the tines can be cut down to about 4" long and the ends filed sharp.

Garden Forks

1. SPADING FORK

2. AMERICAN SPADING FORK

3. ENGLISH GARDEN FORK

4. EVERGREEN GARDEN FORK

1. **SPADING FORK:** Characterized by a narrow head and 4 flat, wide tines with pointed ends that efficiently slide through soft soil, this traditional example of an all-purpose spading fork combines the strength and digging capabilities of a spade with the agility of a fork. A YD-grip and smooth hickory handle attached by solid-socket construction to a forged, carbon steel head make this fork suitable for serious digging and tilling. The wide space between tines and the cant mean less dirt actually gathers on the head during digging, so less effort is expended when turning a bed or grubbing out bulbs, roots, and stones. This is an indispensable tool in the garden and should last a lifetime with proper care. LENGTH 40¾", WEIGHT 5 LBS., HEAD 7¾" × 11¼".

2. **AMERICAN SPADING FORK:** Used primarily to dig and break up soil, this spading fork has the customary 4 flat tines; a narrow, straight head; and little cant. It functions as an all-purpose fork, but reaches farther into the soil and so may be more appropriate in areas with soft or loamy soil. The steel YD-handle makes it surprisingly easy to use, while the wooden grip centerpiece is easy on the palms. The tanged head is driven deep into a long, curved, and tapered ferrule, while the forged steel head contributes durability to this reasonably priced variation. Its larger size may make it inappropriate for smaller users. LENGTH 42", WEIGHT 4.75 LBS., HEAD 7½" × 11".

3. **ENGLISH GARDEN FORK:** This form of the classic English digging or garden fork was invented in 1851 and has been used by farmers on both sides of the Atlantic since then. It is an all-purpose tool, suitable for digging in almost any soil, and features a splayed head, 4 square tines with chiseled edges, and an angled cant. The tall, broad head penetrates a wider, deeper area of soil when digging, but narrow tines won't break healthy roots or disturb sensitive, beneficial subterranean organisms. Fashioned with the best materials, this fork features solid-socket construction, a forged steel head, and a varnished hickory handle. A large tool, best suited for tall users. LENGTH 44", WEIGHT 5.5 LBS., HEAD 8" × 11½".

4. **EVERGREEN GARDEN FORK:** This tool is used for the same tasks as the English Garden Fork but may be more appropriate for the average-size user or for the horticultural hobbyist. Solid-socket construction and a forged carbon steel head mean durability is not sacrificed for size, while the smooth polypropylene grip is replaceable over time. This variation is slightly more affordable than forks made with one-piece wooden handles. LENGTH 39", WEIGHT 4.4 LBS., HEAD 7½" × 11½".

5. **SOLID-STRAPPED GARDEN FORK:** A professional-quality garden tool of unusual strength. Square English tines and triple-riveted straps combine to produce a tool suitable for every cultivating task. Like its companion, the Solid-Strapped

Broadfork

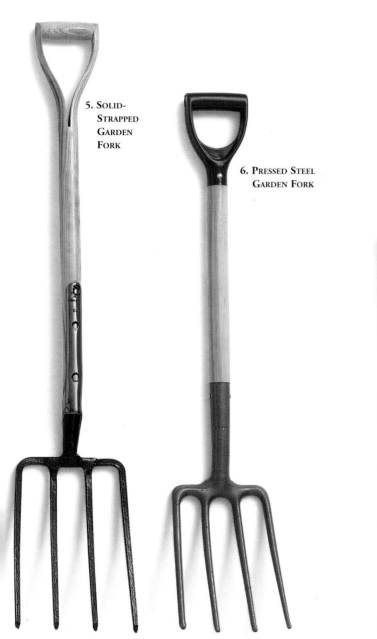

5. SOLID-STRAPPED GARDEN FORK

6. PRESSED STEEL GARDEN FORK

7. BROADFORK

7. **BROADFORK:** This interesting tool is also known as a cultivating fork. Some version of it has been used by horticulturists and small farmers throughout the ages to aerate and amend by hand already broken topsoil. Derived from the digging stick, the original gardening tool, the Broadfork has two wooden handles connected to a broad head with widely spaced steel or wooden tines. Using both hands, the user inserts the fork into the ground and, with a rolling motion, turns the soil—allowing moisture and air to penetrate the fertile top layer without disturbing the less beneficial subsoil. This version sports solid ash handles and gently curved, forged steel tines. The head is attached to the handles by two screws and wedges.
LENGTH 58",
WEIGHT 10 LBS.,
HEAD 9½" × 18".

Garden Spade (see page 36), this fork is intended for the professional nursery worker, landscaper, or gardener.
LENGTH 42½",
WEIGHT 5 LBS.,
HEAD 7½" × 11¼".

6. **PRESSED STEEL GARDEN FORK:** Significantly lighter than the average digging fork, this is an excellent option for those who prefer to heft less. The shorter handle and tines mean less effort is required to turn over soil. The pressed steel head has short, blunt tines that will not damage tender vegetables and bulbs. For this reason, it is an ideal tool when grubbing out predug beds or working around existing plants with sensitive roots. Rust-resistant and easy to care for, this is a good, average tool.
LENGTH 38½",
WEIGHT 3.1 LBS.,
HEAD 7½" × 10¾".

Specialty Forks

1. **KID'S FORK:** A nice companion to the Junior Spade (see page 36). This fork is fashioned from the same superlative materials as "adult" forks but is much shorter and lighter. The ash handle with T-grip is easier for small hands to grasp; the head is solid-forged steel. Also well suited for those who plant in containers, or for patio and rooftop gardeners. LENGTH 32", WEIGHT 2.75 LBS., HEAD 5" × 7".

2. **STAINLESS STEEL BORDER FORK:** The deluxe version of the Solid-Forged Border Fork, featuring a polished stainless steel head attached to a varnished hickory handle by solid-socket construction. Durable yet elegant, this small fork is used primarily in small spaces and predug beds, or for digging around existing plants. It is light and agile and often favored for all-purpose work by users who find the average-size fork too heavy and unwieldy. LENGTH 37", WEIGHT 2.75 LBS., HEAD 5½" × 9".

3. **FIBERGLASS GARDEN FORK:** This tool's handle is crafted from molded fiberglass resin, which allows it to be lightweight and almost unbreakable. Originally designed for use by public utility crews, it is very tolerant of abuse and is specifically suited to perpetually damp or tropical environ-

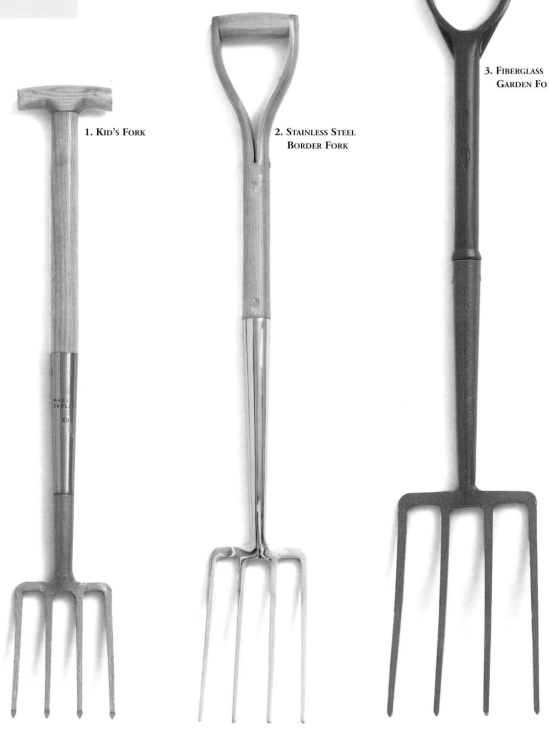

1. KID'S FORK

2. STAINLESS STEEL BORDER FORK

3. FIBERGLASS GARDEN FO

ments. The head is made of forged carbon steel; the fiberglass handle is replaceable and is connected by socket construction halfway down the shaft. If used appropriately, this fork could last forever. LENGTH 39½", WEIGHT 4.8 LBS., HEAD 7½" × 11½".

4. **COMPOST FORK:** Better for turning and aerating compost than the narrow digging forks with 4 tines, this tool has 5 oval tines and a T-grip handle. Bridging the distance between a digging fork and a manure fork, it stretches over a 9"

span, which allows the user to grab a large amount of material with each gesture. When thrust into the middle of a compost heap and lifted or pulled, the spaces between tines allow important organisms to remain undis-

turbed while air penetrates to the compost's core. This particular version is characterized by solid-socket construction, a forged carbon steel head, and an ash handle. LENGTH 43", WEIGHT 5 LBS., HEAD 10¼" × 13¼".

5. **SOLID-FORGED BORDER FORK:** This junior version of the traditional English Garden Fork (see page 46), this tool is used for the same tasks—only on a smaller scale. It is suited to prepared beds and borders, containers, or areas around existing

4. COMPOST FORK

5. SOLID-FORGED BORDER FORK

6. DIGGING FORK

plants as its compact size makes it a precise but more delicate tool. It is preferred by many users who find the weight and length of average-size forks uncomfortable and clumsy. Manufactured with the same superlative materials as the larger version, with

solid-socket construction, a forged steel head, and a varnished YD-grip hickory handle.
LENGTH 37",
WEIGHT 2.75 LBS.,
HEAD 5½" × 9".

6. **DIGGING FORK:**
A hybrid of the American and English styles. This tool combines the benefits of long, square tines that act like an English garden fork with the larger head and chiseled edges of a digging fork. A forged solid steel head is

attached to a wood handle by a tang that is surrounded by a long, tubular steel ferrule. The wood grip and centerpiece protect palms from chafing. A good, affordable fork useful for a variety of tasks, from digging and lifting to sifting

through predug soil and prying stones and roots from a bed. LENGTH 43",
WEIGHT 4.5 LBS.,
HEAD 7½" × 11½".

Bedding and Manure Forks

1. **10-TINE BEDDING FORK:** Traditional bedding forks, also known as mulch forks, look more like rakes with tightly set tines. Combining the advantages of a manure fork and a scoop fork, this tool is a versatile, sturdy, 10-tine version designed to help the gardener turn predug soil, sift through compost, and spread mulch or manure. Forged steel head and tang-and-ferrule construction make this a good-quality, affordable, all-purpose choice. Thick, tines resist bending. Solid ash handle. LENGTH 61", WEIGHT 6 LBS., HEAD 11½" × 13½".

2. **4-TINE SCOTTISH MANURE FORK:** Although this tool is labeled a manure fork, it more closely resembles a hayfork, or pitchfork. The durable, solid ash YD-handle is useful when pitching hay and straw and is attached to a long-lasting, forged steel head by solid-strap construction, which allows for a strong but light tool. The 4 delicate, oval tines pierce dense manure easily without bending or breaking and can be used to turn and sift compost. An indispensable tool, and this particular version is a high-quality option. LENGTH 44", WEIGHT 3.6 LBS., HEAD 8½" × 13½".

3. **5-TINE MANURE FORK:** Manure forks may have 4, 5, or 6 tines depending on their origin, although 5 is more common in the U.S. This fork is fashioned from affordable materials: an enamel-coated, carbon steel head and solid-socket construction reinforced by an aluminum collar. A smooth ash handle is characteristic of a classic manure fork (as opposed to a YD-handle) because the long, slender tines of a manure fork are suited for sifting through and moving around lighter material, not digging. This fork may be used for composting, spreading mulch, or sifting through debris. LENGTH 61", WEIGHT 4 LBS., HEAD 9" × 13".

4. **LIGHTWEIGHT BEDDING FORK:** This tool is an interesting variation of the 10-Tine Bedding Fork. Slender round tines are more delicate but are welded together with an additional brace for extra strength. The polished handle is cut from sturdy ash and connected to the carbon steel head by tang and ferrule. A smaller, lighter head makes it more appropriate for spreading lightweight mulching material such as leaf mold. LENGTH 60", WEIGHT 4.2 LBS., HEAD 10¾" × 13".

5. **6-TINE MANURE FORK:** A traditional manure fork with 6 pointed tines. Appropriate for spreading soil amendments and mulch, it is generously sized and ideally suited for its intended tasks. The head, fashioned from enamel-coated carbon steel, is fastened to a smooth hardwood handle by solid-socket construction with a reinforced collar. LENGTH 60", WEIGHT 4.1 LBS., HEAD 9" × 13".

6. **MANURE DRAG:** This heavy-duty, claw-shaped tool has been around since the Middle Ages, when it was used by farmers to pull manure from the dung cart onto the fields before planting. The current variation has 4 thick tines, bent at a 90° angle to make a rake. A polished hickory handle is attached to the enamel-coated steel head by a solid socket and reinforced collar. This is also an ideal compost tool and soil cultivator. LENGTH 55", WEIGHT 4.2 LBS., HEAD 5½" × 9".

1. 10-TINE BEDDING FORK

2. 4-TINE SCOTTISH MANURE FORK

AMES

**3. 5-Tine
Manure
Fork**

**4. Lightweight
Bedding Fork**

**5. 6-Tine
Manure
Fork**

**6. Manure
Drag**

Scooping Forks

**1. COTTONSEED
SCOOP FORK**

**2. 6-TINE BEET
FORK**

**3. BARLEY
FORK**

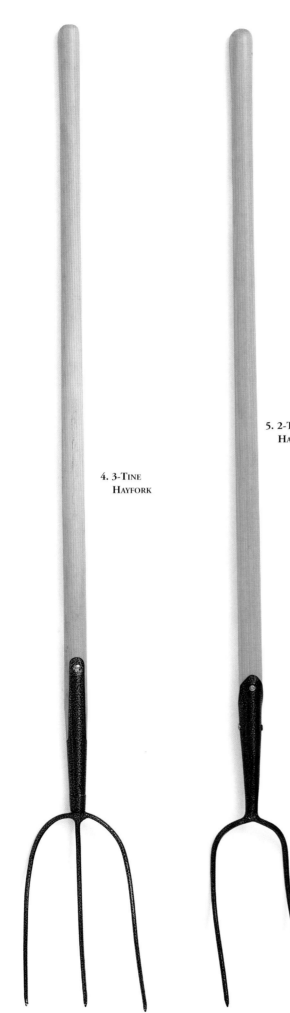

4. 3-TINE
HAYFORK

5. 2-TINE
HAYFORK

1. **COTTONSEED SCOOP FORK:** This wide, 10-tine scooping fork is used more like a shovel to transfer loose material, such as grain or fertilizer, from one place to another. The deeper cant and scoop allow the user to grab larger quantities, while the YD-handle and dull-edged tines are designed to help reach into the center of a large pile or hill. Solid-socket construction and carbon steel blade make this a good-quality choice in a specialty item.
LENGTH 46",
WEIGHT 7 LBS.,
HEAD 14" × 18½".

2. **6-TINE BEET FORK:** This solid-strapped, best-quality fork is used traditionally to grub out beets, potatoes, and other roots and tubers from the soil without damaging their flesh. The forged steel head has 6 long, widely spaced tines that hold produce while allowing dirt to pass through. Dull oval tines will not pierce the vegetables' tender skin when fork is used to dig through the garden patch. Splayed shape of the head covers more surface area per stroke.
LENGTH 60½",
WEIGHT 4.8 LBS.,
HEAD 13½" × 17".

3. **BARLEY FORK:** An oversize specialty fork, traditionally used to lift and transfer barley and other lightweight grains. Its long, slender tines are not appropriate for any heavy lifting as they will bend out of shape. Solid-socket construction with reinforced aluminum collar resists breaking at the joint. Large size may overwhelm smaller gardeners, but this tool is actually remarkably light. Tapered ash handle.
LENGTH 72",
WEIGHT 5 LBS.,
HEAD 14¼" × 19".

4. **3-TINE HAYFORK:** Commonly known as a pitchfork, this tool is used on farms and in gardens to lift and transfer hay, compost, manure, and other lightweight materials. A nimble, easy-to-heft option, it doubles as a great compost tool. Best-quality forged steel head is given extra strength with a socket-and-strap connection secured by a bolt.
LENGTH 60",
WEIGHT 2.6 LBS.,
HEAD 5" × 11½".

5. **2-TINE HAYFORK:** The 2-Tine Hayfork is very common in Europe and is of similar construction to the 3-Tine Hayfork. Also known as a farm fork, this tool is slightly lighter than its 3-tine relative but may be used to accomplish the same tasks. Smaller gardeners will appreciate its easy maneuverability.
LENGTH 60",
WEIGHT 2.8 LBS.,
HEAD 5" × 11½".

THE MATTOCK AND THE PICK

The mattock and the pick are the handiest rough tools in the gardener's shed. "Go break up land/Get mattock in hand," recommended Thomas Tusser in 1573, and his advice has not gone out-of-date. A mattock can be used like an ax or a hoe; a pick, like a giant chisel. Large tools of this kind are heavy enough to sever large roots and prize up boulders the size of watermelons. Small models are excellent cultivating tools.

CHOOSING A MATTOCK OR PICK

A soil laced with tough roots is best cleared with a cutting mattock, available in two weights: 2½ lbs. and 5 lbs. The hoe-shaped end of the lightweight version is also an excellent tool for digging shallow planting trenches in the vegetable garden or turning over sod for naturalizing bulbs. The hoe end gets a good bite of soil with every strike and also digs a straight trench about 4" wide.

A pick is for stony soil, not roots. To avoid those annoying wrenching moments that occur when the pointed end gets caught under a stubborn root, never use a pick to get out roots—backs are damaged that way. But for stones, the heavy pick is the best lever there is, next to a long iron bar.

USING THE MATTOCK OR PICK

When using a mattock, make sure to draw all your swinging power from the legs and knees, following through with your entire body. Don't ever hoist or lever the mattock with your back; instead, step toward the digging area when loosening soil or stones.

Because of their heaviness and because their heads are inserted into their handles through an "eye" joint, mattocks and picks must be thoughtfully used and maintained. One theory holds that the best way to use either tool is to raise it repeatedly to eye level and plunge it into the soil. However, a better rhythm can be achieved if the tool is swung in a rough circle. A good mattock or pick user even reverses hands periodically, swinging first on one side, then on the other. The trick is to let the lead hand slide up and down the shaft while the trailing hand holds firmly. (This method has the added virtue of keeping the handle firmly attached to the head.)

Mattocks and pick handles must always fit tightly to the eye, lest the heavy head fly off. Furthermore, if the handle gets wet, it is important to knock the head loose after use. (This can be done by holding the head at both ends and pounding the end of the handle against a hard floor.) Let the mattock or pick dry out before putting it away; otherwise, it may develop dry rot inside the handle (providing the next user with an unpleasant and dangerous surprise).

THE ALL-PURPOSE MATTOCK: This is the old standard and probably the best, most versatile choice among mattocks. With a lateral cutting blade on one side and a chisel-pointed pick on the other, it's a good combination tool for attacking roots and boulders. It has both a lateral and vertical cutting blade, making it best for work in soil full of roots and brambles of different sizes and textures. If matted roots won't yield to the swing of the lateral blade, they will certainly give way to what amounts to an ax cut delivered with the vertical blade. It is also fine for breaking sod.

HAND MATTOCKS: Also called "Southern Belles" or "weeding hoes," these small mattocks have either a pick and a mattock end or a pick and a two- or three-pronged end. Heavier than other weeders, they are nonetheless a pleasure to swing. The pick or prong end goes deep for stubborn weeds; the lateral mattock end gets surface weeds and stirs the soil. And the tool is small enough to be worked into fairly tight corners.

THE WEED WRENCH: This ingenious tool was invented by an old sailor from the toothed jaws that hold the ropes for sail tension. A set of these movable jaws is affixed to a long pole and a flat transverse piece of steel is set at the bottom for leverage. Grasp the base of a weed sapling firmly in the jaws, pull back on the handle, and watch the sapling pop out of the ground.

GRUBBING MATTOCKS: These lighter-weight mattocks can be used to cultivate lighter ground. Typically, they weigh 5–7 lbs., though their handles are the same length as those of full-size mattocks. In fact, though they are called mattocks, these tools are really more appropriate for weeding and loosening the soil than they are for clearing. They can, however, be used for heavier work like removing shrubs in hard soil or smaller rocks. The shorter blade has an axlike end and an adze-shaped end, making it not only lighter than its full-size cousin, but easier to wield.

THE PICK: A pick is as much a part of American folklore as it is a useful tool. Still, if you get the rhythm of swinging one of these 8-lb. steel heads, you may find yourself looking for further projects that will require one—like digging a garden pond or creating that asparagus bed. Be sure to select one heavy enough to do the job. Smaller, lightweight models are really meant only for cultivation.

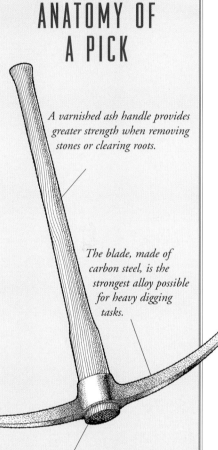

ANATOMY OF A PICK

A varnished ash handle provides greater strength when removing stones or clearing roots.

The blade, made of carbon steel, is the strongest alloy possible for heavy digging tasks.

Connected through an "eye" hole on the handle, the head can be removed and replaced easily.

Picks, Mattocks, and Land-Clearing Tools

1. ALL-PURPOSE PICK

2. PICK-AND-HOE

3. GRUBBING MATTOCK

1. **ALL-PURPOSE PICK:** Also known as a clay pick, this classic landscape and construction tool is used for heavy-duty groundbreaking tasks, such as digging through hardpan and clay soil and prying up serious rocks and stumps. The solid carbon steel blade has a narrow pick on one side and an adze-like blade on the other. It is connected to the varnished ash handle with an eye socket, enabling the user to replace or substitute the handle if necessary. A pick is swung over the shoulder like an ax and requires a fair amount of strength to use.
HANDLE LENGTH 36",
HEAD LENGTH 24¾",
WEIGHT 8.7 LBS.

2. **PICK-AND-HOE:** This smaller, lighter hand version of the All-Purpose Pick has a narrower adze that can be used as a hand hoe due to its length, and may be used as a weeder as well as a lever. A fundamental tool for breaking up ground to make garden beds and borders, the Pick-and-Hoe is agile enough to be used around existing plants. A solid carbon steel head and hardwood handle stand up to rough treatment, while the lighter heft is easy on the back.
HANDLE LENGTH 13½",
HEAD LENGTH 10¾",
WEIGHT 1.3 LBS.

3. **GRUBBING MATTOCK:** An ideal tool for removing tough shrubbery and roots from unbroken ground. A somewhat abbreviated version of the traditional mattock, this specialty blade features a short, axlike blade on one side and an adze-shaped mattock on the other. The adze can be used as a lever to remove rocks, as a draw hoe to shore up or flatten dirt, or as an ax to accomplish serious chopping of hard soil or roots. Solid-forged carbon steel and a varnished ash handle are connected by an eye socket and secured with a bolt.
HANDLE LENGTH 36",
HEAD LENGTH 16½",
WEIGHT 7.1 LBS.

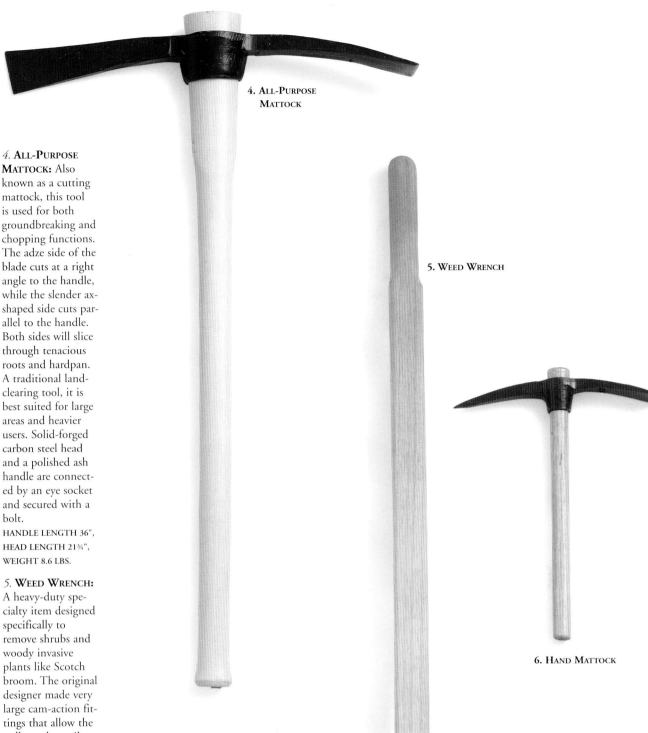

**4. ALL-PURPOSE
MATTOCK**

4. **ALL-PURPOSE
MATTOCK:** Also
known as a cutting
mattock, this tool
is used for both
groundbreaking and
chopping functions.
The adze side of the
blade cuts at a right
angle to the handle,
while the slender ax-
shaped side cuts par-
allel to the handle.
Both sides will slice
through tenacious
roots and hardpan.
A traditional land-
clearing tool, it is
best suited for large
areas and heavier
users. Solid-forged
carbon steel head
and a polished ash
handle are connect-
ed by an eye socket
and secured with a
bolt.
HANDLE LENGTH 36",
HEAD LENGTH 21¾",
WEIGHT 8.6 LBS.

5. **WEED WRENCH:**
A heavy-duty spe-
cialty item designed
specifically to
remove shrubs and
woody invasive
plants like Scotch
broom. The original
designer made very
large cam-action fit-
tings that allow the
puller to be easily
and quickly clamped
onto a trunk up to
about 1½" in diam-
eter. The long lever
arm then pulls the
trunk up easily. A
simple sidewise pull
clears the tool's
mouth for the next
big weed. Contoured,
polished hardwood
handle eliminates
blisters.
HANDLE LENGTH 44",
HEAD LENGTH 10",
WEIGHT 6.6 LBS.

5. WEED WRENCH

6. **HAND MATTOCK:**
This classic mattock,
scaled down to fit in
the palm, is useful
for smaller ground-
breaking tasks. It has
a sharp adze designed
for grubbing out
roots and stones and
a pick-shaped edge
for breaking up clay
soil. The Hand
Mattock is a cheaper
alternative to the
Pick-and-Hoe but
essentially is used for
the same tasks. Solid
construction consists
of a carbon steel head
and hardwood handle.
HANDLE LENGTH 13¼",
HEAD LENGTH 10½",
WEIGHT 1.5 LBS.

6. HAND MATTOCK

CHAPTER THREE

CULTIVATING

The best soils belong to nature, created over the span of millennia by growing plants and the falling rain. The plants clothe the ground— both with their live bodies and with the leaves and stems they drop—and interrupt the rain so that it soaks the earth in a gentle shower. The rain builds channels in the soil, carrying organic matter from the surface and blending it slowly with mineral grains. Plant roots follow these channels, stabilizing the earth as they absorb nutrients, air, and water. When the ground heats up in a dry spell, the cooling leaves and the organic mulch form a barrier to evaporation, helping to keep sufficient water in the soil.

> "When a man does a piece of work which is admired by all, we say that it is wonderful; but when we see the changes of day and night . . . and the changing seasons upon the earth, with their ripening fruits, anyone must realize that it is the work of someone more powerful than man."
>
> —CHASED-BY-BEARS,
> SANTEE-YANKTONAI SIOUX

The moment the natural cover is removed, whether it be prairie, forest, or savanna, the process of destruction begins. Rains fall straight onto the bare soil, puddling and eroding the topsoil. When the soil dries, what is left forms a crust that will prove even more difficult for the rain to penetrate on the next occasion. Hardy weeds that tolerate disturbed soils—that outsprout, outgrow, and overshadow other plants—will appear in numbers to cover the land. Hans Jenny, who studied Missouri soils during the 1920s, noted that virgin prairie soils were more than twice as fertile as those that had been cleared for less than a decade, even though the two soils lay right across the road from each other.

Once the ground has been dug, it is the gardener's responsibility and delight to find ways to help the soil mellow and mature. In *Walden*, Thoreau spoke of his bean field and noted that his daily work was to "make the yellow soil express its summer thoughts in bean leaves and blossoms, rather than in wormwood and piper and millet grasses." But how is the gardener to accomplish this when the garden patch may be relatively bare for weeks, even after the seeds and the seedlings have been planted in the ground?

THE PERSISTENCE OF WEEDS

In the garden plot, hands and tools must substitute for the canopy of plants, breaking the soil surface where it crusts and quickly rooting out aggressive weeds. The healthiest, richest soil in the world is useless to plants if the passageway between them is blocked. A soil that is impermeable or choked with weeds will not produce plants that bear lovely flowers or plump fruits.

In this imperfect world, stirring the soil and weeding are almost always part of the same operation. Together, they promote the freest passage of water and air from the atmosphere to the plants' feeding roots. This laborious process of cultivating the ground often yields unexpected delights as well. While you may not be as lucky as Thoreau, who turned up arrowheads while hoeing in his bean field, there are still wonders to be found: a chip of mica, a bottle shoulder of old blue glass, the seashell from an Indian midden.

No matter how cleanly you clear the ground and how carefully you prepare the soil, it will grow weeds—those aggressive plants that usually end up pushing out all others. Birds and animals will drop the seed with their scat; the wind will bring more weeds; still others will creep along or under the ground by stolons and rhizomes from a neighboring patch. And the majority of weeds will simply grow from seeds that the very act of digging has brought to the surface—perhaps after a sleep of 100 years.

The thing about weeds, whether annuals or perennials, is that they are terribly hardy. They grow like mad, and they just won't quit. One reason for their success is that they are prolific; a single cocklebur plant, for example, produces 8,500 seeds. Weeds also steal nutrients and water that would otherwise reach your plants. And because they start faster than most cultivated seedlings, they can rapidly shade out your crops.

For a gardener, the best and only answer to the weed is to be just as persistent and a shade smarter. In many cases, the best way to prevent weeds is to preempt them. In a warm climate, a spring mulch of black plastic sheets, when heated in the sun, will effectively destroy many weed seeds. Mulches of grass clippings, wood chips, compost,

For a gardener, the best and only answer to the weed is to be just as persistent and a shade smarter.

cocoa shells, and alfalfa hay can all keep the interlopers down simply by smothering them. It's even possible to enlist the services of the less hungry and thirsty of the weed tribe—a gentle ground cover like chickweed (*Stelleria media*), for instance—to act as a living mulch against Johnsongrass, Bermuda grass, chicory, dandelions, and other more noxious cousins.

TOOLS FOR CULTIVATION

Most gardeners need at least a couple of hoes and hand weeders and one long-handled, tined cultivator. For simple cultivating, the good old-fashioned hoe is nowhere near as versatile as the shovel is for digging. In fact, the most popular hoes—whose cheap stamped-metal, tang-and-ferrule heads so often fall from the handle and lie there uselessly—are a great deal better for mixing concrete than they are for cutting weeds.

Fortunately, as much human ingenuity has been expended in the pursuit of better weeding tools as in almost any other tool-making endeavor. The precise choice of weapon depends on the scale of the garden and the nature of the weeds that grow there. A big vegetable garden with open rows needs either a wheeled cultivator, which can be pushed along between the rows, or a large, heavy, well-balanced tool like an "eye" hoe (sometimes called a grub or a grape hoe). These hoes are distinguished by the blade, which is fitted onto the shaft by means of an oval "eye" forged into the blade. Eye hoes are by far the most versatile of hoes. (Old-timers say that a man could even knock the head off such a hoe at lunchtime and use it to fry up a corn cake—hence the term "hoecakes.") A gardener in California found one of these hoes behind her house, where it had lain rusting long enough for the handle to rot out; a quick brushup and a new shaft brought it back to life, and now it's her favorite tool.

The long-handled cultivator is an excellent choice when you want to both stir the soil and pull out seedling weeds. Like so many tools that were once forged by the local blacksmith, the cultivator has been made with as many as seven tines and as few as one. Mass manufacturing has limited cultivator options, but there are still many more choices than you might expect. Broad, flat, or triangular tines with chisel ends take hold in tough soil and will not bend as they break the crust. Oval- and round-tined models penetrate quickly and

FOUND WEEDERS

Some great weeding tools are designed, others are found. Older gardeners in particular—for whom stooping low is a serious proposition—often find a good strong set of barbecue tongs to be an invaluable aid for spot weeding. Just bend slightly at the waist and snag the rogue weed between the powerful jaws.

move swiftly through lighter soils, mixing in compost and pulling out the seedlings of annual weeds. There is even a wonderful old model—usually made with three tines—that has finger-like steel pads at the end of each tine to better aerate the soil.

Even a smaller eye hoe or a cultivator with 3" tines is too big to fit among perennials or other tightly planted beds and borders, or to cultivate among shallow-rooted plants like corn. Specialized hoes can work well in such situations. There are two basic kinds: the draw hoe and the push hoe (as well as a few push-pull hoes). In either case, the blade should be relatively shallow and steeply angled so that whether push, pull, or both, the sharp edge of the hoe will skim along just beneath the surface of the soil to slice off weeds but not damage the roots of desirable plants. Among the more effective draw hoes are the onion hoes (the most popular is the Union draw hoe) and Warren hoes. Push or scuffle hoes (the Dutch hoe is a common version) come in any number of ingenious shapes; most useful among them is the putter-shaped "swoe." You should be able to use any one of these hoes while standing upright, sharpening them periodically as you work.

In tighter spots, raised beds, and lawns, the hand weeder is the best choice. One new hand weeder is probably invented somewhere every day of the year, but a select few are so admirably adapted to the purpose that they keep selling year after year. Weeders with spring-steel tines are very effective; sometimes they seem to "pop" weeds right out of the ground. Little, curved hoelike implements like the Cape Cod weeder give fingertip control over weeds in tight places. And to get the taproots of dandelion or chicory, there is nothing like a fishtail weeder. (There are gardeners, of course, who get great pleasure from extirpating every iota of a dandelion's roots. Fishtails, grubbing knives, and other slender, deep cultivators are the best tools for this practice.)

Be sure the soil is moist when you weed, since roots cling less tenaciously to damp soil. Deep roots acquire free phosphorus in the subsoil and can help to make compost very healthful for the plants you want to prosper.

WHEN TO WEED

Whether annuals or perennials, weeds have to be caught before they set seed, lest your efforts actually serve to propagate new weeds. It's almost always best to cut annuals off before they establish themselves. At this time a gentle swipe—not a strenuous chop—will destroy them. Perennial weeds need even more precise timing if they're to be weakened and ultimately eradicated. Perennials that spread by stolons or rhizomes must be cut relatively early in spring; wait until five to seven true leaves are on the plant. This is when the roots have used almost all their available energy and before they have begun to build and store energy from the leaves.

Bulb-forming perennial weeds like buttercup oxalis and nutsedge should be cut just before flowering, when the bulbs are at their weakest. Deep-rooted plants like dandelion, chicory, and dock should be cut back frequently to keep them from storing energy in the roots.

HISTORY OF CULTIVATING

The theory behind cultivation seems to change at least once every century, but the practice is remarkably uniform. As the Renaissance English herbalist John Evelyn put it, "There is in truth no compost or lactation whatsoever comparable to this continual motion, repastination, and turning of the mould." (Translation: Get out there and cultivate, because it makes the soil happy.)

According to Virgil, whose *Georgics* was at once one of the great poems and one of the most influential agricultural manuals of Augustan Rome, it was the goddess Ceres who first "instructed mortals to upturn the earth with iron." The great Roman poet had a passion for hoeing and for mixing compost and ash into the land, and he clearly understood the importance of the soil's structure, noting, in fact, "the ducts and blind pores that carry her juices to the fresh herbiage." When his writings were rediscovered in the Middle Ages, European gardeners and farmers took readily to the poet's recommendation to "labour the earth incessantly." (For hundreds of years, English farmers followed the somewhat sanguine Virgilian advice to plow fields not only by length but by width as well.) But the question remained: Why does all this stirring of the soil make the earth so fruitful?

To the great natural philosopher Francis Bacon, along with a whole school of Renaissance scientists, the answer was water. Bacon conceded that each plant sucked some "particular juyce" from the soil itself, but argued that the real function of dirt was to pass water to the roots and so into the plants. If a stirred soil improved the flow of water, he reasoned, then stirring was the right thing to do.

In time, the notion that worked soil produces more of some mysterious "stuff" that plants need began to gain support. To some students of the soil, the material was saltpeter; to others, it was some *magma unguinosum*, and to still others it was simply "the juices of the earth." Jethro Tull, the celebrated inventor of the mechanical seed drill and horse hoe—both of which revolutionized farming and paved the way for modern mechanized farms—had an even simpler model. In his view, the cultivator simply chopped up the soil into small bits that would fit into

NO-TILL TAPESTRY

Up until a few decades ago, nobody ever suggested that it was bad to cultivate the soil. Then came people like Wes Jackson and Masanobu Fukuoka, who contended that soils should be neither plowed nor cultivated, but maintained as living tapestries of useful plants. The stationary composting of dead leaves and stems would fertilize the soil; the meshwork of roots and the covering vegetation would keep the earth open and well structured; and people would harvest fruit or seed without ever removing the perennial plantings.

For large-scale agriculture, this approach would surely be a blessing. Yet the gardener whose work is not for profit, but for the pleasure of standing in Nature's place and admiring her ways, will always stir the soil.

circle exactly as you would a mattock.

When slicing, keep the hoe blade shallow so it doesn't hang up in the soil, and keep it sharp. (A light draw or push hoe will not work on full-grown weeds in rough or compacted soils.) At the beginning of the day, set the hoe in a vise and use a mill bastard file, sharpening with the existing bevel in a motion that goes smoothly away from the body. Carry the file with you in the garden to touch up the blade every few hours. Do this by stabilizing the blade against your body, a stable boulder, or a bench, and sharpen by stroking away from the body with the file.

THE BASIC HOE: The common hoe is serviceable for many tasks, but not really ideal for any. The head is usually set at a 90° angle to the blade, attached directly or with a swan neck that keeps soil from building up on the tool. (Not that it isn't great for mixing concrete to lay the deck footings. The hoes with two holes in a large blade are also particularly useful for this task.) The basic hoe does a tolerable job of cultivating, but it makes weeding painful and more laborious than necessary. The standard version is about 6" wide and 4" tall. A ladies' or floral hoe is about a third smaller in the same proportions.

One way to improve the basic hoe is to serrate the backside. A company called I-Tech in Davis, California, suggests using an electric grinder to make grooves $\frac{1}{32}$" deep, $\frac{5}{8}$" long, and $\frac{1}{2}$" apart on the face of the hoe that points toward the user. Each groove slants toward the center point at a 20° angle. When the blade is sharpened on its opposite face, the hoe will acquire sharp serrations that make it cut more efficiently.

THE UNION DRAW HOE: The Union draw hoe (a member of the onion hoe family) is a better draw hoe than the common type because its blade is long and narrow—about 6" × 3". It makes shallower incisions in the soil and thus is suited for cultivating among shallow-rooted plants and root crops like onions (hence its familiar name). It's also lighter and the blade is usually sharpened on three sides, making it a versatile and maneuverable weeding tool.

THE STALHAM HOE: The most beautiful of draw hoes, the Stalham hoe (a member of the swan-neck hoe family) is arguably the best light weeder. Its gracefully arched neck terminates in a long, slender

ANATOMY OF A BASIC HOE

The best hoes have hickory handles that are heavy and add heft and durability to the overall tool.

Attached to the tapered shaft with rivets, the head is unlikely to weaken and fall off.

The replaceable forged steel blade is versatile and adept at chopping, weeding, and grading.

transverse blade—about 6" × 2". The blade is angled back sharply toward the gardener so that it naturally slices weeds just beneath the soil surface.

THE WARREN HOE: Ideally meant for opening furrows to plant seeds, the Warren hoe has a triangular or heart-shaped blade. Open the ground with the pointed end, put the seed in, then flip the tool over and cover the furrow with the two-lobed end. It's also a great spot weeder, and one of the few stand-up weeding tools that gets to the roots of chicory or dandelion. Its narrow blade makes it easier to get into tight spots and break into stiff ground.

THE EYE HOE: Eye hoes and other heavy-duty hoes, including the grub hoes, grape hoes, Canterbury, Scovil, and field hoes, are affixed to their flared shafts by inserting them through oval "eyes" that are forged as part of the blade. As much like mattocks as ordinary garden hoes, these are nevertheless the very best tools for large-scale cultivation, for digging, and even for prying out boulders.

The average blade of an eye hoe is 7½" × 6¾" and constructed of solid steel. Lighter ones are longer in the tooth, at 4"–5" × 7"; the true grape hoe, used for weeding and cultivating in vineyards, is a whopping 8" × 7" or 8" × 8". (Nearly all have shafts that are at least 54" long; the grape hoe's shaft is 41" long.) Different manufacturers give similar names to different heads, so it's best to try out the tool you want to buy. The only really distinctive eye hoe is the Canterbury hoe, which amounts to a very heavyweight three-tine fork with prongs in hoe position. A well-constructed Canterbury hoe is capable of spading, tilling, cultivating, and even removing small rocks from the soil.

Even a light eye hoe has heft to it. Lift it and drop it, and you'll likely find the blade more than half buried in the soil. Its weight and balance make this hoe extremely popular.

THE WHEEL HOE: Even a small wheel hoe, or wheel cultivator, is a behemoth to the average home gardener. Wheel hoes are best used for large-scale home vegetable patches—1,500 square feet or larger. (Organic market gardeners swear by them.) A good one can cultivate between or even among rows, but it's lost if there is no clear path for the wheel.

There are two basic choices in wheel hoes: the high-wheel type has a wheel about 2' in diameter; the low-wheel model has a wheel slightly less than half that diameter. The latter is more efficient, since the force of your push goes directly to the cutting edge. (The effort to push a large-wheel hoe goes directly into the hub of the wheel.) Both styles are offered with smooth-operating rubber wheels (in the old days, the wheels were flat steel bands), and both can be found with

Hoes are used for a range of tasks, but there are two distinct motions. For chopping, the hoe is first raised to head level, then thrust downward in an arc toward the body.

adjustable steel handles to make the tool long (or short) enough to prevent back strain.

An advantage to the low-wheel style is that it has an oscillating, stirrup-shaped blade instead of a plow or a multi-tine cultivator blade. The blade may be as slender as 4" and as wide as 16", which makes the tool an excellent row-weeding device. The slight curvature of the blade allows it to cut less deeply near the plant's roots than it does in the middle of the row. The low-wheel hoe works smoothly, with less strain on your back, and is even available in a two-stirrup model for hoeing two rows at a time.

THE DUTCH HOE: There could not be a better common name than "scuffle" for this whole class of push hoes. The simplest of these, the Dutch hoes, resemble sharp shuffleboard sticks, but others look like flying saucers, putters, fighter airplanes, rising moons, or sharpened pieces of lasagna. The great advantage to all of them is their sharp edge; the gardener can push, slide, angle, and "scuffle" them into all kinds of spaces and crannies in the garden.

The diamond-head hoe, sharp on all four faces, can be "scuffled" in any direction. Properly used, it fairly slides through the soil. The swoe is shaped like a stretched and warped parallelogram; sharp on three sides, it can literally be wrapped around a plant to cut down weeds near a plant's stem.

THE OSCILLATING HOE: The various names of this hoe attest to the way it works. Some call it the action hoe or hula hoe because its cutting mechanism is attached to the handle with a hinge, so it swings as you push and pull it along the soil surface. The shape of its two-edge blade has also inspired the name stirrup hoe. All oscillating hoes look basically the same, but they can vary greatly in size. The widest stirrups are 7" or more across, while the narrowest are only about 2".

The steady back-and-forth motion of the arms and whole body lends an almost restful quality to working with an oscillating hoe. However, this hoe can be tiring to use since it requires lots of arm motion. Some people complain that, while it works well for established weeds in fairly hard soil, it tends to get stuck in light soils and on mats of weeds. Also, because it's always moving, it's harder to corner or to hit a precise, small area.

Swivel the hoe in a small arc or broomlike motion at ground level, to slice plants off just below the top layer of soil.

ON A ROLL

The wheel hoe is ultimately the brainchild of eighteenth-century gentleman inventor Jethro Tull. How the traditionalists swore and stormed when Tull introduced the horse-drawn machines that would entirely replace broadcast seeding and hoeing by hand! Of course, his inventions paved the way for the monster machines that now trample and degrade the landscape, but they also inspired the wheeled machines that are marvels of appropriate technology.

Hoes

1. NARROW FIELD HOE: This light, narrow, goosenecked draw hoe is used to weed in cramped spaces—in beds and borders, between rows and vegetable hills. The deep blade is ideal for carving out furrows and for backfilling over seedlings in already prepared beds. Although a good choice for sandy soil or loam, the delicate nature of this hoe is not suited to hard or rocky soil. It has an enameled steel blade, socket joint, and curved hickory handle. LENGTH 51", WEIGHT 2.3 LBS., BLADE 3⅞" × 3".

2. STALHAM HOE: A classic example of an all-purpose draw hoe, used to push and pull soil as opposed to chopping it. This version, with a long gooseneck and strong socket joint bolstered by a screw, is designed for use in garden loam. The broad blade is fashioned from enameled steel and will slice through weed heads with a single stroke. A long hickory handle means the user can stand upright, lessening back fatigue. This particular hoe is somewhat lighter than the common draw hoe. LENGTH 60½", WEIGHT 2.6 LBS., BLADE 6" × 2¼".

3. UNION DRAW HOE: A slightly shorter neck and heavier weight characterize this standard draw hoe. Similar to the classic onion hoe, it is a good tool for heavy-duty weeding, cultivating, and hilling up, especially in clay soil. The forged steel blade has a sharp slicing edge and solid-socket handle. This is an example of an affordable yet readily accessible option available in most hardware or garden supply stores. LENGTH 58", WEIGHT 2.5 LBS., BLADE 6" × 3½".

4. WARREN HOE: This is a unique draw hoe with a Warren pattern blade designed for close weeding and cultivating. The point has no cutting edge, making it an excellent tool for carving furrows for seedlings without the danger of cutting into tender roots. The Warren Hoe also excels at grading and preparing beds, and backfilling to cover seeds. Top-quality manufacturing includes a tempered steel head attached by tang and ferrule to a hickory handle. LENGTH 60", WEIGHT 2.5 LBS., BLADE 4¾" × 6".

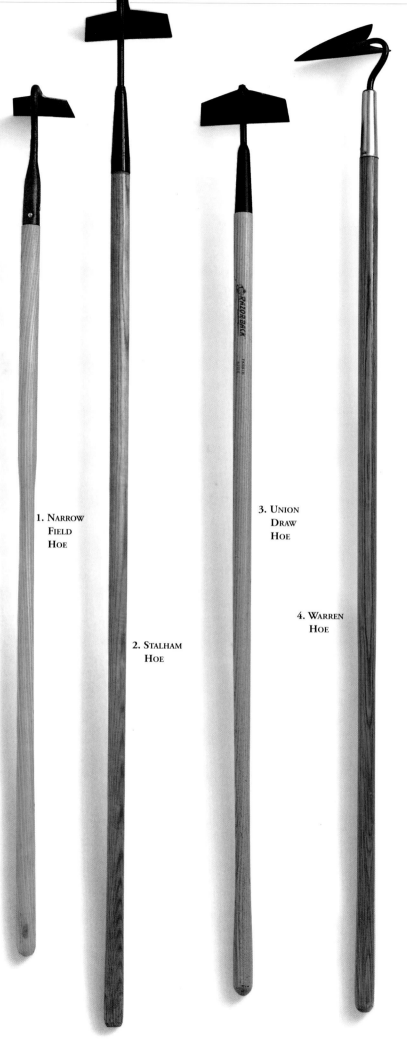

1. NARROW FIELD HOE

2. STALHAM HOE

3. UNION DRAW HOE

4. WARREN HOE

5. HAND FORK

6. HAND HOE

7. HAND PLANTER

meant to cultivate and weed. These hand tools are no less durable than the bigger hoes and may be preferred by smaller gardeners. With solid ash handles, eye-and-socket joints, and enameled steel blades. LENGTH 15" EACH, WEIGHT 0.7–1.1 LBS., FORK BLADE 3½" × 4½", HOE BLADE 3½" × 4½", PLANTER BLADE 2½" × 5½".

8. **OSCILLATING HOE:** Also called an action hoe because the blade moves approximately ½" back and forth as the hoe is pushed or pulled, this tool has a double-edged blade that cuts in both directions and is self-cleaning; with each back-and-forth motion, debris slips off. As a result, the gardener is rewarded with double action without expending extra energy. The forged steel blade sits perpendicular to the soil and cuts weeds off at the crown without chopping. A lightweight, ergonomic option with a long hardwood handle and solid-socket joint that connects the galvanized steel frame to the blade with two replaceable bolts. Maintenance requires periodic oiling of moving pieces. LENGTH 48", WEIGHT 2.3 LBS., BLADE 7" × 1".

9. **COLLINEAR DRAW HOE:** Invented by renowned organic farmer and nurseryman Eliot Coleman, this straightedge hoe resembles the traditional onion hoe with one important difference: unlike all

5. **HAND FORK;** *6.* **HAND HOE;** *7.* **HAND PLANTER:** Used in tandem or alone, these light, precise hand cultivators are good for working amid rows and beds, but due to their short handles, sitting or kneeling is almost mandatory for the gardener. Japanese in origin and beautifully designed to nestle in the palm, they are extremely effective choppers and reward the user with surprising agility, sharpness, and force. The narrow planter is ideal for setting out seedlings and transplants, while the fork and hoe are

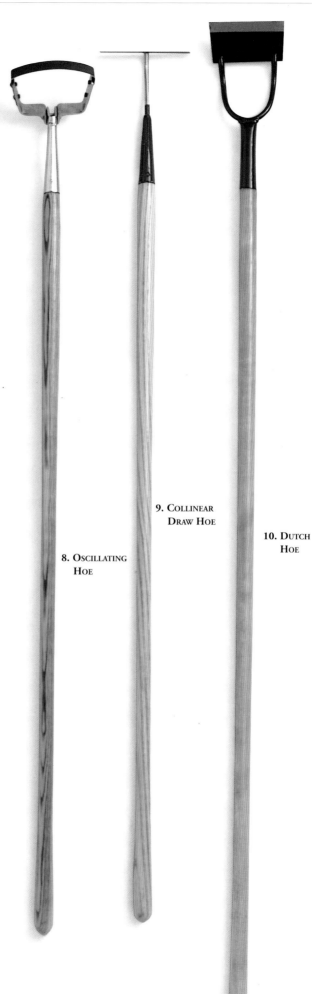

8. OSCILLATING HOE

9. COLLINEAR DRAW HOE

10. DUTCH HOE

other hoes, this hoe is used with the thumbs pointing up the shaft (all other hoes are used with the thumbs pointing down). The motion is much like that of using a regular broom as opposed to a push broom. Ideally suited to weeding in tight spaces, this hoe allows the user to stand up straight. Its edge stirs the soil as it cuts, eliminating newly germinated weeds as well as those on the surface. The stainless steel blade is joined to a long ash handle by a precisely curved shank and welded socket. LENGTH 58", WEIGHT 1.7 LBS., BLADE 6½" × 1".

10. **DUTCH HOE:** This traditional thrust or push hoe was developed by the Dutch to kill weeds and loosen soil that will be raked smooth. Also called a scuffle hoe, the tool is pushed in front of the user while the blade skims the top ½" of soil, removing weeds and gently aerating. The forged, enameled steel blade is slightly splayed at the edge and braced by two steel brackets connected to a socket joint. A long hickory handle allows a user of any height to stand fully upright. Because a pulling motion requires less energy than a pushing motion, the Dutch hoe is better suited for lighter work in cultivated or previously broken soil. It may also be used as an edger. LENGTH 67½", WEIGHT 2.3 LBS., BLADE 5" × 2¾".

Eye Hoes and Wheel Hoe

1. **Scovil Hoe:**
Hoes and hand tools of the traditional eye-and-socket construction have been traced back to the Romans. This hoe is used primarily as a chopping tool for breaking up hard soil, grubbing out stubborn weeds and roots, and hilling up around vegetables. The hickory handle is thickest at the bottom, where the "eye" of the blade rests. The Scovil pattern blade is typical of the most widely available grub hoes, but eye-pattern blades come in a wide range of shapes and can be interchanged to suit specific tasks. The replaceable blade is forged steel painted black. LENGTH 58", WEIGHT 4.4 LBS., BLADE 7½" × 6".

2. **Field Eye Hoe:**
This handy tool bridges the gap between a hand tool and a regular hoe. Originally intended to help clear fields for plowing, it has a semicircular blade pattern and is designed for heavy-duty cultivating and chopping. It can also be used for weeding or grading. The replaceable forged steel blade is painted black; the handle is hickory. LENGTH 46", WEIGHT 3.1 LBS., BLADE 5½" × 6".

3. **Swedish Tree-Planting Hoe:**
Also used as a professional bulb planter. The blade on this hoe scoops a generous portion of earth with each gesture. Combining both digging and chopping functions, it was developed for the Swedish Forestry Service to aid in replanting saplings. An axlike hardwood handle is connected to a forged steel scoop by a solid socket secured with two bolts. LENGTH 36", WEIGHT 2.8 LBS., BLADE 3¾" × 6".

4. **Grape Hoe:** Just as the grapes grown on the West Coast are naturalized immigrants, so too is this hoe, brought to California by Italians specifically to cultivate their beloved vineyards. Both the grapes and the hoe took root. This specialized tool is also called an Italian eye hoe, or a West Coast grape-pattern hoe. The slightly scooped, butterfly-shaped blade is geared toward heavy-duty or professional cultivation and chopping. Squared-off handle ends and a square eye mean that it cannot be interchanged with the more available round-eye sockets. Because the polished hickory handle is short, the user has to stoop. The blade is fashioned from forged steel and painted black. LENGTH 42", WEIGHT 4.7 LBS., BLADE 7" × 8½".

5. **Canterbury Hoe:** Hailing from England, this tool fuses the chopping action of a grub hoe with the spading and tilling motion of a fork or cultivator. A good choice for eliminating stubborn, deep-set weeds or rocks, it breaks up tough soil—even hardpan. The forged steel blade with 3 sharply pointed tines and eye socket connects to a polished hickory handle; the longer handle means less back fatigue. LENGTH 48", WEIGHT 2.8 LBS., BLADE 7½" × 4½".

2. Field Eye Hoe

1. Scovil Hoe

3. Swedish Tree-Planting Hoe

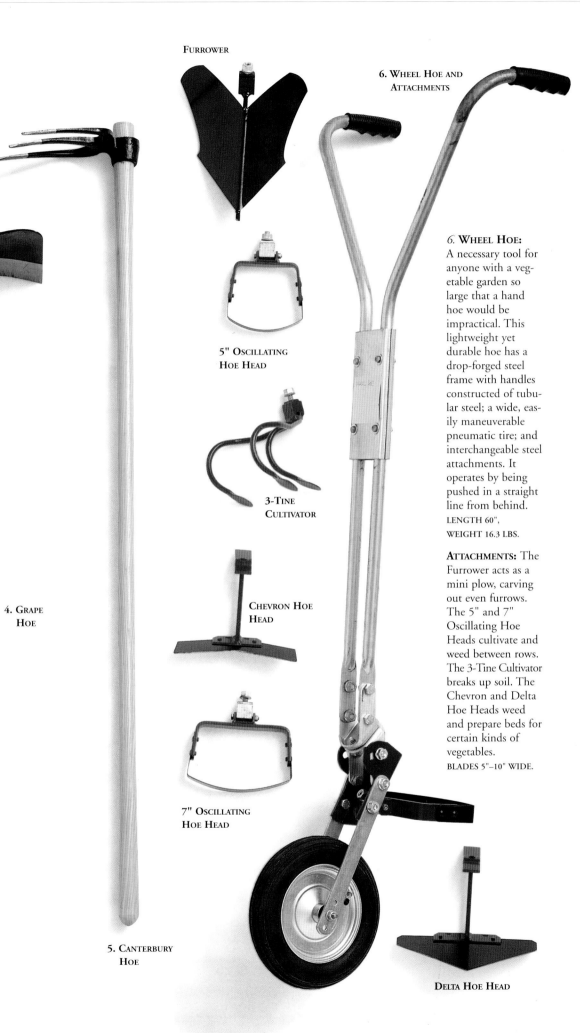

FURROWER

6. WHEEL HOE AND
ATTACHMENTS

5" OSCILLATING
HOE HEAD

3-TINE
CULTIVATOR

4. GRAPE
HOE

CHEVRON HOE
HEAD

7" OSCILLATING
HOE HEAD

5. CANTERBURY
HOE

DELTA HOE HEAD

6. **WHEEL HOE:**
A necessary tool for
anyone with a veg-
etable garden so
large that a hand
hoe would be
impractical. This
lightweight yet
durable hoe has a
drop-forged steel
frame with handles
constructed of tubu-
lar steel; a wide, eas-
ily maneuverable
pneumatic tire; and
interchangeable steel
attachments. It
operates by being
pushed in a straight
line from behind.
LENGTH 60",
WEIGHT 16.3 LBS.

ATTACHMENTS: The
Furrower acts as a
mini plow, carving
out even furrows.
The 5" and 7"
Oscillating Hoe
Heads cultivate and
weed between rows.
The 3-Tine Cultivator
breaks up soil. The
Chevron and Delta
Hoe Heads weed
and prepare beds for
certain kinds of
vegetables.
BLADES 5"–10" WIDE.

THE WEEDER

The hand weeder comes into its own when the work is close to plants or in other restricted zones—in perennial beds, for example, or in raised beds or pots. There are more kinds of weeders than you can imagine. One model uses a ball to fulcrum weeds out of the soil; another has a spring mechanism that's supposed to shoot weeds up into the air (so you can catch them on the fly). One looks like a witch's claw, another like a beckoning finger.

All weeders multiply the native capabilities of the human hand. One class chops or pulls through soil like fingers shaped into a claw, taking up mats of weeds and breaking the soil crust. A second class acts like the edge of the hand, bent into a U or a V at the first joint and sharpened for slicing off weeds. The third and smallest class, which mimics the hand's ability to pinch, includes weeders that grasp weeds firmly and yank them out of the ground.

CHOOSING A WEEDER

Because most weeders are small hand tools, often used by people on their knees, manufacturers assume that they will be subjected to much less stress than larger tools. Therefore, most handled weeders are of tang-and-ferrule construction. In some cases, the tang is reinforced with a type of screw end that makes it less likely to pull out and the ferrule is through-riveted.

The weakness of most hand weeders lies in the metal head, where hard prizing—especially of stones or other larger impediments—leads to bending, weakening, and ultimately breaking. Therefore, good hand weeders have a certain amount of spring built into them so they can give and rebound against obstacles. The best weeders are constructed of forged steel, but even stamped ones can work well provided that the steel is of a good, sturdy gauge. There is no manufacturers' rating system for weeders. Particular styles—like Cape Cod weeders— are often used by more serious gardeners and therefore tend to feature better construction.

USING A WEEDER

Most hand weeders are meant to be used on your knees; however, some popular and broadly useful models are available with long handles for people who find kneeling difficult. If you're working for any length of time, it's best to kneel (not stoop) or at least squat. The strain on your lower back is reduced this way, and you bring more force to bear upon the weeds. Furthermore, kneeling creates the stablest platform for

All weeders multiply the native capabilities of the human hand.

reaching into crowded beds and pulling aside plants with one hand while wielding the weeder with the other.

COLLINEAR HAND WEEDER: This weeder is one of the kindest to your hands. It's precisely designed to catch weeds just below the surface of the soil. The long neck and blade are angled so that no extra maneuvering is necessary when attacking weeds. The hourglass handle is also a particular delight to hold when weeding for long stretches.

Gardeners who really like to get out every last bit of root tend to prefer other weeders, but the collinear hand weeder is the popular choice for those who want to scrape the soil of weeds. This tool was developed by Eliot Coleman and mimics his design for the similarly named hoe (see page 71).

THE FISHTAIL AND DANDELION WEEDER: The business end of the fishtail weeder (or asparagus knife) is shaped in a sharp inverse V to catch a taproot deep and ease it out of the ground or cut it off at the roots. Gardeners who love this tool are delighted by the chance to really root out a weed; others lament that the narrow blade never gets the whole root, and the weed just comes back again. The dandelion weeder, a longer version of the tool, has a 3' handle that allows you to work in a standing position.

THE CAPE COD WEEDER: This tool is an excellent handheld weed slicer, but much to the dismay of left-handers it exists only in a right-handed version. The shape of a Cape Cod weeder is like a finger bent at the first and second joints, with the inner edge sharpened, so it's great for reaching in among growing plants to extirpate hidden weeds. For precise reach, it's hard to beat. It's also heavy enough to stand up to all soil types and pernicious enough to extract big weeds.

THE HAND WEEDER: This is the most versatile tool of those meant to get weeds in narrow spaces. Available in both right- and left-handed versions, it consists of a thin sharp blade set at an angle. By pulling and sliding it gently, you can slice off even well-hidden weeds with no damage to other plants. It also has a pointed end that makes it good for crack and crevice work.

THE FARMER'S WEEDER: Sometimes called a hori-hori knife, after its Japanese name, this weeder is a big knife with a slightly dished end—one sharp blade and one serrated blade. It's great for heavy-duty weeding, especially for rooting out perennials, and is tough enough to go after brambles. Some people swear by it in place of a trowel and will even use it for planting seedlings.

THE CRACK WEEDER: This type of weeder comes in different shapes, but each is designed essentially to cut out weeds or moss in narrow cracks like those between stones and bricks.

Though there are many stand-up weeders available, the surest technique for weeding involves getting down near the soil in a crouch or on your knees.

One method of weeding involves slicing weeds off at their base in a swivel motion from the side.

Weeders

1. DANDELION WEEDER

1. DANDELION WEEDER: For help in removing weeds with deep taproots, such as dandelions, this specialty tool is an ergonomic gem. The gardener drives the 2-prong mouth down over the weed; pulling on the long hardwood handle draws up the lever to lock the prongs around the taproot; completing the horizontal motion of the handle pulls the weed out, taproot and all. The cast steel blade with rust-resistant enamel finish is connected to the handle by a solid socket and secured with a bolt. The hinged lever is also constructed of steel. LENGTH 46½".

2. FISHTAIL WEEDER: Commonly known as an asparagus knife or asparagus weeder, this essential hand tool is used to remove a variety of weeds by cutting them off at the roots. Originally designed to harvest asparagus shoots, the Fishtail Weeder is now a very popular option for weeding in tight spaces, especially in rock gardens or in and around crevices and paving stones. Fashioned from forged carbon steel with enamel finish and connected to a polished hickory handle by a solid socket, this particular version should last a lifetime. LENGTH 15".

3. TAPROOT WEEDER 1: One of the most basic designs in weeders. This forked tool is constructed of a stamped-steel alloy and connected to the hardwood handle by a sturdy tang and ferrule. The short neck and bulky handle add stability, while the long blade allows the weeder to be inserted deeply alongside a tenacious taproot. The bend in the body of the tool creates a fulcrum for prying up the taproot. LENGTH 10½".

4. CRACK WEEDER: Ideal for weeding in crevices, stone walls, and other small areas, this relative of the Cape Cod Weeder is designed to scrape up weeds growing in deep and narrow places. An affordable option constructed of stamped-steel alloy with a painted wood handle. LENGTH 10½".

5A. LEFT-HANDED HAND WEEDER; 5B. RIGHT-HANDED HAND WEEDER: Used like miniature hoes, these premium weeders are designed to scrape just under the surface of the soil, severing off weeds with one stroke. Lightweight and easy to manipulate, they can be used in existing beds around individual plants without disturbing healthy roots. Solid carbon steel blade and shank is inserted deeply into the hardwood handle for surprising stability. Left-handed weeder is angled slightly to the right, vice versa for right-handers. LENGTH 18", BLADE 4¾" × 2".

6. FARMER'S WEEDER: Used by some home gardeners to grub out weeds. This weeder doubles as a knife and is a handy all-purpose tool that combines many functions in one, such as digging small holes, planting bulbs, prying up rocks, and cutting troublesome roots. The 6" blade sports a smooth, tapered slicing edge on one side and a serrated cutting edge on the other. Hardwood handle. LENGTH 11½".

7. CAPE COD WEEDER: Popular with home gardeners, this L-shaped original is used like a hoe to cut weeds off at their roots. The narrow head allows the user to work in very tight spaces around existing plants. This particular version is geared more toward a right-handed user. Forged high-carbon steel blade is inserted into a polished, contoured ash handle and secured with epoxy and a steel pin. The entire joint is reinforced by a brass ferrule. A leather loop allows for easy storage. LENGTH 13".

8. COLLINEAR HAND WEEDER: This unique hand tool was invented by master gardener Eliot Coleman, based on his design for the Collinear Draw Hoe (see page 71). It alleviates wrist torque by shaving just below the surface of the soil, allowing the user to hold the tool at a natural angle while kneeling. A lightweight steel alloy blade is attached to a slender steel shank, which is inserted into a hardwood hourglass-shaped handle. LENGTH 14", BLADE 7" × 1".

9. STIRRUP WEEDER: The popular Stirrup Weeder is designed to uproot or pull weeds at their roots by slipping just below the surface of the soil. This particular version is fashioned from one piece of lightweight aluminum and is especially handy for users who suffer from arthritis or other wrist discomforts. May also be used to lightly cultivate topsoil. LENGTH 10½".

10. JEKYLL WEEDER: This deluxe hand weeder is a reproduction of the famous horticulturist Gertrude Jekyll's favorite weeder. Good for uprooting many tough weeds, it is constructed of the best material available. A polished stainless steel forked blade attaches to the beech handle by tang-and-ferrule construction. Useful as a small hand cultivator or grubbing tool, this particular weeder nestles snugly in the palm and makes an elegant presentation. LENGTH 10".

11. TAPROOT WEEDER 2: A unique-looking tool that features a forked head for removing weeds with deep taproots. Supported by a sturdy steel fulcrum, this weeder makes it easy to remove stubborn roots with a gentle downward push on the handle, eliminating any strain or torque on the wrist. The patented Vistaflex cushion-grip handle adapts to individual palms, protecting against blisters and chafing. Enameled steel with rubber grip. LENGTH 12½".

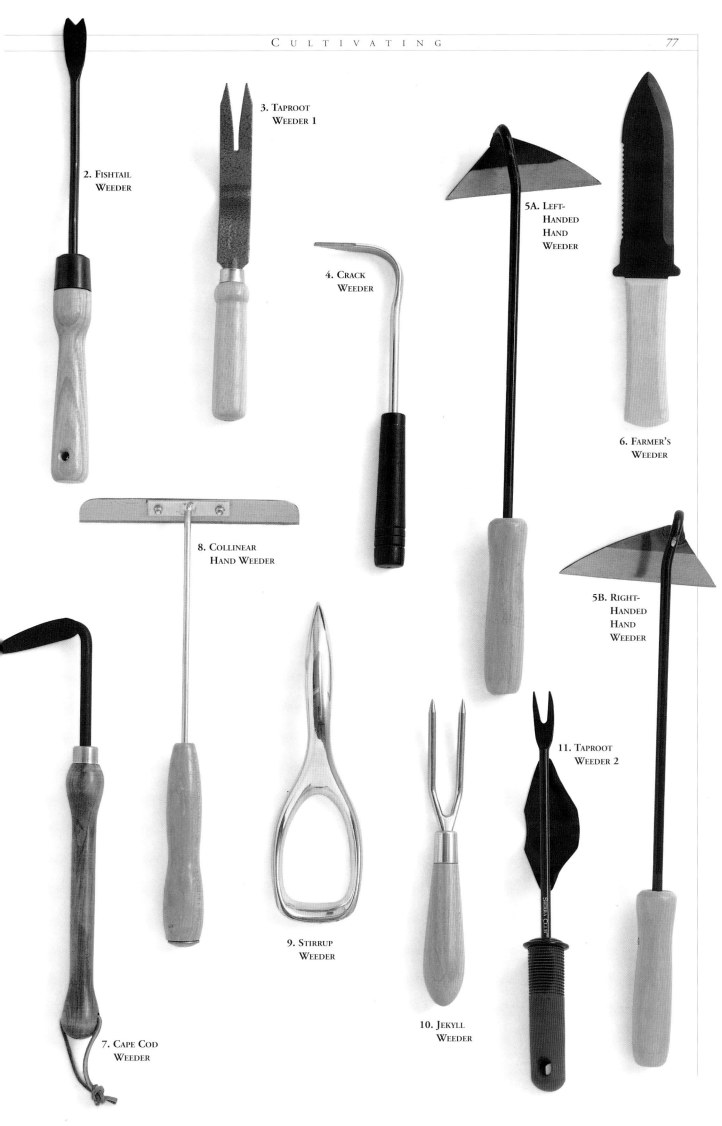

2. FISHTAIL WEEDER

3. TAPROOT WEEDER 1

4. CRACK WEEDER

5A. LEFT-HANDED HAND WEEDER

6. FARMER'S WEEDER

8. COLLINEAR HAND WEEDER

5B. RIGHT-HANDED HAND WEEDER

7. CAPE COD WEEDER

9. STIRRUP WEEDER

11. TAPROOT WEEDER 2

10. JEKYLL WEEDER

THE CULTIVATOR

Cultivators are tined tools, usually with long handles. (The hand fork is actually a small cultivator.) The tines are always bent at an angle so they can be dragged through the soil. There may be one prong or as many as seven.

A cultivator is most useful in the medium-size or larger vegetable patch, or in garden beds where there is enough room to maneuver a large tool. It stirs the soil and pulls up young weeds between the rows quickly and efficiently. It's also useful when you want to incorporate compost or manure that you've already broadcast on the soil's surface. According to how much pressure you apply to the tool, it can work to differing depths.

CHOOSING A CULTIVATOR

A cultivator is a heavy-duty pull tool. The more you draw it through the soil, the more the tines and the shaft tend to pull apart from the stress. Therefore, if you want a cultivator that will last a lifetime, check to see that the head and tines are solid and securely affixed to the shaft.

The head and tines should be forged from a single piece, not spot-welded together. There is nothing worse than a gap-toothed cultivator—one whose welds have failed because you happened to yank the tool against a heavy stone. A solid socket, through-riveted to the shaft, makes the optimum connection between head and shaft. Though solid-socket cultivators are hard to find and cost more than the other models, they're well worth the search and the higher price.

Most manufacturers use a tang-and-ferrule construction to secure the head to the shaft. The quality of this connection varies incredibly with different models. The cheapest ones are awful; after a year or two of use, the head loosens and falls right off. (You can hang the tool next to your beheaded hoes.) At the other end of the spectrum is the highest-quality tang-and-ferrule work, tight-fitting and nailed in place, almost the equivalent of a solid socket. You can often tell the quality by feel and heft, but if you have any doubts go for the top of the line in any given brand.

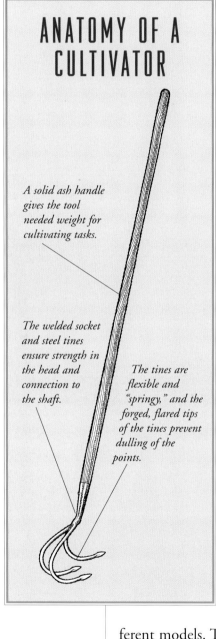

ANATOMY OF A CULTIVATOR

A solid ash handle gives the tool needed weight for cultivating tasks.

The welded socket and steel tines ensure strength in the head and connection to the shaft.

The tines are flexible and "springy," and the forged, flared tips of the tines prevent dulling of the points.

Though different garden situations call for different cultivators, there are three important parameters to consider: tine shape, width, and depth.

Cultivators are manufactured with tines in a variety of cross sections, from rectangular or triangular to round or oval. The broader and flatter cultivators have greater strength and are capable of working heavier soils. The round- and oval-tined models are more appropriate for working lighter soils and for incorporating compost or other soil amendments.

The cultivator you buy should have a width to match your garden practice; the choice varies from a wafer-thin, single-tine biocultivator to a 9"-wide, four-tine manure hook. Generally, the more open space in your garden (unplanted soil in a specimen border or rows in the vegetable garden), the broader the cultivator you will want. The best compromise is in the 4"–5" range.

There is also a wide choice of depths. The longest tines will go 9" down into your soil; the shortest will go only about 3". You can, of course, vary the depth of penetration by adjusting the pressure that you apply to the tool, but the shallower cultivators are preferred for perennial beds, where you don't want to disturb a root system. The deeper ones are actually meant to grub out roots. In fact, one model, the potato fork, was invented for digging potatoes, but it also does a good job of loosening heavy soils.

USING THE CULTIVATOR

A garden fork is to a spade as a cultivator is to a hoe. The tines help to more thoroughly stir the soil, and they will penetrate where a solid edge may not. Nonetheless, the tined and edged tools work in precisely the same manner.

To use a tine cultivator, hold it with your thumbs open on your fist and pull it through the soil as if you were using a draw hoe. Be sure to choose a model whose handle is long enough so you won't have to stoop to work it.

THE THREE-PRONG CULTIVATOR: "Claw" is an apt nickname for this cultivator, since it holds its three flexible tines in a clenched array with the middle tine well ahead of the other two. In some versions, the prong ends come to a smooth point; in others, they terminate in three V-shaped or spoon-shaped ends, each of which acts like a miniature plow.

There are two great virtues to the three-prong cultivator. First, the arrangement of its tines allows you virtually to make two passes with a single pull. The lead tine stirs the soil and turns it in revolving-door

The cultivator you buy should have a width to match your garden practice.

fashion through the tines that follow, resulting in a particularly fine crushing of clods. The second advantage is the narrow width of the head, seldom more than 3½", which makes it possible to work where rows are narrow in the vegetable garden or in closely planted garden beds.

THE BIOCULTIVATOR: The single-prong cultivators are even better than three-prong models at cultivating right up against the stems of your plants. Shaped more or less like a finger, the single prong allows the most exact control possible over where you turn the soil.

There are two versions of single-prong cultivators: one crooked like finger against a trigger, the other poised like a finger on a keyboard. There is not a great deal of difference between the two, except that the former likes to scuff the soil near the surface while the latter can drive as deep as 6" into the ground.

The biocultivator has a copper rivet feature that penetrates the soil with every thrust, reportedly leaving traces of copper there. Since copper is known to act as a fungicide, proponents of the biocultivator claim that it may help to reduce the local population of soil fungi and thus serve to increase the crop.

THREE- AND FOUR-TINE CULTIVATORS: These tools are the workhorses when it comes to making a fine dust mulch. They are narrow enough to get into most rows, yet long, heavy, and sharp enough to penetrate and break the soil. Unlike three-tine cultivators, the four-tine models have prongs that are all in a single line—a propitious arrangement for dragging up small stones and other impediments along with burgeoning weeds.

The ordinary three- and four-tine cultivators are made with round or oval prongs, sharpened at the ends. For heavy soils or heavy-duty use, there are also models made with sturdy oblong prongs that come to a diamond point. The latter are essentially strong garden forks whose prongs have been bent over during forging. Their weight and strength make them an excellent choice for working heavy or rocky soils.

1. **3-Prong Cultivator:** This tool features many of the same benefits as the 3-Prong Arrowhead Cultivator with the added beauty and high-quality construction of a Swiss design. The forged, polished steel head has narrow diamond-point tines, good for blending amendments into predug soil, loosening topsoil before planting, and weeding. This delicate-looking tool's hardwood handle and solid-socket construction guarantee a lifetime of use. Taller length and head angle enable the user to stand fully upright when cultivating. LENGTH 65", WEIGHT 2 LBS., BLADE 4¾" × 9".

2. **3-Prong Arrowhead Cultivator:** A good, intensive soil cultivator. The heavy-duty head, made of forged carbon steel and featuring 3 diamond-point tines especially suited to amending dense clay soil, is bolted to steel pads and then to a hardwood handle. The angle of the head makes it easier to stand upright, alleviating back strain. The shorter length may be preferred by some users. LENGTH 54", WEIGHT 2.3 LBS., BLADE 6" × 11½".

3. **Biocultivator:** A unique Swiss design, this specialty tool is meant to cultivate in small areas by mixing compost and organic amendments with surface soil. The single steel blade gently loosens and aerates the top 6" of soil (twice as deep as other culti-

vators) without damaging existing roots or inverting soil. Especially good when used in intensively planted or narrow vegetable or flower beds, it is easier to control than 3- and 4-prong versions but is not appropriate for large jobs. A steel blade with flared edge is attached to the hardwood handle by solid-socket construction. A copper rivet is embedded in the blade to deposit trace elements in the soil—a practice said to reduce fungi and increase yields in heavy or acidic soils. LENGTH 64", WEIGHT 2 LBS., BLADE 1" × 13".

4. **4-Prong Cultivator:** This cultivator has been used for centuries to mix compost, manure, and amendments into predug soil. A sturdy, tough, multipurpose tool constructed with forged steel tines and a solid-socket joint, it is the optimal choice for weeding and cultivating in one stroke. It may also be used to aerate soil around trees and shrubs, drag compost when turning the pile, or break up dense topsoil. LENGTH 55½", WEIGHT 4 LBS., BLADE 5½" × 9".

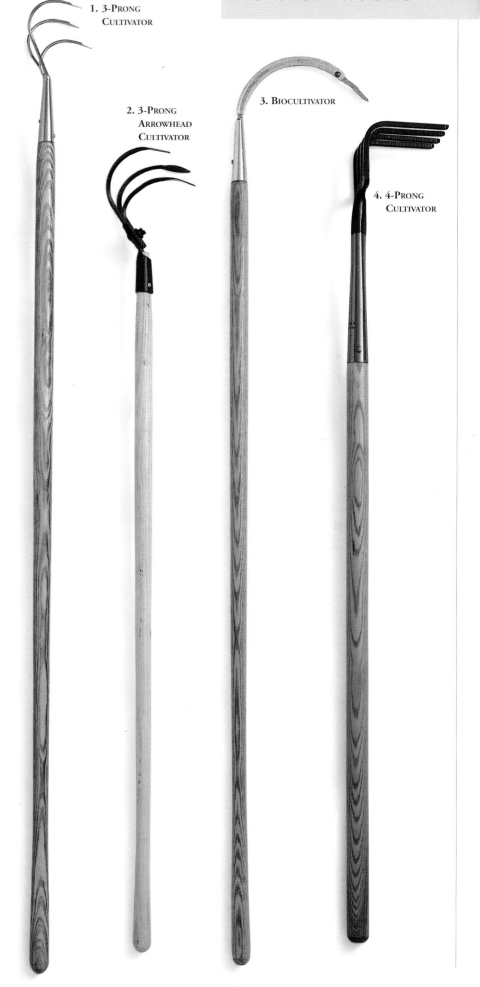

Cultivators

1. 3-Prong Cultivator

2. 3-Prong Arrowhead Cultivator

3. Biocultivator

4. 4-Prong Cultivator

CHAPTER FOUR

PROPAGATING

One could do worse than to define beauty as the growing of a seed or the regeneration of a whole plant from a bit of stem, tuber, or leaf. And to assist in these events is the gardener's greatest privilege and pleasure. Through these simple sproutings is shown the essential and harmonious structure of the living, growing world.

The events that take place in propagation are plainly miraculous. Where before there was apparently a loose part—an ovoid seed the size of a dust mote or as large as a cannonball, or perhaps a severed stem, leaf, or root—suddenly there is a whole plant. One minute, the wind might blow the loose piece around the corner, but suddenly roots go down and the fragment is no longer a fragment. A new plant has been born, and the world is green again.

Nature has her tools—sun, wind, rain, weather, animals, insects, and weeds—but so does the gardener. In addition to know-how, helping with the birth and rebirth of plants from slips, cuttings, or seeds requires good sense in choosing the right tool for each delicate step. The kitchen counter or the garage tool bench is not the place to mix potting soils, set the seeds in their temporary beds, or make cuttings. A well-organized potting bench is required for efficient and sanitary propagation. And though you may start seedlings in old margarine tubs or milk cartons, it's likely that you'll look into highly efficient soil blockers if you're serious about propagation. Finally, when you go to plant out the seedlings early, you had best have a good cloche, row cover, hot cap, or cold frame to protect them from the frost.

"The Norwegians have a pretty and significant word, 'Opelske,' that they use in speaking of the lure of flowers. It means literally 'loving up,' or cherishing them into healthy vigor."

—CELIA THAXTER

Propagating for the garden is real midwifery and calls upon the traditional midwife's skills: faith, patience, cleanliness, steadiness, and meticulous care. Just as a human mother needs constant assurance in clean and comfortable surroundings, so do seeds, cuttings, and grafts need a clean, well-made bed, consistent care, and a steady period of weaning. In any kind of propagation, the basic steps are the same. First the raw materials—seeds, stem cuttings, roots, graft scions, and stock—are separated from the parent and prepared to sprout on their own. Second, a suitable environment for the birth to take place must be readied. The third step is weaning, the gradual preparation for the new plant to live on its own.

Whole arts are devoted to all three of these processes. Each gardener stratifies some seed just so; each likes a particular medium for rooting different plants; each insists upon making the stem cutting at a particular angle. And most important, each appreciates the need for special propagation tools.

HISTORY OF PROPAGATION

Pre-Christian civilizations were wont to credit gods or demigods as the first propagators. That you could take a single seed from an ear of wheat, plant it, raise it, and get sixty more seeds from that original seed was, after all, a momentous discovery. To primitive man, it was little short of a miracle.

In a way, world history itself might be called a footnote to this discovery. The finest practical minds of each century—people like Aristotle, Cato the Elder, Virgil, Walafrid Strabo, Francis Bacon, Alexander von Humboldt, Ralph Waldo Emerson, and Luther Burbank—all studied plant propagation with a view toward improving the quality and variety of useful plants. As horticultural knowledge advanced, civilizations rose and flourished. When the rural arts declined—in Mesopotamia with soil destruction, in Rome through ruinous policies—so did entire cultures.

The principles behind today's propagation practices were understood long ago. The ancient Irish, who appreciated the virtue of a well-drained seedbed, propagated seeds by setting them into a square turf turned upside down; when transplanting time came, there was no need to knock the tender seedlings out of a box, and therefore transplant shock was reduced. Another practice, still in use today, is every bit the equal of a soil block or propagating pot. For centuries, housewives have saved their eggshells to serve as containers for seedlings. They can be planted straight into the garden soil, which not only reduces shock, but also provides calcium and other valuable plant nutrients through the shell.

The importance of maintaining the right temperature for seeds and seedlings has also long been appreciated. Native American gardeners

As horticultural knowledge advanced, civilizations rose and flourished.

started pumpkin seeds in bark baskets filled with a rich compost from dead tree stumps. To speed germination, they hung the baskets over a low fire, much the way a heating mat or cold frame is used to raise germination temperatures. The technology of the hotbed—essentially a cold frame set over a bed of manure whose decomposition creates heat—represents the same idea.

The lore of the cloche is unique. In medieval times, the cloche was an alchemist's tool, useful for isolating chemical reactions. How it got into the garden is unknown, but its properties are still plainly alchemical: while the rest of the soil is still bare and black, the dirt under the warming cloche is rich with greenery. Once, garden cloches all had the distinctive bell shape and were made of glass. In the nineteenth century, Paris and other French cities were fairly surrounded with cloches in early spring and in fall. (Imagine what tunes could have been played upon those thousands of bells!)

Knowledge of propagation by cuttings may go all the way back to the time of Noah, who is supposed to have grown the first grapevine. Notoriously easy to increase by cuttings, vines were already grown in a bewildering array of varieties long before "scientific" propagation. Early experiments may have involved the severing of promising mutations, or sports, from an existing vine, planting them on their own, and evaluating the new plant that resulted. Similarly, hedgers have always depended on the fact that easy-to-reproduce plants such as willow will grow up to form a hedge if vigorous cuttings are taken from an existing specimen and planted all in a row.

Of course, one of the chief problems with reproduction by means of cuttings is that the fat ends, once inserted into the earth, may rot before they can sprout roots. To prevent this, the Greek philosopher Theophrastus suggested thrusting cuttings into a squill bulb. Later gardeners evolved an ingenious technique of planting slips through holes drilled into a willow branch on the theory that the branch would act as a sleeve to protect the buried portion while roots developed.

Today we use a rooting powder combined with a chemical fungicide, both to stimulate root growth and to keep away rot fungi. But even

THE ANCIENT ART OF GRAFTING

St. Paul's mention of an olive graft in his epistle to the Romans suggests that grafting was already a practice of long standing. The idea was to graft the desired scion onto a wild olive root so that the former acquired the latter's hardiness.

By the age of the Renaissance, grafting was a high art, and there were numerous "magical" tinctures for protecting the graft union from infection while the two plants knit into one. Among the most odorous and entertaining of these mixtures was one composed of alcohol, pine pitch, beeswax, and talc. Even today, despite the presence of effective rubber bands that seal the graft union, there are propagators who still prefer carefully prepared grafting wax. One suspects that it's as much the smell and feel of this process that excites them as its hygienic advantage.

this high-tech solution has its clear precedent. Renaissance gardeners used any number of mysterious tinctures that, when painted over the end of the cutting, were meant to prevent rot. Some were the mere essence of cow dung, while others included everything from wax and pitch to aloe juice.

In the ensuing centuries, little changed in the propagator's art. Rooting hormones improved the ability of cuttings to thrive, and rubber bands replaced wax on the grafter's bench. Cloning, or reproduction from the cells at a plant's growing tip, has dramatically changed commercial propagation, but not the home gardener's propagating procedures or the joy of creating new life where none existed before. As Angelo Pellegrini wrote in *The Food Lover's Garden,* "There is a special delight in observing the progress of propagation; in following the course of a plant's development, day by day; in contemplating a healthy, well-nourished plant in soil properly cultivated and free of weeds."

PROPAGATION TOOLS

The tools used for propagating may look like generic tools, but they are primarily selections or adaptations developed especially for the purpose. A border fork or perennial spade is a smaller version of the usual models, especially useful when working down on your knees near a clump of roots. A dibber for sowing in flats is a mere shadow of the big, bulbous tools used for planting out. Potting mediums, such as vermiculite and perlite, are intentionally different from soils, and floating row covers are a far cry from the plastic sacks that line a trash can.

True enough, some propagating tools may share duty as digging or cultivating implements. And, conversely, a border fork or spade can be used for dividing roots, as can well-sharpened and disinfected bypass pruning shears be used to take cuttings or scions. In fact, the occasional propagator can usually get by with little more than a pocketknife and some margarine tubs.

But if you're serious about this pleasure, make sure you have the right tools. The result will be less infection, less rot, and a greater number of healthy new plants.

Propagation Tools

1. **PRESSER BOARD:**
Used to tamp down
moist topsoil over
recently planted
seeds or to prepare
seed trays before
seeding.
3½" × 10" × 3".

2. **PENCIL-SIZE
DIBBERS:** These
make individual,
small seed holes in
small pots, seed flats,
or peat pots.
⅝"–¾" DIA. × 5½"–9".

3. **BORDER FORK:**
Small and easy to
manipulate, this dig-
ging fork is invalu-
able for a myriad of
soil preparation and
cultivation tasks dur-
ing propagational
planting. Ideal for
separating roots and
bulbs when dividing
plants. LENGTH 37",
WEIGHT 2.75 LBS.,
HEAD 5½" × 9".

4. **PERENNIAL SPADE:**
A small, heart-shaped
tool designed to dig
around existing beds
and in tight spaces.
Useful for getting at
the rootball of peren-
nials that propagate
through dividing.
This version features
open-socket construc-
tion with a forged
steel blade and hard-
wood handle.
LENGTH 20¼",
WEIGHT .75 LB,
HEAD 4½" × 4¾".

5. **CONSERVATORY
SPRAYER:** A throw-
back to the Victorian
era, with a solid brass
tank, brass pump
body, and hardwood
handle with fully

**1. PRESSER
BOARD**

**2. PENCIL-SIZE
DIBBERS**

**3. BORDER
FORK**

7. SHEARS

**9. GRAFTING
KNIFE**

8. SHARPENER

**11. GRUB
KNIFE**

**10. BUD
KNIFE**

articulated nozzle, this gentle mister does not disturb tender seedlings and cuttings.
6" DIA. × 13".

6. **MISTERS:** Small glass or plastic misters are convenient for the home gardener and are available in any garden supply store.
3⅛" DIA. × 6";
2¾" DIA. × 5¾".

7. **SHEARS:** All-purpose utility shears with wide handle loops are useful for a variety of propagation tasks, from trimming extra foliage on cuttings to snipping twine and floral tape.

These shears feature 2" forged chrome-plated blades with a serrated edge.
LENGTH 8¾".

8. **SHARPENER:** An essential tool on any propagator's bench, a sharpener keeps the blades of a knife, scissors, or shears clean and sharp for optimum use. Proper care of blades controls the spread of diseases and pests.
LENGTH 9½".

9. **GRAFTING KNIFE:** A standard grafting knife for preparing scions and rootstock. With a folding forged steel blade

and polished walnut handle, it also makes a superb general-purpose knife.
BLADE 2¼", HANDLE 4".

10. **BUD KNIFE:** Used with roses, fuchsia, fruit trees, or other species that

are propagated by cuttings. The rust-resistant forged steel blade allows the user to make clean, precise cuts that will not damage bark. It has a flared section at the top to lift the bark while grafting, and folds into a black resin handle.
BLADE 1¾", HANDLE 4".

11. **GRUB KNIFE:** An essential tool for digging up bulbs, tubers, and corms to be divided. Also useful for opening up holes for transplanting seedlings, and for light cultivating and sawing. BLADE 6", HANDLE 5½".

12. **RIGHT-ANGLE TROWEL:** Useful for transplanting seedlings and sprouts, especially when using a Modular Soil-Blocking System (see pages 104–5).
HEAD 5¾", HANDLE 4¾".

5. CONSERVATORY SPRAYER

4. PERENNIAL SPADE

6. MISTERS

12. RIGHT-ANGLE TROWEL

SPECIALTY KNIVES

Cutting and dividing tools may be as simple as a safety razor blade, a craft knife, or an old kitchen knife. Yet the most delicate and exacting work of the propagator is accomplished by tools designed for a specific purpose. A grafting or budding knife, for example, is thinner in the blade than an ordinary pocketknife, and often features a little blunt protrusion for lifting a flap of bud. The knives are so beautiful that it's hard to choose among them, particularly when they're laid out together. All are made of fine carbon steel, and the bevels on the blades are steep and sharp. The handles are shaped to hold still in the hand. Although any one of them would work well for taking cuttings, propagating knives can be divided into three categories, according to the job they do best.

With your fore-finger supporting the stem tip below the cutting area, draw the blade toward you in a horizontal motion. Use the thumb of the hand that holds the knife to balance the stem and help center the cut.

THE PRUNING KNIFE: Characterized small hooked blades that look like diminutive billhooks, pruning knives have probably been in existence since the Renaissance. They are, in fact, scaled-down versions of big, sharp hooks used to prune, incise, and tip-layer hedging plants to create the broad thick hedges that still characterize the boundaries of European farm fields.

Pruning knives are excellent for scoring, wounding, and girdling, and for taking cuttings and slender wood scions. Their curved blades, however, are not appropriate for working directly on the propagating bench or for making cuts that need to be straight and precise.

The best and most costly blades are hand-forged, though less expensive stainless steel models hold almost as fine an edge. Some are sheath knives, but most fold up like a pocketknife. For the right feel, look for a solid walnut handle with a brass recess to receive the folding blade. The shapes and curvatures of the blade vary a great deal from brand to brand, so try a variety in your hands before you buy.

THE GRAFTING KNIFE: Grafting knives may be the purest and most businesslike small knives in the world today. Blunt-ended but slender in cross section, the best are hand-forged and hold a razor-sharp edge. The flat blade is best for working directly on the bench and for smoothing the cuts that match cambium to cambium.

There are both fixed-blade and folding versions. The folding ones, with their shapely walnut and brass-fitted handles, are a delight to look at, hold, and use. For grafting, however, this is not merely a creature comfort. A blade that slips may slice at the wrong angle, or worse, may tear the bark. Both mistakes can be fatal to the graft, since only a smooth, impermeable joint between scion and stock will produce a successful result.

THE BUDDING KNIFE: The budding knife has a blade precisely like that of a grafting knife but features a slender, smooth knob on the dull side at the outward extreme. When open, the budding knife looks something like an alligator in profile, with only the eye and snout appearing above the water.

What is the use of this little knob? It holds open the cut on the stock so the gardener can smoothly insert a single bud for grafting. This appendage is crucial, particularly for T-budding, when you must gently fold back the bark without tearing it. It also supplies a smooth but not sharp appendage on which to balance the tender slice of bud into the cleft. In addition, it works well whenever you want to make fine adjustments to fit scion and rootstock together.

THE THREE-IN-ONE KNIFE: In the constant push to combine and diversify, many fine knife companies now make three-bladed, folding horticultural knives that combine a hooked pruning blade, a blunt straight grafting blade, and a short, stubby dull blade for budding. These are good knives—made as carefully as their single-purpose cousins. The questions to ask when you consider buying one are: Does it feel right in my hand? And does it really do that much more than a good budding knife?

In each case, the answer may indeed be no. Everybody loves a good Swiss Army knife for its versatility and the huge range of functions combined in one small implement. But when it comes to precise budding and grafting, the tool ought to fit your hand as smoothly as a good glove. Why clutter it up with multiple functions that only make the handle too thick and increase the likelihood of a wobbly connection between blade and handle?

MULTIPURPOSE KNIVES: For the first-time propagator, a knife devoted to one single propagating operation may not be the best choice. Pruning knives are not delicate enough for grafting, and budding knives are generally not sturdy enough for rough-and-ready pruning in the garden. Instead, gardeners planning their first forays into various propagating techniques can choose from a range of multipurpose knives.

One option is the picnic knife, which is handy for various gardening tasks from simple budding to cutting twine or even fresh cucumbers from the garden. Most versions are folding and have a locking ring to keep the blade in place. And there is always the ubiquitous Swiss Army knife, a dependable option for very rudimentary cutting, including opening a cool bottle of soda on a hot day.

ANATOMY OF A BUDDING KNIFE

The nub, called a "bark lifter," is adept at peeling back bark for easier grafting.

A stainless steel blade resists rust and is easily sharpened.

The walnut handle is not only beautiful but durable and smooth to the touch.

Knives

1. **FRENCH PRUNING KNIFE:** A curved, high-carbon steel blade is the backbone of this handy, affordable option in pruning knives. The 2⅞" blade folds and locks into the 4⅜" hardwood handle, making it a good all-purpose pocketknife. A twisting ring called a Viro lock secures the blade when it is open.

2. **SWISS BUDDING KNIFE:** A good knife for fruit tree propagators, this tool has a 1¾" curved, stainless steel blade and bark lifter. The 4" handle is lined with brass.

3. **PICNIC KNIFE:** This versatile pocketknife is appropriate for most medium-level cutting tasks, from twine to cheese. It features a high-carbon 3¼" blade with a 4⅜" hardwood handle and locking ring.

4. **TINA PRUNING KNIFE:** A standard, all-purpose, folding pruning knife with a 2¾" curved, forged steel blade. The 4" handle is walnut with brass lining. Also useful for cutting flowers to make indoor arrangements.

4. TINA PRUNING KNIFE

3. PICNIC KNIFE

2. SWISS BUDDING KNIFE

1. FRENCH PRUNING KNIFE

5. OTTER PRUNING KNIFE: A professional-quality knife with a 3" thick, curved, forged steel blade that folds into a 4½" brass-lined hardwood handle. Larger than standard pruning knives, this is a good choice for heavy-duty tasks.

6. SWISS NURSERY KNIFE: This multi-purpose knife has a 2¾" straight, high-carbon stainless steel blade that's good for deadheading, pruning, and cutting. The blade is beveled on one side and flat on the other for easy sharpening. It folds into a 4" black nylon handle with brass lining.

7. SWISS ARMY KNIFE: A pocket-knife almost any outdoorsman wouldn't be without, this classic multi-purpose implement has six stainless steel blades that fold neatly into the renowned red nylon 4" handle. This example features an all-purpose blade, a small blade, a flat screwdriver, a Phillips screwdriver, an awl, a bottle opener, and a can opener.

8. TINA GRAFTING KNIFE: A superior grafting knife with a 2¼" forged steel blade that folds into a 4" polished walnut handle.

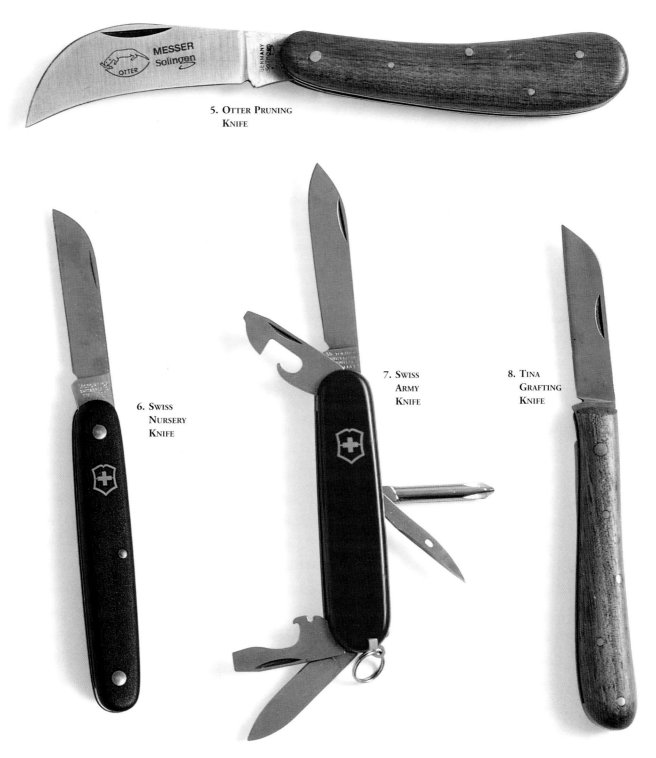

5. OTTER PRUNING KNIFE

6. SWISS NURSERY KNIFE

7. SWISS ARMY KNIFE

8. TINA GRAFTING KNIFE

THE POTTING BENCH

The potting bench is the birthing room for most of your new plants, whether you're starting from seed, cuttings, or scions. The bench itself must be capacious, clean, orderly, and properly stocked. Nothing is more frustrating than not finding the whetstone, when you're ready to graft a scion to rootstock, misplacing the dibber in the midst of transplanting a seedling, or losing the sprayer when you're readying a flat for germination.

A fine potting bench is fitted with at least one shelf (two is better) for stacking pots, peat pots, pellets, and trays, and for storing grafting wax, wound dressing, fungicidal powders, soluble fertilizers, and the like. It should also have a broad work surface at a comfortable height—just the height your hand reaches when your forearm is held parallel to the ground.

The work surface ought to be closed at the back so you won't lose half-filled pots or dibbers in your haste to make room by pushing things aside. The surface should be deep enough to fit an array of sprayers, watering cans, small pots, whetstones, lubricants, knives, dibbers, labels, and clippers behind the space where you actively work. This way, the tools will be handy when they're needed.

The space under the bench is often left open so that you might have sacks of peat and perlite at one moment and a pile of riddles, tampers, and flats the next, all depending on the job at hand. The dream potting bench, though, has a couple of large shelves for the riddles and the tampers, as well as flat files for the glass covers that go on top of seed flats. You can stack the flats themselves in an open corner, but there should be bins for the components of your favorite potting soils, making it a simple matter to put together the ingredients you need while keeping the rest well sealed in their bags.

PROPAGATING FROM CUTTINGS

The truly unbelievable act of propagation occurs when you take a cutting near the tip or even the middle of a woody plant's stem, plunge it into a sharp medium, and wait for roots to grow. The stem cutting itself is 2"–6" long and includes the growing tip as well as at least one leaf and a bud. The cut must be made straight across the stem, using a sharp pruning knife or bypass shears. Do not tear or shear the exposed cut.

Immediately touch the cut end to a small plate of rooting hormone laced with a fungicidal powder. Then insert the cutting into the medium up to approximately half its length, or until it stands firmly. Once all cuttings are in place, wet down the medium thoroughly to secure them. Put the cuttings in bright but not direct light.

To prevent drying out, use a cold frame or a barn cloche (see pages 106–11). As new shoots and roots appear, the structure can begin to be opened for longer periods, and by autumn the new plants can go into the garden.

Potting Bench

POTTING BENCH:
A traditional workbench constructed of rot- and weather-resistant wood, such as redwood or cedar, is an important planting and storage tool. Having a comfortable place to work with accessible supplies encourages efficiency and productivity. This top-quality, recycled-redwood version features a bottom shelf for storing pots and other implements, while topsoil and amendments may be stowed underneath. A deep, rectangular counter is located at comfortable standing height (32"–36" high) to facilitate potting and propagation tasks. An upper shelf provides easy access to smaller items. The best potting benches are easily assembled and able to withstand a lifetime outdoors. WORK TOP 48" × 22½", UPPER SHELF 6" DEEP, HEIGHT 33".

POTTING BENCH

PROPAGATION SUPPLIES

Propagating supplies include hardware and software. A finely made cut, whether for layering, propagation by cuttings, or grafting, is the beginning of a healthy new plant. But without the soft materials that form the planting medium, you end up with nothing more than rotten plant debris. Aside from all the potting mediums for germination, cuttings, or layering—vermiculite, perlite, peat, coir, sand, compost, and soil—soft materials such as fungicides and rooting hormone are needed to cleanse the cuts and encourage them to flourish. Finally, propagating supplies include the string, tapes, and waxes that bind and seal a graft, excluding air and infection.

The serious propagator will have all these materials on the bench, ready for use as the season begins.

SOILLESS MEDIUMS: Every propagator develops his or her own favorite recipes for germinating, potting, and cutting mediums. The point is to keep the seed or the cutting evenly moist, not damp, and to allow plenty of air to the roots. This being so, the mediums may even change from batch to batch.

Still, each material will be added for its particular quality. Perlite is used for its porosity; sharp sand improves drainage; peat moss holds water in reserve, as does the coconut fiber called coir; vermiculite is a wonderful substance made out of a clay that has been heated to 2000°F. Not only does the heat sterilize the material, but it also causes the clay to explode and exfoliate into onion-like layers. Each layer holds moisture evenly and uniformly. Furthermore, vermiculite has a fair amount of body and heft, so it stabilizes any medium.

ROOTING HORMONE: A rooting hormone is a chemical powder or liquid that stimulates auxins, organic chemicals that are already present in the cut stems. When activated, the auxins in turn encourage root growth.

The chemicals in rooting hormone have unpalatable names like indolebutyric acid (IBA, for short), indoleacetic acid (IAA), and napthoxy-acetic acid (NAA). The last of these is the one most often found in commercial rooting powder, diluted to about 0.8% concentration in a medium of powdered talc, water, or alcohol. In choosing a rooting hormone, knowing the active chemical is less important than checking to see if a fungicide has also been included; if so, you won't need to add any before you dip your cuttings.

There are two important things to remember when you use rooting hormone. First, never dip a cutting directly into the jar. Take a small amount of hormone, mix it with a dash of fungicide (if not already

Rooting hormone, applied to freshly cut stems, encourage good results from hard-to-root species.

included), and perform the operation in a shallow dish or on a piece of paper. This way, an infected cutting will not harm the whole jar of hormone. Second, dip only the exposed cut end of the cutting. A little rooting hormone goes a long way.

Liquid formulations are a little messier to use, but according to some reports they allow improved penetration of the chemicals and so encourage better rooting.

FUNGICIDAL POWDER: There are few things more annoying than seedlings that rot at the base and topple, or cuttings that wilt instead of rooting. Usually, the cause is one of the many soilborne fungi with nasty names like rhizoctonia.

Good cultural practices help. Clean your containers in a 10% bleach solution and don't overcrowd seeds or cuttings. Be sure that flats, trays, or pots are well aerated. If problems do occur, Benlate or captan fungicides will get rid of them. Use fungicide only as a last resort. All fungicides are in fact growth inhibitors, and will slow the plants you want to encourage in the process of killing the bugs.

GRAFTING TIES, WAX, AND TAPE: The procedure for sealing a graft generates as much controversy as any other slightly esoteric art. Jute, raffia, and waxed twine each have their adherents. Others swear only by rubber strips, and still others toss them all out, substituting biodegradable grafting tape. The truth is, each has its virtues.

All tie materials, including elastic bands, are supposed to biodegrade, making physical removal unnecessary. A slow-to-rot band, however, can leave an unsightly mark at the graft union. Experienced grafters will typically cut away the tie, whatever its material, one to two months after the graft has been made.

Except for grafting tape, all ties require a good coat of wax over the top to seal the graft fully. Commercially prepared grafting waxes are usually based on some combination of beeswax, paraffin, or resin. You can warm and soften them by rolling a wad in your hands and pressing it around the graft union but it's better to heat the wax gently over a burner until it's just barely liquid. The latter method makes it easier to spread the wax so that it fills all the cracks and crannies where the tie winds around the graft.

You can also use pure paraffin or beeswax, although each of these has to be melted. It's also a good idea to mix in a teaspoonful of captan or another fungicide with each batch.

Supposedly, grafting tape seals the graft all by itself and does not require waxing. Be careful, though, when grafting a plant that calluses quickly and grows very fast. Kousa dogwoods, for example, will callus so fast that the tape is liable to burst before the union is fully accomplished.

Propagation Supplies

1. PLANTING MEDIUMS: Peat, vermiculite, perlite, and sterilized soil are the primary choices used when propagating by cuttings. Constant moisture is essential for proper rooting, and these disease-free mediums drain quickly but retain adequate moisture.

2. FERTILIZER: Standard organic fertilizer, available in any garden supply store, is diluted and used to encourage healthy sprouts and seedlings.

3. PLANT SUPPORTS: Bale twine, bamboo stakes, and green floral tape are all used to tie up and support tender seedlings and encourage upright, vigorous growth.

4. GRAFTING WAX: Seals new grafts against moisture loss and protects from infection. Often melted and brushed on.

1. PLANTING MEDIUMS

2. FERTILIZER

4. GRAFTING WAX

5. TREE SEAL AND BRUSH

8. SOIL AND SOIL MARKERS

3. PLANT SUPPORTS

6. SOIL STAPLES

7. FUNGICIDE AND HORMONAL ROOT PROMOTER

BONIDE
SULFUR
PLANT FUNGICIDE
MICRONIZED SPRAY OR DUST

3. PLANT SUPPORTS

Geranium (cranesbill) 'Johnsons Blue' 4/10/96

CUTTING TYPE(S)
· Soft wood 4/10/96

ROOTING MEDIUM
· one part coarse sand
· one part vermiculite
· rooting hormone used

CLIMATE
· cold frame 65-75°
· bottom heat mat

POTTING TIME LINE
· 5/10 - 5/15
· Pot up into sterile soil peat pots.

9. PROPAGATOR'S NOTEBOOK

5. **TREE SEAL AND BRUSH:** Used to seal and protect large, open wounds on plants and trees from which cuttings have been taken.

6. **SOIL STAPLES:** A simple way to encourage a plant to reproduce is by "stapling" a branch or stem to the ground to encourage it to take root on its own.

7. **FUNGICIDE AND HORMONAL ROOT PROMOTER:** These items are now commonly used when propagating by cuttings to encourage healthy root growth and eliminate the spread of disease from generation to generation.

8. **SOIL AND SOIL MARKERS:** Sterilized soil promotes healthy germination; reusable markers remind the gardener of what has been planted since many sprouts look alike.

9. **PROPAGATOR'S NOTEBOOK:** A simple loose-leaf binder will encourage the propagator to write down each season's attempts, methods, successes, and failures.

SEED FLATS, TRAYS, POTS, AND PELLETS

These small containers are the cradles of young plants, and regardless of aesthetics they must be sturdy, clean, and roomy enough to let the plants achieve the desired growth. For centuries, gardeners have been trying to approximate all these conditions in a single ideal container.

FLATS AND TRAYS: Wooden flats are hardy and stable. They can take a full load of potting soil without breaking, and (provided the bottom is slatted) they drain well. But they are also prone to picking up disease and can wick moisture away from the plants' roots. Plastic flats, on the other hand, hold moisture and temperature higher than wooden versions, and they are very easy to clean in a 10% bleach solution. Unfortunately, they are often less stable than wooden trays and frequently must be replaced. The sturdiest are made with long indented channels in the base, but even these are not as easy to hold and carry as a lovely redwood seed tray.

No matter what its material, planting directly into a flat is probably not a good idea. In a flat full of soil and seedlings, it's harder to separate out individual seedlings at transplanting time. And a disease that strikes one or two of the seedlings is liable to carry off the whole flat. A better way to use the flat is to let it serve as a tray and insert individual pots for each seedling.

PLASTIC POTS: Like plastic trays, plastic pots have the virtues of being reusable and easy to clean. However, these pots are not good for young plants. When roots reach the pot edge, they rebound and begin to wind around the rim, making girdling circles and developing a habit that discourages healthy growth when transplanted into the garden. In fact, much of what is usually called "transplanting shock" occurs because of the roots' discomfort.

A new generation of modular plastic lattices are made without bottoms, so that roots can at least grow freely downward. These models are also often fitted with a sort of ejection mold that hugs tightly to the walls of the lattice, thereby reducing transplant damage.

SOWING SEED

Tiny seeds like ageratum, snapdragon, and petunia can be sown directly onto the surface of the medium and pressed gently into it with a plastic label. Larger seeds can be distributed into little furrows or tiny, shallow holes, made with a small dibber, and lightly covered with medium.

Water the medium with a fine mist from a bulb sprayer or a watering can with an upward-pointing, oval rose. Setting the whole potting flat in a larger flat full of water that will percolate up through the roots is also effective. In either case, cover the flat or pot with a sheet of glass or seal it inside a plastic bag. This keeps moisture constant and maintains gentle pressure on the seed coat to soften and yield.

Most seeds like a soil temperature of at least 68°F for healthy germination. Placing the covered tray in a room that remains at 70° is adequate, but the temperature inside the medium is typically 5° to 10° lower than the surrounding air. Though setting the flat on top of the refrigerator will help, heat from a thermostatically controlled electric coil or tray set beneath the flat is the most dependable.

PEAT POTS AND PELLETS: These containers are supposed to largely eliminate transplant shock. They cost more than plastic pots, and they cannot be reused because you plant the seedling pot-and-all, but they do allow the roots to grow right to the border of the pot or pellet. When planting out, the seedling's roots are meant to penetrate the peat envelope and extend immediately into the surrounding soil. Sometimes, however, the peat is slow to decompose in the surrounding soil, making it just as hard for the roots to expand normally. Moreover, you must be careful to bury the *entire* peat pot in the soil, or the protruding rim will wick moisture away from the roots.

Various peat substitutes present the same problems as peat pots. For gardeners who are concerned about the potential environmental damage done by mechanical peat harvesting, the choice of a waste material like coir, a by-product of coconut production, is probably better. (If the coir were not turned to use as a peat substitute, the material would be entirely wasted.) A question remains as to what the ecological consequences are to the coconut grove when a substantial fraction of its organic matter is removed and exported. Furthermore, the fact that coir must be transported halfway around the world to reach us may negate its other ecological advantages.

PAPER POTS: Another apparently elegant and ecologically friendly solution is the paper pot, which can be made two different ways. The first is a latticework of recycled paper that resembles a big sheaf of paper dolls or paper party decorations. It fits directly into the seed flat, creating many modular "pots" that, when the seedlings have matured, can be parted and planted directly into the garden.

The second style is the newspaper pot, which also gives the gardener the pleasure of doing the recycling personally. The idea is marvelously simple: by lining a cup with old newspaper (never colored newspaper, whose dyes may harm the soil) and pressing a close-fitting wooden plunger into the cup, quite a sturdy little pot can be made. Filled with potting soil, it will grow any seedling, and the result can be planted directly into the garden without removing the pot.

As environmentally lovely as they may be, however, paper pots have the same limitations as peat pots. The whole pot must be buried in the soil to avoid wicking, and you likely will find that the roots have trouble breaking through the thin paper layer.

Seed-Planting Supplies

1. SOIL-TESTING KITS

1. SOIL-TESTING KITS: Soil testing used to be done in laboratories. Now, home-testing kits are available in any hardware or garden supply store. The best kits will test the soil's pH balance and test for the presence of the nutrients potassium, nitrogen, and phosphorus. The directions should be clear and concise and the results easy to read.

The kit on the left comes in its own storage box and features a detailed analysis more appropriate for serious or large-scale gardeners. The kit on the right is a more affordable version that may suit the average user. Both contain enough material to test several areas of soil.

2. **PLASTIC TRAY WITH COVER:** Plastic trays and covers come in a wide variety of sizes and protect tender seedlings by keeping them warm and moist. This small one features adjustable air vents to control moisture and air circulation.

3. **PEAT POTS AND PEAT TRAYS:** Peat is a marvelous substance for planting containers. Individual 2"-round pots and linked 2"-square trays are widely available. If the peat container is kept moist, the roots of the seedling can grow through it and into the surrounding soil after it is set out, making for less disturbance of the seedling. Peat containers also benefit the garden by adding organic matter to the soil.

4. **POT MAKER:** This simple but clever device allows the gardener to make 2¼" paper pots out of newspaper and almost any other waste paper. Surprisingly durable, paper pots last just long enough to get a seedling off to a great start before setting out. The Pot Maker is turned from hardwood and stands about 5" tall.

5. **DIBBER:** This D-grip dibber is the heaviest of hand dibbers. It features a solid steel body and fabricated steel stirrup supporting an oval hardwood handle. At over 2 lbs., the weight alone is enough to penetrate most soils. LENGTH 9½".

2. PLASTIC TRAY WITH COVER

3. PEAT POTS AND PEAT TRAYS

4. POT MAKER

5. DIBBER

6. POTTING TIDY

6. **POTTING TIDY:** A portable, plastic planting surface useful for anyone who doesn't have the space for a permanent potting bench. Affordable, longlasting, and lightweight, the extrathick, polypropylene plastic won't rust or rot and cleans up with the squirt of a hose. High back allows the tray to be hung up for storage, while flat front facilitates clean up.

SOIL BLOCKERS

Press the soil blocker into the planting soil by its handle and fill the blocks. Release the soil blocks by squeezing the plugger.

The best solution to date is actually an old one: the best pot is no pot at all. Market gardeners who need a long season for temperature-sensitive crops like melons have always given them a head start by planting the seed into an inverted square of turf. The block of turf is then planted seedling side up in the soil.

The advantage of this system is clear. The seedling soil is not substantially different from the surrounding soil, so roots will sense little change in environment as they expand. Furthermore, because there is no pot boundary except for the air itself, there is no barrier to turn the roots from their straight course into girdling circles.

Not many people have a handy supply of invertible turf, but a European manufacturer has developed a system that allows you to make stable, freestanding soil blocks. It is one of the prettiest combinations of appropriate engineering and gardening sense that can be imagined. The device, called a soil blocker, comes in four sizes, from a ¾" germination block to a broad 4" block for large seedlings. Generally speaking, the later a seedling is to be planted in the garden, the larger the block it will require, and in any case it's always a good idea to use the largest block that is practicable. Large blocks are richer in nutrients, and you can grow the seedling without the need for added soluble fertilizer.

The molding system looks rather like the detonator for an old-fashioned blasting system. You press down on the T-handle, pushing it into the blocking soil mix. The result is an array of freestanding blocks, each with a depression in the top to receive the seed. The larger sizes can even press out a hole in the top of the block, perfectly fit to receive seedlings grown in smaller blocks, for potting on before planting out.

ANATOMY OF A SOIL BLOCKER

A dimple fitting within the cube cells automatically prepares a hole for seeds or very young seedlings.

Constructed of solid zinc, a soil blocker can last for years if maintained properly.

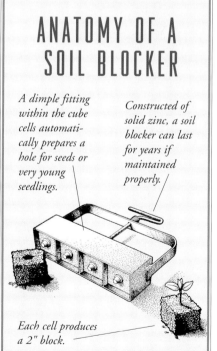

Each cell produces a 2" block.

Modular Soil-Blocking System

1. **MINI SOIL BLOCKER:** The initial tool used in the system when starting seeds. Makes twenty ¾" cubes in an area 3" × 4", a ratio that promotes maximum growth in a minimum of space. After seeds sprout, transfer cubes to the Soil Blocker to establish roots. Zinc-plated steel handle and washable plastic cube mold.
4" × 3" × 5".

2. **SOIL BLOCKER:** With one stroke, this tool makes four 2" blocks of soil, dimpled on top and ready for seeds. An optional cube attachment prepares blocks with a hole ready to accept the tiny ¾" cubes from the Mini Soil Blocker, thus allowing continuous seedling growth without disturbing tender roots. Zinc-plated steel.
8" × 2" × 8¾".

3. **MAXI SOIL BLOCKER:** This tool is used to make single 4" blocks that will accommodate transplants from the Soil Blocker or other late-planted varieties that need a larger module. Zinc-plated steel.
4" × 4" × 12½".

4. **STAND-UP SOIL BLOCKER:** This tool enables the user to stand while making many soil blocks in rapid succession. Each punch creates twelve 2" blocks. Zinc-plated steel.
8" × 6" × 31".

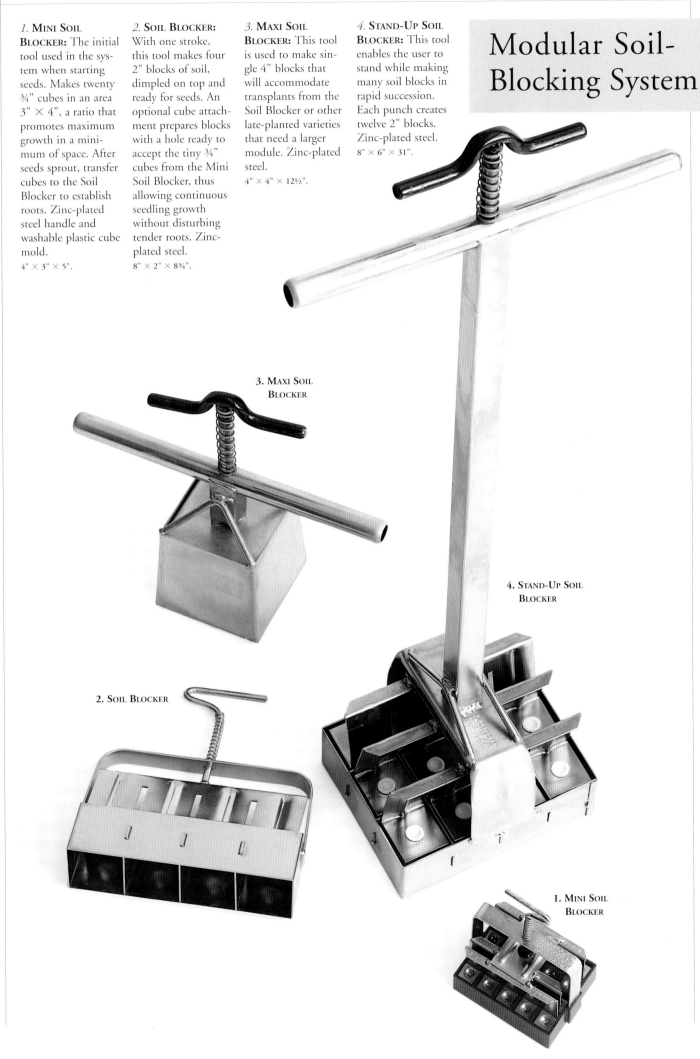

3. MAXI SOIL BLOCKER

4. STAND-UP SOIL BLOCKER

2. SOIL BLOCKER

1. MINI SOIL BLOCKER

COLD FRAMES

The definition of "hotbed" as a place that fosters ferment is thought to come from the widespread practice of propagating early vegetables, and even rooting cuttings, in heated garden frames called hotbeds during the eighteenth and nineteenth centuries. Before any other plant poked its nose through the winter soil, the hotbed would be seething with growth. Once, the source of heat was a layer of fresh manure in the bottom of the bed. These days, gardeners are more likely to use electric heating coils embedded in sand or depend exclusively on the warmth generated by the sun coming through the slanted glass window, or "light," that forms the hinged top of the bed. In the latter case, the hotbed becomes a cold frame, but it is by no means sodden and dead.

A good cold frame that captures the south light of late winter is at least as effective as a cloche in promoting early growth. In some respects, it's also more versatile, since you can open it a little at a time to let plants acclimatize to the outer air. Though somewhat heavier than cloches, cold frames can nevertheless be moved around the garden, used where needed, and removed when not in use. New lightweight frames made of efficient synthetic materials are especially appealing.

Indeed, cold frames are far more commonly found than hotbeds today. All types work on the principle of maximizing light while maintaining even warmth. They are frequently made with wooden or brick walls, whose insulating properties help maintain the interior temperature. The top "light" is hinged and covered in glass or acrylic.

Some cold frames have clear or translucent walls as well as tops. These are intended for northern latitudes, where the early spring sun strikes the ground at a low angle. More light reaches the seedlings earlier, improving their ability to photosynthesize. In the past, such cold frames usually lost too much heat through glass sides to be viable, but new heat-retaining plastic materials have made the clear frame a very useful tool for northern gardeners.

As the days warm and lengthen, the real problem for a cold frame is that it can get too hot. Several days of full sun in April in an unventilated cold frame will cook and wilt tomato seedlings. For this reason, every cold frame has a hinge that allows at least two or three different open positions. Generally, as the days lengthen and planting-out time approaches, the frame is left open for longer periods during the day. Of course, this requires monitoring. A wonderful hinge is available that senses the frame's interior temperature, opening it at 72°F and closing it again at 68°F. It is nonelectric, which is a small miracle.

A good cold frame that captures the south light of late winter is at least as effective as a cloche in promoting early growth.

Cold Frames

1. **RECYCLED REDWOOD COLD FRAME:** This durable, split-window cold frame is constructed of clear-heart redwood recycled from old wine vats. Mildew- and rot-resistant, it is designed to be placed directly over a seedling bed or used with three standard-size nursery flats. The lid is clear, shatterproof acrylic that allows light and heat in while keeping pests and frost out.
4' × 2', ANGLES FROM 7" TALL IN FRONT TO 12" AT BACK.

2. **WOODEN SEEDLING FLAT AND ROW COVER:** This is a low-tech, home-made variation on a cold frame, featuring a reusable redwood seedling flat that holds plantable peat pots and seedlings. Lightweight polyester-mesh row cover protects against frost and disease while retaining moisture and allowing light and heat to penetrate. A good, portable alternative to a cold frame for patio, deck, and rooftop gardeners.
12" × 24" × 6".

3. **DANISH COLD FRAME:** For those who live in regions with long nights and a short growing season. This cold frame makes the most of every bit of light by allowing exposure from every angle with its translucent 3½-mm-thick poly-carbonate structure. The frame is aluminum and the lid adjusts to varying heights.
35" × 21" × 12".

1. RECYCLED REDWOOD COLD FRAME

2. WOODEN SEEDLING FLAT AND ROW COVER

3. DANISH COLD FRAME

CLOCHES AND OTHER SEASON EXTENDERS

The word "cloche" comes from a French word meaning "bell." Indeed, "bell jar" is another name for this clear-walled device that fits neatly over one or more tender plants, protecting them from cold, wind, insects, and birds. You can plant out tender crop plants like tomatoes, melons, and peppers two to three weeks earlier when using a cloche. You can also start lettuce, strawberries, and similar cool-season crops earlier in the season and keep them on later into the fall.

After World War II, the rise of reliable clear plastic made all styles of cloches available in cheaper, plastic models. There are plastic bells, caps, cones, pyramids, tents, and barns. They pass light as well as the glass models do, and they are less liable to break. The single abiding difficulty is that plastic eventually degrades under the ultraviolet rays of the sun. Otherwise, the only reason to choose glass over plastic is an aesthetic one. Once, glass was slightly more impervious to frost, but now even that advantage is gone.

Gardeners claim mircles for both glass and plastic cloches. There is hardly a serious market gardener in the northern third of the United States who cannot tell you a story about a continuous cloche that saved 100' of young tomatoes, lettuce, scallions, cabbages, or strawberries in a snowstorm.

THE PLASTIC CLOCHE: Everything from jam jars to clear milk containers has been used to give vegetables a head start in the garden, but plastic cloches are cheap and do a better job because they can be ventilated. Tomato, pepper, eggplant, or melon seedlings can be set out weeks earlier than usual when protected under such a cloche. Its wide lower lip, when piled around with soil, holds the light cloche in the soil. The top should have a ventilating cap or a few holes to prevent overheating.

It's a good idea to place the cloche in the garden two weeks before planting, so the soil beneath has plenty of time to get warm. The only problems with cloches come when the days are too hot and the sun is

THE BELL JAR

The old-fashioned glass cloche is a thing of beauty. Once blown by hand in low, fat shapes like dowagers in skirts, bell jars are costly items in antique stores, but they are still manufactured today. If you choose to use one in the garden, the better choice is a style with a removable top that permits ventilation. An unventilated bell jar must be propped up against a small stone to ease the flow of air and heat.

Among the loveliest of the antique bell jars are those that incorporate a knobby glass handle at the top. Presumably, this made it easier to lift and place large quantities of bell jars into the field at once. But the handle can act as a magnifying glass, burning the plant within, so these bell jars in particular are better used as ornaments for the terrace or as covers to protect an elegant patio picnic. Indeed, in a spring or autumn potager, a bell jar can look more elegant than almost any statuary intended for the garden.

too strong. On these occasions, a cloche needs to be vented if the plants are to survive the heat. Old-fashioned glass cloches had to be propped up one at a time, using a stone or a brick. Newer ones often have some means of ventilation through the top or the side. It is also important that no plants growing inside cloches have their leaves touching the clear covering, since the contact will scorch the leaves.

FORCING POTS: If you hunt garden antiques, you may come upon earthenware pots that resemble bell jars. Unlike the latter, however, they are entirely opaque. They were intended to exclude light from maturing plants—especially rhubarb, sea kale, endive, and chicory—whose leaves and stems are tastier if the plant is blanched.

Also like bell jars, forcing pots usually have a removable lid, both to reduce midday heat and to let the gardener check the progress of the blanching process.

HOT CAPS: Many plastic cloches are made from recycled plastic, but a more ecologically appealing alternative is the wax-paper hot cap. Each cap fits on a little wire frame. When placed over a seedling tomato plant, the cap looks like a coffee filter set upside down in the vegetable garden. As the days warm, you can tear the top off the cap for ventilation, while leaving the side walls to protect the plant from drying winds.

THE WALL O' WATER: Invented by a Utah man in the early 1980s, the Wall O' Water is a simple and powerful concept. Like an ordinary plastic cloche, it has a basic conical shape and surrounds the young plant, leaving an opening for ventilation at the top.

The difference is that the Wall O' Water is actually a conical reservoir that holds 3 gallons of water in a protective wall around the plant. The effect is to moderate temperature changes. In the daytime, the water absorbs heat, so that the plant stays cool and moist; in the night or in cold weather, the water radiates up to 900,000 calories of heat to keep the tender seedling from freezing. An ordinary cloche can extend the planting season by three weeks on either end. A Wall O' Water can extend it up to eight weeks.

CONTINUOUS CLOCHES AND ROW COVERS: Since the early twentieth century, cloches have been transformed. English gardeners finally tired of the "one bell to one plant" approach and invented the continuous cloche, an open-ended structure capable of covering whole rows of

ANATOMY OF A WALL O' WATER

The top can be left open to allow seedlings to receive sun and ventilation, or bent closed for very young seedlings.

All the cylinders put together hold 3 gallons of water.

The base is 6" in diameter.

strawberries, lettuce, or other crops. The first continuous cloches were shaped like A-frame tents and could be connected one to another to make as long a row as desired. This construction was fine for small seedlings and narrow single rows. The barn cloche is more capacious with a shallowly pitched "roof" that permits two rows of taller plants.

As beautiful objects, the barn and tent cloches cannot compete with bell jars. Instead of turning the market gardener's field into ranks of shiny bells, they convert it into a massive parking garage or miniature flea market. Still, they are much more effective and easy to use, covering whole rows instead of individual plants.

With the advent of flexible polyethylene sheeting, it became possible to make tunnel cloches as long as the field required, usually out of a single piece of fabric. Sure enough, the place looked like an army barracks full of little Quonset huts, but the result was far earlier production and a better livelihood for the early farmer.

As simple and light as it is, the plastic tunnel cloche looks like the miracle of the modern age, but in fact its ancestors date back at least to the eighteenth century. Gardeners in England and in colonial America developed simple portable cloches out of wooden hoops covered with oiled paper.

This practice has been revived at Colonial Williamsburg in Virginia, where melons are started and rosemary overwintered in paper cloches. The gardeners bend oak slat into hoops fixed to a frame 10' long by 2½' wide. In the traditional manner, they cover these with a fine and costly linen paper impregnated with linseed oil for waterproofing.

Today's home gardeners can easily follow the same procedure with modern versions of the tunnel cloche. Wire or plastic hoops are driven gently into the ground, spanning the desired width of row. (There are large enough hoops available to cover even the wide rows of intensive-bed cultivation.) The plastic sheeting is spread over the hoops, and its edges are anchored in the soil at the bed's edge or tacked down with broad, blunt "earth staples."

The system is quite simple. What is impressive is the array of covering materials tailored for different garden needs. All the covers are woven specifically to transmit water and vapor through tiny pores,

WHY SEEDLINGS LIKE IT WARM

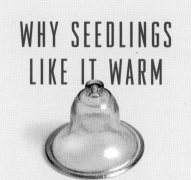

In a living system like the soil, the coming of warmth in spring is like the start of a symphony as the conductor lifts the baton: The ground opens, the soil softens, the rains soak the earth; water penetrates the seed coat and the leaves and roots begin to unfurl, often carrying the softened seed coat aloft on the cotyledon.

Now is the time when, with the aid of a cold frame, a cloche, or a row cover, early crops like lettuce and broccoli may be directly seeded into the soil. Any translucent material—glass, plastic, or slitted polyethylene film—that covers the open soil will keep it both warm and evenly moist. In this way, market gardeners get a two- or three-week jump on the coming vegetable season.

without leaking or tearing. Some will keep plants safe down to 24°F, but the trade-off is reduced light. Good extra-early-season row covers typically transmit 50% of available light, as opposed to the 90% for row covers that will protect your plants to 29°F.

Summer row covers serve two purposes. Lightweight types are mainly for insect protection: a covered row fends off root maggots, leaf miners, cabbageworms, and some vine borers. Specially formulated shade cloths intentionally reduce the transmission of solar energy to the soil by 50%. In many areas, this will make it possible for gardeners to keep growing sweet and tender salad greens throughout the warm, summer months.

One kind of row cover is so light and flexible that it doesn't even require hoops to be supported over plants. The so-named "floating row covers" (Reemay is the best-known manufacturer) are almost transparent, and they need only be draped directly over seedlings with their edges held down by soil. They don't provide quite as much frost protection as hoop-mounted covers, but they will withstand light frosts and protect tender leaves from wind and insects.

On the other hand, you might consider following the old-fashioned method. Why not make cloches that are ecologically sound? Lath can be substituted for oak, and butcher's paper or even brown wrapping paper can stand in for linen. When torn or broken, the cover can be recycled immediately, even composted, and not simply thrown away.

Plant Protectors

1. ENDIVE BLANCHING POT

1. ENDIVE BLANCHING POT: Many vegetables, such as endive, chicory, rhubarb, celery, and leek, need to be sheltered from the sun to improve their taste or appearance —or in some cases be edible at all. This terra-cotta pot is a great way to blanch vegetables without going through the effort of hilling up or other methods. The removable lid allows the gardener to check on growth and progress. 15" DIA. × 20".

2. GLASS BELL CLOCHES: The classic bell-shaped glass cloche was developed by French gardeners at the turn of the century. More portable than cold frames, bell cloches protect seedlings from cold and pests while ensuring maximum light exposure. Some have removable handles for ventilation. LARGE CLOCHE 14" DIA. × 10½"; MEDIUM CLOCHE 11" DIA. × 9"; SMALL CLOCHE 7¾" DIA. × 5¾".

3. WINDOWPANE CLOCHE

2. GLASS BELL CLOCHES

3. **WINDOWPANE CLOCHE:** A modern variation of the traditional English cloche design that incorporated malleable steel and waxed paper, this cloche features lightweight aluminum and glass. Unique in that it has a wider base than the bell-shaped cloches, this may be more useful when protecting a wide area of seedlings. Pyramid shape mimics a greenhouse. 18" × 18" × 9".

4. **PLASTIC BELL CLOCHES:** These bell cloches serve the same purpose as their traditional glass cousins but are more affordable and lightweight, which makes them more appropriate for large areas of seedlings.

Of translucent, reusable plastic, they may have a small removable handle or a hole at the top for ventilation. 12" DIA. × 10".

5. **WALL O' WATER:** A unique crop protector, this item insulates the soil and tender seedlings from frost, which enables the user to extend the growing season by as much as six to eight weeks. Each one holds 3 gallons of water in vertical cells, capable of transferring 900,000 calories of heat—enough to melt snow as much as 3' around. At first, seedlings are placed inside with the top edge closed (like a tepee). As the plants grow and the sun heats up, the top is opened to allow in more light. These protectors are especially useful for growing heat-loving plants like tomatoes and roses. Reusable, flexible plastic. 12"–16" DIA. × 18".

6. **PLASTIC GREENHOUSE:** These widely available plastic protectors are more sightly than homemade versions (usually fashioned from plastic beverage containers cut in half and turned over) and provide the same benefits. They allow light in and retain heat and moisture while guarding against pests and frost. Airholes allow ventilation. Plastic Greenhouses frequently come in multipacks and may be useful when covering many seedlings; however, they are made from thin plastic and may have to be replaced more often than the bell-shaped varieties. 8¼" × 8¼" × 10".

4. PLASTIC BELL CLOCHES

5. WALL O' WATER

6. PLASTIC GREENHOUSE

CHAPTER FIVE

PLANTING

There is a smell in the air each spring. It's the bittersweet smell of impending growth as billions of hungry bacteria perfume the warming soil. Now is the time to plant. Where just a month before it might have taken a backhoe to part the frozen ground, no matter how fertile it may have been, now even a single thumb can do the job. Gardeners break out their dibbers and trowels. They stir the soil in old containers or tap them empty and pour in a fresh mix. The seeds and the young transplants stand ready . . .

> "Therefore every gardener and owner ought to be careful and diligently to foresee that the seeds committed to the earth be neither too old, dry, thin, withered nor counterfeited . . . that the wind at the instant blow not from the north but rather from the south or southwest, nor the day be Very cold; for in such seasons and days (as all the skillful report) the earth, as then timorous and fast shut, hardly receiveth and nourisheth the seeds. . . ."
>
> —DIDYMUS MOUNTAIN

The first and biggest wave of planting takes place in the spring, but there is more to do every month or two. Radishes are almost continually sown, and the early lettuce must be followed by a later planting of heat-tolerant varieties. Many annual flowers and perennials are best planted after the soil warms. Broccoli and the coles can be planted again in late summer, and the smart gardener who has propagated corn seed in peat pots may even venture a second crop of corn for early fall.

Then, when the air cools and the garden begins to decline toward winter, comes the biggest planting task of all. With trowel and bulb planters, the gardener makes new beds of daffodils to naturalize, installs a patch of snowdrops and crocuses, puts irises around the pond, or fits fritillaria and allium into the perennial border.

Every act of planting has three rhythmic steps: stoop and open, insert and close, and firm the surrounding soil. The movements are so fluid that in many cultures they have also become dance steps. In Malaysia and other parts of the world, farmers still sow to the beat of drums.

HISTORY OF PLANTING

Planting is the central ritual of human culture. It is the assurance that not only plants, but families and communities as well will continue to have the sustenance they need to grow and thrive. To plant is to take part in an intimate act, one that draws the sower very near to the ground. Though huge, impersonal planting machines have been invented for agricultural use, the best garden-sowing tools are still hand tools, little changed from the time of their origin.

SEED PLANTING

First recorded in Roman times and virtually unchanged since, the dibber is only slightly more formal than a digging stick. Indeed, old-time gardeners have always recommended the simple sharpening of a handle from a broken-down spade or rake to make a serviceable dibber. Only with the onset of the Renaissance did dibbers become an item of manufacture, some iron-shod models for penetrating the harder clay soils.

Earth-opening ability is only half of the seed-planting equation. Seed carrying is the other. A dried corn husk or a catalpa leaf served native gardeners, its pointed end encouraging the release of only one seed at a time. In 1670, Leonard Meager recommended exactly the same process to English gardeners: "If you put your seeds in a white paper," he wrote, "you may very easily and equally sow them by shaking the lower end of your paper with the forefinger of the hand you sow with." So, as another early writer put it, might the seeds "be workmanlie bestowed in their beds."

This method was fine for the small seeds of vegetable, herb, and flower plants, but transplants and bulbs needed more depth. Large trees, of course, could be transplanted using spades or shovels, but seedlings, bulbs, and corms were too big for the digging stick and too small for the shovel.

LARGE-HOLE PLANTING

Today, one would scarcely suspect the common parentage of the trowel and the bulb planter. One looks like a big tongue or a small shovel, the other like a giant cookie cutter with a handle. Until the end of the first quarter of the nineteenth century, however, the two tools closely resembled one another. Trowels looked like a half tin can cut lengthwise,

A dried corn husk or a catalpa leaf served native gardeners, its pointed end encouraging the release of only one seed at a time.

while bulb planters resembled the whole can. The function of both tools was to remove a measured circle of earth so that transplants or bulbs might be efficiently placed at a single depth.

Following its transformation into a small steel tongue, the trowel could still be used to dig a uniform, measured hole. (Today, some trowels even come with inch markings stamped into the blade.) But the new shape would be less liable to spill its load and more capable of shaping a wide variety of holes. Its round-pointed end could mark a shallow line in the soil, and with the whole tool a gardener could work around rocks or other obstacles and shape the hole to exactly fit the rootball of a transplant.

The trowel had to await the invention of hard, lightweight steel before it could come into popular fashion. Earlier examples were heavy, shaped lumps of iron, whose weight made them vulnerable at the connection between blade and handle. The steel trowel could be forged, fitted with tang and ferrule, or made in a single piece to never break.

But hand tools would not do for field crops. For centuries, the sowing of large fields was done by broadcasting seed. Once the soil had been dug, the planter would hang a quantity of seed in a basket or box from his waist. With vigorous and rhythmic motion, he would walk the plowed field, throwing handfuls of seed left and right like a man beating time or conducting an orchestra. Still, though it may have been beautiful to watch a team of sowers advancing in unison across the landscape to scatter the glittering seed, their method was not very efficient. The sowing was never very even, and the exposed seed remained prey to birds and the wind until germination.

PLANTING RITUALS

In ancient Japan, the act of planting was so central that it was initiated each spring by the emperor himself, who ritually made love to a woman in the first opened furrow. Native American women, while planting different vegetables together, sang to the seeds that would ultimately produce them. The Hebridean farmer invoked religious protection of the Holy Trinity, the archangel Michael, and Mary the Mother of God to watch over the planting hole, the seeds, and the seedlings—even the tools and the hands of their users.

Most native peoples have used digging sticks for planting. Hopi women used a pointed stick of piñon pine to plant hills of corn seed, one color for each of the four sacred directions. Iroquois women used a similar stick, made of maple or ash instead of pine, to plant the mixture of corn, beans, and squash that characterized the eastern native polyculture.

Jethro Tull, an eighteenth-century British estate holder, watched this process with a mixture of admiration and frustration, looking to improve its efficiency. The mechanically minded Tull designed a remarkably simple and effective horse-drawn machine that could perform all the required seed-planting functions at once: a simple plow opened a shallow furrow; a geared wheel dropped measured amounts of seed into the hole; a gentle harrowing chain followed, covering the seed over, and a flat-faced wheel firmed the soil. There was even an attachment to mark out the next row to the left, making it possible to create evenly spaced, perfectly seeded rows. The Tull seeder has long been superseded for large-scale planting, but a hand-driven wheeled seeder of precisely the same design is now the preferred sowing device for a big vegetable garden.

CONTAINER PLANTING

For most planting, the soil is the given quantity. In an age of paving, it's too easy to forget that almost the entire surface of the earth's dry land is covered with soil. When it comes to tender or invasive plants, however, it often becomes necessary to plant not in the ground but in containers. Furthermore, there are those gardeners who simply prefer the wonderful interaction of a delicate flower or pattern of branch and foliage with the warm red circle of a terra-cotta pot or the rough grace of a redwood planter. For it is only with container planting—when the soil, the air, and the water are all our responsibility—that we experience the full human daring of planting.

To plant in containers is to adopt a whole small world, with all its attendant responsibilities. Yet for all the comparative difficulties, gardeners have been planting in containers for as long as there have been gardens. A talismanic stone pot from a Maltese temple dating back to 2000 B.C. has cut into its face a bas relief of a plant growing in a pot. The Egyptians used terra-cotta pots, as did the Mesopotamians and later the Greeks. Beginning in about the sixth century before Christ, Athenian women annually forced lettuce and herbs such as fennel in containers, only to let them wither and die intentionally. Called Gardens of Adonis, these plants were meant to celebrate the death and resurrection of that handsome mythological figure. As the forced herbs perished, they were replaced by the crops that rose from the warming ground.

Even to this day, there is a ceremonial feel about a potted plant. It stands usually between house and wilderness as a kind of sentinel or symbol, sending the silent message that architecture is a part of nature. It reminds us of John Gerard's sanguine hope: "It were to be wish'd that Houses were built for the Gardens, and not Gardens made for the Houses."

A potted plant usually stands between house and wilderness as a kind of sentinel or symbol.

THE DIBBER

The dibber, or dibble, is perhaps the simplest garden tool. Its only job is to poke holes. But in doing so, it also begins the transformation from bare dirt into a thriving garden.

Dibbers are good for planting seeds, small seedlings, or little bulbs. A succession of pokes, thrusting the tip to the required depth, opens the holes instantly. (Particularly for seedlings, this takes a little practice, because it's important not to open a hole deeper than the root mass, lest harmful air space is left beneath the plant.) Once the seeds are sown, the holes are covered with a quick swipe of the hand.

CHOOSING A DIBBER

The skinnier dibbers are useful for seeds or small seedlings; fat ones serve for bigger seedlings or small bulbs. Practical gardeners often take the broken shafts of spades or hoes and sharpen the end to make a serviceable planting tool. Some people like to use D-handles so the tool won't fall from their hands, even if the grip slips or if they've grown tired from a whole day's planting.

Most gardeners prefer a short-handled dibber, which allows them to get down next to the soil. (A homemade version is nothing but a sharpened broomstick 4"–5" long.) The best models have a shaped ash handle and a sharp, forged carbon steel prod. Pistol grips let you use the tool almost as if it were a screw gun, and your hand is much slower to tire.

Lightweight metals and shaping technologies have taken the dibber to new heights. A few models are actually narrow trowels, but other types have a flange scooped out of the tip so the tool can penetrate the earth more easily and provide a channel for the displaced soil.

TO MAKE A MULTI-DIBBER

Dibbers are subject to all kinds of invention. By fitting a set of sharpened dowels to a piece of Peg-Board and fastening a C-shaped handle to the opposite side, you can create a "multi-dibber" that will make a dozen holes with every poke.

USING A DIBBER

It's hard to misuse a dibber, but not impossible. Watch your planting depth carefully, and don't get carried away by the pleasure of the poking. It's little use to plant seedlings, seeds, or bulbs too deep. In fact, mistaken planting depth is a leading cause of seedling mortality.

If you use a short-handled dibber, don't try to do it by stooping. You'll tire quickly and end the day with an aching back. Squat or sit instead. This is where kneelers or tiny gardener's stools are truly useful.

Dibbers

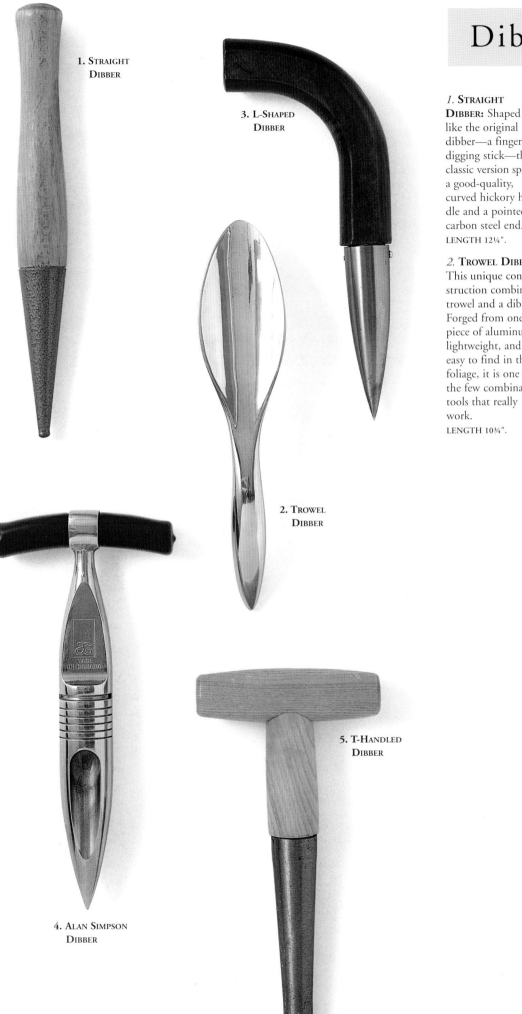

1. STRAIGHT DIBBER

3. L-SHAPED DIBBER

2. TROWEL DIBBER

4. ALAN SIMPSON DIBBER

5. T-HANDLED DIBBER

1. **STRAIGHT DIBBER:** Shaped like the original dibber—a finger or digging stick—this classic version sports a good-quality, curved hickory handle and a pointed, carbon steel end. LENGTH 12¼".

2. **TROWEL DIBBER:** This unique construction combines a trowel and a dibber. Forged from one piece of aluminum, lightweight, and easy to find in the foliage, it is one of the few combination tools that really work. LENGTH 10¾".

3. **L-SHAPED DIBBER:** Used like a claw to open a hole in the soil, this tool has a rosewood handle attached with a bolt to a pointed steel end. LENGTH 10¼".

4. **ALAN SIMPSON DIBBER:** The Cadillac of dibbers, this tool is a unique—and handsome—step above the standard garden-variety dibber. The polypropylene handle is securely socketed into the solid chrome base. Divets on either side allow the shaft to penetrate the soil with less effort. This tool is featured in the Smithsonian for its beautiful design. LENGTH 10¾".

5. **T-HANDLED DIBBER:** Fashioned from best-quality carbon steel and solid ash, this dibber has a T-grip that fits nicely in the palm with minimum torque in the wrist. The user is able to exert even pressure, resulting in a consistent hole depth. LENGTH 10¼".

THE TROWEL

Next to the round-point shovel, the trowel is probably the most indispensable garden tool. Excellent for planting and transplanting seedlings, as well as for stirring the soil and lifting out stubborn dandelions or other deep-rooted weeds, a trowel can be used to make a hole, excavate and shape it, then smooth the soil back over once the planting is complete.

CHOOSING A TROWEL

Most trowels today are manufactured with an elliptical cross section that allows them to penetrate the soil and carry a good panful without spillage. Often they have a depth gauge worked into the metal itself, a particularly useful feature if you're interplanting two different sets of bulbs or seedlings at different depths.

While common trowels are dished and round-pointed, some models are made with a broad V-shaped cross section and a sharp point. These tools are intended for digging in tougher ground and are sometimes used by foresters and others who work in less-than-tame landscapes. The main differences between common trowels and the V-shaped versions are the width of the blade and the material of construction.

Big, broad trowels are the most versatile, but they are also the heaviest and can be too unwieldy for small hands. Narrower trowels are excellent for transplanting material grown in the average peat pot, soil blocker, or nursery six-pack. (Often, these are called "transplanting trowels.") The narrowest versions, sometimes called "weeding trowels," do double duty, enabling you to plant small seedlings and extract obstinate weeds. A strong trowel of this sort is a surer bet than most dandelion weeders because you aren't as likely to miss the weed's taproot.

One peculiar-looking trowel is perhaps the best for transplanting seedlings into the vegetable garden. Called the "right-angle trowel," it looks like a cheap tool that somehow got badly bent out of shape, but it's a marvelous thing to work with. Just insert the blade into the soil and pull it toward you with a smooth short jerk to open a small hole just the right size to receive the seedling; then insert the rootball and backfill. As awkward as it may look, this trowel is one of the best designed of single-purpose hand tools.

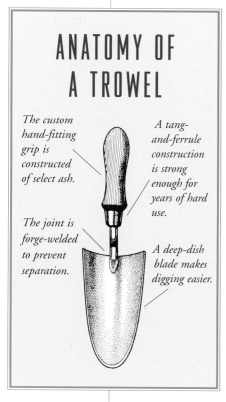

ANATOMY OF A TROWEL

The custom hand-fitting grip is constructed of select ash.

A tang-and-ferrule construction is strong enough for years of hard use.

The joint is forge-welded to prevent separation.

A deep-dish blade makes digging easier.

Cheap trowels are made from stamped metal, hammered into the wooden handle in a simple tang-and-ferrule design. Sometimes the tang pulls out; more often the ferrule loosens and rattles around on the shank in an annoying manner. But most often a cheap trowel bends at the shank or even at the blade.

A better choice is the one-piece aluminum trowel, which will never bend or lose its handle. Some gardeners object to the cold feel of uncoated aluminum, but there are rubber and PVC-coated one-piece trowels that are more pleasant to grasp. In fact, one trowel—marketed as an "ergonomic trowel"—is made of one piece coated with a shaped, flexible material like that used on many of the European-style scissors.

Not all wood-and-metal trowels are cheap. Perhaps the best trowels of all are those of forged carbon steel. A good steel trowel may indeed have a tang-and-ferrule design, but it will be well anchored in an ash or hickory handle, sometimes riveted. The very finest are fitted with a solid socket to an ash handle, precisely as if they were small spades.

The trowel is one tool that you may wish to buy in stainless steel. Though the stainless models are about twice as costly as carbon steel, the tool is small so the price is not too outlandish. The great advantages are that the trowel is simple to clean, rustproof, and easy to spot if you leave it lying in a furrow.

USING THE TROWEL

The word "trowel" comes from an old word that meant "ladle," and its etymology is a clue to its function. The trowel virtually ladles up small quantities of soil, stirs the earth in narrow spaces, and roots up weeds. Trowels are not intended for levering out stones or other heavy materials in the soil. Indeed, the main cause of death among trowels is the gardener who tries to use them as prying implements.

When using a trowel it's best to squat, sit, or kneel. Never stoop for trowel work. Scoop to the proper planting depth, place the seedling, then use the back of the trowel to firm the soil around the seedling's rootball. You can poke the surrounding earth gently with the tip to make sure that any large air pockets, which are injurious to transplants, have been eliminated.

The trowel is also very handy for adding an amendment—a little bonemeal, for instance, or a thimbleful or 5-10-5—to the planting hole. Use the tip to ladle in a small amount, then stir it gently to mix in the bottom of the hole. Place the seedling atop this well-stirred mixture and proceed as above. When using the trowel as a cultivating tool, stab the soil gently and repeatedly, twisting slightly with each prod. The result will be a broken soil surface, ready to receive the rain.

Scoop down into soil at a slight angle and remove dirt to the proper planting depth. Place your plant or seedling in the hole and fill it in, slightly jabbing the soil around the transplant to eliminate air pockets.

Trowels

1. **LONG-HANDLED TROWEL:** With a longer handle attached to an all-purpose, medium-dish head, this trowel eliminates the need to kneel when digging or setting out plants in hard-to-reach places at the back of large borders and beds. The narrow, epoxy-coated, carbon steel blade pierces the soil easily, does not bend, and cleans up with minimum effort. Durable, polished hickory handle guards against splinters and callused palms. Leather loop allows for easy hanging. LENGTH 17¼".

2. **STAINLESS STEEL TROWEL:** The deluxe edition of the Standard Hand Trowel. Polished stainless steel lends an elegant, rust-resistant finish to this hardworking tool and makes it easy to find amid the foliage. Polished ash handle is shaped to fit in the curve of the palm. LENGTH 12½".

3. **BIG AMERICAN TROWEL:** Forged carbon steel blade with a solid-socket hardwood handle makes this trowel a top-of-the-line, heavy-duty, long-lived option for all-purpose planting, transplanting, and digging. The slightly pointed edge is good for breaking through hard or rocky soil. Deeply dished, oversize head and longer length allow the user to scoop more soil with less effort. Priced slightly higher than the average trowel, but the absolute best choice for the serious gardener.

At almost a pound, its heavier weight may make it unsuitable for smaller gardeners. LENGTH 14¼".

4. **TRIGGER GRIP TROWEL:** This ergonomically sound invention, cast in one piece from aluminum alloy, is extremely tough yet very lightweight. A depression in the handle guides the thumb to the proper place while a unique trigger provides a better grip for the forefinger, eliminating the need to use a lot of wrist action for good leverage. Smaller dish means a lighter load, which is also better for the wrists. Available for both right-handed and left-handed gardeners. LENGTH 10¾".

5. **STANDARD HAND TROWEL:** This tang-and-ferrule trowel is the standard from which all other trowels evolve. More of an investment than the similarly shaped, run-of-the-mill trowels sold in every garden supply and hardware store, this particular trowel is superior because it is made with the best materials. A sturdy ash handle attached to an epoxy-coated carbon steel blade promises a lifetime of precision digging with maximum flexibility, absolutely no bending, and minimum torque in the wrist. The smooth 5" handle resists splintering and protects against blisters. LENGTH 12½".

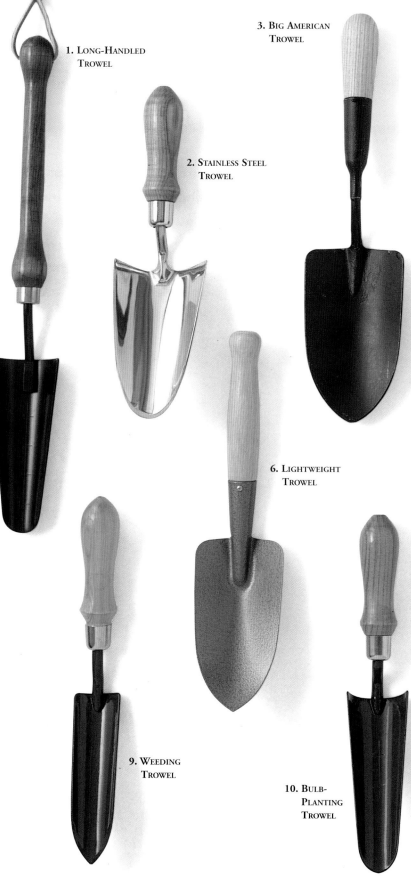

1. LONG-HANDLED TROWEL

3. BIG AMERICAN TROWEL

2. STAINLESS STEEL TROWEL

6. LIGHTWEIGHT TROWEL

9. WEEDING TROWEL

10. BULB-PLANTING TROWEL

6. **LIGHTWEIGHT TROWEL:** This lighter trowel has a longer handle and a shallower blade, making it ideal for general garden digging and planting. The stamped steel blade is secured to a polished wood handle by a single rivet. Solid construction eliminates bending, a problem with many lightweight hand tools. LENGTH 11¾".

7. **ERGONOMIC TROWEL:** This trowel is constructed with a cast aluminum blade surrounded by a unique, cushioned rubber grip. The padded rubber absorbs shock and allows the fingers and palm to be squeezed into proper alignment, alleviating stress on the wrist. Solid, one-piece construction and a long, pointed blade facilitate heavy digging without any risk of bending or breaking

4. TRIGGER GRIP TROWEL

5. STANDARD HAND TROWEL

7. ERGONOMIC TROWEL

8. TRANSPLANTING TROWEL

11. RIGHT-ANGLE TROWEL

12. JEKYLL TROWEL

Hand Trowel, the Weeding Trowel has a narrower, longer, pointed blade designed to reach into crevices of rock gardens and grub out tough weeds like dandelions. Its smaller size and lighter weight make it a more useful tool for indoor and potted gardens, as well as for gardeners with smaller hands. LENGTH 12".

10. **BULB-PLANTING TROWEL:** The narrow, epoxy-coated steel blade is specifically designed to plant bulbs—measurements etched into the blade help in planting particular varieties in their required depth of soil. A lipped collar lets the gardener put more muscle into digging, while the padded rubber handle absorbs shock and prevents slipping and blisters. Designed to pierce the soil in one strike (when held like a dagger) and open a pocket for the bulb when pulled forward in the ground. LENGTH 13".

11. **RIGHT-ANGLE TROWEL:** This uniquely shaped, Swiss-engineered trowel is also called a "dipper." The pointed stainless steel blade is bolted perpendicular to the colorful plastic handle. The shape mimics how the human hand digs, allowing the gardener to open a hole in the earth with one stroke. The 4¾" right-angle handle is easy on the wrist, while its bright color makes finding the trowel a snap. HEAD LENGTH 5¾".

12. **JEKYLL TROWEL:** A top-of-the-line, standard-shaped trowel inspired by the famous horticulturist Gertrude Jekyll. Polished stainless steel head, solid brass collar, and smooth beech handle lend an understated luxuriousness to this tough tool. It is the most expensive tool pictured here, but the extraordinary design and excellent materials make gardening with this trowel an art. LENGTH 12¼".

the blade. Rubber will deteriorate after many years, but otherwise a long-lasting, durable, and reasonably priced choice. Hole in handle allows for easy storage. LENGTH 13¾".

8. **TRANSPLANTING TROWEL:** The long, tapering blade of this specialty trowel is intended to carve a rootball out of the soil or pot with minimum effort or damage to the plant or its environment.

Its sizable dish makes it a good implement for digging deep, narrow holes in which to plant seedlings. The epoxy-coated carbon steel head with rubber handle will not break or bend. A useful

tool of quality to add to a basic collection. LENGTH 12".

9. **WEEDING TROWEL:** Fashioned from the same superlative materials as the Standard

BULB PLANTERS

For obvious reasons, these tools are sometimes called "hole-in-one" planters. No one knows when bulb planters were invented, but they probably evolved from the innovation of hollowing out dibber prods. These modified dibbers made straight-sided holes of even depths—perfect for planting the larger bulbs.

CHOOSING A BULB PLANTER

Don't bother with the cheap, stamped-metal bulb planters that are prevalent at garden centers in autumn. A lasting carbon-steel bulb planter is an excellent investment. It's less liable to break and can hold an edge, saving a great deal of strenuous pushing on a day when you're planting, say, five hundred tulip bulbs.

A long-handled version can be operated from a standing position by pushing your foot against a tread like that of an old-fashioned shovel. This model is particularly effective when there are many bulbs to plant. You can scatter the bulbs, make the holes, and plant in three successive operations. Or if you're working with friends, you can designate one hole digger, one bonemeal applier, one bulb dropper, and one soil firmer. Only the "firmer" needs to squat.

USING THE BULB PLANTER

Planting bulbs is strenuous exercise because the gardener seldom plants fewer than a dozen and usually more than a hundred. Resist the temptation to rush the job and plunge in with the planter. Instead, take time to plan each section. Scatter the bulbs experimentally and imagine what they'll look like with their heads nodding high in the air next spring. Make patches of different colors, or arrange patterns and rows for a parterre. (The bonemeal that encourages proper rooting also makes a good white marker material for your pattern lines.)

Once the holes have been dug and prepared, it's time to sit or kneel with your bulb planter and get to work. Develop a rhythm: plunge, extract, drop a dribble of bonemeal, plant the bulb, cover, and firm. After each section is planted, take a break to go check the watering or rake a path. At the end of the day, you will have done a satisfying job of work with minimum strain.

Easily operated on your knees, the bulb planter is simply plunged into the soil, twisted slightly to secure the clump of dirt, and removed.

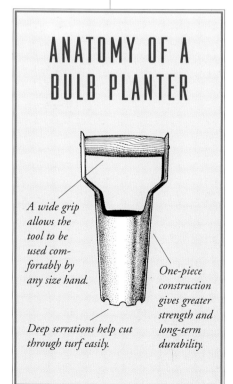

ANATOMY OF A BULB PLANTER

A wide grip allows the tool to be used comfortably by any size hand.

Deep serrations help cut through turf easily.

One-piece construction gives greater strength and long-term durability.

Bulb Planters

1. QUICK-RELEASE BULB PLANTER: This hand bulb planter features a handle that squeezes together to grip a core of dirt 2½" in diameter and then releases, which may make it easier for those suffering from wrist fatigue. It has a stainless steel coring tube with polypropylene handle.
LENGTH 9",
WEIGHT .75 LB.

2. HEAVY-DUTY BULB PLANTER: This professional-quality alternative in long-handled bulb planters is used primarily for mass plantings over wide areas. Fabricated from solid carbon steel, it will not bend or break. The extra-wide T-handle has padded rubber grips while the 7" coring tube features a heavy-duty foot tread and cuts a core 2½" in diameter.
LENGTH 36",
WEIGHT 5 LBS.

3. LONG-HANDLED BULB PLANTER: A high-quality bulb planter that allows the user to cut into soil or grass just by pressing down on the foot tread and twisting the handle. The enamel-coated, solid-forged steel blade is connected to an ash T-grip handle. The coring tube is 2½" in diameter.
LENGTH 39",
WEIGHT 4 LBS.

4. HAND BULB PLANTER: For those who prefer to get close to the soil, this American-made tool is the companion to the Heavy-Duty Bulb Planter. It features the same stout construction and will easily last a lifetime. Made of fabricated steel with a wooden handle, it cuts a core 2½" in diameter.
LENGTH 10",
WEIGHT 1.5 LBS.

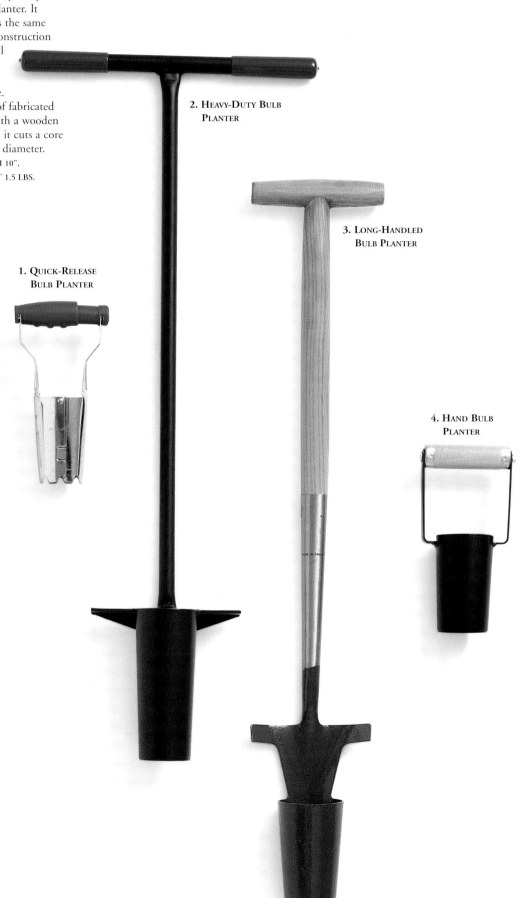

2. HEAVY-DUTY BULB PLANTER

3. LONG-HANDLED BULB PLANTER

1. QUICK-RELEASE BULB PLANTER

4. HAND BULB PLANTER

SEEDERS

A good precision seeder is one of the most admirable mechanical tools made in our machine-mad age.

For many gardeners, the usual seeder is the corner of a hoe and a seed packet. The hoe draws out a shallow furrow, and the seed is gently tapped into it from the cut end of the packet. But a great deal of waste can be avoided if the seed is well spaced from the start. This way, the seedlings won't have to be thinned and each small plant will have a better chance of survival.

Choose a seeder according to how much you plant. If you do nothing but a few rows of tomatoes, cucumbers, lettuce, and radishes, you can simply pour the seeds out of the edge of a neatly cut packet. For larger vegetable gardens, a handheld seeder will reduce waste and the need for thinning. For a big garden—the sort that supports the family table with most of its vegetables, herbs, and cut flowers—a mechanical seeder is not only more efficient but also a great deal of fun to use.

HANDHELD SEEDERS: The simplest handheld mechanical seeder looks like a pillbox with a dispenser attached. Into the covered wheel goes a packet of seeds; a dial is adjusted to match the exit hole to the seed size; and voilà, you can dispense single seeds as you walk the row. One variation is nothing but a deep trowel with a small dam in it. The dam opens just large enough at the center to admit single seeds through the hole. The trouble is that while a radish seed may easily pass through, a corn seed almost certainly will lodge.

MECHANICAL SEEDERS: The serious vegetable gardener should invest in a mechanical seeder. Not all such seeders are alike, however. With some you mix the seed into a kind of stiff slurry and then extrude it into the rows like toothpaste from a tube. Others work on the principle of a revolving belt or wheel, but can distribute only one or two sizes of pelleted seed. Leave these models to the market gardener. Your own best choice, and the most admirably simple in principle, is a wheeled seeder that can accommodate naked seeds of many different sizes.

A good precision seeder is one of the most admirable mechanical tools made in our machine-mad age. As you push it in front of you, the foremost part of the machine opens a small furrow while to its right, at a fixed distance, a pointed stake gently traces the line of the next row. A revolving disk, calibrated precisely to accept the particular size of seed that you're sowing, drops individual seeds at exact intervals, then a chain and roller cover the seed and firm the soil.

Versatility is the precision seeder's second advantage. With at least half a dozen interchangeable disks for seeds of different size, this tool allows you to seed everything from the diminutive radish or lettuce to corn and peas.

Seeders

1. SINGLE-ROW SMALL-SEED PLANTER: This seeder plants one row of seeds at a time. When pushed through the soil it makes a furrow and drops a seed, leaving regular spacing and needing only a light raking to cover. Plated steel construction with wooden handle. Sows three sizes of seed.
7" × 4" × 6",
HANDLE 48".

2. PRECISION GARDEN SEEDER: A very efficient single-row seeder for planting vegetables. It features an aluminum frame and plastic wheels and hopper, and has interchangeable seed plates for different seed sizes and spacings. It makes a furrow in prepared soil, drops the seed, back fills, and marks the next row up to 30" in one automatic operation.
8" × 30" × 13",
HANDLE 26".

3. FOUR-ROW GANG SEEDER: This seeder will do four rows spaced 2¼" apart. Depending on which hoppers are used, it will also do two rows 4½" apart, or two rows 6¾" apart. It is excellent for seeding and reseeding crops like lettuce or carrots, which can then be continuously harvested.
4" × 4" × 4",
HANDLE 48".

2. PRECISION GARDEN SEEDER

1. SINGLE-ROW SMALL-SEED PLANTER

3. FOUR-ROW GANG SEEDER

CONTAINER GARDENING

Providing plants with a natural transition, container gardening is the best way to make the move from outdoors to indoors. Pots of annuals and half-hardy perennials and shrubs can be placed on south-facing terraces and patios, extending nature into the paved places near the house and making an environment for outdoor eating. Baskets can hang from trellises or canopies, and some pots are designed to hang from walls, bringing the garden to eye level. Jardinieres and étagères—plant stands that rise in tiers above the ground—make it possible even to create whole theme gardens by assembling and planting a variety of pots.

And if there is no space near the house for the kitchen garden, a nest of pots can contain herbs, small lettuces, and cherry tomatoes. Strawberry pots—large earthenware pots with many pocket-like openings in the sides—are excellent not only for strawberry plants, but also for a selection of herbs mingled with nasturtiums and other edible flowers. Pots are also the safest way to deal with mint and similar invasive herbs that, when planted in the open garden, can even find their way into cracks in the pavement.

CHOOSING A CONTAINER

When you purchase a container, or make one out of a discarded tub or an old pair of sneakers, your choice involves three different factors. The first is aesthetic: how will the container look in this or that part of the garden, and will it set off the intended plants? The second regards water: will the material of the container hold water or transmit it? Will it need extra care to keep it from drying out, and are there drainage holes to keep it from getting water-logged? The third is about buffering: will the material of the container allow it to respond more or less quickly to changes in the surrounding climate?

People sometimes treat aesthetics as though it were of minor importance, but with pots it's a primary concern. One of the great features of the simple terra-cotta pot is that it ages and weathers so well, often acquiring a mottled coloration or a beard of lichen and moss. The usual terra-cotta pots, with broad, simple rims, were developed with ease of shipping in mind—the rims help to stack numbers of pots without breakage. A striking terra-cotta

A SMALL WORLD

Each pot, urn, and hanging basket exists in its own microclimate. Where the earth nearby is living its long, slow life, changing gradually from cold to warm and wet to dry, the soil in the container is undergoing much more rapid change, responding with almost breathless haste to variations in its climate. Too little water and the fuchsias wilt, while all around the garden is doing fine. A sudden early frost and the cherry tomatoes wither, while those out in the vegetable garden hang on.

variation called the long tom, however, has no rim at all. Intended for taproot plants, these tall, slender earthenware pots are a striking accent when assembled in a group.

Almost any material used for potting can be shaped, figured, and molded. Terra-cotta and "cast stone," a sort of concrete, make wonderful urns of almost any shape and size. They may be festooned with swags, cast as the face of a faun, or shaped to resemble classical vases and amphora. Generally, a cool-colored material lends itself to more formal situations, marking an entry to a terrace or outlining the bounds of a formal garden.

Among containers, wood is a compromise material. Slatted redwood pots look as rough, lovely, and relaxed as any terra-cotta planter. But a fine-planed redwood or cedar planting box—sometimes painted white or garden green—can be as formal as the grounds of the Governor's Palace at Colonial Williamsburg. Indeed, many of those four-square planting boxes, with spherical finials, are copied from eighteenth-century designs.

Cedar and redwood are the best woods for containers because they naturally resist rot. Old oak whiskey or wine barrels also make fine containers; the wood is impregnated with alcohol and resins that help them to survive the weather. These containers should be washed thoroughly before use, but once prepared they can even be used for a small water garden—the planks will swell and seal the joints to make the container leakproof. Teak is a beautiful and costly material for containers, but since it means cutting into the rain forest, sensitive gardeners may wish to avoid it. Similarly, pressure-treated lumber is imbued with toxic preservatives and is therefore not the best choice for a planter, even though it may be cheaper. (If you must use treated wood, be sure it has no pentachlorophenol in it.) Whatever you may choose, never use lumber treated with creosote, which is directly toxic to plant roots.

Plastic is the most malleable material for pots, window boxes, and any general container. Practically anything can be extruded—from a simple rimmed brown pot to a great white urn replete with lions holding rings in their mouths. You will, however, have to weight down plastic urns so they don't tip over in a high wind. Also, from an aesthetic point of view, there's a problem with the way plastic feels to the touch. The truly awful thing about this material is that it feels greasy and lifeless—a sore disappointment if you're used to the cool damp of terra-cotta.

On the other hand, plastic in an excellent choice when it comes to water-holding qualities. Almost all other materials, with the exception of metals and glazed pottery, lose water through the walls of the con-

A grouping of different containers and plants provides a nice flash of artistry to any garden, deck, or patio.

tainer itself. The soil in a terra-cotta pot for example, will dry much more quickly than that in a plastic pot. If your climate is warm and dry, this can make the difference between a withered plant and a living one, particularly if you go away for a long weekend. Surprisingly, a wooden container holds water better than terra-cotta and most pottery materials. Whichever material your container is made from, be certain that there are drainage holes in the bottom. Terra-cotta and plastic pots usually come with such holes, but many ceramic, glazed, and wooden containers do not.

Holding water effectively is only a relative benefit. In a damper climate, retained water militates against your plants. In the microclimate of a container, too much water is as dangerous as too little, and a worried novice is as likely to drown the plants as to starve them. In such a case, the more porous materials, like terra-cotta and wood, are far more capable of shedding excess water and protecting the plants.

It's easier to determine when a terra-cotta pot needs water. In fact, one of the great pleasures of gardening is to tap the sides of your terra-cotta pots. A nice dull thud means that everything is fine inside that little world; only when you hear a clear open ring is it time to water.

As buffers against waterlogging and sudden temperature changes, the natural materials are also superior. Though plastic is impermeable to water, it's a poor insulator. This means that temperature changes will more quickly be transmitted to the soil within a plastic pot.

USING CONTAINERS

There is far more to the millennial lore of container gardening than can be hinted at here, but if you don't actually wish for your plants to wilt and wither like those of the classical Greeks, you must be most careful about water and winter.

Natural in-ground dirt is a terrific buffer. It mitigates the effects of drought, freezing, and the stresses that lead to disease. In the little world of the container garden, the balance is far more delicate and disaster much nearer at hand. To maximize watering efficiency, place your pots in the garden where they will get sufficient sun, but keep them

PLANT STANDS

A whole range of devices allow you to raise your container plants to new heights. The columnar plant stands called jardinieres usually have platforms or holes at one or more levels to receive pots. Etagères are broader—sometimes in half- or quarter-round patterns to fit onto walls or corners—and may step back like a pyramid through three or four levels. Most sold today are steel and painted garden green, but you can find old Victorian ones made with filigree work and daring curves executed in whited steel rods and wires, or even in painted wicker. When well planted with a variety of flowers, herbs, and perhaps an orchid or two, they become the centerpiece of a patio.

away from the hottest corners. Choose the largest pot that you can find, with the most space for soil. Most important, create a soil that can be watered a lot without becoming compacted. "Soilless" mixes made of peat, vermiculite, perlite, and such are designed specifically for this purpose, but you can also use ordinary garden soil as long as you lighten it with peat, sand, and compost.

Winter stress is another headache if you live in a cold climate. Annuals or herbs can be replanted each spring, but perennials and woody plants need some protection to keep from heaving right out of their pots during winter freezes and getting dried out in periods of alternating freeze and thaw. To keep evergreens from losing too much moisture through their leaves, spray the leaves with an antidesiccant. To protect all woody plants from heaving, shield both pot and plant with protective layers of burlap.

HANGING BASKETS

Traditionally made of wood, hanging baskets are now commonly available in plastic to make them lighter. Almost as light and much prettier are the so-called "hayrack" planters, consisting of an open frame of coated steel wire filled with a peat or coco-fiber liner. The hangers themselves are usually triangular or S-curved to hold the container away from the adjoining wall. A simple, almost invisible variation consists of a clip or a circle of black steel that holds the rim of a terra-cotta pot and is affixed with a nail or screw to the wall. Window boxes are often held in place by a double-L arrangement, one side of which hooks over the window ledge while the other hooks under the base of the planting box.

Hooks that affix a hanging basket to the hanger are often wired into the side of the containers, but one ingenious solution is a slender wire that runs right up through the hole in the bottom of the container, providing a hook that appears to exist without any means of support.

Plant Containers

2. GLAZED EARTHENWARE STRAWBERRY JAR

4. TALL TERRA-COTTA POT

1. CAST-STONE PLANTER

3. VASUM POTS

5. BASKET-WEAVE POT

1. **CAST-STONE PLANTER:** This ornate, highly detailed mortar planter can be cast in a range of designs. Frost-proof when empty, it can be left outside in winter. Because of it's heavy weight, it is best used as a stationary planter, and can support a range of plants or small trees.

2. **GLAZED EARTHENWARE STRAWBERRY JAR:** Traditionally used for growing strawberries, this planter will not withstand frost. Open pockets are located randomly around the pot's outer structure, and an assortment of herbs and lettuces as well as succulents look charming in it. For use outdoors in spring and summer.

3. **VASUM POTS:** These terra-cotta pots are sturdy but not frost-proof. Almost anything can be planted in them, and they're inexpensive enough to keep on hand for seedlings. Often used effectively to line a driveway or stairway.

4. **TALL TERRA-COTTA POT:** This traditional pot is hand thrown and frost-resistant. The simple, strong shape doesn't detract from plants.

5. **BASKET-WEAVE POT:** Constructed of frost-resistant terra-cotta, this pot is hand thrown at Whichford Pottery in the Cotswolds, England. Its shallow shape is well-suited to a variety of colorful annuals or bulbs.

8. LEMON POT

6. CAST-STONE URN

10. GUY WOLFF LONG TOM

7. CEDAR PLANTER

9. SMALL GLAZED POT

6. **CAST-STONE URN:** The cast of this urn has a long heritage and has graced countless gardens for centuries. It is particularly handsome when used in pairs, flanking a front door or stairway. A tall plant in the center with low plants cascading over the edges makes a striking arrangement. Frost-proof when empty.

7. **CEDAR PLANTER:** Equally attractive when used as a window box or deck planter, this pot looks lovely left natural or painted. It is deep enough (6") to make daily watering unnecessary unless there is a long spell of high temperatures.

8. **LEMON POT:** Named for the European tradition of overwintering citrus trees in large pots indoors. The shape is also well-suited to roses, small trees, and topiary. Traditionally made of unglazed terracotta, this pot is not frost-proof. If left outdoors during winter, invert the empty pot when snowy conditions arrive.

9. **SMALL GLAZED POT:** This takes on the look of a very old, unglazed pot covered with minerals and mold. It is primarily used as decoration because the beauty of the pot often competes with the plant growing in it. Not frost-proof.

10. **GUY WOLFF LONG TOM:** Designed to accommodate plants with long taproots, the Long Tom pot is very strong but not frost-proof. It is made of porous white clay, usually unglazed.

CUTTING

Cutting takes courage. Removing part of a growing plant means interrupting nature's plans and substituting your own. To deadhead a marigold or remove that big, diseased limb from the maple is to modify the plant's growth habits. To cut down a tree for firewood is to change the shape of the landscape, letting in more light.

And to harvest fruit, flowers, or stalks of grass is to remove living things from the earth.

> "*I am persuaded that pruning is not only a very useful but also a curious thing, and capable of affording pleasure to those that understand it. But at the same time, it must be acknowledged that it is likewise pernicious or dangerous when performed by unskilful hands.... Everybody cuts, but few prune....*"
>
> —DE LA QUINTINYE

Each cutting task has an implement dedicated to it, and this means that more than one cutting tool is needed in the garden. Deadheading and the harvesting of flowers require a delicate pair of shears that are light and fine enough to cut without crushing or tearing tender herbaceous stems. Shrub pruning usually calls for a sharp pair of hand pruners (also known as secateurs or clippers) that can sever woody stems without damaging the remaining plant. Big stems—up to 3" in diameter—require a high-leverage pair of loppers.

Trees have an enormous variety of cutting tools dedicated exclusively to their care. Whole catalogs exist to serve the needs of arborists and foresters who, like old-fashioned physicians, respond to most health problems of their patients by cutting away the offending parts. In the home garden, you will not have much use for a chain saw, but a fine, curved-blade pruning saw will cleanly cut branches up to 6" in diameter. For working higher up, a pole pruner fitted with either a remote-control lopper or a saw (sometimes both) lets you reach the problem without climbing into the tree. And when timber is on the ground in big, heavy rounds, the ax, the maul, and the wedge help you reduce the hunks to fireplace sizes that the hatchet cuts down into kindling.

The oldest of cutting tools, now called billhooks, brush hooks, and clearing axes, were once widely used for pruning and hedging but today are reserved almost exclusively for land clearing. Swung against a sapling, the long, sharp blade of such a tool can mow it down in a single cut.

The most beautiful of all cutting tools, and perhaps the loveliest tool ever invented, is the scythe. Specialized for cutting hay and mowing grass, it has been almost wholly supplanted by automatic, mechanical mowers. Nonetheless, it is still possible to find one, and if you have even a few hundred square yards of rough grass on your property—an area too rocky or rough for the mower—you should give the scythe a try.

HISTORY OF CUTTING

It is almost certain the first woody plant to be intentionally pruned by man was the grapevine in Armenia around 6000 B.C. Curiously enough, this date roughly coincides with the beginning of the modern era, and as civilization spread west through Babylonia, Egypt, Greece, and Rome, the grape and its pruning tools went along. One hundred years before the Christian era, the vine had reached all the way to Britain.

Through these six millennia, until the Renaissance in Europe, basic pruning tools remained virtually the same. Either long- or short-handled, the falx of the Romans and the pruning hook of the Britons were tools with a sharp, recurved blade like that of a modern billhook. There were versions that came complete with a pike for poking and an ax for chopping, but the central purpose of the tool was neatly to sever limbs and woody stems, both large and small. Descendants of the falx were the basic tools used for espalier, or training the branches of fruit trees to grow a flat pattern that would give each spur equal access to the sun.

The scythe, the archetypal grain-harvesting tool, evolved from a long-handled falx. The earliest farmers harvested wheat by pulling the plants out by the roots. The Middle Eastern cultures in Mesopotamia began to harvest by cutting. Not until the Roman Empire, when maximum efficiency was required to harvest large and undermanned estates in Gaul and other provinces, did a version of the modern scythe

THE FIRST PRUNER

As recorded in *The Compleat Gardener* (1693), the story goes that a wild ass got into vineyard somewhere in a ancient Greece and gnawed a few grapevines back to their main stems. The gardener's rage turned to delight when he found that the gnawed vine regenerated quickly and produced far more fruit than the untouched vines. He began intentionally to cut the vines, an experiment attended with so much success that "to express their acknowledgement of so fine an Invention, they erected in one of the finest places of that province, a marble statue to that animal as the author of pruning vines, that is, to the author of the abundance of wine."

evolve. Though it was unlike our scythe and had no grips, the tool was long, had a transverse blade, and was operated by a farmer who walked through the field, swinging the tool with a supple motion of his waist.

The scythe was a prize possession, often the only metal-bladed tool of many European peasants. More valuable than any of their livestock, the tool cost, by one estimate, a quarter of the medieval farmer's annual income.

The great innovation in cutting tools continued with the invention of clipped hedges. The wall-like effect of a well-trimmed hedge led to a popularity explosion in the fifteenth and sixteenth centuries, and tools had to be developed to cut hedge plants smoothly and efficiently. A simple falx was hard to use on stems of many different sizes, and it tended to gouge. It's unknown who invented hedge shears. They were, however, the first garden tool based on the scissor principle and were thus ancestors of modern shears, hand pruners, and loppers.

Not until the nineteenth century did the full panoply of modern garden cutting tools appear. In 1822, the first edition of J.C. Loudon's *An Encyclopaedia of Gardening* reported not only the pruning-bill, descendant of the falx, but also all kinds of chisels, axes, saws, shears, scythes, garden scarifiers, bark scalers, and moss scrapers. The real gems of nineteenth-century industrial craft were the French hand pruners, or *secateurs*, scissor-action tools that rested lightly in one hand yet could cleanly sever stems more than 1" in diameter. The principle of the French pruners was expanded quickly. It was applied to long-handled loppers that could cut larger stems, and the same design was fitted to a long pole and operated with a remote-control puller to become the fearsome averruncator.

The only cutting implement that has not changed is the ax. The fact that it has changed little from its form of 8,000 years ago makes it one of the world's most stable and traditional tools. Otherwise, of the cutting tools that we use today in the garden, few resemble their original form. The venerable falx—now called a billhook or a brush hook—has been reduced to a minor role clearing overgrown fields.

THE SCISSOR PRINCIPLE

All shears, hand pruners, and loppers are based on the scissor principle, according to which two blades are joined at a central pivot and brought together to cut. Usually, the two blades pass each other in the cutting process to sever the stem more cleanly. Tools that bring a sharp blade down against a flat "anvil" crush the edge of the stem they're cutting; such tools should be used only on deadwood, where their slightly greater biting power outweighs the raggedness of their cut.

The main differences among pruners have to do with scale. It's important to choose the right length and shape of blade and handles. Delicate ikebana shears will prove almost useless for pruning plum trees, while a pair of loppers will butcher a hedge. Secateurs may serve for cutting flowers, but their strength is overkill. The longevity of both flower and plant will be improved if lightweight flower shears are used.

FLOWER SHEARS

In the traditional kitchen of a suburban home, there is often a nest of Mom's crucial things: needle and thread, a clean cup, the kids' vitamins, and a little pair of flower shears. These diminutive red-handled scissors go with her several times each day to deadhead, clip, and cut the flowers in her garden. And along the way, they might come in handy if she sees a wild branchlet among the junipers or something amiss in the pots of Japanese maples.

CHOOSING FLOWER SHEARS

The choice of flower shears depends on your need. Often a serious gardener may have two pairs: one that gives fingertip control for cutting flower stems to size on the potting bench, and another with a long, precision reach to get at the flowers out in the garden. Specialized shears with blunt ends are made for harvesting fruits; other models, with small but with powerful levering action, precisely prune the delicate woody stems of bonsai trees. Think before you choose. Those pretty ikebana shears may turn out to be a fat-bodied nuisance in dense perennial beds. And not every good-looking tool has the proper weight and feel.

Test the pivot of the blades to be sure it operates smoothly, without wobbling, and verify the quality of materials and construction. Flower shears once had steel or alloy handles coated with a plastic or vinyl material to make them more pleasant to the touch. Today, composite plastic materials may be used for the entire handle, which makes the tool lighter without sacrificing strength. Some gardeners still like the businesslike heft of the metal-handled tools, but many now prefer the light feel of the composite materials.

USING FLOWER SHEARS

When cutting from the garden, be sure to leave the longest stems possible so you'll have more choice of height for the flower arrangement. And be certain that the clippers are sharp. A ragged cut distorts and closes the intrastem vessels that carry water into the flower, shortening its life.

The simplest and most versatile flower shears have straight carbon or stainless steel bypass blades 2"–5" long. Both handle and blades are slender, letting you work among tight clumps of stems, and the bypass action gives a smooth precise cut on live stems. Because florists use such models, they often have a notch near the pivot of the blades for cutting either tougher stems or florist's wire.

Some gardeners still like the businesslike heft of the metal-handled tools, but many now prefer the light feel of the composite materials.

THINNING SHEARS: Though not quite needle-nosed, these longer-bladed shears can actually single out each delicate stem in a dense stand of cornflowers. Blunt-ended instruments called grape shears, developed to harvest fruit that might be damaged by a pointed tip, have the same virtues as thinning shears but are also less liable to bruise.

DEADHEADING SHEARS: These stainless steel tools have long handles with loops for thumb and forefinger, and the blades are very short but straight and needle-pointed. As delicate as they may look, these are tough, high-leverage tools. Bonsai makers use them to cut small wood stems when there is no room for the slightest error.

IKEBANA SHEARS: With their stubby curved carbon steel blades and butterfly handles, ikebana shears are a sight to behold. The thick handles prevent them from getting into tight spots in growing plants, but they are excellent for recutting the stems of cut flowers, blossoms, and small woody branches for flower arrangements. Your fingers and thumb won't lose their hold on the handle no matter how strange an angle you cut.

CUT-AND-HOLD SHEARS: Too often, you find yourself at full arm's length trying to get at a flower deep in the border; if you stretch to the maximum, you can just barely get the shears around the stem, but you can't possibly reach your other hand to keep the clipped flower from falling. Cut-and-hold shears, uncanny instruments that resemble flower shears except for a little extra fold of metal in one blade are able to gently grasp the clipped bloom and keep it from falling.

DEADHEADING

The simplest form of pruning is deadheading. If the spent blooms of annuals are removed before they can set seed, the plant will continue to flower. Once seedpods begin to establish, the plant signals the remaining blooms to give way to the production of seed. Often, you can simply pinch off the dead flower, using the thumb and forefinger. A neater and less destructive method is to cut with slender, straight flower shears that are not much bigger than sewing scissors.

Flower Shears

1. **DEADHEADING SHEARS:** Originally used by bonsai gardeners, these handsome, lightweight, shears are made of high-carbon stainless steel. The small blades make precision cuts while the looped handles fit hands of any size. A great choice for thinning out prized perennials. LENGTH 7⅛", WEIGHT 3.2 OZ., BLADE LENGTH 1½".

2. **BIG-LOOP SHEARS:** A handy, all-purpose scissors, good for both indoor and outdoor use. Large looped, vinyl-covered handles are comfortable for any user; sharp stainless steel blades resist corrosion. Ideal for cutting twine, paper, and other materials in addition to stems. LENGTH 6½", WEIGHT 2.1 OZ., BLADE LENGTH 1¾".

3. **FISKARS FLOWER SHEARS:** Light, elegant thinning shears of superior construction. The short, precise blades with a bypass action are fashioned from carbon steel. The straight handles are cushioned for a firm but comfortable grip. This is a good choice for light pruning, thinning, and flower cutting. LENGTH 6", WEIGHT 1.8 OZ., BLADE LENGTH 1½".

4. **FRUIT AND FLOWER SHEARS:** Heavy-duty shears designed for more demanding tasks than the average thinning shears. The blades are fashioned from high-carbon forged steel and will cut through thicker fruiting and flowering branches. Simple bypass construction and handle lock. LENGTH 8¼", WEIGHT 5.4 OZ., BLADE LENGTH 2½".

5. **IKEBANA SHEARS:** These unique, butterfly-handled shears, used predominantly by ikebana practitioners, are very useful to the home gardener for cutting flowers to make indoor arrangements. Sharp precise blades cut both herbaceous and woody stems with ease. LENGTH 7½", WEIGHT 8.2 OZ., BLADE LENGTH 2⅛".

6. **THINNING SHEARS:** The slender, more delicate cousin of the Fruit and Flower Shears, these Japanese thinning shears are the right tool for deadheading, trimming, and precise thinning. Also handy for picking fruit and flowers because the pointed blades reach through vegetation. High-carbon steel blades, bypass action, simple handle lock. LENGTH 7", WEIGHT 3.6 OZ., BLADE LENGTH 2".

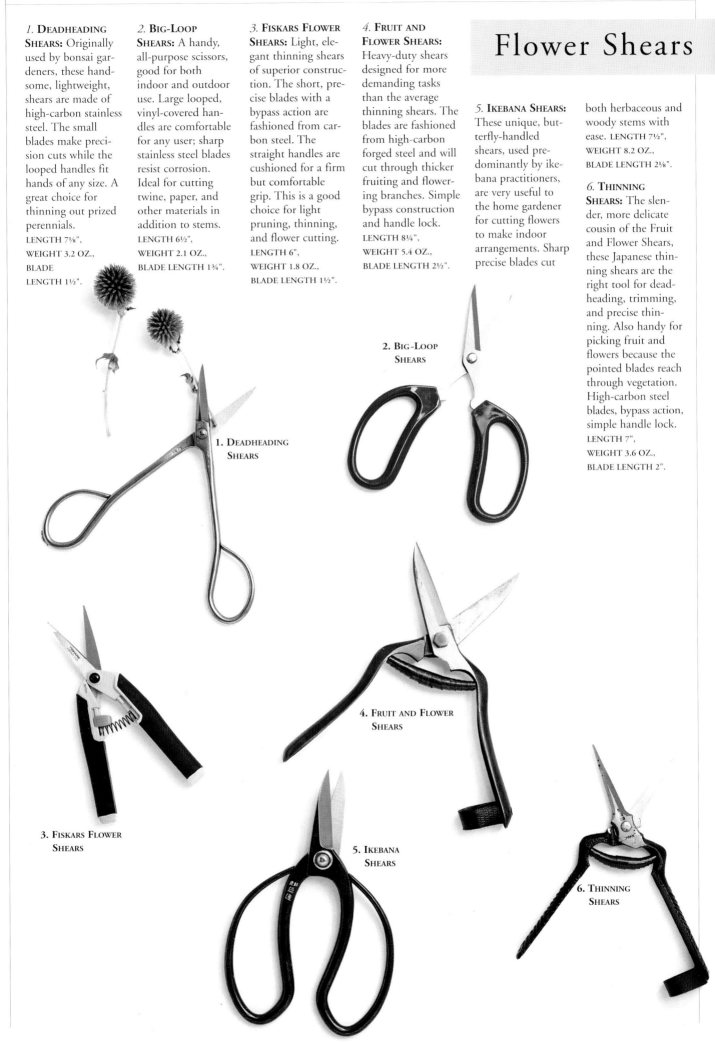

2. BIG-LOOP SHEARS

1. DEADHEADING SHEARS

3. FISKARS FLOWER SHEARS

4. FRUIT AND FLOWER SHEARS

5. IKEBANA SHEARS

6. THINNING SHEARS

HAND PRUNERS

The secret of the nineteenth-century *secateurs,* or French hand pruners, lay in precision-cut and precision-fit blades that scissored cleanly past each other when the handles were squeezed in a "bypass" action. The slightly curved shape of the cutting blade also encouraged a smooth "draw cut," in which the blade slides knifelike through the wood, rather than a wounding "crushing cut."

Today, of all garden cutting tools, these hand pruners are the most essential. Though intended primarily for the light pruning of woody stems, whether on rhododendrons, apple trees, or blue spruces, they also make fine tools for taking cuttings to propagate new plants. And in a pinch, they can be used to cut flowers for the table, to extirpate brambles, to prune the dead leaves off the strawberries, or to harvest the tomatoes.

Gardeners are fiercely loyal to their hand pruners. Just watch what happens if you have the temerity to borrow someone else's favorite pair; more than likely, you'll find the lender surveilling you with a baleful eye, lest you lose or purloin such a precious possession.

To keep your own pruners from getting lost, it's worth investing in a little leather holster that attaches to your belt. The pruners are small enough to shove into your back pocket, but once you've ripped the seams out of three or four pockets you'll see the wisdom of carrying them in a holster. Furthermore, the heft of the holster on your belt gives you the comfortable feeling that the tool is on your person and not lying somewhere else in the garden.

CHOOSING HAND PRUNERS

For most garden tools, there is an often unspoken but very real distinction between "homeowner" quality and "professional" quality. The former is adequate at best, but the latter is durable and always effective. Interestingly, when it comes to hand pruners, the best professional models are also those most popular with home gardeners—despite the fact that the major manufacturer never made "homeowners" a target market.

Hand pruners are the most frequently used cutting tools, so design and quality are both crucial elements. For a rough-and-ready

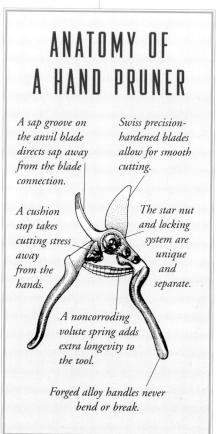

ANATOMY OF A HAND PRUNER

A sap groove on the anvil blade directs sap away from the blade connection.

Swiss precision-hardened blades allow for smooth cutting.

A cushion stop takes cutting stress away from the hands.

The star nut and locking system are unique and separate.

A noncorroding volute spring adds extra longevity to the tool.

Forged alloy handles never bend or break.

test, hold the tool in your hand and flex it. Does it have the right weight? Does it feel comfortable in your hand? Will you be able to use it in tight spots without striking other branches? Does it open and close without sticking? Is the safety latch that locks the tool positioned conveniently, and does it work well with a flick of the thumb? The best hand pruners feel so good that an arborist hanging upside down 60' off the ground in an oak tree feels reassured when grabbing the tool from its holster to cut away a few pesky root suckers or watersprouts.

When assessing the quality of hand pruners, you should also be sure that the blade is made of tempered carbon steel and is easily replaceable. (You can sharpen the blade, of course, but eventually you may wish to replace it without having to discard the tool.) The best handles are made of vinyl-coated aluminum alloy that is both light and strong. The safety latch should click in and out easily, and the spring that holds the pivot under tension should operate smoothly, without friction. Ideally, the bottom blade will mesh snugly with the cutting blade, and it will have a groove that carries gummy sap away from the tool.

Another advantage of the best-quality hand pruners is that they have replaceable parts. They can be disassembled with little fuss, any part can be replaced, and the whole tool can be reassembled in just a few minutes if you have the spare part handy.

For most garden tools, it makes no difference whether you're right-handed or left-handed. Not so for hand pruners. The cutting blade is beveled on one side only, and that side must rest on the inside of the cut nearest to the tree; in other words, the blade that makes the cut smooth is always between your hand and the parent stem or trunk, assuring a smooth-edged cut. If you're a lefty, don't fail to get a left-handed pruner.

WHEN TO PRUNE SHRUBS

You can encourage better flowering of shrubs by cutting back the spent flowers at the right time. Late-flowering shrubs like hydrangea bloom on wood that has grown in the current year and therefore should be pruned back hard in early spring. Shrubs that bloom in spring and through the month of June should be pruned after they flower. Flower shears will do for smaller twigs, but the best tool for this work is usually a good pair of hand pruners. Their sharp, curved blades are capable of making precise cuts on everything from the slenderest twig to a stem ½" in diameter.

USING HAND PRUNERS

The only way to misuse these tools is to try to make them cut something too big or too tough for them. In fact, it's comical to watch a gardener attempt to get through a big stem with a pair of hand pruners. The hand twists this way, then that way, as though there were a tug-of-war going on between the gardener and the plant.

The results of such a confrontation are detrimental to both plant and pruners. The cut usually tears bark from the stem, increasing the possibility of infection, and the tool has been subjected to torsion that can ultimately loosen the picot or bend the blades so they no longer pass each other smoothly.

For cutting dead stems, which tend to be tougher, it may be better to choose specialized hand pruners such as the anvil models. On these tools, the cutting blade meets a small anvil, and you get more cutting force with less need to twist.

When you need to cut really large stems, it's time to put away the hand pruners and get out the loppers.

BYPASS PRUNERS: For general pruning of woody stems up to ¾" thick, your best bet is the bypass pruner. This tool works like a pair of scissors, except that the blades are slightly curved to hold a stem or branch in place and to make a cut that slices rather than crushes (thereby inviting infection). Its cutting blade is usually beveled and hollow-ground on the outward-facing side only. The inward-facing side slides smoothly and seamlessly against the face of the unsharpened bottom blade, creating a neat and even slicing action. The slenderness of both blades means that you can cut right at the bark branch collar without leaving a stub.

The bypass pruners made by Felco—a Swiss company founded in 1945 by Felix Sclisch to make *only* garden shears—are the standard against which all others are measured. Many imitations, more or less successful, are available from other manufacturers. There are even lightweight bypass pruners that are little different from flower shears. Of the really serviceable models, however, the majority work just like Felco pruners.

One exception is the Sandvik line of bypass pruners. On these tools, the pivot is offset from the center line of the two blades. The effect of this design is an increase in the force that a given hand pressure will exert on the branch to be cut. The tool seems to lean slightly downward into the cut, gently forcing the blade into the stem. In sum, this means that Sandvik hand pruners exert slightly greater force per unit of pressure on the handles.

The pattern for these pruners is said to have been created by Felco designers back in the 1920s. Curiously, the company never chose to go forward with the pattern. Some time later, however, the people at Sandvik—a larger tool company, better known in Europe for its drill bits and belt sanders—made the decision to get into the garden tool business. They asked Felco to manufacture the unused design and license it to Sandvik. Felco declined but informed them that the design

The bypass pruners made by Felco are the standard against which all others are measured.

was not protected by a patent and that they could go ahead and make the tool themselves.

ANVIL PRUNERS: The poor anvil pruner has come into a lot of bad press, but it is not without its uses. Approximately the same size as bypass pruners, anvil pruners are based on an entirely different principle of design. Instead of slicing, the cutting blade comes down on a finger-width "anvil," cutting the stem as if it were lying on a small chopping block. The drawback to the design is the width of the anvil, which makes it impossible to work right up to a bark branch collar. This means that a short stub will remain behind, providing a potential place for disease to enter the plant. Also, the cut is more likely to crush the stem than slice it, thereby radically increasing the avenues for infection.

For pruning tough, lignified deadwood, however, there is nothing like the anvil pruner. Your hand doesn't have to twist and push to force the two blades past each other. Instead, all you have to do is push the blade into the brass anvil.

The ratchet-action pruner. This version of the anvil pruner is a revolution in hand pruner design. Its ratchet action increases cutting force by as much as 30%, allowing even very weak hands to cut live branches up to ¾" in diameter and deadwood more than 1½" thick.

The rolcut pruner. This beautiful tool, with its scroll-decorated metal body, is reminiscent of an old nickel-plated revolver. It's the cleanest-cutting of the anvil pruners because it takes a gentle saw to the wood. When you press on the handles, the cutting blade draws back through the wood while the anvil blade cleanly slides forward.

BEWARE OF BUDS

The three kinds of buds must be taken into account even before pruning begins. Cutting terminal buds, or those that grow at the ends of stems, will direct the plant's energy to growth along the stems and thereby increase its bushiness.

Conversely, cutting buds that grow laterally on the stem will divert energy to the terminal bud and encourage a taller, skinnier shape.

Latent buds, which are seen as nubbins on the stem, will sprout only when higher growth is removed.

Hand Pruners

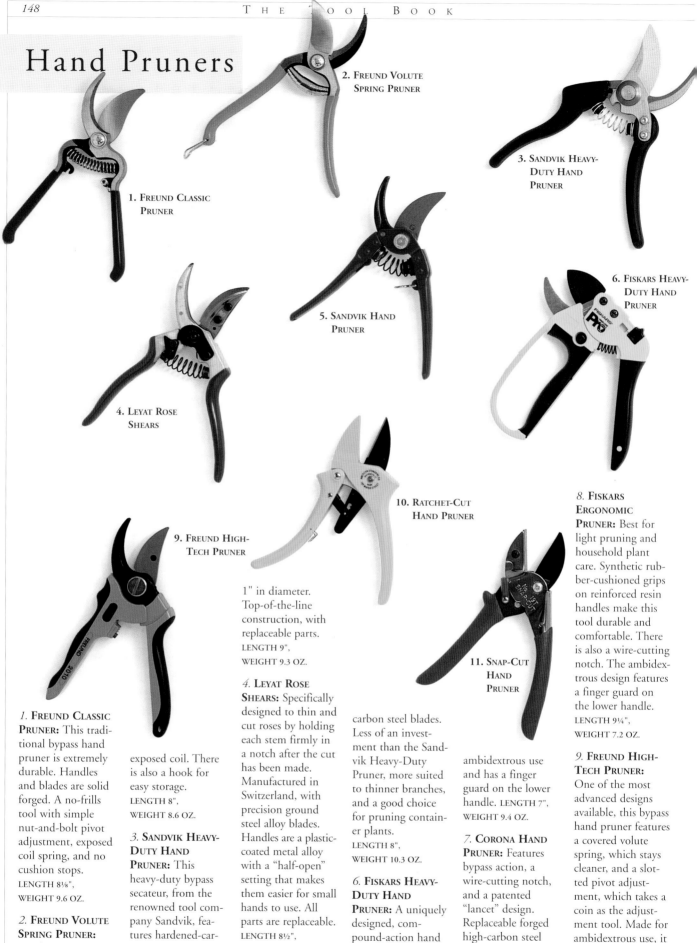

2. FREUND VOLUTE SPRING PRUNER

1. FREUND CLASSIC PRUNER

3. SANDVIK HEAVY-DUTY HAND PRUNER

5. SANDVIK HAND PRUNER

6. FISKARS HEAVY-DUTY HAND PRUNER

4. LEYAT ROSE SHEARS

10. RATCHET-CUT HAND PRUNER

8. FISKARS ERGONOMIC PRUNER: Best for light pruning and household plant care. Synthetic rubber-cushioned grips on reinforced resin handles make this tool durable and comfortable. There is also a wire-cutting notch. The ambidextrous design features a finger guard on the lower handle. LENGTH 9¼", WEIGHT 7.2 OZ.

9. FREUND HIGH-TECH PRUNER

11. SNAP-CUT HAND PRUNER

1. **FREUND CLASSIC PRUNER:** This traditional bypass hand pruner is extremely durable. Handles and blades are solid forged. A no-frills tool with simple nut-and-bolt pivot adjustment, exposed coil spring, and no cushion stops. LENGTH 8⅛", WEIGHT 9.6 OZ.

2. **FREUND VOLUTE SPRING PRUNER:** Similar in design and construction to the Freund Classic, this simple, basic pruner features a volute spring instead of the traditional exposed coil. There is also a hook for easy storage. LENGTH 8", WEIGHT 8.6 OZ.

3. **SANDVIK HEAVY-DUTY HAND PRUNER:** This heavy-duty bypass secateur, from the renowned tool company Sandvik, features hardened-carbon steel blades with xylan (an antifriction, antirust coating), and a sap groove, and a quick-release safely catch. Cuts branches up to 1" in diameter. Top-of-the-line construction, with replaceable parts. LENGTH 9", WEIGHT 9.3 OZ.

4. **LEYAT ROSE SHEARS:** Specifically designed to thin and cut roses by holding each stem firmly in a notch after the cut has been made. Manufactured in Switzerland, with precision ground steel alloy blades. Handles are a plastic-coated metal alloy with a "half-open" setting that makes them easier for small hands to use. All parts are replaceable. LENGTH 8½", WEIGHT 8.5 OZ.

5. **SANDVIK HAND PRUNER:** A bypass pruner for smaller hands, featuring steel handles and carbon steel blades. Less of an investment than the Sandvik Heavy-Duty Pruner, more suited to thinner branches, and a good choice for pruning container plants. LENGTH 8", WEIGHT 10.3 OZ.

6. **FISKARS HEAVY-DUTY HAND PRUNER:** A uniquely designed, compound-action hand pruner with synthetic rubber-cusioned grips and reinforced resin handles. Like other Fiskars models, this one is made for ambidextrous use and has a finger guard on the lower handle. LENGTH 7", WEIGHT 9.4 OZ.

7. **CORONA HAND PRUNER:** Features bypass action, a wire-cutting notch, and a patented "lancet" design. Replaceable forged high-carbon steel blade cuts branches up to 1" in diameter. Vinyl-covered alloy handles cushion hands. LENGTH 8¾", WEIGHT 0.7 LB.

9. **FREUND HIGH-TECH PRUNER:** One of the most advanced designs available, this bypass hand pruner features a covered volute spring, which stays cleaner, and a slotted pivot adjustment, which takes a coin as the adjustment tool. Made for ambidextrous use, it has a cushion stop and internal latch. LENGTH 8½", WEIGHT 10.4 OZ.

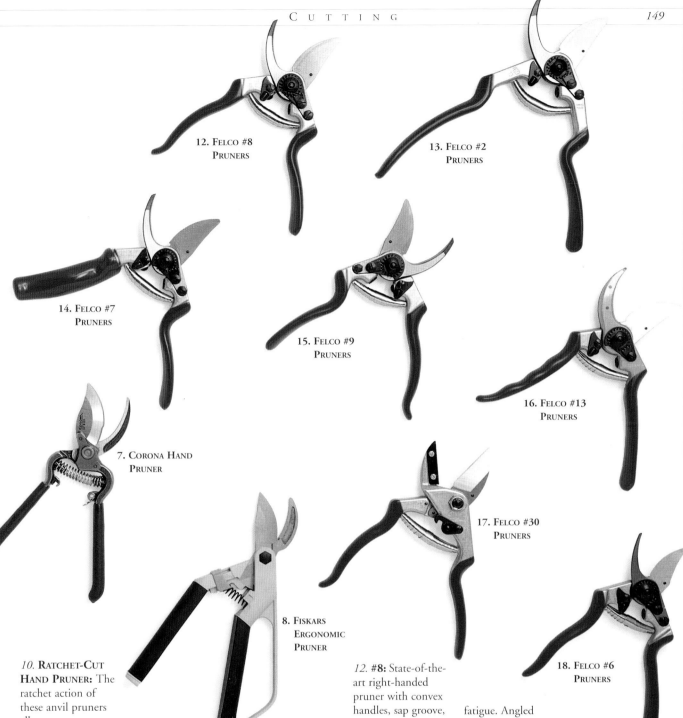

12. FELCO #8 PRUNERS

13. FELCO #2 PRUNERS

14. FELCO #7 PRUNERS

15. FELCO #9 PRUNERS

16. FELCO #13 PRUNERS

7. CORONA HAND PRUNER

17. FELCO #30 PRUNERS

8. FISKARS ERGONOMIC PRUNER

18. FELCO #6 PRUNERS

10. **RATCHET-CUT HAND PRUNER:** The ratchet action of these anvil pruners allows even very weak hands to cut branches up to ¾" in diameter. With a unique, patented design based on the principle of a lever, the pruner grips the stem, allowing the user to make progressively deeper cuts. Features Teflon-coated, hardened steel blades and tough, brightly colored plastic handles. An affordable, lightweight choice that many gardeners will prefer.
LENGTH 7¼", WEIGHT 3.9 OZ.

11. **SNAP-CUT HAND PRUNER:** This is a professional-style anvil for cutting branches up to ¾" in diameter. An affordable option with better-than-average construction, featuring a Teflon S-shaped 1½" blade, vinyl grips, and a reversible and replaceable brass anvil. A good choice for thinning dead branches. LENGTH 8", WEIGHT 10.9 OZ.

FELCO PRUNERS
Felco pruners are of the highest quality and feature replaceable high-carbon steel blades for the cleanest, closest cuts. The ergonomic handles are made of forged metal alloy and padded with soft rubber. These Swiss-made pruners are expensive but they are worth every penny. Felcos come in an array of sizes and forms—following are several of the most-asked-for designs.

12. **#8:** State-of-the-art right-handed pruner with convex handles, sap groove, anvil action, separate locking segment, cushioned stop, and a noncorroding volute spring.
LENGTH 8¼", WEIGHT 8.7 OZ.

13. **#2:** The most popular Felco design with sap groove, wire-cutting notch, tempered bolt, cushioned stops, volute spring, and bushing to prevent blade spreading.
LENGTH 8½", WEIGHT 8.7 OZ.

14. **#7:** A rotating handle brings fingers into the palm, reducing hand fatigue. Angled blade for close cutting, wire-cutting notch, sap groove.
LENGTH 8½", WEIGHT 10.7 OZ.

15. **#9:** The same tool as #8, but for left-handed users.

16. **#13:** This new Felco, developed in collaboration with occupational medicine specialists, bridges the gap between one-handed pruning shears and two-handed loppers. When cutting thick branches, the extra-long left handle lets the user overlap both hands. This ensures full cutting capacity with a 25% reduction in muscular exertion.
LENGTH 10¾", WEIGHT 10.7 OZ.

17. **#30:** Felco's high-tech concept of an anvil pruner, with ergonomic grip and replaceable blades. A good all-purpose cutter.
LENGTH 8½", WEIGHT 7.8 OZ.

18. **#6:** A classic Felco design made for smaller hands.
LENGTH 7⅞", WEIGHT 7.7 OZ.

HEDGE SHEARS

When professional gardeners are called in, the first sound you hear is the buzz and rattle of half a dozen motors: leaf blowers, lawn mowers, string trimmers, rototillers, and chain saws. This is when you find yourself longing for the days that preceded the age of power tools, when a gardener's presence might be signaled by nothing louder than the rhythmic snick of hedge shears opening and closing.

Long-bladed hedge shears are perhaps the greatest touchstone for memory in the garden. Cutting the hedge was a privilege earned by many sons and daughters. Even as a young gardener, you had to be reliable, steady, and comfortable on a ladder, and you had to stick to it until the unruly mass of uneven shoots emerged in the clean shape of a well-clipped hedge. While the little groundlings were pushing the (hand) lawn mower, edging the grass, or sweeping the pine needles from the driveway, you would lean out dangerously and deliciously over the top of the great hedge, half wishing that the ladder would throw you into its cool deep green.

CHOOSING HEDGE SHEARS

The earliest garden shears were nothing more than outsize versions of sheep shears. Made of a single piece of metal, these primitive shears consisted of two long, triangular blades joined at their base by a metal spring. Tiring to use and limited in size, they were soon replaced by two-bladed shears joined at a fulcrum point in the middle. The handles were made of wood, so the tool could be longer and lighter, and the fulcrum increased its power and efficiency.

The blades of a modern pair of shears should be stainless steel or forged carbon steel. Ash handles are the best choice, since they absorb the shock of cutting and can accept a reliable tang-and-ferrule connection to the blades. Even high-quality models sometimes have through-riveted tangs, but shears that are well made seldom give way at the handle. More important to the construction is an effective stopper between the blades. This part of the tool ensures a soft final contact when the handles are brought together.

Long-handled hedge shears improve your reach from ground level (though in many cases a ladder works just as well). One long-handled model sets the blades at an angle to the handles. This tool is often used

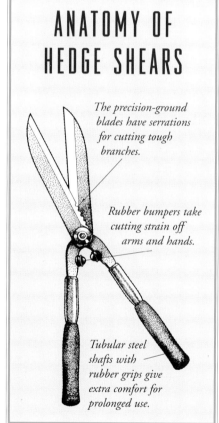

ANATOMY OF HEDGE SHEARS

The precision-ground blades have serrations for cutting tough branches.

Rubber bumpers take cutting strain off arms and hands.

Tubular steel shafts with rubber grips give extra comfort for prolonged use.

by gardeners who want to trim grass edging without stooping, but it also comes in handy if you want to reach over and smooth the top of a tall hedge.

USING HEDGE SHEARS

Working with these tools is a continuous learning process, and the number of gouged hedges that result is directly proportional to the degree of experience. In fact, the unsightly "mistakes" often made by beginners using hand shears is one of the chief reasons that so many people convert to electric hedge trimmers.

The electric versions may seem superior because the blade is very long and flat, but often you only trade one problem for another. So what if the hedge lacks the formal regularity of Versailles? Electric hedge trimmers are even more likely than hand shears to commit the really unfortunate error of cutting the hedge "upside down."

To maintain healthy growth from top to bottom, hedges must be trimmed to a shape like a truncated pyramid or cone. The bottom of the hedge should be slightly wider than the top, allowing all the leaves to receive adequate light. Hasty hedge trimmers, unwilling to pause, stoop, or sight along the hedge to see that it's properly shaped, usually carve an inverted pyramid instead. The unfortunate result is a hedge that appears to have been set on stilts because its lower branches died for lack of light.

The best way to trim a hedge is to take your time and maintain the proper general shape. Keep the shears at a comfortable distance from your chest and maintain that set distance. To cut higher, lower, or side to side, adjust your arms rather than your body. And when you go low, squat in order to maintain the shape. In this way, you won't scalp the hedge or cut it upside down, and the minor imperfections of your cutting will be lost in the overall impression of a healthy, thriving colony of plants.

KINDS OF HEDGE SHEARS

Hand shears have improved in quality over the years despite the rise of motor tools. The best models have always been made of drop-forged carbon steel, with the handles carefully attached and through-riveted in place. When you were a child, the shears that you used probably had two straight, sharp blades and, if you were lucky, a notch near the pivot to deal with the occasional thick stem. Much time and annoyance often went into trying to capture one unruly pittosporum sucker that seemed to dart out from between your blades as though it were the unruly cowlick on a cartoon character that would not lie down.

A number of brilliant solutions have since appeared to make hedge

The most important aspect of using hedge shears is to move your body instead of extending your arms for hard-to-reach areas. This insures even cutting over the length of the hedge.

pruning a much less frustrating and often inconsistent endeavor. Clever blade designs and a wider range of sizes give the gardener more options from which to choose. Serrated and wavy-edged blades help hold branches in place, eliminating the common frustration of errant, unruly branches that appear to resist being cut by conventional blades. Smaller models of hedge shears provide more mobility and precision.

SERRATED BLADES: The first solution is obvious: if you want a blade to hold, serrate the edge. You lose some smoothness in the cut, and the serrations (located on one blade only near the blade connection) have an unfortunate tendency to gather sap and detritus, but a serrated blade will fix the most unruly stem so you can cut the hedge evenly. One long-handled pair of shears with a serrated edge at the joint can hold branches up to ½" in diameter for a clean cut. Better still is the wavy-edged blade, a specialty of the German firm True Friends.

WAVY-EDGED BLADES: Hedge shears whose blades feature this unique pattern will hold the stem without gathering dirt or roughening the cut. The serrations, which run the length of both blades, however, can often leave a ragged cut.

MINI HEDGE SHEARS: For the dense hedge— or the hedge that requires delicate pruning—there are small versions of all-purpose hedge shears available. One particular design of Japanese origin resembles a wishbone when open. Its smaller size makes it adept at snaking into even the most overgrown hedges. The traditionally designed hedge shears are also available in miniature models.

TO PRUNE A HEDGE

The point in pruning a hedge is to cut back many stems of different sizes in order to maintain a smooth exterior surface of dense, healthy growth. Hedge shears have long blades that make it easy to shape a hedge, encouraging a truncated wedge shape that is wider at the bottom than at the top.

Though it's possible to prune hedges more than once during the growing season, it's best to stop pruning by the end of July so that new growth has a chance to mature and be less susceptible to damage from the first frost.

Hedge Shears

1. All-Purpose Hedge Shears

2. Japanese Hedge Shears

3. Long-Handled Hedge Shears

4. Wavy-Blade Hedge Shears

5. Two-Handed Hedge Shears

6. Mini Hedge Shears

4. **Wavy-Blade Hedge Shears:** A wavy-patterned blade that helps keep branches in place distinguishes this hedge shears. Drop-forged, hollow-ground steel cutting blades are plated with rust-resistant chrome. Blade tension is adjustable and locks in. The hardwood handles have cushioned bumpers to absorb impact.
LENGTH 22",
WEIGHT 3 LBS.,
BLADE LENGTH 9".

5. **Two-Handed Hedge Shears:** This example features a longer blade in a lightweight, agile hand shears. Superior construction, including heavy-gauge, hollow-ground steel cutting blades coated for easy slicing action, makes this tool better than the all-purpose variety. The joint is assembled with a locking pivot bolt and the handles are sturdy tubular steel with padded rubber grips. Also features rubber shock absorbers and a cutting capacity of ⅝".
LENGTH 22",
WEIGHT 2.4 LBS.,
BLADE LENGTH 9½".

6. **Mini Hedge Shears:** A smaller version of the All-Purpose Hedge Shears, featuring the same manufacturing. A good choice for restricted areas.
LENGTH 15",
WEIGHT 1.2 LBS.,
BLADE LENGTH 5½".

1. **All-Purpose Hedge Shears:** The standard in shears design, this affordable tool will prune the average home gardener's shrubbery with ease and precision. Forged carbon steel blades, heat treated to hold a sharp edge, are well balanced by a single-bolt joint. Hardwood handles distribute weight evenly across both hands.
LENGTH 19½",
WEIGHT 1.8 LBS.,
BLADE LENGTH 8".

2. **Japanese Hedge Shears:** This classic Japanese-inspired hedge shears boasts light aluminum alloy construction with Teflon-treated blades that are shaped to lock down a cut for precise work. A pivot bolt adjusts the blade tension, while the thin, resin-coated, aluminum-pipe handles exert maximum control and balance with minimum weight. This tool is best suited to close-in tasks.
LENGTH 20",
WEIGHT 1.2 LBS.,
BLADE LENGTH 6¾".

3. **Long-Handled Hedge Shears:** This is a top-quality hedge shears, designed in France. The long handles allow farther reach without sacrificing balance or weight distribution. The blades, crafted from hardened carbon steel, are precision ground and finished to reduce friction. A serrated edge at the joint holds branches up to ½" in diameter for a clean cut; a steel bearing helps keep the blades perfectly aligned. Handles are coated with rust-resistant orange epoxy and feature rubber grips and buffers.
LENGTH 30",
WEIGHT 3 LBS.,
BLADE LENGTH 10".

LOPPERS

People who have never used loppers are inclined to regard them as superfluous tools. If the stem is small enough for clippers, they say, then why not use a hand pruner? And if it's too big for a hand pruner, what's wrong with using a pruning saw?

These people are usually found in one of two characteristic positions. In the first case, they can be seen pushing and twisting a pair of hand pruners with all their might, straining every muscle to get through the lignin; in the second, they're madly chasing a whippy branchlet with the pruning saw, trying in vain to keep the saw in the kerf.

True enough, loppers are limited to a single purpose. But that purpose is a noble one: to cut medium-size branches too large for the hand pruners and too small for the saw. Loppers were perfected in vineyards and orchards around the world to accomplish the majority of the growers' yearly pruning needs. Even in an ordinary garden, perhaps one-third of all the branches you ever have occasion to cut—on shrubs, in orchards, or on small ornamental trees—belong to this unglamorous category.

Don't contort your body when using loppers. Attempt to stay level with the cutting area, and use a relaxed, smooth cutting motion to avoid tiring.

CHOOSING LOPPERS

Superior reach and leverage are the two basic advantages of loppers over hand pruners. The loppers' blades are virtually identical to those of hand pruners (both bypass and anvil models are available), but the handles of loppers are typically 16"–36" long. With handles like these, you can reach higher and deeper into the plant, and when you push on them the leverage is enormous.

Shorter models usually have steel handles, whereas the longer versions have handles made from aluminum or an aluminum alloy. No matter which handle length you choose, the tool should have durable stoppers made of rubber or another flexible material. These stoppers end the cut when the blades are closed. Even without ratchets, gears, or compound-cutting action, a lopper can cut stems twice as thick as those cut by a comparable hand pruner.

Like all other garden tools designed for cutting, loppers should have a cutting edge made of a fine carbon steel, and the blades should be durably affixed to the handles. Also, before you decide on a new purchase, it's important to examine the pivot point between the two blades to see that it allows smooth action. Be sure, too, that the juncture between the blades is solid. Lastly, consider the cutting capacity of the tool in reflection to your needs.

USING LOPPERS

Loppers are heavy tools compared to hand pruners. You must relax to use them effectively, since tense, hunched-up shoulders will soon tire. Also, it's important to get yourself into a comfortable position when you make your cut. Don't think that you're saving time by contorting your body to get at that extra branch. Move into the correct position and then make the cut.

Never chomp down with the loppers. Set the blades precisely where you want them, and follow through with a single, firm scissor stroke. If the blades don't part the wood, check to see that the tool is sharp. If it's not, don't get stubborn about it; sharpen the tool before you try another cut. Otherwise, switch to a pruning saw.

BASIC LOPPERS: There is a constant effort to expand the capabilities of loppers. So far, the limit is a branch 3" in diameter, which can be cut by a 37½"-long Corona model. This tool, used by foresters to clear saplings, must be a tough one to operate; in fact, it's often sold with a shoulder harness for support.

The main distinction among ordinary loppers is the shape and purpose of the blades. Some are narrow to permit access to branches in tight quarters; others are blunt-ended and parrot-beaked, capable even of dehorning cattle.

SPECIALTY LOPPERS: Clever physicists have discovered ways to increase the cutting power of shorter tools by working in ratchet gears or compound fulcrums. Wilkinson Sword and HK Porter make lovely anvil loppers that include a second pivot to complete the cut. The wildest-looking of the loppers is the so-called maxi-ratchet lopper, a serious hickory-handled pruner that can cut branches up to 2" in diameter with a series of easy motions. The jaws of the tool call to mind a snapping turtle about to bite.

Geared loppers are comparable to ratchet loppers, except that the mechanical advantage is gained automatically, without your having to "pump" the handles more than once.

ANATOMY OF A LOPPER

Deep-forged, precision-ground blades stay sharp longer.

A sweeping curve hook and blade make for easy cutting.

Rubber bumpers automatically stop the handles once the cut has been made.

Tubular steel shafts with rubber shock-absorbing handles alleviate cutting vibrations on the hands.

Loppers

1. ALUMINUM BYPASS LOPPER:
Lean and light, these Corona bypass loppers cut branches up to 2½" in diameter with less effort due to the unique construction. The drop-forged carbon steel blades are coated with a slick resin to help draw material in and cut it with one-third less force than is required by other blades. Lightweight aluminum handles have cushion bumpers and rubber grips. A good-quality choice, especially for those who prefer the control of a less hefty tool. LENGTH 26", WEIGHT 2.6" LBS.

2. COMPOUND-ACTION LOPPER:
This rugged lopper combines the easy slicing action of a bypass version with the additional mechanical advantage of a linkage of levers. The construction creates a compounding of power, much like a lower gear on a bicycle. The heavy-gauge tempered steel cutting blade has a chrome hook for drawing in a branch up to 2" in diameter. Padded oversize rubber grips extend halfway up the steel handles for additional comfort when pressing. A professional tool. LENGTH 32¼", WEIGHT 3.3 LBS.

3. TIMBERLINE ANVIL-ACTION PRUNER: For those who prefer an anvil-action tool, this example features top-of-the-line construction with a 1¾" cutting capacity. The cutting blade is made of Teflon S-coated hardened steel, and the anvil blade is brass; both are replaceable. This lopper also has gear action for more cutting force, and hardwood handles. Heavier than others pictured here, it is best suited to tasks that don't require precision cutting. LENGTH 30", WEIGHT 5.25 LBS.

4. 5' LONG-REACH PRUNER: Longer than the 2' Pruner but not as long as the examples on page 159, this may be the ideal pole pruner for home gardeners, offering both extension and precise control. Both the 2' and 5' models feature a hard chrome-plated steel blade that snips the branch and then grips it for removal. This example has the trigger grip preferred by many users as it reduces arm fatigue. Fiberglass pole. LENGTH 5', WEIGHT 1.4 LBS.

5. VINEYARD PRUNER: These handsome loppers boast both durability and artistry. Initially designed for pruning grape vines, they combine a more delicate and precise cutting action with the reach of a standard-size lopper. Forged carbon steel blades are replaceable. Solid hardwood handles add heft while helping to distribute weight more evenly. Best suited to the thinner branches of fruit and flowering shrubs. LENGTH 25¾", WEIGHT 2.3 LBS.

1. ALUMINUM BYPASS LOPPER

2. COMPOUND-ACTION LOPPER

7. 2' LONG-REACH PRUNER

6. FELCO #21 LOPPER

8. LARGE BRUTE SANDVIK BYPASS LOPPER

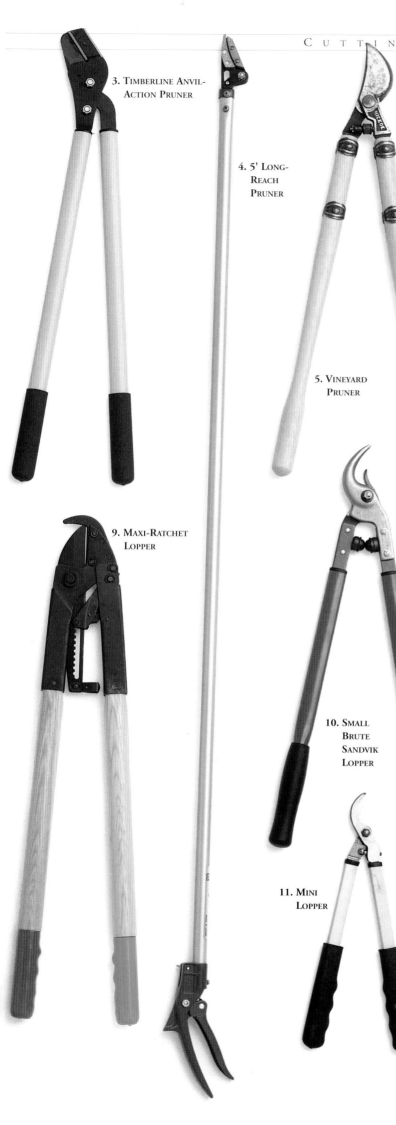

3. TIMBERLINE ANVIL-ACTION PRUNER

4. 5' LONG-REACH PRUNER

5. VINEYARD PRUNER

9. MAXI-RATCHET LOPPER

10. SMALL BRUTE SANDVIK LOPPER

11. MINI LOPPER

6. **FELCO #21 LOPPER:** Manufactured with the same excellent standards as the Felco hand pruners, these bypass loppers feature forged alloy handles with a red plastic grip. Cushioned stops absorb cutting impact, while hollow-ground steel blades cut branches up to 1½" in diameter. Anvil-action blades have a sap groove and are joined by a star nut and separate locking segment. LENGTH 25", WEIGHT 4.8 LBS.

7. **2' LONG-REACH PRUNER:** This tool serves as an extension of the user's arm to prune branches up to ½" in diameter with one hand. It has a lightweight fiberglass handle with chrome-plated steel blades. Trigger grip reduces arm fatigue. LENGTH 2', WEIGHT 0.8 LB.

8. **LARGE BRUTE SANDVIK BYPASS LOPPER:** This heavy-duty bypass lopper is crafted from the best materials and is priced accordingly. Originating in the wine-growing regions of France, it is able to cut branches up to 2" in diameter without crushing plant tissue. Features steel construction with replaceable high-carbon steel blades with two cutting radii: One makes the initial cut with a deep-slicing action; the other finishes with a shearing cut. This model has aluminum handles with rubber grips and cushioned stops. LENGTH 31", WEIGHT 3.9 LBS.

9. **MAXI-RATCHET LOPPER:** Based on the same principle as the Ratchet-Cut Hand Pruner (see page 149), this heavy-duty tool is the largest ratchet-based pruner available and will cut branches up to 2" in diameter with minimum effort. The user presses the hickory handles together—it takes several strokes—and with each progressive push, the heat-treated steel alloy blades slice into the branch a little farther until the cut is made. This tool is an excellent, less physically demanding option for those who have a large area to prune. LENGTH 27¾", WEIGHT 3.5 LBS.

10. **SMALL BRUTE SANDVIK LOPPER:** A smaller edition of the Large Brute Sandvik Bypass Lopper, this tool has a cutting capacity of 1¼" in diameter and a more controllable reach for smaller users. The only other major difference is that the steel handles are coated with rust-resistant red epoxy. LENGTH 23", WEIGHT 2.3 LBS.

11. **MINI LOPPER:** A good choice where hand pruners are too short but standard loppers are too long or unwieldy. This tool features forged carbon steel cutting blades, bypass action, and steel alloy handles with padded rubber grips. LENGTH 16½", WEIGHT 1.9 LBS.

POLE PRUNERS

To prune high up in a tree or to harvest fruit on a big, old apple tree, for instance, you need either a ladder or one of the long-handled tools that extend your reach. These tools include the pole pruner itself as well as the fruit picker and the pole saw.

The pole pruner is essentially a lopper on a stick, but the stick (with a telescoping feature or an extension) can be up to 16' long. The pruners have hooked ends that drape over the branch and right up against the bark branch collar. A sharp, movable steel blade is drawn through the wood by means of a pulley-mounted rope.

A good pole pruner can cut wood up to a thickness of about 1½" thick, and some models are combined with a pruning saw so that you can tackle both medium and large branches with the same tool. The trick when operating a pole pruner is to make good clean cuts without standing in the way of falling wood. The arborist's customary cry when dropping wood out of a tree is "Headache!" (If you're hit by a falling branch, you will definitely get one. Or worse.)

To get that tiptop, tastiest apple—the one that has had the greatest benefit of the sun all year long—a pole pruner won't do you much good. You can cut it all right, but the beautiful fruit falls heavily to the ground. Fruit pickers are far better for this purpose. These tools come in lengths from 2' to 5', and they not only cut that distant prize but hold on to it in a basket attachment until you've brought it down.

WHEN TO PRUNE A TREE

When you cut a two-by-four piece of lumber, it stays cut because the wood is dead. But when you cut the end of an oak branch, it sprouts three or four new stems in its place. Every time you prune, you must know what effect your cuts will produce. Trees can be pruned anytime, except during the first flush of growth in the spring. But to discourage suckers and water sprouts—those little ugly branches that rise straight from the ground or upright from a branch—you must wait until late summer when the tree is storing up energy. Unless you intend to make a particular effect (like European gardeners who pollard their trees, repeatedly cutting back to radiating nodes of small branches), cut tree branches back to the stem where they originate.

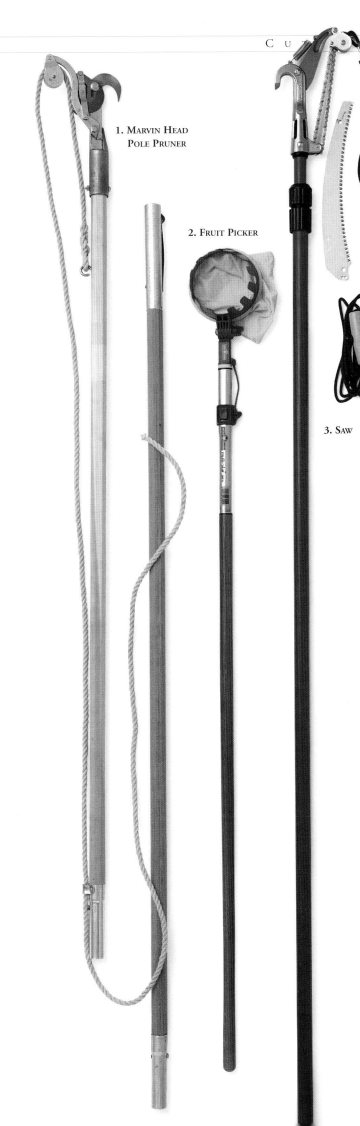

1. MARVIN HEAD POLE PRUNER

2. FRUIT PICKER

3. SAW

Pole Pruners

1. **MARVIN HEAD POLE PRUNER:** A sturdy but lightweight Douglas fir pole is matched with carbon steel blades and aluminum sockets in the manufacture of this long-reach pole pruner. The pole may be used with a forged steel Marvin head lopper or a saw, depending on the task. The Marvin head attachment with an additional extension pole is featured here. The pulley assembly has nylon rollers and high spring tension. Cuts branches up to 1¼" in diameter. Pole reaches to 6' alone, to 12' with extension. **WEIGHT 2 LBS.**

2. **FRUIT PICKER:** The basket attachment for catching fruit can be used alone or in conjunction with a fiberglass extension pole. A plastic rim holds the cloth mesh bag open, and upward-projecting fingers gently pluck fruit from stems. **WEIGHT 2 LBS.**

3. **SAW:** This telescoping fiberglass option features a chrome hook and a tubular steel adapter that will accommodate the forged carbon saw head. A professional-quality pruner. The pole reaches to 14', fully extended. **WEIGHT 5 LBS.**

PRUNING SAWS

The most dangerous of all gardening tools, pruning saws are the closest thing we have to the old knight's broadsword, knife, and lance. Though tree professionals will often use chain saws to cut bigger branches, they still prefer the wonderfully fast and silent cutting of a quality tri-edge handsaw—a short saw for fine cutting, a 2'-long curved Tuttle-toothed saw for big 8" lateral branches, or a pull saw on the end of a pole for those stems that can't be reached by any other means.

The principle of cutting was established early on in human history: the thinner the blade, the more force per unit of area and thus the greater cutting power. The moment that flint was discovered and chipped to a fine edge, it became possible to cut, rend, and scrape—to part the molecules that bind fibers together.

In order to make a saw, however, it was necessary to repeat this principle at equal and opposite angles all the way down the length of a long blade. Perhaps it's true that the inventors were inspired by the jawbones of animals, but the reality of a saw is much more complex. The blade must be thick enough not to bend too much when pushed or pulled. The teeth must be angled out from the center line to gouge a lane, called the kerf, for the saw's breadth to run through without binding. They may be angled forward or backward so the tool cuts on the push or pull stroke. Sometimes a deeper tooth, called the raker tooth or the Tuttle tooth, is employed to help clean the sawdust out of the kerf.

As simple as it looks, the pruning saw is a triumph of practical physics and engineering. It has to be. While the carpenter calmly crosscuts a prefinished length of lumber, the pruner must calculate how to get a branch that weighs maybe 200 pounds to fall where it should, when it should, and without tearing the bark of the parent trunk. The pruning saw, therefore, has to be able to snake its head into a tight branch crotch, to cut smoothly through knots or included bark, to work upright or upside down or at an angle, and to make a cut that is smooth and precise enough to leave no ragged bottom edge.

WHY CUT CLEAN?

Every flaw in a pruning cut is a highway for disease to enter a tree. The whole circulation of a tree takes place in a slender band of tissue between the bark and the trunk itself. (The heartwood and the sapwood serve only for stability and food storage.) To rip part of the bark off with a cut or to leave a ragged edge of half-pruned bark is to provide disease organisms with direct access to this system. It's much the same as a person getting a deep cut and failing to clean and protect it: disease enters and infection follows.

To protect a pruning cut, Band-Aids won't help. All the asphalt-based wound dressings developed to keep out bacteria won't help, either; in fact, they simply seal in disease. The best protection is a clean cut, because it mimics the best case in nature, when the branch breaks clean at the collar. In and beneath the collar, the cells are specialized to shut off the wound from the rest of the tree—a process called compartmentalization—and to cover over the wound naturally with a nice even roll of callus.

CHOOSING A PRUNING SAW

A good saw is a pleasure to wield, but a poor one can lead to mishaps—if not actual bodily injury. Hardened, tempered steel blades are crucial. (To determine whether a blade is tempered, flick it with a fingernail. It will produce a ringing tone if it's tempered.) In addition, the connection between the blade and the handle must be solid. This is especially true for folding saws, some of which have a tendency to loosen dangerously at the blade-handle junction.

Many saws are now manufactured with plastic handles. Wooden handles are more comfortable, and they absorb shocks that plastic would transmit directly to your hand. The open "banana" handle is commonly found on small pruning saws and, undeniably, it is a pleasure to grasp. (Some such handles even have indentations to cradle your fingers!) But from a practical point of view, a closed D-shape handle is the better choice, because whether you hold it upside down or right side up, it will not fall from your hand.

Always support the branch with your free hand when cutting with a pruning saw.

USING A PRUNING SAW

When properly used, a pruning saw is invaluable for shaping trees and keeping them in good health. Improperly used, this tool is responsible for more horticultural disasters than any other garden implement.

You must be certain to cut only dead, crossing, diseased, or hazardous branches. The cut should, in most cases, occur at the bark branch collar, not flush to the trunk or halfway out on the stem. And the cut should be made cleanly. If the limb is short and light, support it with your free hand; for larger limbs, use the three-cut method (see page 162).

Often, a branch is pruned just to get it out of the way. It's impending over the driveway, or maybe it's brushing against the roof tiles or scratching at the front door. In these cases, many people will cut the branch back only as far as needed to make it less intrusive. This way, they mistakenly think, the least damage has been done to the tree.

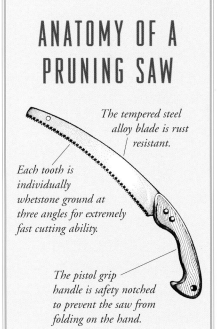

ANATOMY OF A PRUNING SAW

The tempered steel alloy blade is rust resistant.

Each tooth is individually whetstone ground at three angles for extremely fast cutting ability.

The pistol grip handle is safety notched to prevent the saw from folding on the hand.

Unfortunately, within a year, the end of such a cut will sprout three or four fresh branchlets that will ultimately treble or quadruple what was once a solitary problem. Not only will the branchlets quickly return to the invasion, but their attachments to the parent limb will now be considerably weaker. When they become sizable branches, they might well pose a significant hazard that would not otherwise have existed.

BASIC PRUNING SAWS: Blades are the most important element to consider when choosing a pruning saw. As a general rule, longer blades with fewer teeth per inch and deeper-cut teeth are capable of cutting thick living branches fast. Shorter saws with more teeth per inch make finer cuts on smaller branches.

Not too many years ago, almost all pruning saws were lance-toothed. Each tooth was triangular in shape, and a good lance-tooth saw had each tooth beveled on one face; the poorer versions had unbeveled teeth. The large-size saws featured deep grooves—gullets, rakers, or Tuttle teeth, depending on the pattern—that alternated with each set of lance teeth. These grooves set the depth of the cut and served as "rakes" to sweep the sawdust out of the kerf.

There are still lance-tooth saws (both good and bad) on the market, but they have been joined in recent years by saws that feature a wonderful development called the "tri-edge" or "Japanese" blade (all the blades are imported from Japan). Each tooth on a tri-edge blade has three bevels. The teeth are self-cleaning because the body of the blade tapers upward from the tooth to the back of the saw. This means that sawdust thrown up by the teeth travels up the blade's back and out of the kerf. These saws are extraordinarily fast and smooth. Most arborists swear by them.

CURVED PRUNING SAWS: These pruning saws cut on the pull stroke. A small size (around 13" is average) works best for light pruning jobs, but for serious pruning a 2' blade is the more appropriate choice. If you have a lot of trees, it's a good idea to own both sizes. Some professionals recommend buying one double-edged saw that has fine teeth on one side and coarse teeth on the other.

The danger of cutting the wrong branch with the opposite set of teeth makes these saws a questionable choice for all but experienced users. If you buy two decent handsaws, keep them in a two-saw leather scabbard.

THE THREE-WAY CUT

To cleanly cut a large branch, it's necessary to begin by removing most of its length. The three-cut method protects both the pruner and the tree. Begin with an undercut at least a few inches beyond the bark branch collar. Cut upward at least one-third of the way through the branch. (Watch out: if you go much farther, the weight of the branch may force it downward, binding your saw blade.) Another inch or two beyond the undercut away from the trunk, make your second cut all the way through so that the major part of the branch comes down. Any bark tearing, however, will stop at the undercut. Finally, make the third cut at the bark branch collar.

With any pruning, you must be responsible to see that no part of the branch is under tension that might cause it to spring forcefully loose. You are cutting so as not to let the branch fall either on anyone or on anything valuable.

Folding saws. Gardeners who have only an occasional need to prune might prefer a saw that needs no scabbard at all. This is when folding saws are used to best advantage. You can carry a folding saw in your pocket and store it away safely until the next time it's needed. The trick is to find a model that locks securely in both the closed and open positions. This safeguard not only makes it harder for kids to hurt themselves playing with the tool, but also prevents damage to the pruner while cutting. A wobbly blade is an invitation to a ragged pruning cut or a wounded finger.

STRAIGHTEDGE PRUNING SAWS: You can buy a small straight-edged pruning saw with either lance or tri-edge teeth. But there is little reason to recommend a straightedge saw over a curved saw. A pruning saw with a curved blade helps force the wood into the teeth, which makes cutting easier and faster. Curved models are also more effective when you need to insinuate the tip of the saw into a tight or awkward spot.

CROSSCUT SAWS: The largest saws are the one- and two-man crosscut saws, among the few pruning saws that are made with a straight blade. These saws cut on both the push and the pull stroke, and are meant chiefly for felling trees or cutting large branches. Among the cutting lance teeth are deep gullets to carry away the big curls of sawdust. Better versions now feature a blade that tapers like a tri-edge blade and helps to prevent the saw from binding in the kerf. It is said that a good sawyer can almost outpace a chain saw with a crosscut saw. And the lance teeth are much easier to resharpen than are the teeth of a tri-edge or chain saw.

THE BOW SAW: For cutting logs into rounds, most gardeners tend to prefer the bow saw. The slender, gullet blade of this saw is supported under tension between the two arms of a light metal "bow" or arch. The tool cuts very quickly, and its only drawback is the width of the bow itself. If the wood that's being cut is 1' or more thick, the blade is liable to run up against the back of the bow; at that point, it can cut no farther.

The classic lance-tooth (top) blade is quite serviceable if its triangular teeth are beveled on one side; larger saws have Tuttle teeth (middle), or grooves in between sets of teeth to rake out excess sawdust from the cut; "tri-edge," or Japanese blades (bottom), have gained popularity for their superior cutting action and self-cleaning teeth.

Pruning Saws

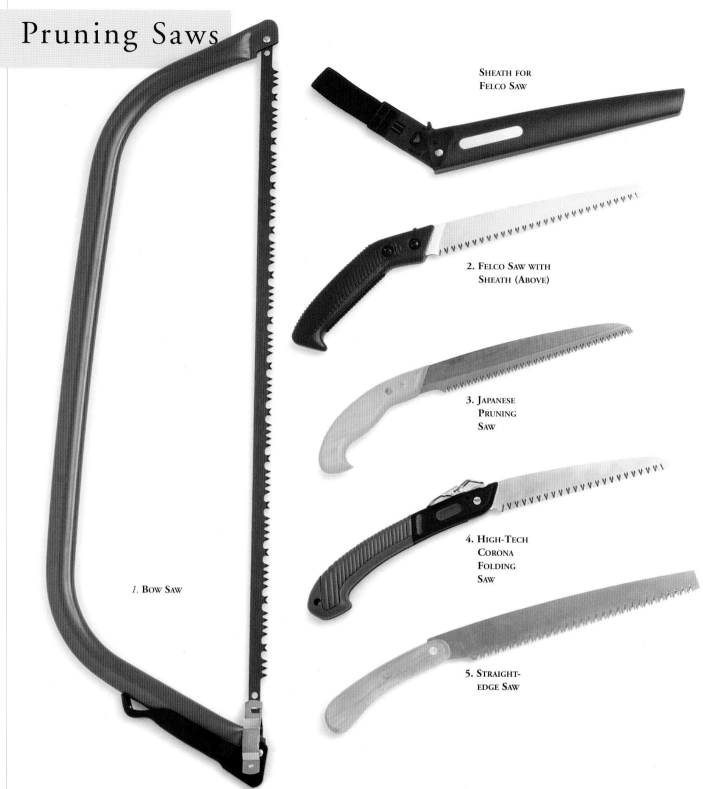

SHEATH FOR
FELCO SAW

2. FELCO SAW WITH
SHEATH (ABOVE)

3. JAPANESE
PRUNING
SAW

4. HIGH-TECH
CORONA
FOLDING
SAW

1. BOW SAW

5. STRAIGHT-
EDGE SAW

1. **BOW SAW:** Best used on thick branches and logs, this finely honed bow saw cuts with both push and pull strokes. It is an essential tool for big pruning jobs. This good-quality version features mechanical levers and a rigid steel frame, which keep the 30" steel blade taut. LENGTH 33".

2. **FELCO SAW WITH SHEATH:** A straight-edge stationary pruning saw protected by an attractive, easy-to-find red plastic sheath. This saw features a patented, antifriction, 9½" taper ground blade that cuts limbs up to 6" in diameter on the pull stroke. The blade is replaceable. LENGTH 16½".

3. **JAPANESE PRUNING SAW:** This classic pruning saw features a polished wooden handle and uniquely angled blade with teeth that cut precisely on the pull stroke. A beautiful saw that feels good in the palm but is more expensive than other stationary saws. The blade is 8½" long. LENGTH 14".

4. **HIGH-TECH CORONA FOLDING SAW:** A quick-action folding saw featuring a 7" replaceable steel alloy blade that cuts branches up to 4" in diameter on the pull stroke. The teeth are impulse hardened and taper ground on three angles for faster cutting action. Poly-propylene handle is ergonomic and locks in place. LENGTH 16".

5. **STRAIGHTEDGE SAW:** A long, fine-toothed stationary saw for clean cuts on the pull stroke. The 10½" cutting edge is connected to a hardwood handle for extra momentum. LENGTH 16".

6. **TRADITIONAL JAPANESE FOLDING SAW:** The Japanese make some of the most beautiful pruning tools, and this saw is no exception. It features a long, smooth, straight handle made of hardwood and a 9¼" steel blade that cuts cleanly on the pull stroke and folds neatly into the handle. Cuts branches

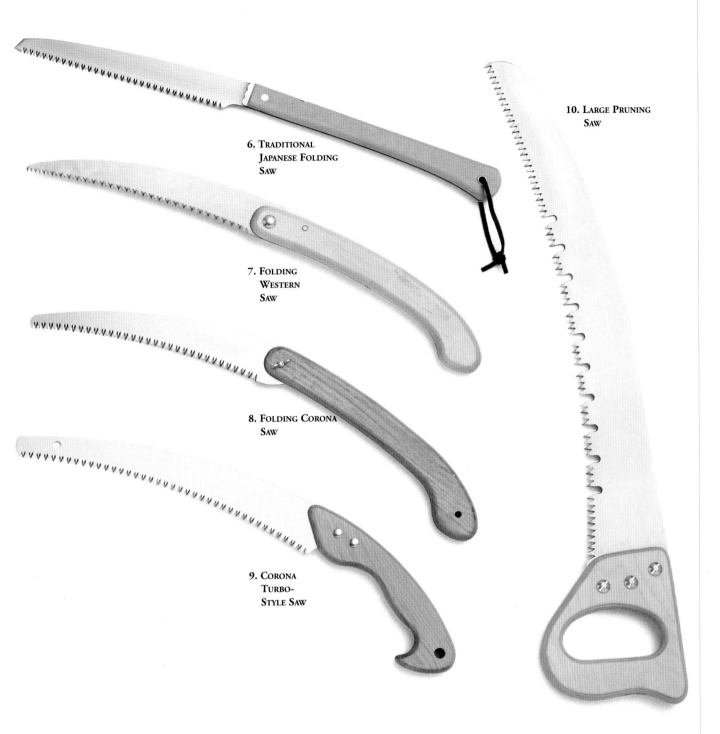

6. Traditional Japanese Folding Saw

7. Folding Western Saw

8. Folding Corona Saw

9. Corona Turbo-Style Saw

10. Large Pruning Saw

up to 4" in diameter. Leather loop is attached to end for carrying or storing. LENGTH 21½".

7. Folding Western Saw: Another variation of the folding pruning saw. This Western-style saw is characterized by simple, triangle-shaped teeth that are sharp on one edge only and are set bent out of line a bit. The 9¾" blade cuts on the pull motion. Once a popular version, it has been almost entirely replaced by saws with Japanese-style teeth. LENGTH 21".

8. Folding Corona Saw: Another classic Japanese-style folding saw, this tool features a curved blade. It cuts on the pull stroke with a 13" precision-ground blade. LENGTH 20½".

9. Corona Turbo-Style Saw: A long, curved cutting edge features impulse-hardened teeth that have been individually whetstone ground at three angles for a cutting action that is twice as fast as traditional saws. The tempered steel alloy blade, 13" long, resists rust and cuts branches up to 10" in diameter.

This saw cuts on the pull stroke. The hardwood pistol grip handle is safety notched and has a hole for hanging. LENGTH 20".

10. Large Pruning Saw: A full-size, good-quality saw designed to quickly cut large limbs with precision due to individually ground teeth that cut on the push or pull stroke. This saw features a 22" steel blade, with crosscut-style teeth and large, chip-clearing gullets. Hardwood handle. LENGTH 28½".

WOODLOT TOOLS

On the back roads of southern Europe or deep in the British country-side, you can still find whole groves of polled oaks that have stood for centuries, their trunks thickening and their branches await-ing harvest every few years for firewood. The trees look beautiful, well ordered, and ancient. They have seen the whole modern history of axes, saws, sledges, wedges, and mauls.

The woodcutter who once minded these lots, or who wandered deep into the old forests felling, cutting, and splitting wood, was so familiar a character that he figures prominently in many fairy tales.

His task was difficult and did not pay well, but like the work of the farmer, the herbalist, and the builder it was crucial to the continuation of everyday life.

Woodcraft was then a much more common pursuit than it is today. (Perhaps the belief in wood sprites, or forest gnomes, existed because in those days there was frequent occasion to meet them!) Today, the man or woman who chooses to cut fire-wood by hand not only participates in an excellent form of aerobic exercise, but also begins to recover this ancient knowledge.

The old saying "Wood should be split before Easter" meant that trees were traditionally felled in late winter or early spring. A fresh-felled tree is almost half water. Before it will be useful firewood, it must dry at least over the summer, until the water content drops to 25% or less. A good woodchopper cuts the wood into rounds and splits the rounds as soon as possible to facilitate drying. The wood is easier to cut when it's green, and it seasons faster after the cut edges have been exposed to the air. The quicker drying also gives less opportunity for the wood to become vulnerable to molds and rot. If a branch is too small to split, a strip of bark can be removed with a hatchet to expose the raw wood.

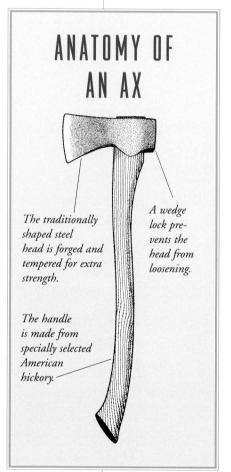

ANATOMY OF AN AX

The traditionally shaped steel head is forged and tempered for extra strength.

A wedge lock prevents the head from loosening.

The handle is made from specially selected American hickory.

THE AX

Over the years, the favorite shapes for axheads have changed. The straight-bladed Dayton or Ohio pattern axes (called "Yankee axes" in Europe), first made to cut hardwoods and conifers on the west-ern frontier of the United States, were big, solid felling tools. Cruiser axes, which have a moderate cutting flair and a somewhat shorter handle, were first used by "cruisers"—the logging scouts who went into uncut areas to map and evaluate the timber. These scouts needed a tool that was less cumbersome, but big enough to clear a path and take timber for evaluation. The sinuous Hudson Bay ax has a blade that is almost wasp-waisted, an excellent configuration for biting into and pulling out of soft-wooded conifers.

For every pattern that has been preserved into the age of mass production, a dozen have been lost. Assembly-line axes are usually ground, painted, and varnished to give a uniform look. Now that certain axes are no longer used in commercial forestry, a few companies have decided to return to the tradition of the craft (Gränsfors Bruks axes are made from start to finish by one craftsperson), so that each ax is made by a single craftsperson at a forge. The beautiful, rough, unpainted surface of these axes, combined with their extraordinary heft, gives you the eerie feeling that you're handling a tool as old as humanity.

Whether hand-forged or machine-made, a good ax can be recognized by a few simple elements. If the head has been painted, check to see that the paint doesn't conceal the ragged lines of forging flaws. If the metal is not smooth and unblemished, it's likely that a crack or chip will eventually occur at the weak point. Look closely at the handle. Though other hardwoods are adequate, hickory is the best wood for ax handles. No matter what kind of wood it's made from, be sure the grain is even and there are no knots visible. Variable-grain wood, which probably came from a tree under drought stress or other weakening conditions, is liable to split along the thin grain, and knotty wood can break at the knot.

Try out the tool to be sure it's scaled to your size and weight. Axes come in sizes from 15" in length with a 1¼-lb. head, up to 30" in length with a 3½-lb. head. Don't assume you know the right size just by looking at the selection. It's no good buying a fine ax, only to find that you can't work with it for more than ten minutes at a time.

The trick to using an ax is the proper swing. Start by bending your knees and sweeping the ax over your head in a broad, strong, and well-controlled arc. When you're cutting rounds, aim for the bottom of the round you're working on, not for the top. Intentionally visualizing the log "cut-through" helps both the aim and the force of the blow. Of course, to be able to cut with such authority, you have to be sure the piece is resting on a stable chopping block. Nothing dulls an ax blade faster than having its edge repeatedly rammed into the dirt.

Be patient. It takes a lot of practice to get really good with an ax and to learn to use it safely.

Proper use of an ax begins with your hands spaced apart on the backswing, bringing them together at the base of the handle before the arced downswing. Be sure to bend your knees slightly and follow through by lowering your shoulders toward the cutting area.

BASIC AXES: There is no simpler, more elegant tool than the ax. With its delta-shaped head and gently contoured handle, a good ax looks as if it could actually fly by itself.

Until this century, most axes were made by local blacksmiths, at first by custom order and then in accordance with the popular patterns that evolved in different parts of the country and around the world. The "Yankee" pattern, for example, has a straight, no-nonsense bit with little flair in the face or the cheeks; the taper of the head is neither fat nor thin, so the ax can be used for both splitting and cutting. Conversely, the "Michigan" pattern is hollow-ground in the cheeks to prevent binding.

THE DOUBLE-BIT AX: Paul Bunyan's ax was a double-bit version. A big, heavy tool for felling, cutting, splitting, and even for throwing, this ax was once the symbol of the logger's strength. It also requires care and skill to use properly. Two sharp edges are better than one, but the second edge is a danger to anything (or anyone) behind you. If you intend to fell trees by chopping, this is the tool for you. Otherwise, a single-bit ax will do the job.

THE SINGLE-BIT AX: This ax is the workhorse of the woodpile. A good woodsman can use it to split most rounds of softwoods and many hardwoods. And for cutting kindling and smaller logs out of presplit wood, the single-bit ax is unsurpassed.

THE SPLITTING AX: For splitting hardwood—rock maple, for instance—the best tool you can use is a splitting ax. This ax weighs as much as the heaviest single-bit ax, with a 3½–4-lb. head, but the head flares broadly from edge to butt. This shape allows the tool to push the fibers apart strongly as it penetrates, making it easier to split the wood.

THE SPLITTING MAUL
AND THE SLEDGEHAMMER

The maul and the sledgehammer are the heaviest tools in the woodlot, and they're used for the toughest splitting jobs. Though a splitting ax is strong enough on its own, it can't take a hammer on the butt without breaking. A maul, on the other hand, weighs 2 lbs. more in the head than the ax does. It has the force of a sledgehammer when it strikes a round; moreover, should it become wedged in the wood, it can be hammered without any damage to the head. You can also turn a maul around and use the butt end as a sledgehammer for driving an independent wedge.

The sledgehammer-and-wedge combination is slightly less versatile because you must find a way to set the wedge in the round before you whale away with the sledge. This procedure works fine if there is a good crack to receive the wedge, or if the wood is soft enough to admit the wedge tip with a light blow or two. But it can present an annoying problem when the round is tight and hard.

THE HATCHET

Hatchets resemble axes in every respect but size. An ax takes two hands to wield and a hatchet chops with one, making the latter an excellent tool for tasks like cutting up kindling, sharpening tomato stakes, or other jobs that require holding the piece that you're working on with one hand while you cut with the other.

Most people buy an all-purpose hatchet, adaptable to many tasks, but individual models are best for specific tasks.

THE SCOUT HATCHET: There are few Boy Scouts who have not experienced the longing to have a scout hatchet. Also called a camp ax, this small, light tool is frequently made of a single piece of tempered steel with a rubber handle wrapped around it. It's a very versatile piece of camping equipment, able to limb small branches, cut up kindling, sharpen tent pegs, and drive the pegs into the ground. Some versions even have a notch in the bottom for pulling nails.

THE KINDLING HATCHET: Designed specifically for making kindling, this hatchet has a broader edge than most. It's usually bent more than average at the end-knob, making it easier to hold when you're trying to get all the kindling in before winter arrives.

THE JAPANESE HATCHET: The only dramatically different entry among the hatchets is the Japanese hatchet. Made by hand, this bright, laminated-steel tool looks like a cross between a meat cleaver and a samurai sword. Not only are these hatchets able to perform all the tasks accomplished by other hatchets, but they can also be used for clearing brush since they have long blades that cut on the outswing as well as the downswing.

Chopping and Splitting Tools

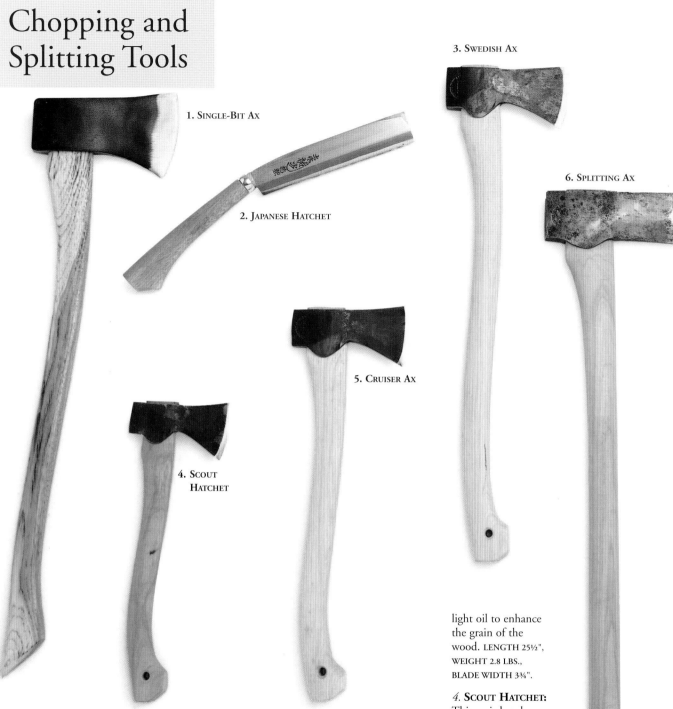

1. SINGLE-BIT AX

2. JAPANESE HATCHET

3. SWEDISH AX

6. SPLITTING AX

5. CRUISER AX

4. SCOUT HATCHET

AXES, HATCHETS, AND MAULS

A premium ax or hatchet is an investment that will last for decades. The best axes are individually forged and balanced, not machine-made. Axes and mauls are good for splitting logs and chopping large trees and brush. The butt end, or poll, can be used as a driver. Hatchets are more suitable for chopping kindling or pointing stakes. The following tools are examples of the finest craftsmanship and are highly recommended.

1. SINGLE-BIT AX:
A superb example of the modern American-style ax. Sometimes called a Michican pattern ax, it features a broad blade, a poll (the flat butt or hammer side) deep enough to do light driving. Drop-forged and then ground smooth. LENGTH 29¼", WEIGHT 4.5 LBS., BLADE WIDTH 4¾".

2. JAPANESE HATCHET:
Shaped more like a cleaver than a hatchet, this tool is of elegant Japanese design but is actually a hard-working chopping implement. The highly polished, laminated steel blade is attached to a hard-wood handle by a pinned tang and ferrule. Individually made by a craftsman; comes with a carrying case. LENGTH 16½", WEIGHT 1.1 LBS., BLADE LENGTH 8½".

3. SWEDISH AX:
This is an example of tool craftsmanship at its finest, with beauty and utility perfectly married. Each ax is individually forged by hand by a blacksmith in Sweden, who stamps his or her name into the head. With the exception of the edge, no grinding, polishing, or painting is done that would obscure the beauty of the tool. The handle is finished with a light oil to enhance the grain of the wood. LENGTH 25½", WEIGHT 2.8 LBS., BLADE WIDTH 3¾".

4. SCOUT HATCHET:
This ax is hand-forged in Sweden. Very light in weight it is intended for camp chores or very light chopping, splitting, or limbing duties around the home. LENGTH 14½", WEIGHT 1.5 LBS., BLADE WIDTH 3".

5. CRUISER AX:
This ax falls between a full-size ax and a hatchet. Because of its light weight and compact size, it is perfect for household or camping use. The shorter handle requires a careful chopping technique. LENGTH 21", WEIGHT 2.2 LBS., BLADE WIDTH 3¼".

6. SPLITTING AX:
This ax falls between a splitting maul and an ax. It's sharp enough to cut and heavy enough to drive a wedge to split tough rounds. The unique flaring blade shape forces

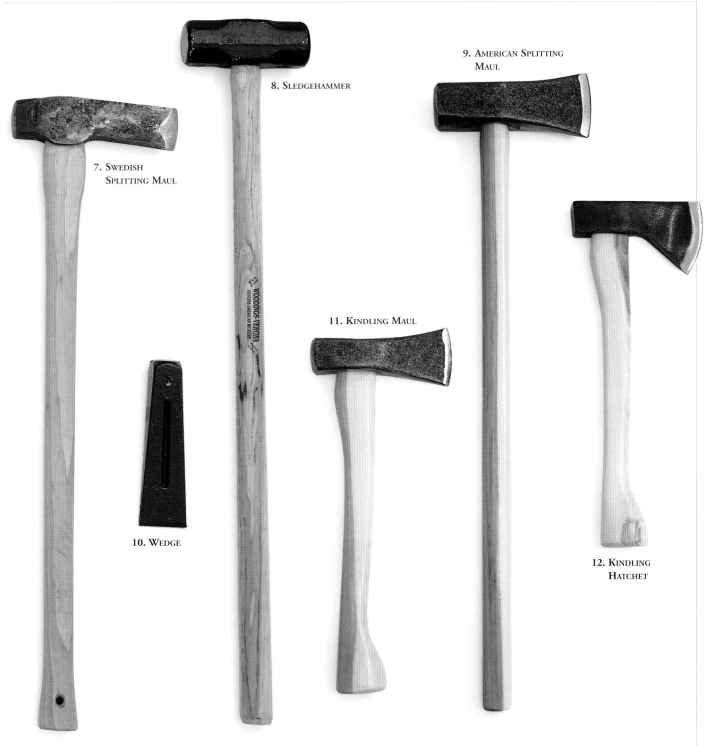

7. Swedish Splitting Maul

8. Sledgehammer

9. American Splitting Maul

11. Kindling Maul

10. Wedge

12. Kindling Hatchet

wood apart and prevents the head from becoming wedged. LENGTH 29½", WEIGHT 4.8 LBS., BLADE WIDTH 2½".

7. **Swedish Splitting Maul:** Splitting mauls split wood with the grain and are usually used for chopping firewood. This hand-forged Swedish version has a head that forces the grain apart; the blade is ridged to provide an easy pivot to work

the tool back out of the wood if it isn't split on the first stroke. The head is precisely angled to concentrate the force of the blow, and the poll is strong enough to drive steel wedges. LENGTH 31¼", WEIGHT 7.5 LBS., BLADE WIDTH 2¼".

8. **Sledgehammer:** A drop-forged head and hickory handle make up one of the simplest of all tools. With an 8-pound head and 32½" han-

dle, this one can drive stakes and wedges and break up rock and concrete. LENGTH 34¾", WEIGHT 9.1 LBS.

9. **American Splitting Maul:** The 7-pound head on this maul is the perfect weight for splitting firewood. One study has indicated that it is possible to expend less energy splitting a cord of wood with this maul than with any other tool.

LENGTH 31", WEIGHT 7.7 LBS., BLADE WIDTH 3½".

10. **Wedge:** This is the standard forged-steel splitting wedge, used to drive into small cracks in log ends and split the toughest logs and rounds. At one time wooden wedges were the norm, but today splitting wedges are of steel. LENGTH 8¼", WEIGHT 3.8 LBS., BLADE WIDTH 2½".

11. **Kindling Maul:** This tool acts like a miniature splitting maul and is intended for one-handed use. It is extremely useful for the homeowner or gardener who burns wood. Made in Maine, with a drop-forged carbon steel head and very shapely hickory handle. LENGTH 17¼", WEIGHT 4.6 LBS., BLADE WIDTH 3".

12. **Kindling Hatchet:** A widely flaring blade and shaped handle that flares at the butt make this light-weight tool a specialist in light splitting chores. Drop-forged carbon steel head and hickory handle. LENGTH 17¼", WEIGHT 2.3 LBS., BLADE WIDTH 3⅞".

CLEARING TOOLS

There is a machine called the brushhog. You drive this machine onto a piece of land, and it roars, belches smoke, and grinds up everything in its path. But if all you want to do is clear small parcels on your land, you can get a few good hand tools and experience the same toil and pleasure enjoyed by early gardeners.

Imagine a row of mowers coming across the crest of a hill in evening light, their scythes flashing in the westering sun and the grain stalks standing momentarily in the air before they fall with a soft swish. The men come first, working at a whirling, rhythmic pace; behind them are the women and children, who rake up the hay into ricks with wooden rakes or bind the wheat into sheaves or shocks.

Consider the hedger with his billhook, like some medieval warrior, stooping to cut into, but not all the way through, the flesh of the hedge, bending over the canes and burying the growing tips in the earth to make the hedge grow thick and full. (This practice is the origin of the phrase "To hedge your bets," meaning to straddle them across an area so your chances are enhanced.)

It is indeed hard work to use hand tools to clear land or mow down the weeds. But there is satisfaction in using a fine tool to good effect—and in the tiredness of the body, used to equally good effect. (A mineral-salts bath after a day of hand clearing affords a pleasurable sensation like no other.)

CHOOSING CLEARING TOOLS

Where the nineteenth-century farmworker cut grain and sugarcane or hedged and cleared wasteland, you will mainly use clearing tools to remove the second growths that take over disturbed and disused lands. A machete, brush hook, clearing ax, or billhook will take down woody shrubs, vines, and saplings; a scythe or grass hook can mow the weeds on the property's edge before they can set seed; and a swing blade or grass whip is good for getting into those weedy corners where nothing else can reach.

All clearing tools are heavy-duty implements, possessing carbon steel blades and the firmest possible connection between handle and head. The chief differences among such tools lie in the length of the individual handles. Short-handled clearing tools—the billhooks and machetes, for example—are designed to cut at close quarters. With these tools, you grasp the offending plant in one hand while swinging and cutting with the other. Longer-handled tools, such as brush hooks, Yorkshire billhooks, and scythes, require plenty of room to operate effectively, but they can take more down at one time with their wider swing.

USING CLEARING TOOLS

Scythes are the cleverest of clearing tools: the rotating motion of the mower throws the blade into the grass, at a tangent to the legs, so it's difficult to cut yourself by accident. The same is not true of billhooks, brush hooks, machetes, and clearing axes, all of which can be extremely dangerous when carelessly used. It's most important never to swing such tools in any arc that might end with your own arm or leg. (This is just common sense, but at the end of a long day of clearing it's sometimes tempting to make one or two cuts back toward the body.) The key to efficient work with all clearing tools is relaxation, especially at the shoulders, elbows, and waist. The implement should swing freely in an even motion that comes from the waist as opposed to the arms.

For clearing underbrush, weeds, and vines, and especially for nasty customers like bramble canes, a machete or billhook is the best tool. Both tools are short-handled and long-bladed, allowing you to grasp canes with one hand while swinging the blade with the other. Both are heavy enough to get through tough woody branches, but the billhook blade has a curved hook end that catches and holds the material to be cut. Extreme care must be taken with these tools, given the fact that the good ones are made of tempered steel and can be razor-sharp. Indeed, machetes are commonly used by nursery and Christmas tree growers, who shave off new growth with the big, sharp blade.

The clearing ax represents an effort to make a tool powerful enough to whack back thick canes, with blades that are less liable to nick you. It resembles a cross between an ax, bow saw, and bush hook. Wielded with one or two hands in a golf-stroke motion, it will clear anything up to sapling size.

If you're taking back an old field choked with the saplings of ailanthus, black cherry, box elder, or acacia, a long-handled version of the billhook gives you a decided advantage. Sometimes called a bush hook, brush hook, or Yorkshire billhook, this sharp, curved cutting tool has a contoured shaft like that of a shovel. You can swing it easily with both hands, never stooping to reach at the bases of stubborn saplings, cutting them down with a single smooth motion. The curve of the blade not only helps hold the wood being cut, but also keeps the sharp face of the blade out of the dirt.

Bend your arm slightly at the elbow when holding the upper nib, or grip, of the scythe, allowing your other arm to extend fully and hold the lower grip. Keep the scythe at a 30°–45° angle to the ground and swing it in a slight arc with your hips only.

THE SCYTHE: With their curved blades and sinuous handles, the scythe and its cousin the sickle once looked as much like some exotic shorebird as they did like masterpieces of the blacksmith's and joiner's art. The blades were made of custom-forged metal, made by mixing steel and iron in laminates to get sharpness from the steel and malleability from the iron. A fine scythe or sickle would cut a ribbon in the air, but the blade would dent against a hidden rock instead of breaking.

Modern scythes are much lighter. Stamped-bladed, ash-handled scythes are adequate, but the best are hand-forged Austrian scythes. The blades have a wonderful curve, dipping near the junction with the snath (called the beard). The snath itself may be a comparatively slender wand of ash or lighter aluminum.

A light scythe blade handles grass, and a heavier one can even deal with small underbrush. It is important to remember that a scythe's power depends on the steady, twisting motion of the user. If you're stopped dead by a heavy stem, the tool will certainly jar your body. Nonetheless, it's often better to experiment with a scythe in rough country underlain with stones or other hard debris. A power tool might be dangerous on such land, but a scythe sweeps up and over the obstacles, laying down the grass like a blanket on the land.

THE SICKLE: The same advantage holds true for the sickle (or its cousin the grass hook), but it's a one-handed tool that must be used when stooping. When you have a limited area of grass or weeds to cut down, the sickle is a joy to swing. It sings through the air, cutting off stems like a hot knife through butter. Since you work lower to the ground, it's best for working through very rough patches where boulders or other impediments may be lurking beneath an apparently clean mound of grass.

THE SWING BLADE: The jester among grass-cutting tools is the swing blade or grass whip. It's a comical-looking instrument, rather like a golf putter with a double row of grinning teeth. The teeth are the two sides of serrated blades, and when you swing it like a golf club, it miraculously cuts grass with a vengeance. It's best attibute is the serrated blades that don't let the grass escape—a decided advantage over the scythe.

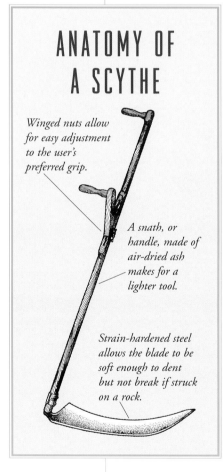

ANATOMY OF A SCYTHE

Winged nuts allow for easy adjustment to the user's preferred grip.

A snath, or handle, made of air-dried ash makes for a lighter tool.

Strain-hardened steel allows the blade to be soft enough to dent but not break if struck on a rock.

Scythes

1. **STRAIGHT-SNATH SCYTHE:** A superior example of a two-handled European-style straight snath made from light-weight ash and attached to a right-handed, hardened-steel cutting blade, or scythe. A good tool for clearing large areas with high grass. Left-handed blade is also pictured. LENGTH 63", WEIGHT 4 LBS., BLADE LENGTH 25".

2. **WHETSTONE AND SHEATH:** The plastic sheath is kept full of water and is carried on a belt, making it easy for the user to sharpen the scythe blades frequently while cutting.

3. **ANVIL AND HAMMER:** An anvil and hammer is used instead of a grinder to straighten the blade on certain scythes.

4. **AMERICAN-STYLE SCYTHE:** This is a modern rendition of the traditional, American-style bowed snath. It is stronger than wood, fashioned from exceedingly light-weight, low-mainte-nance aluminum. This particular example is shown with three American pattern blades that can be alternated, depending on the area to be mowed. LENGTH 59½", WEIGHT 5 LBS., BLADE LENGTH 30", (MEDIUM 26", SMALL 20").

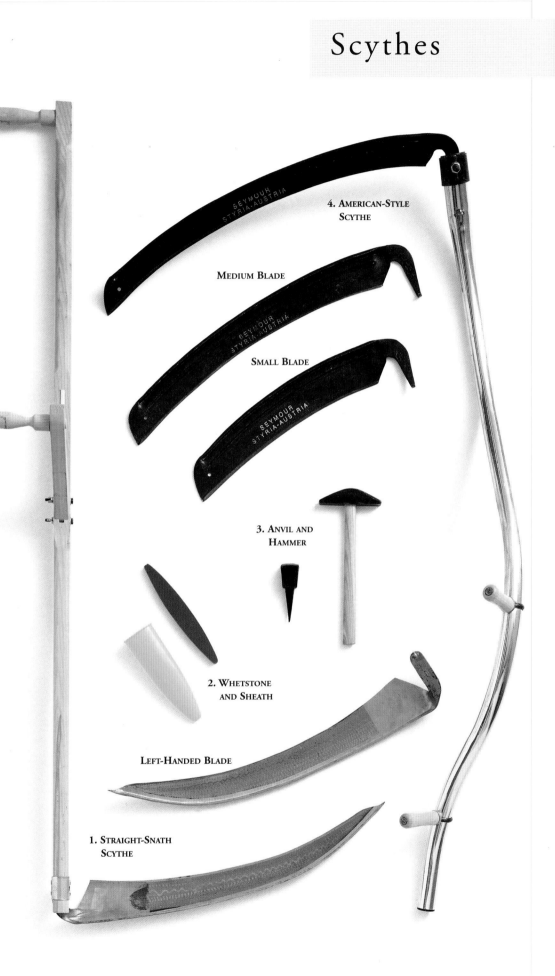

4. AMERICAN-STYLE SCYTHE

MEDIUM BLADE

SMALL BLADE

3. ANVIL AND HAMMER

2. WHETSTONE AND SHEATH

LEFT-HANDED BLADE

1. STRAIGHT-SNATH SCYTHE

Brush Cutters

1. **AMERICAN BRUSH HOOK:** A formidable land-clearing tool that does not find its way into many home gardeners' hands, this hook is designed to mow down in one swipe large bushes and trees measuring up to 1½" in diameter. Generally used by firefighters and other professionals, it is extremely durable and features a double-edged, solid-forged steel cutting hook bolted to a thick, flat hickory handle.
LENGTH 52",
WEIGHT 4 LBS., BLADE
LENGTH 14".

2. **IRISH BRUSH HOOK:** This versatile tool accomplishes a variety of heavy clearing work, from cutting and pruning to clearing brush and stripping fallen trees, and it is more manageable for most home gardeners than the American Brush Hook. Top-notch construction includes a tempered carbon steel blade, straight-grain ash handle, and a solid-socket collar.
LENGTH 53",
WEIGHT 4 LBS., BLADE
LENGTH 14".

3. **SWING BLADE:** Another heavy-duty clearing tool for large projects, this tool is shaped like the Jungle Knife but is larger and more ponderous to use. It is better suited to large gardeners and thick bush. A solid-forged carbon steel blade is bolted to a hickory handle and cuts in either direc-tion when swung back and forth.
LENGTH 41¾",
WEIGHT 3.8 LBS.,
BLADE LENGTH 11¾".

4. **JUNGLE KNIFE:** Also known as a grass whip, this agile tool is an affordable, lightweight choice for clearing high grasses (especially around trees and rocks), but may not be suited to heavier tasks. The serrated blade cuts in either direction and is connected to a steel handle with a contoured grip.
LENGTH 42½",
WEIGHT 1.5 LBS.,
BLADE LENGTH 9½".

5. **SERRATED GRASS HOOK:** This tool is a serrated variation of the traditional hand sickle. Its teeth will help hold thicker brush (like bamboo) for easier cutting. Tempered, hand-sharpened steel blade with hardwood handle.
WEIGHT 0.4 LB.,
BLADE LENGTH 17",
HANDLE LENGTH 5".

6. **UTILITY MACHETE:** This all-purpose clearing tool is suitable for medium-weight tasks when a traditional machete is too daunting. Useful for chopping, heavy pruning, and clearing thick bush and bramble, it can be wielded by amateurs with ease. Hand-sharpened steel alloy blade and contoured beech handle.
LENGTH 17",
WEIGHT 1 LB.,
BLADE LENGTH 11¾".

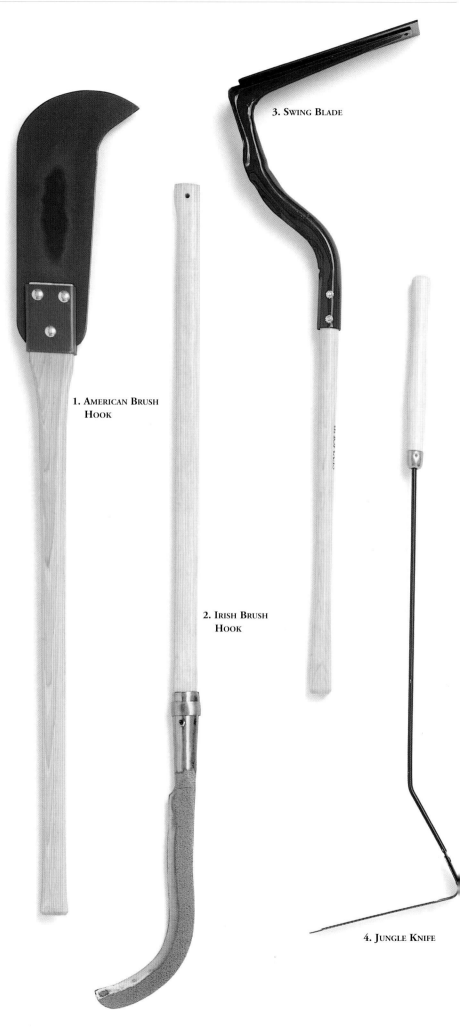

3. SWING BLADE

1. AMERICAN BRUSH HOOK

2. IRISH BRUSH HOOK

4. JUNGLE KNIFE

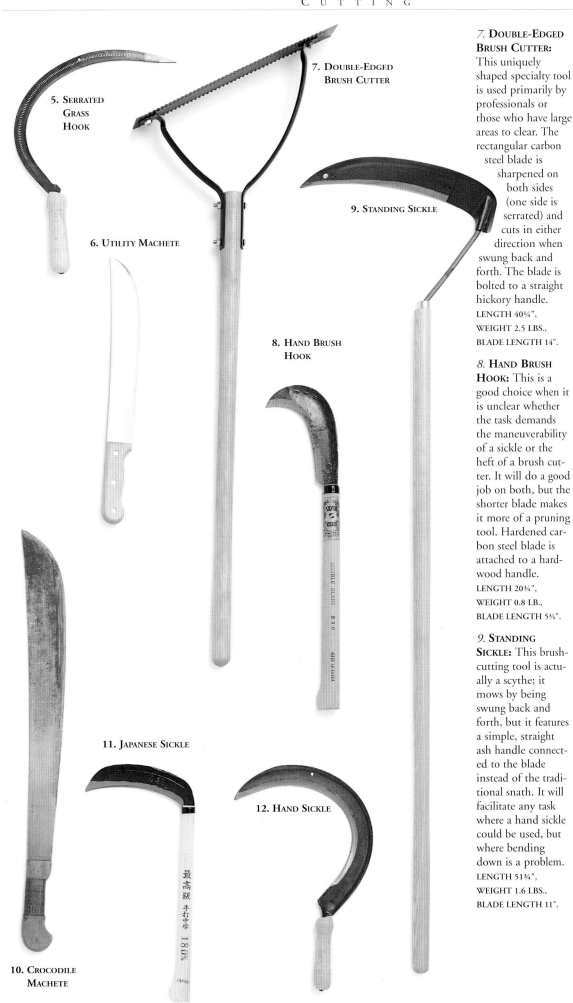

5. SERRATED GRASS HOOK

7. DOUBLE-EDGED BRUSH CUTTER

6. UTILITY MACHETE

9. STANDING SICKLE

8. HAND BRUSH HOOK

11. JAPANESE SICKLE

12. HAND SICKLE

10. CROCODILE MACHETE

7. **DOUBLE-EDGED BRUSH CUTTER:** This uniquely shaped specialty tool is used primarily by professionals or those who have large areas to clear. The rectangular carbon steel blade is sharpened on both sides (one side is serrated) and cuts in either direction when swung back and forth. The blade is bolted to a straight hickory handle. LENGTH 40¼", WEIGHT 2.5 LBS., BLADE LENGTH 14".

8. **HAND BRUSH HOOK:** This is a good choice when it is unclear whether the task demands the maneuverability of a sickle or the heft of a brush cutter. It will do a good job on both, but the shorter blade makes it more of a pruning tool. Hardened carbon steel blade is attached to a hardwood handle. LENGTH 20¾", WEIGHT 0.8 LB., BLADE LENGTH 5¾".

9. **STANDING SICKLE:** This brush-cutting tool is actually a scythe; it mows by being swung back and forth, but it features a simple, straight ash handle connected to the blade instead of the traditional snath. It will facilitate any task where a hand sickle could be used, but where bending down is a problem. LENGTH 51¾", WEIGHT 1.6 LBS., BLADE LENGTH 11".

10. **CROCODILE MACHETE:** Not for the fainthearted, this large, affordable machete will hold up under years of hard work, stormy weather, and large, thorny brush. Manufactured in England, it boasts a rust-resistant carbon steel blade that is hand-rolled into shape. The beech handle is wrapped with copper wire. LENGTH 27, WEIGHT 1 LB., BLADE LENGTH 22".

11. **JAPANESE SICKLE:** Known as a *kama,* this light-weight hand sickle of Japanese design is a superior choice for cutting grass when a brush cutter or scythe is too large. A short, hand-forged laminated steel blade offers optimum control. LENGTH 15½", WEIGHT 0.5 LB., BLADE LENGTH 7".

12. **HAND SICKLE:** This example high-lights the classic English hand sickle, used for centuries to clear areas of high grass where a scythe could not go. The hardened carbon steel blade is sharpened on both sides, making it appropriate for both left- and right-handed users. The handle is made of polished hickory. WEIGHT 0.5 LB, BLADE LENGTH 14", HANDLE LENGTH 5".

CHAPTER SEVEN

WATERING

There is nothing quite like the intimacy of carrying a pair of watering cans to the garden to water your plants by hand. You fill the cans at the tap and carry them balanced in each hand the way farmers once toted two buckets hung from a yoke across their shoulders. You set them down near the shrub or the seedlings that need your help, then gently pour, watching the water divide into a thousand tiny streams and rain lightly onto the ground. You are so close to the action that you can watch the earth drink up the droplets and see the shine of water reflected off a young green leaf.

We plough the fields,
*   and scatter*
The good seed on the
*   land,*
But it is fed and
*   watered*
By God's Almighty
*   Hand.*
He sends the snow in
*   winter,*
The warmth to swell
*   the grain,*
The breezes and the
*   sunshine,*
And soft refreshing
*   rain.*

—JANE MONTGOMERY CAMPBELL

You can also see most intimately and truly how your plants are doing under your care. Here a leaf is browning, there a slug has gobbled a corner. Here the weight of the water almost topples a yellow lily: perhaps the stalk needs support. There grow the first tendrils of purslane: you must dig them out immediately.

An old cliché says that, when watering, you want to act like the rain. No way. The water you give to your garden must be steady, gentle, and consistent. It must not beat down young shoots, rip at the leaves, or puddle on the surface of the ground. It should be more caressing and fructifying than nature's rain which may fail to come for weeks and then drop 5" in an hour, or blow in sideways at 50 mph under the influence of gale.

There are few things lovelier than a well-watered, healthy young plant. Water provides the nutrients it needs from the soil. Water reacts with carbon dioxide to make the sugars that feed the plant and fuel the cells.

The cells themselves fill with water and swell, becoming juicy and resilient to the touch. In a fast-growing plant like corn, you can almost see the changes happen. The leaves arch upward out of the ground, bending slightly at the tips as though from the speed of their climb. But without water, the leaves droop lower, the tips brown, dust gathers, and the plants' growth skids to a halt.

KNOWING YOUR GARDEN

The great art and pleasure of watering is to keep your plants happy even when nature seems to turn its back on them. A part of the intimacy of this gardening task is learning when and how much to water. Rules of thumb do little good here. You must get to know your garden, square foot by square foot, through constant attention. Where is the soil light, and where is it heavy? Where are the low-lying spots and the high spots? Where is the sun strongest and the shade deepest?

The aim is to maintain just the right amount of water in the soil. There should be plenty available for plant growth, but not so much that the water drives out air and suffocates the roots. The magic saturation point, known to scientists as "field capacity," varies with soil texture, humidity, and individual plant needs. To measure whether you have watered enough, dig down 6" into the soil with a trowel and feel the bottom of the hole with your fingers. If it's moist, no more water is needed. If it's dry, you must water.

AN ALTERNATE SOIL-TEXTURE TEST

Squeezing a lump of soil in your hand is a simple way to loosely determine your soil type. If a little sticks to your hand and the lump holds loosely together, you have loam soil. If the lump holds firmly together and is slightly greasy to the touch, your soil has a higher proportion of clay. If it will not stick together at all, it is sandy soil.

To learn the proper amount of water to give, you must get to know the soil. A clay soil may need to be watered very slowly and less frequently than a loam soil, since it holds water readily and grows waterlogged easily. A sandy soil, on the other hand, passes water so quickly that it needs frequent, deep watering. Better yet, adding a good amount of finished compost can improve the texture of either kind of soil, bringing it closer to the happy medium of a loam.

To decide on the frequency of watering, you must also factor in the air. It isn't easy to determine the humidity on a given day, but it's important to know that wilting of tomato leaves, for example, may have more to do with a hot day of low humidity than with lack of moisture in the soil. Dry air increases the rate at which water rises through the plant's tissues and evaporates through the leaves' tiny pores. The available soil water may be fine, but it may not be able to climb fast enough to keep the leaves healthy. In such a climate, periodic sprinkling that wets the leaves may not be a bad idea, since it increases the humidity of the air.

LEARNING YOUR SOIL

You can test the relative amount of sand, silt, and clay in an area of soil by filling two-thirds of a mason jar with water and adding a trowelful of the soil. Cover the jar, shake it until all the soil is dissolved, and set it down. After two minutes, mark the level of the soil that has settled out. This is the sand fraction. After three hours, mark the level to which the soil has risen. The space between the first and second marks measures the silt fraction. Finally, the next morning, measure the level again. The space between the second and third marks gives the proportion of clay in the soil. Roughly equal amounts of all three indicate a loam soil, but a proportion weighted to either sand or clay indicates soils that will pass water more or less quickly than loam. Use this process to make a rough map of the soil in your garden.

In one regard, however, it is simple to measure the air. Set an empty open jar in the garden and measure it at the end of a week. If there is at least 1" of water in the jar, then the garden probably has all the moisture it needs.

When all is said and done, the best way to tell if a plant needs water is intimately to know your plants. A certain rose or zinnia may like water not on it leaves but at its base. The tomato loves to be sprinkled all over but sends deep roots, so it needs water less frequently than do the cabbages and the onions that grow nearby.

The experienced gardener takes all these factors—soil, air, and plant needs—into consideration when choosing different tools to water effectively. Watering cans give the best control over how much water you give to a small area and how quickly you give it, but they must be refilled frequently. The garden hose, fitted with a nozzle or a water breaker, lets you provide any amount of water exactly where you want it. (And unlike the watering can, you can simply turn it on and leave.) Sprinklers are fine for turf since they provide very even coverage to the whole area at their best. Where drought is a concern and you want to encourage good deep root systems, particularly for vegetables and specimen plants in the border, a soaker hose or a drip-emitter system is the best choice.

HISTORY OF WATERING

Watering and gardening go hand in hand. Indeed, agriculture initially began and thrived along the edges of great rivers where Nature herself taught gardeners how to water.

Perhaps the most successful long-term agriculture in the world belongs to the Nile Basin of Egypt, where prosperity depended on the river's annual flood. Far from a feared event, this flood was eagerly awaited and in fact worshiped, for it brought to the earth not only water but a layer of fertile organic residue that annually renewed the soil. In the valley of the Tigris and the Euphrates, the two great rivers supplied successive civilizations with abundant water for the first large-scale irrigation in the western world.

Still, although rivers brought water, it was up to gardeners to apply it, particularly during the dry seasons when untended plants might wither and die. For centuries, water was lifted from streams by hand, by means of levered buckets, or by ingenious contraptions like the spiral-shaped Archimedes screw, which distributed water to fields via channels, furrows, or pipes. Gravity moved the water, and it was applied to soil beside the plants. Where row cropping was not possible, the only alternative was to carry water in wheeled carts, dipping buckets into them and distributing the water by hand. Though these means were able to put water where it was needed, the application rate was often too fast or too slow, and too coarse. In furrows, the plants nearer to the source got more water than those at the end of a row. With hand watering, the roughly poured stream from the bucket often was powerful enough to wash away seedlings or bubble and run off instead of percolating into the soil.

Modern watering tools have pushed gardening out from the dooryard into the surrounding landscape, transforming gardening from the pursuit of a wealthy few—who could afford the team of gardeners with watering engines and buckets—to the delight of anyone with the means to buy a hose. The great innovations, none of which existed before the late sixteenth century and most coming into their own toward the end of the nineteenth century, are the watering can, the hose, the sprinkler, and most recently, drip irrigation.

EARLY WATERING CANS

As simple as it looks, the watering can is actually a masterpiece of appropriate technology. There have been buckets since humankind first realized it had hands, but a bucket is a crude tool. It can hold water all right, but try to pour it gently. The simple genius of the watering can is that it fills quickly and holds plenty but releases slowly like a gentle rain. And it puts water only where you point it, reducing the likelihood of errant weeds from large-scale watering.

The watering can did not spring into being as it is today. A century before the first cans, there were a number of valiant experi-

EMERGENCE OF THE WATERING CAN

The watering can looks like an ancient tool, but the first mention of it in the Oxford English Dictionary dates only from 1692. More than a decade later, a garden writer was still compelled to explain just what the tool was: "It imitates the rain falling from the Heavens," he noted. "When being bended down, it spouts forth water thro' a thousand holes, in a sort of Head that's made to it."

ments. One was an earthenware pot that resembled a very large, hollow artichoke filled with small perforations; the trick was to keep your thumb over a hole at the top while you filled it, then remove your thumb to break the vacuum and release the flow of water. The spray was gentle, but it must have released half the water on the gardener's feet.

The first spouted watering pot was also earthenware. The rose and spout were formed as part of the pot. The holes were far too large, and it looked like a gall or carbuncle at the end of a branch, but it was a vast improvement over earlier versions.

During the nineteenth century, after many further improvements, a lively debate raged as to whether the French or the English watering can was superior. English cans were big and burly with two handles, one across the top and one at the back. They were (and still are) measured in imperial gallons, each containing five quarts. You could carry a can in each hand to balance the load, but you had to put one down to operate the remaining can with both hands.

French cans tended to be oval in shape, which made them easy to carry without constantly brushing them against your legs and knees. Their real superiority, however, lay in the handle: there was only one, gracefully arched from the top front of the can to a point midway on the back of it. You could work the can simply by hiking one hand back along the handle until water began to spout from the rose.

The controversy was not to be decided in favor of the French. In 1885, a failed colonial vanilla bean planter named John Haws introduced a novel watering can that combined the virtues of both the French and English cans. What he lost in vanilla, he more than made back in watering cans: the Haws name, with its distinctive hawthorn berry emblem, has become synonymous with the finest watering cans. Haws cans are designed with two handles, making them easy to carry, but the back handle is arched like French versions, so each can may be poured with one hand. The can is oval shaped and so is the raised bib by which you fill it. This design allows for the can to be filled extremely fast. When cans were filled by dipping them into a big water cart, you could fill a 2-gallon Haws can in 5 seconds, and a pair of them in 15 seconds.

PRESSURIZED WATERING

Around 1850, when pressurized water systems first appeared in Europe and America, the rubber hose was already an important firefighter's tool. Suddenly, when it was attached to the home faucet, it liberated ordinary men and women to garden as though they were wealthy.

In 1885, a failed colonial vanilla bean planter named John Haws introduced a novel watering can that combined the virtues of both the French and English cans.

People like Andrew Jackson Downing inspired the American suburban garden, with its broad lawns, specimen trees, little groves, and beds of flowers spread across the landscape. A short time later in Britain, the great Edwardians, led by Gertrude Jekyll and William Robinson, extended the English cottage garden away from the dooryard and into the woods. The hose behooved all their efforts.

Once it was possible to deliver water under pressure, hundreds of inventors went to work inventing ways to use pressure to distribute water. Late nineteenth-century landscapers' catalogs are full of the results, some of which closely resemble today's sprinklers and others that look more like alien spaceships.

As entertaining as many sprinklers are—even today—some are terrible wasters of water. In semi-arid California, where many of this century's watering innovations originated, many people who once used the impulse sprinkler now swear by drip irrigation. Where a whirlybird sprinkler works hard and fast, a drip system works slowly and steadily.

DRIP IRRIGATION

Modern drip irrigation did not become popular until the 1960s, when plastic molding technology made it possible to make flexible pipes with hundreds of tiny emitters that would not clog or burst.

The concept of slow, underground irrigation had many historical precedents. In 1570, Thomas Hyl described the best way to water seedlings. He suggested using a dibber to poke a hole leading from the surface of sloped soil toward the roots "and so water the root underground, for water rotteth and killeth above the ground." He also recommended placing a container of water with a wick in the bottom next to plants so that the slowly released water would steadily feed the roots. Clever tomato growers have done the same for more than a century, jabbing a couple of small holes in a tin can and setting it into the ground beside the tomatoes.

Drip irrigation is simply a way to accomplish the same end with a specially designed hose, so the watering can continue over a large area without constant attention. The Israelis, who live in a land of little water and salty soils, were true water pioneers. In fact, is said that drip irrigation began when an Israeli engineer who had an orchard noticed that a tree near a leaky spigot thrived in comparison to the others. This

THE ELUSIVE HOSE

Two thousand years ago, water was being carried to plants through irrigation ditches. The ancient Romans used lead or clay pipes to conduct water, as did medieval monks in their cloisters. The great Moorish gardens of the Generalife in Granada had half-pipe stair banisters that brought water from the high hill to the heart of the garden. But until the mid-nineteenth century no one had ever come up with a flexible, portable device that could instantly lead water 100' or more from its source.

led to a twenty-year effort to design "leaky pipes"—usually plastic tubes perforated with hundreds of small water-emitting fixtures—that would release a slow, steady volume of water into the soil. Water thus delivered had two benefits: it went straight to the plant's roots instead of leaching away, and it drove salts and other harmful minerals lower in the water table away from plant roots.

The only innovation to beat drip watering has to do not with technology but with savvy. If you set out to apply the minimum irrigation possible when you're making a garden, you will purposely choose plants that are well adapted to growing in your climate without a great deal of extra watering and you will have to prepare the soil well and mulch thoroughly. Perhaps you'll decide to do away with the guzzling lawn and with water-loving exotics among your flower beds, emphasizing drought-tolerant, deep-rooted native plants. In this way, you would be returning to the system of the ancient Egyptian, who cooperated with Nature instead of replacing her.

THE PRINCIPLES OF WATERING

If watering is an art, then gardeners, like artists, must choose the tools that best accomplish their ends.

If watering is an art, then gardeners, like artists, must choose the tools that best accomplish their ends. A careful artist would never choose a cheap brush or a palette of poor, ill-mixed paints, and neither should the gardener settle for less than those tools best suited to the garden's needs.

There are four principles of watering. First, water should be distributed in streams sufficiently fine that they do not damage plants or cause soil to puddle or run off. Second, water must be spread gently and evenly to all the roots that need it. Third, water must extend as far into the garden as needed; and fourth, it must be applied to the soil in a way that wastes as little as possible.

In choosing and using watering tools, the question is always which of the four principles will be your responsibility and which will be the tool's. A watering can, for example, makes a fine spray and allows you to put water where it's needed, but *you* must carry the can and pour the water with care. A hose or sprinkler will transport the water for you, but you may have to do a great deal of adjusting to see that the spray is fine enough and the water goes where you want it to go. Even a drip system, convenient as it is, requires monitoring to ensure that no emitter has clogged or the line has not been severed by an errant thrust of the spade.

THE WATERING CAN

Watering cans do not make for light labor, but they are a pleasure to use because they bring you out into the garden close to your plants. And once there, you may notice not only what is beautiful, but also what other tasks urgently need your attention.

A purist may love to heft a big Haws can everywhere in the garden, but even the laziest gardener will want a can or two for patio and terrace plants or hanging baskets. The advantage of using a watering can for these purposes is that you quickly come to know how much water is needed for each plant and can provide it accordingly. Even if you're going away for a week, you can give precise watering instructions without fear that someone might leave a hose running into the cymbidiums and forget about it for the rest of the day.

CHOOSING A WATERING CAN

The important aspects of a good watering can are the spout and the rose. The spout must be slightly higher than the can itself, so the can may be filled to the brim. The quality of the spray depends ultimately upon the rose, the perforated piece at the business end of the spout. A cheap plastic rose, no matter how many holes it may have, is not going to last a very long time. The holes will widen with use, and they will often clog. The best roses are made of brass. The holes do not get reamed out, and they can be easily cleaned.

ANATOMY OF A WATERING CAN

Two hand grips make for easy balancing.

The domed lid prevents spilling when watering.

Made of galvanized steel, the can is durable and relatively lightweight.

A removable rose allows for a range of finer-spray adjustments.

Roses for watering cans come in two shapes: round and oval. The former look stolid and give their cans a businesslike air; on better cans, they may be made to face up or down. Round roses produce a gentle stream for seedlings, whereas the oval types can give you a more forceful stream when you're watering the base of a big shrub, for example.

Far more graceful in appearance and action, the oval roses revolutionized the watering can when they appeared under the name "Money's Inverted Rose Watering Pot" in 1830. When pointing skyward (hence the name "inverted rose") the oval puts out the gentlest possible stream of water. Owing to the water pressure in the spout, the stream slows slightly as it emerges from the rose. For this reason, water never falls with more than its own weight. When the oval faces down, it pours with more force at a greater rate, yet the streams are still gentle enough to water the seedlings.

Two specialized watering cans require different roses. The mister actually atomizes the water it emits; it's scarcely ever needed outdoors, but it humidifies the air for indoor and nursery plants, thereby keeping the leaves from drying out too much. Indoor plants and tiny seedlings also respond well to small, rubber-bulb waterers with round roses. By squeezing the bulb at different pressures, you can increase or decrease the rate at which the water comes out.

Once it could be said that all good watering cans were made of either copper or galvanized steel. While copper was strong, however, it dented easily and was quite heavy. Furthermore, it was very expensive. Gardeners seldom use copper cans today, unless they also have some decorative purpose.

Galvanized steel, on the other hand, is still the material of choice for serious gardeners. The can may weigh up to 4 lbs. when empty and may top 20 lbs. when full, but it's beautiful and durable and makes a lovely sound when banged. There is also a rightness to the cool feel of zinc-coated steel in the hand.

Again, it's better to buy two such cans so you can carry one in each hand as a balanced pair. The traditional way is to have one coated with red enamel and the other with green enamel. The red one is for soluble fertilizers, the green for pure water.

For years, plastic cans were looked down upon as a poor substitute, but now even Haws makes them. Not only are they far cheaper to manufacture and therefore much less expensive, but they're also a lot lighter than cans made of any other material—a comparable size may weigh 4 oz. instead of 4 lbs. Moreover, they're impossible to ding and dent.

Generally speaking, plastic watering cans cannot fit a fine brass rose. The plastic roses that come with them, however, will serve well to water patio containers.

USING THE WATERING CAN

The weight of watering cans can be deceptive. When empty, they're so light you can run with them. But once they're filled with water, they can seem as heavy as barbells.

The trick to using a watering can is to relax your shoulders when you pick it up after it's filled. Do not try to heft the can unnecessarily. Fill it while it sits on the ground, then pick it up by bending at the knees. Avoid stooping to lift the can and stooping to pour it. If you want to get right next to the ground when you pour, kneel down or squat.

Always try to balance the load by using two watering cans. Let the weight of the cans extend your arm and shoulders fully.

When pouring, be sure the rose is firmly attached and positioned to give the spray you desire. The upward-pointing rose makes the finest and gentlest spray of droplets. The downward-pointing rose makes a firmer, harder "rain."

THE HAWS METAL WATERING CAN: Easy to carry, fill, and pour, Haws cans are still the standard by which other watering cans are measured. The company now makes them in every material from copper to plastic. If you're looking for a full-size, dependable, efficient can, it's very hard to beat this one.

THE FRENCH WATERING CAN: The French style of watering can is as likely to be made in Taiwan as Lyons, France, but the principle remains the same: there is a single slender, arched handle for both carrying and pouring.

Cans of this type are usually more uncomfortable to use in larger sizes, but the medium and small sizes have great advantages. They're comparatively easy to work with one hand, since the handle can be held at whatever point is most efficient and "hiked" up and down to adjust the pressure on the rose.

One current version of the French watering can harkens back to a classic design of the first watering cans. Its elongated spout tapers at the end so there is no need for a rose. Made of galvanized metal, its stark beauty and simple design make it a favorite for watering indoor and outdoor patio plants.

THE CONSERVATORY WATERING CAN: Like a long, slender arm, the spout of this steel can arches gently over a long distance. Designed for watering in greenhouses and conservatories, the can is ideal for watering plants that are either hidden deep in borders or hanging in baskets.

Like a long, slender arm, the spout of the conservatory watering can arches gently over a long distance.

Watering Cans

1. TRADITIONAL STEEL WATERING CAN: A general-purpose watering can used by horticulturists the world over. Ideal for everyday outdoor use, it is crafted from heavy-gauge galvanized steel, coated with rust-resistant zinc. The spout is supported with a welded brace and the overhand handle is used for toting, the side handle for tipping. This version sports a rubber-backed brass rose. A very affordable metal can. Holds 2½ gallons.

2. **PRACTICIAN POLYETHYLENE WATERING CAN:** A plastic version of the unique Haws design, this can has a right-angled downspout, splashproof mouth, and brass rose. Plastic may be preferred by some users as it is more affordable, rustproof, and easier to clean than steel. Holds 1⅞ gallons.

3. **FRENCH WATERING CAN:** This hot-dipped, galvanized steel can was developed in southern France and boasts a high-sided oval shape with a large mouth and one broad handle that spans the entire length of the can. The unique design enables the user to water with one hand: the can gently tips as the user moves or "walks" his hand down the handle without losing balance or straining the wrist. Large brass rose with galvanized steel backing. Holds 2½ gallons, but is available in several sizes.

4. **HAWS METAL WATERING CAN:** The century-old Haws Company was founded on this top-of-the-line watering can design. The can distributes weight evenly when full and pours in a long, steady stream. The long neck waters difficult areas with ease and creates high pressure on the rose for a big, beautiful spray, while the tall can holds a great deal of water without sacrificing balance. Crafted from heavy-gauge steel, the can is dipped in a rust-resistant zinc coating to ensure years of use. Upturned, removable brass rose allows gentle sprinkling. Holds 2 gallons, but is available in several sizes.

1. TRADITIONAL STEEL WATERING CAN

2. PRACTICIAN POLYETHYLENE WATERING CAN

6. PATIO WATERING CAN

5. CONSERVATORY WATERING CAN

8. HANDY WATERING CAN

5. Conservatory Watering Can: This long-necked, painted, galvanized steel can is designed specifically for watering in greenhouses, conservatories, and other places where a long reach and accuracy are necessary. The brass extension adds inches to the reach, while the small, upturned rose delivers a light sprinkle that won't damage new sprouts. The can holds less water, so it is easy to maneuver around tight spots without spilling. Holds 3 quarts.

6. Patio Watering Can: This small can has an extra-long spout and upturned brass rose to gently water potted and hanging plants. Light and agile, it easily reaches out-of-the-way places. Squat size fits under indoor faucets. Holds 1 gallon.

7. Painted Brass-Handled Watering Can: A more elegant version of the standard metal watering can. Features a painted galvanized steel can with two long-lasting brass handles. Holds 2½ gallons.

8. Handy Watering Can: The best choice for an indoor can, this polyethylene Haws design has all the advantages of the larger varieties, including the right-angled downspout, but in a smaller, easy-to-clean-and-store package. Because it holds less water, it is best suited to watering individual potted plants. Holds 2 pints.

9. Copper Watering Can: A lovely rendition of the standard Haws design, copper has the advantage of aging with a beautiful patina. The spout is located nearer to the base of the can for easier pouring, while the swanlike brass rose extension adds length. The small brass oval rose is meant for sprinkling. Holds 3 pints.

10. French Galvanized Metal Watering Can: A very simple design based on the very first watering cans, this tool sports a tall coffee-can shape, a low-slung, unsupported spout, and a long loop handle. Made entirely from galvanized metal. A good, lightweight choice for watering individual or indoor plants. Holds ½ gallon.

3. French Watering Can

4. Haws Metal Watering Can

7. Painted Brass-Handled Watering Can

9. Copper Watering Can

10. French Galvanized Metal Watering Can

Roses

1. LARGE GALVAN-IZED ROSE: This largest of roses fits the French-style watering cans. It has a much larger than average spout size and uses a section of a bicycle inner tube as a gasket to seal against leaking. The large holes give a coarse spray for very rapid watering. The unperforated section at the bottom of the brass face reduces unwanted drips and drizzles.

2. RUBBER-BACKED ROSE: Possibly the most useful rose in the world. It has a flexible rubber body that fits many if not most watering cans. It gives a great spray and does not ding or chip pots. The solid-brass face snaps in and out for easy cleaning, and the rose itself pulls off easily to water with a straight stream.

3. SCREW-ON HAWS ROSE: A large, round, all-brass rose with a threaded back and face stiffened by concentric corruga-tions, this one fits traditionally styled cans. Classic and functional.

4. OVAL ROSE: The rose that made Haws famous. Used with the solid brass face pointing upward, and combined with the long Haws spout, it gives the most marvelous fountain of fine, very gentle, rainlike spray.

5. STANDARD ROUND ROSE: A solid brass body and face make this Haws rose striking when new and beautiful as it ages and takes on a blue-green patina. Slightly slanted round face projects the water beyond the spout in a fine, even spray, and can be used facing up or down.

6. UPTURNED GALVANIZED ROSE: This brass-faced French rose features a galvanized steel body and fits the smaller French cans. It can be used facing up or down.

7. LONG-REACH EXTENSION AND BABY ROSE: This combination is specifically for the Haws Conservatory Can. The long brass spout is ideal for watering house-plants or conservato-ry plants because it extends the reach and turns down just a bit. The brass baby oval rose fits on the extension and also on all the smaller brass and copper Haws cans.

8. PLASTIC HAWS ROSE: A plastic-bodied version of the classic Haws oval. It fits Haws plastic cans and is intended to be used with the brass face pointing up. High-quality brass face ensures a good, fine spray.

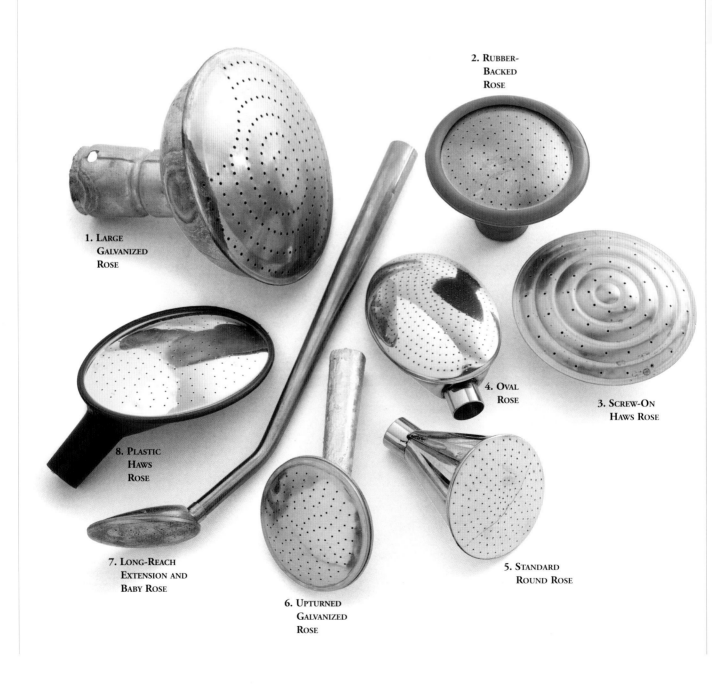

2. RUBBER-BACKED ROSE

1. LARGE GALVANIZED ROSE

8. PLASTIC HAWS ROSE

7. LONG-REACH EXTENSION AND BABY ROSE

6. UPTURNED GALVANIZED ROSE

4. OVAL ROSE

5. STANDARD ROUND ROSE

3. SCREW-ON HAWS ROSE

THE HOSE

Three of the four principles of watering are well served by the watering can: it puts out a gentle and vivifying stream, placing it exactly where the water is wanted, and it covers the whole area evenly. The hitch comes with the fourth principle—to bring water as far as needed into the garden. In this case, heavy cans have to be carried long distances or a large water cart must be wheeled behind to fill the cans.

The garden hose has been a liberator, but it is also the most mischievous of all garden tools. While it admirably fulfills the fourth aim of watering, it has to be tamed by a nozzle, breaker, or sprinkler. And though you can go far with it, you're liable to get tripped or splashed along the way. Sometimes it lies in wait, timing the attack. Turn around to turn the spigot on, and a coil resting in the cabbage bed turns a 180° angle to direct a gentle stream of extremely cold water down the back of your leg. A few moments later, an apparently flat section will ride up against the stake you use as a hose guide, only to form a big kink, jump the stake, and flatten half a row of tender pepper plants.

CHOOSING A HOSE

The great aim of hose makers through this entire century has been to make a strong and lightweight hose that will not kink or tangle. The old rubber hose—an extruded rubber tube with a hole in the middle—not only tangled but was inordinately heavy. Stimulated by the shortage of rubber during World War II, manufacturers turned to synthetics like vinyl and nylon; when layered, such materials could create a hose as strong as a rubber hose but much easier to carry.

For the most part, the best hoses that you can buy are not made of rubber. True, an outer coating of rubber is less liable to degrade in the sun than is a plastic or vinyl one, and rubber has a somewhat higher natural resistance to bursting. But a good 5-ply vinyl-nylon hose is just about as strong and durable as a rubber hose—and very much lighter in weight.

The "plies," or layers, that make up a hose's body determine its quality. The inner ply is always a slim, smooth tube through which the water runs. In all but the cheapest hoses, a second ply made of a spiral or knit mesh fabric lends strength to the inner tube. (In fact, this nylon fabric is the very same material that goes into making the "belts" of car tires.) One or two more plies are meant to give additional strength to the hose and help it resist kinking, and the outer ply is made of a tough vinyl or a vinyl-rubber mix that resists scratching and solar degradation.

The garden hose has been a liberator, but it is also the most mischievous of all garden tools.

The number of layers is not the only feature that makes 5-ply hoses the best. Their composition and the quality of their fittings are also important factors. Better vinyls contain far higher proportions of plasticizing agents and ultraviolet inhibitors to make them more flexible and less liable to weaken in the sun. Although two hoses may look exactly the same, one may kink mildly while the other kinks furiously, and one may burst after a year while the other lasts for a decade.

The fittings are almost always the first place where hose quality suffers. Being run over by a car or even just stepped on can cause a hose to leak forever after—not only out the edges, but from the inner coupling as well. Cheap hoses feature stamped, galvanized steel fittings with O-ring washers that have a tendency to fall out and get lost. A good hose should have brass fittings (the best are individually cast and octagon-shaped), and the washer should be integral to the whole fitting, not just an insert.

Hoses are manufactured in standard working diameters of ½", ⅝", ¾", and 1". The usual range of water pressures at which our faucets deliver—30–50 lbs. per square inch—make the ⅝" diameter the most appropriate choice. A hose of this width will water the garden in about one-third less time than a ½" hose.

USING A HOSE

The first rule is never to leave a hose out in the sun. (It's true that rubber is less liable to degrade in sunlight, but even this hardy material will ultimately crack under the strain of repeated heating and cooling.) The second thing to remember is that hoses are manufactured and laid in particular spirals. Use the hose's memory of its original shape to your advantage by coiling it accordingly. To help preserve an even coil, use a hose caddy (see page 290). Kinks will tend to work out, and the smooth-coil memory of the hose will be reinforced.

Some hoses will never kink because they have no length or stiffness. The shortcut hose, a 3' or 4' length of hose with brass couplings at either end, is good for filling up watering cans or washing up after working. A "shortie" can also be fitted with a second spigot, so you can use it to run the control of your water out from an inaccessible faucet.

If all else fails, there is always the flat hose. A few canvas ones can still be found, though these are very likely to decay unless they're dried after each use. Vinyl versions with brass couplers fill and swell with water, then sink down with a sigh when you shut the pressure off. They are flexible and do not kink, because they have no internal structure. When you have limited storage space, they are also a good choice because they can be folded up small.

The fittings are almost always the first place where hose quality suffers.

IRRIGATORS

An effective drip-irrigation system waters the soil slowly, continuously, directly, and with minimal evaporation. It places the water directly adjacent to plants and never wets the leaves, flowers, or fruit. And like a plain hose, it can extend more than 100' into the landscape.

The system can be as simple as a soaker hose or as complex as a vast network of pressure-regulated plastic lines fitted at intervals with tiny brass couplings. A soaker hose is fine for a short run of vegetables or garden plants, so long as the hose lies in a roughly straight line on flat ground. For bigger gardens and sloping ground, choose a system that actively corrects for pressure differentials, giving each plant the same amount of water. A more elaborate system also allows you to apply liquid fertilizers simultaneously with the watering.

Soaker hoses sometimes build up mineral deposits, and drip emitters become blocked. If you notice incipient wilt in certain plants, check the system for clogs. Drip systems are also vulnerable to breakage. You can't hoe with wild abandon in their vicinity, or you'll chop off a feeder line and end up with a big puddle instead of watered plants.

THE SOAKER HOSE: The oldest viable drip systems, soaker hoses were once made of canvas to leak water all along their length. Canvas hoses can still be found, but they have two defects. They rot quickly in the soil, and they drip far more water at the start of the hose run than at the end.

DRIP-SYSTEM HOSE: These are extraordinary tools for pinpoint watering. A pressure regulator at the spigot end of the hose prevents backflow and steadies the pressure coming from the main source. Each emitter valve in the system (up to several hundred can be inserted in the flexible vinyl lines) contains a pressure compensator to ensure uniform drippage. The lines can be snaked through the garden, but they are best used for row crops. There are also ring and cul-de-sac drip-system hoses that distribute water from a series of side lines that go straight to the roots of a shrub or a clump of perennials.

True drip systems can work at an ordinary hose pressure of 30 psi. This means that a small change in pressure from the main source (plus or minus 2 psi) has a smaller effect on water delivered when compared with a soaker hose that runs on only 10 psi pressure.

ROOT FEEDERS AND TREE GATORS

They don't exactly drip, but root feeders for trees and shrubs share the virtues of drip-system hoses by supplying water directly to plant roots. Better yet, they contain a chamber for soluble fertilizer, allowing you to water and feed roots at the same time.

Even young trees have drip irrigators specially designed for them. For spring-planted trees, which suffer enough stress without having to contend with occasional summer droughts, the "gator" is a sleevelike, zip-on bag with a few small holes in the bottom. Fill the bag with water and replenish it every week or two, or when the bag is empty.

Hoses

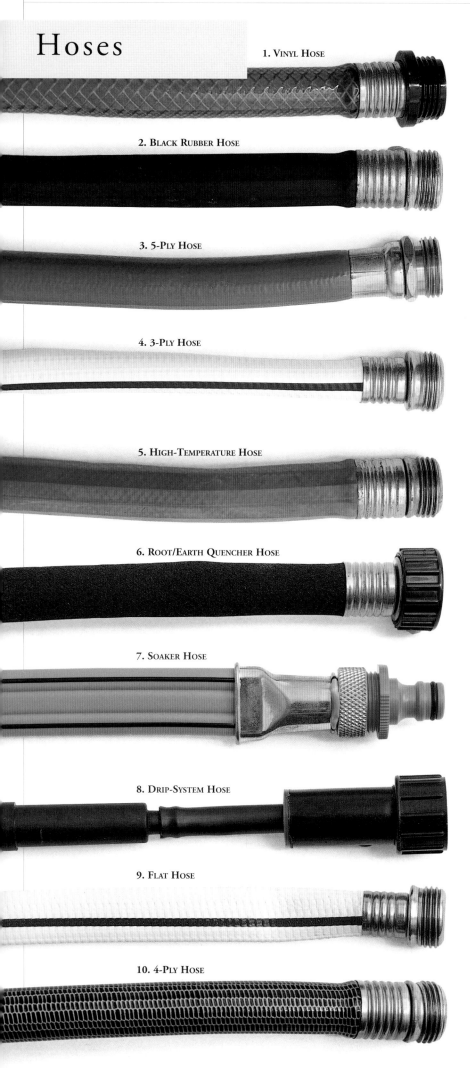

1. Vinyl Hose

2. Black Rubber Hose

3. 5-Ply Hose

4. 3-Ply Hose

5. High-Temperature Hose

6. Root/Earth Quencher Hose

7. Soaker Hose

8. Drip-System Hose

9. Flat Hose

10. 4-Ply Hose

1. **Vinyl Hose:** An example of a hose designed for medium-level watering tasks, this lightweight option is made from dual-radial reinforced tubing covered with flexible vinyl. Easier to maneuver than rubber hoses. At ⅝" in diameter, with nylon couplings, it is burst- and kink-resistant and may be preferred by smaller gardeners.

2. **Black Rubber Hose:** A good choice for professional gardeners, this example is constructed entirely of malleable, reinforced black rubber. This is a best-quality hose, ⅝" in diameter, with brass couplings.

3. **5-Ply Hose:** The best-grade hose available on the market (and also the stiffest), this kink-resistant, 5-ply hose is ⅝" in diameter and features a dually reinforced inner core of PVC tubing covered with heavy-gauge rubber and vinyl. This hose won't burst under pressure or crack in the sun, and it comes with machined brass couplings.

4. **3-Ply Hose:** The minimum recommended ply in hoses, this ½"-diameter example is constructed of lightweight, reinforced vinyl. A good choice when a very portable hose is needed. Brass coupling has a plastic ring for watertight connection.

5. **High-Temperature Hose:** An industrial-strength hose designed to withstand temperatures up to 200°F. A high-temperature inner tube is reinforced and covered with a thick, all-rubber red cover (which helps eliminate confusion). This hose is ⅝" in diameter and features a leak-proof brass coupling.

6. **Root/Earth Quencher Hose:** A ⅝"-diameter hose constructed from 65% post-consumer recycled rubber derived from used tires. Designed to evenly soak areas with vegetation by sweating water either above or below ground. The rubber will not freeze or crack with proper use, and the hose can be connected to other hoses in a network. Also has a removable black end cap.

7. **Soaker Hose:** An essential hose for drought-prone regions, this is a heavy-duty, professional-quality soaker hose designed to water large areas with minimum evaporation. It features 1-ply rubber pierced with tiny holes every 18", and solid brass couplings.

8. **Drip-System Hose:** This hose is fabricated from UV-protected polyethylene tubing with ½ gallon-per-minute drip emitters installed every 18" to slowly water with little evaporation. It connects to other hoses or tubing to water a large area. An affordable option that can be left on the ground over winter.

9. **Flat Hose:** A hose made from cotton canvas that slowly delivers water to surrounding plants. It handles easily, folds flat for storage, and features brass couplings.

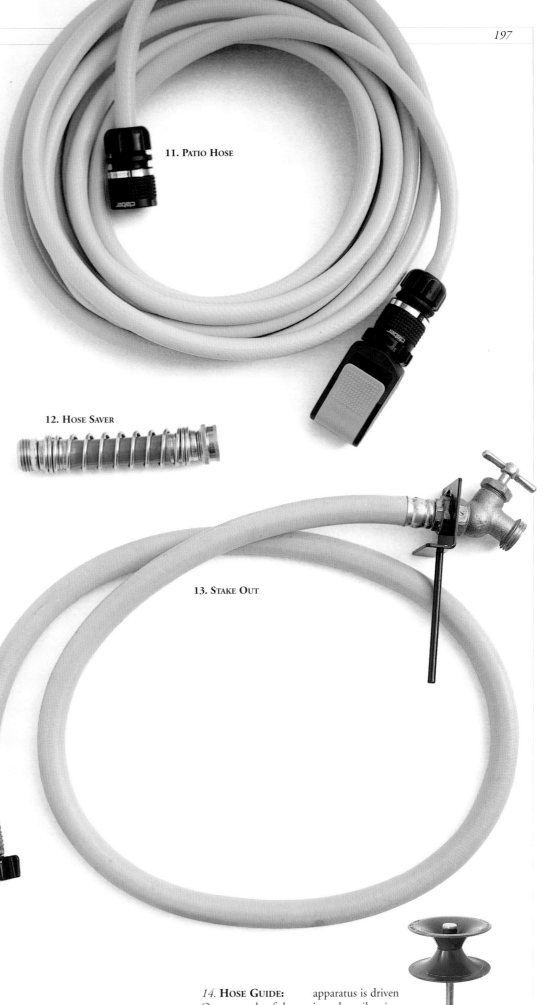

10. 4-PLY HOSE:
This is an example of a good-quality, 4-ply hose. Tougher than 3-ply, but not as strong as 5-ply, it is an adequate and maneuverable hose for most home gardeners. Made of reinforced PVC tubing, this ⅝"-diameter hose has a rubber and vinyl covering. It also features brass couplings.

11. PATIO HOSE: A special cam lock fitting allows this 50' hose to be hooked up to a sink or basin faucet. It is smaller than the average outdoor hose, measuring ⅓" in diameter. It also features snap-on fittings on both ends for quick disconnection.

12. HOSE SAVER:
This specialty hose attachment comprises a sturdy steel spring and solid brass fittings. It screws between the hose and faucet, eliminating the overstretching and kinking that result in reduced water flow and wear and tear on the hose.

13. STAKE OUT:
Outdoor faucets are often rendered inaccessible by shrubbery or other obstacles. This attachment permanently extends faucets to make watering more convenient. The solid brass, corrosion-resistant faucet has a replaceable washer, while the 16-gauge, enameled, rust-resistant steel stake (not shown) stands 17" tall and swivels to eliminate kinks. The 5-ply extension hose spans 5'. The faucet is removable from the stake to allow for filling a bucket or watering can with ease.

11. PATIO HOSE

12. HOSE SAVER

13. STAKE OUT

14. HOSE GUIDE:
One example of the many inexpensive varieties of hose guides available. This polypropylene and uncoated steel apparatus is driven into the soil or into predrilled holes in wood or masonry to keep the hose free of walkways and plants.

14. HOSE GUIDE

HOSE ACCESSORIES

A hose is a wonderful tool for taking water where you want it to go, but without human intervention the steady flow that comes from the end is not suitable for any watering task more delicate than filling a furrow.

For finer work, you can make do by pressing your thumb down over the opening to create a manageable spray. And though you'll end up with a very tired hand, you'll feel the great pleasure of being close enough to the garden to give it the amount of water it needs in exactly the right place. While you're at it, you can tend to other things that need to be done, like staking, dividing, deadheading, and weeding.

You can experience the same intimacy, however, without the wear and tear of managing the water flow personally. Accessories at both ends of the hose can tame it for delicate tasks. At the spigot end, a gooseneck coupling pivots as the hose moves, thereby reducing the tendency to kink. A spiral metal hose saver helps stabilize the very end of the hose, where it's most likely to fold and slow the flow to a trickle. A Y-shaped water distributor, with shutoff valves, lets you hook up two hoses at once while releasing the water through either or both.

The other end of the hose is where memories are made. Nozzles and breakers exist at the very heart of gardening. Few gardeners do not have at least one happy memory of standing with the hose at the edge of a bed, letting the nozzle play across it and watching a rainbow dance in the spray. Or perhaps it was the pleasant task of checking the bubbler, set beneath each rose in turn, to see that it was working slow enough so the water soaked through the odorous layer of cocoa shell mulch and percolated neatly into the soil.

THE NOZZLE: Hose-end nozzles come in two sorts: those that launch water in an atomized spray, going for distance, and those that mix it with air so that it filters gently into the adjacent soil. In either case, the idea is to convert a solid stream of water into a form that reaches the soil where you want it to and in a way that will keep it from running off the surface.

For general watering, the first type will often be your choice. But when you want to keep water away from fungus-prone leaves or have it bubble slowly into the soil, the latter type is best. Another good thing about the second type is that you can place it, set a kitchen timer, and forget about it until the timer rings.

Since you want the water to penetrate the soil, it's important to see that most of it goes there. An imitation of falling rain is not necessary. On the other hand, never use a solid spray from the nozzle to plow the soil.

Nozzles and breakers exist at the very heart of gardening.

The result of a direct spray will be compaction, runoff, and possibly the exposure and death of roots.

The pistol-grip nozzle: Almost everyone these days seems to have the pistol-grip style nozzle. It's great for washing the car and for water fights. Different pressures on the handle produce everything from a wide and gentle mist to a solid projectile stream. But it's not the best nozzle for the garden. You'll get just as tired squeezing the trigger of one of these grips as you would from holding your thumb over the hose end. But it's so much fun to use that it will likely remain the best-seller.

The twist-type nozzle: The oldest and still the best form of garden nozzle is the wonderful brass twist-type version. It's easy to grasp and adjust, and it creates just as wide a range of spray as the pistol grip. If you really want a hardy, steady stream of water (to wash down the driveway, for instance), a jet-spray nozzle is the perfect choice; it resembles a small version of the nozzles that firemen use, and it has the same effect. Conversely, misting heads break the stream into a fine mist for watering tender seedlings.

WATER BREAKERS: Nozzles throw water, but breakers drop it gently in place. The simplest of these is the fan head, which converts water into many fine streams, much like the rose on a watering can. Aerating bubblers and wands mix air with the water, so a large volume can be released with little force. When you want water to percolate into soil around roots, there is no better tool than a bubbler. The wand version makes it easier to reach the back end of a bed without having to traipse in there yourself.

QUICK COUPLERS: The usefulness of these hose-end devices has inspired many companies—Claber and Gardena, among them—to create whole systems that allow you to choose the tool you need for any situation. The nozzle systems are based on quick couplers. Instead of screwing a single attachment into a standard brass coupler, the systems have couplers that snap together with a simple push. It's easy to switch from breaker to nozzle, and even to rotating or oscillating sprinklers. The quick couplers often have shut-off valves at both ends of the hose. The business-end valve is particularly useful since it lets you shut off the water in order to change tools, without having to kink the hose manually or return to the source to shut it off.

HOSE GUIDES

Since no one has figured out how to completely control the coil of a hose, the next best thing is a hose guide. An upright device driven securely into the ground and often sporting a kind of turnbuckle, the guide is placed at the corner of the garden bed. When the hose is dragged around a corner, it's supposed to catch on the upright or turnbuckle.

There are two rules concerning hose guides. First, you have to stake them deeply enough so impetuous hoses can't pull them out of the ground. Second, they have to be tall enough to deal with the deviousness of hoses, which rarely drag flat across the ground. A hose can easily rise up in a coil, jump the guide, and fall gleefully on your plants.

Hose Accessories

1. **RAIN WAND:** A professional accessory used by nurseries to provide a gentle, drenching "rain" suited to seedlings and potted plants. Lightweight and easy to use, it acts as an extension of the user's arm to water inaccessible areas. Thumb-operated shut-off valve, aluminum extension wand, aluminum rose with over 400 perforations.

2. **PATIO WAND:** A shorter wand, appropriate for watering hard-to-reach potted and hanging plants. Aluminum wand, thumb-operated shut-off valve, rubber nozzle and grip.

3. **BRASS SPRAY LANCE:** Similar to the Rain Wand, this trigger-grip tool features a rose that gently mists new sprouts and seedlings. Perhaps the most versatile wand available because of its cone-shaped, soft spray. It throws out a huge volume of water and can spray up to about 8' or fill a tiny pot without blasting the soil out of it. Aluminum wand, brass rose, plastic grip.

4. **TREE AND SHRUB AERATOR:** Extra-long, T-handled spike for watering and aerating the deep roots of trees and shrubs. Hose attaches to aluminum wand to deliver water directly. Good choice for drought-prone areas, as it reduces evaporation.

5. **4-POSITION WATER WAND:** Essentially the same tool as the Rain Wand, the Water Wand has the added benefit of four different water patterns (from mist to stream) that adjust with the flip of a finger. Aluminum extension, polyethylene grip and rose, thumb-operated shut-off button.

6. **SPIKE SPRINKLER:** Heavy-gauge steel spike allows user to deliver water directly to the base of trees and shrubs. When staked and aimed at a target, the sprinkler casts a 90° wedge of rough spray (approximately 20' wide). Best used when the gardener is nearby, as it should be moved often.

7. **WATER DISTRIBUTOR:** Turns one faucet head into two. Made of corrosion-proof, heavyweight plastic with replaceable washers.

8. **FAN HEAD:** An industry standard, this attachment is crafted from die-cast metal and solid brass and attaches to the hose end, turning a stream of water into a drenching rain. Good for intensive watering, but does not have a shut-off valve.

9. **PLASTIC COUPLING:** A long-lasting, leakproof option for connecting two hoses. Male and female varieties.

10. **BUBBLER:** Aluminum orb attaches to the end of any hose and allows water to gently "bubble" up through its perforations. Soaks soil thoroughly and slowly without flattening tender seedlings.

11. **ROUND PISTOL GRIP NOZZLE:** Solid-plastic hose attachment allows user to control water stream by simply pressing and releasing the "trigger." A ratchet holds the trigger open. Heavy-duty polypropylene resists corrosion and leaks. Snaps on and off hose end.

12. **PISTOL GRIP NOZZLE:** A more contemporary version of the traditional

adjustable Jet Spray Nozzle, this attachment may be easier for some people to use. Water pressure is controlled by pressing down or releasing the metal trigger; nozzle

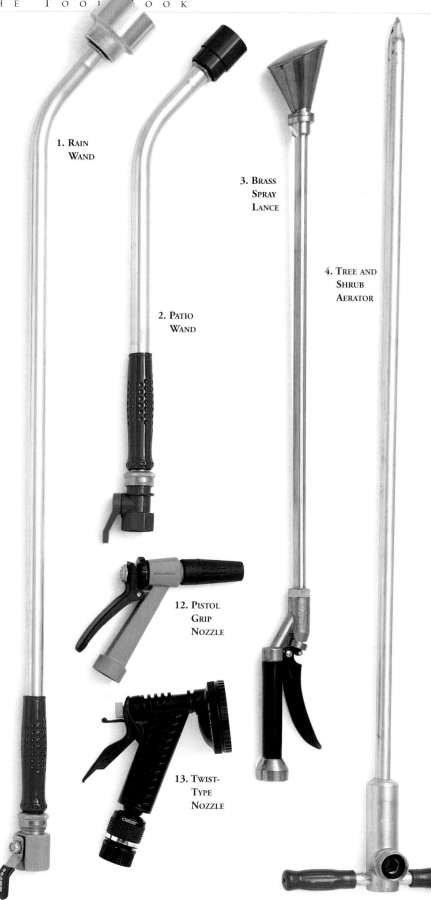

1. RAIN WAND

3. BRASS SPRAY LANCE

2. PATIO WAND

4. TREE AND SHRUB AERATOR

12. PISTOL GRIP NOZZLE

13. TWIST-TYPE NOZZLE

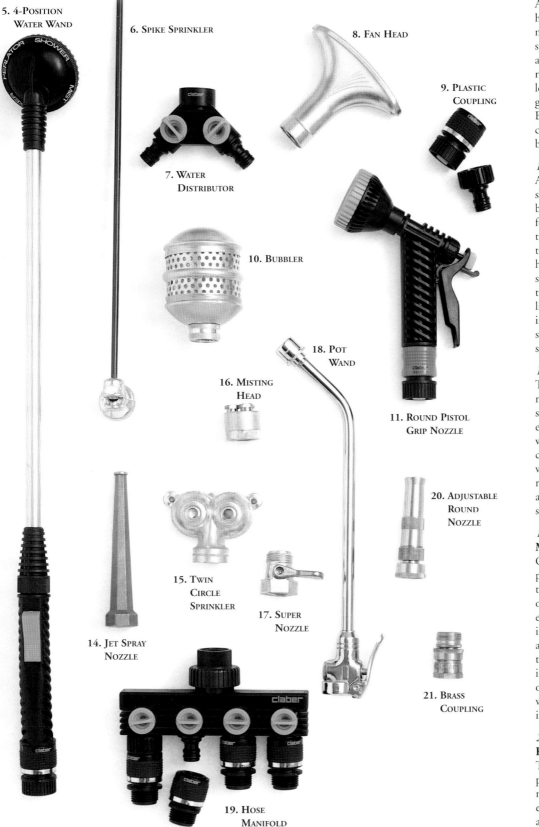

5. 4-POSITION WATER WAND

6. SPIKE SPRINKLER

8. FAN HEAD

9. PLASTIC COUPLING

7. WATER DISTRIBUTOR

10. BUBBLER

18. POT WAND

16. MISTING HEAD

11. ROUND PISTOL GRIP NOZZLE

20. ADJUSTABLE ROUND NOZZLE

15. TWIN CIRCLE SPRINKLER

17. SUPER NOZZLE

14. JET SPRAY NOZZLE

21. BRASS COUPLING

19. HOSE MANIFOLD

16. **MISTING HEAD:** Attaches to end of hose to finely mist new sprouts. This sprinkler is available in several sizes, ranging from ½ gallon-per-minute to 4 gallons-per-minute. Brass-coated, die-cast metal with solid brass jets

17. **SUPER NOZZLE:** A single lever ball shutoff valve with both male and female hose threads that can be attached to either end of a hose. In addition to simple on/off functions, this valve acts like a nozzle, projecting a strong, straight stream, a coarse spray, or a mist.

18. **POT WAND:** This short aluminum wand with a shutoff valve is especially useful for watering in pots and containers. Fitted with a corrosion-resistant plastic-and-aluminum rose to soften the wash.

19. **HOSE MANIFOLD:** Corrosion-resistant plastic attachment turns one faucet opening into four— essential for watering several separate areas without having to add new plumbing. Individual shutoff valves distribute water without reducing water pressure.

20. **ADJUSTABLE ROUND NOZZLE:** Traditional, rustproof, solid brass nozzle attaches to end of hose and adjusts from a fine mist to a sharp stream with a twist.

adjusts from mist to stream. Solid die-cast metal and brass.

13. **TWIST-TYPE NOZZLE:** A round-headed version of the Pistol Grip Nozzle. Similar function, but the

round head features adjustable exit patterns that switch from mist to shower to jet with a twist. Solid plastic with replaceable washer.

14. **JET SPRAY NOZZLE:** Simple brass attachment for hose end that focuses water into a sharp jet. Good for cleaning off pavement and tools.

15. **TWIN CIRCLE SPRINKLER:** This old-fashioned, die-cast metal stationary sprinkler easily screws onto a hose end and is laid in the middle of a garden bed, border, or lawn.

Water exits from the holes in two elegant arches. An affordable and easy-to-maneuver attachment.

21. **BRASS COUPLING:** Solid brass coupling for an almost instant connection between two hoses.

SPRINKLERS

Fixed-spray sprinklers are best for small open areas like a garden corner.

Oscillating sprinklers water in a rectangular pattern, perfect for most lawns.

The rain tower sprinkler as an industrial-size impulse sprinkler for watering very large areas.

Many of us have childhood memories of playing in the water from a sprinkler through a hot summer afternoon. Each kind of sprinkler called for a different game. The fixed-spray ones invited you to simply run in and out of them, whereas you had to circle around the spray of a rotating centrifugal sprinkler. Oscillators were for hurdles: you could outrun the jets of water to the place where they stopped, then double back and run right through them. The impulse sprinklers were thrilling and dangerous—you could run forever without leaving the radius of their throw.

The experience of childhood may well help you decide on the best sprinkler for your garden. In general, choose a model heavy enough not to turn over under pressure. (Light plastic ones often do this.) Also, those with brass or other sturdy metal heads last longer and maintain a more even pattern than plastic-headed sprinklers. Finally, check the couplers to see that they turn freely and hold their washer well. The frequently occurring leak between sprinkler and hose—the connection where pressure is highest—is another area that requires utmost quality.

No matter what kind of sprinkler you buy, you must decide where to place it and how often to move it. With a little practice, you'll learn the length and pattern of water the machine throws. Then you must design the day's watering so that all areas receive equal attention.

This process can be particularly problematic with some sprinklers, because they don't distribute water evenly throughout the whole pattern. With some versions, most of the water falls near the head; others distribute more water toward the edge of the pattern. You can obviate some of these problems by buying the best-quality model of any type. But even with this advantage, you should perform a simple test: place open jars at several different distances from the sprinkler and turn it on; let it run, then turn it off, and see how much water reached each container.

FIXED-SPRAY SPRINKLERS: Fixed sprinklers are best where you have a small, limited area to cover—a corner bed, perhaps, or a spur of the lawn that larger sprinklers miss. They are not good sprinklers to use around trees, since they'll throw water straight up into the foliage, but they drop a fine, gentle rain on flowers, shrubs, or lawns. The chief way these sprinklers betray you is by flipping over on their sides or going belly-up, so choose one made of heavy, noncorrosive metal with a substantial footprint, or base. Some smaller models now offer a variety of "dialable" spray patterns, but they seldom have the pressure to deliver patterns that are really distinct.

OSCILLATING SPRINKLERS: These sprinklers make rectangular patterns and are particularly good for watering the typical American lawn. An oscillating sprinkler worth buying will have small, removable brass fixtures covering each of its fourteen to twenty little nozzle holes to focus the throw of water. Better models also have a dependable mechanism for guiding the movement pattern.

All oscillators are intended to work in one of four modes: full swing from right to left, half swing from center to right, half swing from center to left, and any stationary position. This means you can run them to the edge of trees or even angle them in underneath. Unfortunately, their mechanism is often inconsistent. It's no fun to find that your sprinkler has been watering only half the intended area for the past twenty minutes. Those with external drives are easily damaged by banging about. More dependable models work by means of an internal water turbine.

THE IMPULSE SPRINKLER: For many of us, the word "sprinkler" conjures up the *thwick-tock-tock-tock* sound of the impulse sprinkler, spreading water as fast as it can over the largest possible area. This sprinkler covers a circle up to 100' in diameter but can be adjusted to cover only a section of the whole "pie" and throw at a low enough angle that it can reach beneath trees. Because it's so powerful, however, it needs a stable base; one with a flimsy plastic base can turn over and dig a serious hole in the lawn.

Market gardeners often use special impulse sprinklers mounted on tripods. Called "rain towers," these elevated models solve the stability problem, but the low-throw angle can slam straight into plants. People often try to balance an ordinary impulse sprinkler atop an inverted bucket, but the tower is a far better idea.

TRACTOR SPRINKLERS: Traactor sprinklers can't cover anywhere near the area of the impulse sprinkler in a single circle, but they're more powerful for watering a large, open lawn. They consist of a simple revolving sprinkler mounted atop a tiny

THE "WHIRLYBIRD" SPRINKLER

Perhaps the most useful and clever sprinkler ever made was invented by Orton Englehardt in 1933 to water his friends' lemon grove in California's Central Valley. This rotating sprinkler operates by deflecting a powerful stream of water with a spring-loaded arm. The arm breaks the stream into droplets as it swings back into place, causing the sprinkler to revolve. To this day, "whirlers" are a prominent feature not only in agricultural fields but on home grounds and vegetable gardens.

water-driven tractor that moves slowly over the lawn, guided by the pattern of a laid-out hose. The best ones have three different speeds to water more or less deeply, according to need. One pattern actually rolls up the hose behind it.

Sprinklers

1. TRACTOR SPRINKLER

2. SLED ROTATING SPRINKLER

6. FROG SPRINKLER

9. WHIRLING VANE SPRINKLER

5. SERPENTINE SPRINKLER

1. **TRACTOR SPRINKLER:** The hose that feeds this sprinkler also powers and guides it. The spinning arms are geared to turn a ratcheting mechanism, which drives the wheels. The front wheel straddles the hose and follows its path. Waters a circle 60' in diameter, and crawls forward at three speeds: 30', 45', or 60' per hour. Cast-iron chassis; brass, steel, aluminum, and plastic parts. HEIGHT 10½", ARM SPAN 34'.

2. **SLED ROTATING SPRINKLER:** A rotating sprinkler with a steel base, brass wands, and adjustable spray tips. The sled base allows this sprinkler to be dragged by the hose to a new location while the water is turned on. 9" × 7" × 6½".

3. **PORTABLE SPRINKLERS:** This small system combines several spray sprinklers with short lengths of hose to provide the kind of spray and coverage that an in-the-ground system provides but without the expense. The system can be moved or re-configured at will, and can be joined to multiple systems or other sprinklers for more coverage. Water coverage is 20' circles.

4. **AQUA DIAL SPRINKLER:** To adjust the coverage of most sprinklers, one increases or reduces the flow or dynamic pressure at the spray head; the less pressure, the shorter the throw and the lower the coverage. This interesting sprinkler is adjusted by "dialing" the coverage in. A knob on the top changes the pitch of the nozzle arms and thereby increases or decreases the diameter of the watered area. 9½" DIA. × 9".

5. **SERPENTINE SPRINKLER:** Features a stainless steel and bronze impact head, which can project water 15' to 42'. The spray is adjustable for full- or part-circle operation, with very even and precise coverage. The stand is heavy wall pipe and, because of the wide serpentine, is very stable. 12" × 16½" × 8".

6. **FROG SPRINKLER:** While very decorative, this brass frog is actually a fully functioning lawn sprinkler. Because of its fine spray and limited coverage—10' to 30' in diameter—it is perfect for small or secluded corners of a garden. 6¾" × 7½" × 5½".

7. **SLED IMPULSE SPRINKLER:** A brass impulse head mounted on a powder-coated fabricated steel base offers a new version of an old standard. Because this sprinkler shares the same basic design as the Sled Rotating Sprinkler, it too can be moved without shutting the water off. Water coverage is 60' in diameter. 9" × 7" × 6⅜".

3. Portable Sprinklers

4. Aqua Dial Sprinkler

8. Water Timer

7. Sled Impulse Sprinkler

10. Oscillating Sprinkler

11. Rain Tower

8. **Water Timer:** This water timer is actually a water computer, using solid-state technology to regulate the timing of your watering schedule—and it is far easier to set than the average VCR. Simply choose the coverage you want, from 15 choices that vary from 5 minutes every 2 hours to 120 minutes every week, and then set the dial to the corresponding number.
2½" × 4" × 6½".

9. **Whirling Vane Sprinkler:** A spinning deflector blade, driven by the intense spray of the round nozzle screen, throws water in a perfect circle up to 40' in diameter. Very small and light but stable, this is a good, general-purpose sprinkler. This same type is also available in square and rectangular designs.
5½" × 5⅜" × 3½".

10. **Oscillating Sprinkler:** No summer would be complete without the mesmerizing rhythmic sweep of an oscillating sprinkler on a lazy afternoon. This one features a 5-position adjustment for sweep and a powerful turbine drive, which can be accessed and cleaned if necessary. Aluminum and injection-molded plastic.
19¾" × 8¾" × 4½".

11. **Rain Tower:** A good choice for watering large areas of tall plants, such as those in vegetable gardens, this specialty tool is an impulse sprinkler mounted on a tall, galvanized steel tripod. The bronze sprinkler head waters a full or partial circle that spans a maximum of 80' in diameter. The broad base will not damage newly seeded turf. Height adjusts to 41" or 72".

COMPOSTING

"**S**oil," said the great scientist Hans Jenny, "is a body in nature." It is not an assembly of minerals or a mixture of elements. It is a living entity with musculature and circulation. It breathes, it feeds, and in its various and millennial life, it renews the surface of the earth, making all growth possible.

Compost is the means by which the soil acquires the bulk, fiber, slow-releasing food, trace minerals, and active bacteria cultures to renew itself. Of all garden tasks, composting is the one that makes you feel most connected to the natural world. And nature composts absolutely anything organic.

Home composting is usually modest, but it's still the best, cheapest, and most environmentally responsible way to care for your garden soil. By converting the leavings of all kinds of vegetation and animal manures into rich black humus, compost establishes the ever-renewable basis of healthy, productive garden soil.

> "*Nothing is waste until it's wasted.*"
> —CLARK GREGORY

This concept applies not only to the vegetable garden, but also to flower beds and especially lawns. A fall topdressing with well-finished compost is perhaps the best way to fertilize a small lawn because it feeds the roots of the grass plants and at the same time helps to suppress diseases.

There are at least four important benefits to home composting. First, of course, you recycle and return to the soil all those husks, grounds, stems, clippings, dead leaves, and other remnants that would otherwise go to waste. Dedicated composters do not, in fact, believe that anything can be thrown away.

Second, you dramatically reduce the need for synthetic industrial fertilizers and chemical pesticides. A healthy soil produces happy plants that, experiencing less stress, are not as susceptible to pathogens and pests. Indeed, studies now show that compost-rich soils actively suppress many of the fungi that cause damping-off and other soilborne plant diseases.

Third, you greatly improve the structure of the soil in terms of both its fiber and its circulation. A soil rich in decomposed organic matter is a better conductor of water and air, and makes a better site for the storage of nutritious elements that roots need to absorb. Furthermore, black humus—the end result of the compost process—releases nutrients slowly over the course of the growing season, keeping the growth of your plants even and measured. It also buffers pH, so the soil will be less liable to become either too acid or too alkaline.

Fourth, by using compost, you will create a soil that warms faster in the spring and thus allows you to prepare the garden earlier. The black color of compost absorbs early-season sunlight, and the biological activity of the compost—rich as it is in living and dying worms and microorganisms—generates heat on its own.

HISTORY
OF COMPOSTING

George Washington spoke for every good gardener from Babylonian times to the present when he remarked that a good manager of the land must be "like Midas, one who can convert everything he touches into manure, as the first transmutation towards gold."

Civilization and composting appear to share the same starting point. Every culture known has practiced some form of reclaiming organic materials to return to the soil. Some, like Ibn al Arabi in the eleventh century, went so far as to advocate adding human blood to the mix, along with dungs, lime and mortar, old wool or cotton, wood ash, street sweepings, and almost any other decomposable material.

Indeed, until the end of the nineteenth century, the respect for compost was almost universal. Then came the industrial process of nitrogen fixation from the air, and suddenly it was thought that compost was old-fashioned, outmoded, and doomed to be replaced immediately by man-made fertilizers.

This illusion lasted less than a century. Even in its heyday, the knowledge of compost was still expanding. At the turn of the twentieth

COMPOST IN LITERATURE

There's no doubt that the gardener in the Gospel According to St. Luke is a composter. In one parable, he begs leave to save an unfruitful fig tree by "digging about it and putting on manure."

In Shakespeare's tragedy *Timon of Athens*, the title character pays homage to compost, exclaiming that the earth is "a thief that feeds and breeds by a composture" stolen from organic waste.

Perhaps the greatest literary composter was Walt Whitman, who in *This Compost* remarked that the earth "grows such sweet things out of such corruptions . . . it distills such exquisite winds out of such infused fetor . . . it gives such divine materials to men, and accepts such leavings from them at the last."

century, Sir Albert Howard developed ground rules for the most efficient composting, basing his techniques on what he learned from the traditional practices of the Indian countryside. His "Indore Method," using a three-to-one mixture of plant remains to manure, is still the basis of the modern compost pile.

COMPOST BINS

Good composting involves four simple practices. First, the bin itself must be convenient to the source of the compost ingredients, whether they come from the garden or kitchen, but it must also be well secluded—screened by a hedge, for instance, or hidden by fencing. (The composting process may be beautiful, but the pile itself, mounded up with orange rinds, coffee grounds, and less palatable leavings, is not.)

Second, the compost pile must be maintained at the right size. There must always be sufficient bulk to the pile to keep the digesting microorganisms satisfied with respect to food, air, moisture, and temperature.

Third, the pile must be frequently turned. Sometimes, people build or buy a good container, fill it with the proper amounts of green and brown materials, and then get furious when the process seems too slow or the pile begins to smell. A rank odor in the compost pile is almost always a sign that the heap needs turning. The microbes that do the best job of turning trash to humus are air breathers; if they don't get enough oxygen, they die and their place is taken by anaerobic bacteria, which give off noxious gases in the process of digestion.

The solution is to turn the pile. Perhaps the least popular task in the garden is forking over the compost heap. And over the past decade, a great deal of ingenuity has been exercised to make it easier—by designing both bins that ease the chore and specialized tools to accomplish it.

Fourth, the finished compost should be accessible. It does no good to build and turn the pile if the result is a mixture of fresh, half-done, and fully cooked compost. Planning is needed. One favorite method is to make three adjacent piles, shifting the compost from one bin to the next as it matures. The other choice is to fill each bin and let it rot until the material has fully composted.

In either case, one way to get a little jump on the process is to have

ANATOMY OF A COMPOSTER

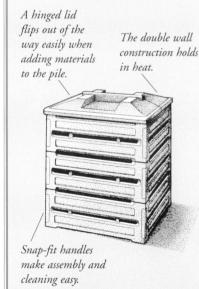

A hinged lid flips out of the way easily when adding materials to the pile.

The double wall construction holds in heat.

Snap-fit handles make assembly and cleaning easy.

a bin that can be opened easily at the bottom. This type of access allows you to remove the more finished and crumblier compost that has sunk to the bottom because it's finer in texture.

Choosing a Compost Bin

If all the different kinds of compost bins invented in the last decade were arranged side by side, the place would look like a playground. True, a few compost bins are just four sturdy walls of metal or wood joined to make an open cube. But there are also closed drums and pyramids, bins with little doors at the bottom, bins made of slats like a wooden fence, bins made of stacking ovals, little boxes full of big red worms, and even a big plastic ball that resembles a space capsule.

All the permutations are meant to meet the four requirements of an ideal compost bin. All the better bins solve the problem of how to remove finished compost from the bottom of the pile while fresh scraps are still working at the top. Additionally, beyond satisfying the four criteria, a good bin will help to make the compost finish faster.

When choosing a bin, look carefully at how it addresses each of these problems.

Using a Compost Bin

Efficient composting is not as simple as leaving a pile of leaves in the sun. Of course, any organic matter will eventually turn to humus; however, to produce a speedy and efficient process that will retain the most nutrients and create the best-textured humus, you will need a bin at least 3' × 3' × 3'.

Properly mixed, a compost pile can yield finished humus in six weeks or less, but only if you mind the size of the pile and its aeration to ensure that it remains continually moist but not sodden. A compost pile must be large enough to generate the internal heat that stimulates microbes to breed and feed, speeding the process of decomposition. This is the reason that home piles are usually in containers, not simply sprawled across the ground. As a general rule, around 25 cubic feet is sufficient. A much smaller bin is possible if you hire the giants of the soil world to mind it. Vermi-composters, which use the enormously enhanced digestive faculties of earthworms, speed the compost process in closed piles scarcely bigger than a bread box.

Bins That Open on One Side: The simplest compost bin to make is one with one side of the cube removable, so that you can get at the whole pile with shovel and fork to turn the compost. The bin can be made with any handy materials, from slats to chicken wire to old construction pallets.

To turn a manageably sized compost pile, simply insert the fork near the base of the pile, pull out a good quantity of degrading compost, and turn it over as you place it on the top of the pile.

Unfortunately, trouble strikes when you try to take finished compost from the bottom of the pile. With the side open, the whole pile takes the opportunity to spill out.

BINS WITH REMOVABLE SLATS: These premade bins represent an effort to solve the problem of getting at the finished compost. One version has a little bottom door that slides open on one face of the cube. This is not a bad idea, but the best compost may be around the other side of the bin's bottom. The vertically slatted composter addresses this problem because in theory any one of the slats can be lifted to get at the best humus. It works fine on level ground, but the slats tend to jam when it's on a slope.

THE BIOSTACK: To date, the best solution to the access problem is the Biostack, which at first blush sounds like a silly idea but is actually an ingenious invention. This composter consists of three rectangular tiers that snap together. When your compost has decomposed to a specified point, you can disassemble the segments, top first; the removed top tier then becomes the foundation of a new pile. Simply take the topmost layer of compost off the first pile and drop it into the new foundation. By the time you reach the third tier of the original stack, you will have both exposed the finest compost and inverted and aerated the entire pile in one continuous and actually not unpleasant operation.

THE CLOSED DRUM: To improve the speed with which finished compost is made, you can simply turn the pile frequently, but this practice is difficult and time-consuming. In closed-system composting, the system itself rotates, working the compost easily. The closed drum is a good solution. Just be sure it's well balanced and easy to agitate. And don't let it get too full.

Stackable composters work by inverting the three tiers of the stack, thereby aerating the pile and allowing access to finished compost.

THE BIO-ORB: The funniest solution to speeding up the composting process is the Bio-Orb, a 3'-diameter black plastic ball that contains up to 13 cubic feet of leaves and other compostable materials. (Because it's closed, this composter can generate the requisite internal heat despite the fact that it's smaller than the recommended size for open composters.) All you have to do to agitate the contents is roll the thing around. Should you be composting on any kind of hill, however, the pile may not be the only thing that gets agitated. It can roll right over your toes or into the neighbors' hedge.

HOMEMADE BINS: For many veteran composters, all the modern inventions are strictly superfluous. The handiest rough-and-ready solution to the compost bin is to nail together four construction pallets or to knit together a strong 3'-high roll of chicken wire.

Neither of these constructions is particularly attractive, however, so some people will either build a simple container from wooden slats, fashion something out of slats and wire, or find another material that is more sightly for a cylindrical pile. One good choice is 50-mil thick black plastic that is filled with a regular pattern of holes. It can be joined together with plastic nuts to form a cylinder about 3' high. Not strong enough for heavy-duty composting, it does fine with leaves, providing you add some light high-nitrogen material to help them along in the decomposition process.

VERMICOMPOSTERS: In an ordinary open compost bin, the active work of breaking down the trash will be done chiefly by microorganisms; worms appear only at the end of the composting process, once the pile has cooled a bit. But if you want fast, rich compost, you can achieve it with vermicomposters, using earthworms that eat and defecate at a much greater rate than any microbe present earlier in the compost process.

But worms won't live on raw leaves. They prefer a diet of good kitchen scraps (but not meat products). A closed worm composter can be placed either right outside the kitchen door—except in freezing weather—or even under the sink. Add scraps as necessary, and regularly sieve out finished compost. The best of these composters are also fitted with a little spigot, so you can draw off rich "compost tea," which is excellent for house plants, without having to open the bin.

SOLVING THE COMPOST EQUATION

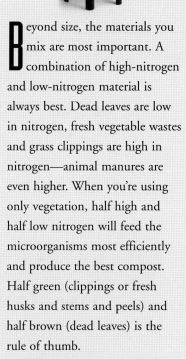

Beyond size, the materials you mix are most important. A combination of high-nitrogen and low-nitrogen material is always best. Dead leaves are low in nitrogen, fresh vegetable wastes and grass clippings are high in nitrogen—animal manures are even higher. When you're using only vegetation, half high and half low nitrogen will feed the microorganisms most efficiently and produce the best compost. Half green (clippings or fresh husks and stems and peels) and half brown (dead leaves) is the rule of thumb.

Where fresh manures are involved, you'll have to experiment. Probably a two- or three-to-one mix in favor of vegetation will be best, because manures are comparatively high in nitrogen. Chicken manure, the "hottest," will make a compost that lets off a warm mist.

Composters

1. Biostack Composter:

Constructed of 60% recycled polyethylene, this heat-conducive plastic compost bin separates into three bottomless parts, making it easy to transfer and aerate compost by stacking and unstacking the components. The hinged lid blocks rain while the side vents encourage air circulation. The whole unit is water-, rot-, and rodent-proof and cleans up with the spray of a hose. 28" × 28" × 34", 13 CUBIC FEET.

2. Bio-Orb Composter:

This uniquely designed compost bin is meant to be rolled every couple of days to easily turn and aerate compost. It is also useful in that it can be rolled over to the debris to be composted. Constructed of 100% recycled polyethylene, it is heat absorbing, UV-stabilized, and resistant to rot, rodents, and rain. 36" DIA. × 30", 13 CUBIC FEET.

3. Oval Plastic Composter:

A small, oval-shaped plastic compost bin that may be preferred as a patio and rooftop composter because it is free-standing, neat, and compact. This 100% recycled polyethylene container with hinged lid retains heat, blocks out rain, and cleans easily. 27" × 17" × 30", 6½ CUBIC FEET.

4. Leaf Composter:

A simple, portable bin designed for breaking down leaves and other bulky debris. Made from 100% post-consumer/post-industrial recycled plastic, this rot-resistant cylinder is actually a single 30" × 118" sheet of perforated 50-mm plastic, fastened at the edges with hand-tightened plastic nuts. Weighs 6 lbs. and rolls into 6" diameter for easy storage. 36" DIA. × 30", 17½ CUBIC FEET.

1. Biostack Composter

2. Bio-Orb Composter

3. Oval Plastic Composter

4. Leaf Composter

5. Wire Bin Leaf Composter

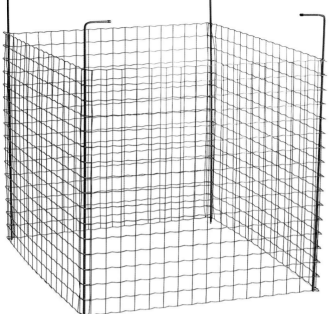

5. Wire Bin Leaf Composter: A variation of the Leaf Composter, this large, no-frills, portable alternative is made from interlocking 2", PVC-coated wire mesh that can be easily assembled anywhere and also folds flat for storage. Good for holding and breaking down large items to be incorporated into a hotter compost pile, this bin weighs 13 lbs. 34" × 34" × 32", 21⅖ CUBIC FEET.

6. Vermi-Composter: High-density polyethylene allows for an odorless, space-efficient composter to be used with live earthworms. A built-in drainage system with tap allows the user to pour out compost tea, while air vents provide much-needed circulation. Light and portable, it can be used indoors or out, in the country or city. This bin sports a hinged lid and interlocking sides. 27" × 17" × 12", 3 CUBIC FEET.

7. Can O' Worms Composter: A larger alternative to the Vermi-Composter, this tiered polyethylene bin stands on four legs and is meant to be used with earthworms. Self-contained, odorless, and easy to use, it may be a bit large for indoor users but ideal for leaving outside the back door. 18½" × 18" ×11", 2¾ CUBIC FEET.

7. Can O' Worms Composter

6. Vermi-Composter

COMPOSTING TOOLS

L et's face it. Turning the compost pile is something that has to be done. No matter how fancy a bin you have, you've got to go out there and tend to its needs. And once it's turned, the temperature has to be monitored so you can judge what stage the process has reached. Finally, if you want to use the fresh humus for a topdressing, the finished compost has to be sieved to remove any undigested bits of twig, bark, or other fragments.

All of these tasks could of course be accomplished with general-purpose tools: a garden fork to turn the pile, a meat thermometer to take the temperature, and a frame fitted with ¼" galvanized hardware cloth to sieve the results. But for efficiency and accuracy, specialized tools do a better job.

TURNING THE PILE

Turning with an ordinary garden fork is just not very satisfying. The middling compost holds nicely on a fork, but the undigested bits of orange rind, eggshell, and celery stalk just fall between the teeth—as, of course, does the well-finished compost. When in frustration you take a shovel to the pile, you find that it goes in a good ways but you can scarcely pull it out.

One thing you can do is get a better fork for the purpose. Traditionally, manure forks were made with more than the standard four tines for precisely this reason—to catch horse droppings instead of allowing them to pass through. Nowadays, a five- or six-tined fork is as likely to be called a "compost fork" as it is a "manure fork," perhaps because the former sounds more savory. It certainly does work well in compost.

ADDING OXYGEN

The fact remains that once you get any fork or shovel deep into a compost heap, the task of pulling it out can seem like a labor of Hercules. The thought of repeating this action several dozen times to turn and aerate the pile is most unpleasant.

Compost aerators are made solely for this purpose. These handy devices consist of a long tube with a 3" folding blade at the end. Push down on the two-handed handle and the blades fold up; pull back and they deploy, raking their way through the heap from a depth of 3' back to the surface again. This tool is far easier to manipulate than any fork.

Once you get any fork or shovel deep into a compost heap, the task of pulling it out can seem like a labor of Hercules.

TAKING THE TEMPERATURE

A good hot pile will steam slightly as it works. And to the practiced composter, this occurrence, along with heat against a finger thrust beneath the surface, may be sufficient to tell what stage the composting process has reached. A new pile should heat gradually from 50°–60°F up to about 113°F—the temperature preferred by the microorganisms that begin decomposition. Once the pile is really cooking, however, a whole second group of bacteria take over. These "thermophilic," or "heat-loving," bacteria work very fast. They thrive in temperatures from 113° to 158°F.

A skilled composter may also be able to tell the temperature by feel. For the rest of us, however, a thermometer is a necessary aid. A good compost thermometer will exactly resemble a meat thermometer except for one thing: the shaft should be at least 20" long so that the sensor measures the temperature in the *middle* of the pile.

SIEVING THE RESULTS

When at last the compost is done, the pile has cooled, and earthworms have begun to inhabit the lower layers, it's time to prepare the newly made humus for the garden. If you plan to till it into the vegetable garden, you can simply apply it directly to the soil surface and let the tiller bury and chop any larger bits that remain in the sweet-smelling black mass.

On the other hand, if you're side-dressing the flower beds or top-dressing the lawn, the effect will be prettier if no shards of sticks or other uncomposted residue remain in the compost. Furthermore, too much undigested material will actually rob nutrients from growing plants, since the bacteria that work to decompose them will take the nitrogen they need from the soil.

To sift out detritus, a sieve or a riddle is your best bet. For small quantities, the beautiful English riddles set in a hoop of willow beech, or elm like large tambourines do a wonderful job. There is also a more elaborate version with legs and a rotary grinder on top—exactly like a food mill, only larger.

But for those of us who use compost in bulk, the best idea is to make a good solid frame at least 2' square, fit it with ¼" mesh, and prop the whole thing securely at a 45° angle over the bare earth. When you want compost, put a tarp beneath the sieve and push shovelsful of compost from the bin through this screen. What comes out the other side will be fine, crumbly, and sweet-smelling enough to serve the garden well.

The beautiful English riddles set in a hoop like large tambourines do a wonderful job.

Composting Tools

1. PLASTIC RIDDLE

2. WOODEN RIDDLE

3. METAL RIDDLE

MESH SCREENS

1. **PLASTIC RIDDLE:** Rustproof, durable, and affordable, this plastic riddle has interchangeable mesh screens (¼" and ⅛") for a variety of sifting tasks. 15¾" DIA. × 3¾".

2. **WOODEN RIDDLE:** A traditional riddle based on English design, this is the best tool for sifting compost and soil, removing rocks, and winnowing seeds or beans. Fashioned from English beech with a ¼" mesh screen. 16" DIA. × 3".

3. **METAL RIDDLE:** Attractive and easy to see in the foliage, this lightweight, sturdy, stainless steel riddle comes with interchangeable screens. 11½" DIA. × 2½".

4. **COMPOST FORK:** This top-quality compost fork features 5 slender, diamond-point tines ideal for sifting, mixing, and separating compost. Solid ash T-handle and wide head allow the user to thrust the fork deep inside the compost pile to turn it without injuring crucial insects and worms. Solid-socket construction with forged carbon steel head. LENGTH 44", WEIGHT 1.5 LBS., HEAD 9¾" × 13½".

5. **AERATOR:** This specialty compost tool is constructed of ¾" galvanized steel tubing with retracting 3½" blades. It is used exclusively to aerate compost. The blades close as the user inserts the rod into the pile, and open when the tool is withdrawn. LENGTH 34", WEIGHT 1.5 LBS.

6. **THERMOMETER:** A 20"-long stainless steel thermometer to penetrate deep into the center of a compost pile for accurate temperature readings. Measures 0°–220°F (plus or minus 1°).

7. **BIOACTIVATOR:** A fully organic medium containing enzyme-producing bacteria to help break down compost.

4. COMPOST FORK

5. AERATOR

6. THERMOMETER

7. BIOACTIVATOR

CHAPTER NINE

LAWN CARE

A decade ago, the big lawn was king. After all, a lawn is the only plant community both tough enough to jump on and soft enough to lie comfortably upon. And when well adapted, it grows very well without heaps of water or pest killers. But today the American lawn is under attack, and hardly anyone sings its praises anymore. For in the wrong surroundings, and tended by the wrong hands, it must guzzle water and chemicals to achieve the greenness and purity of a long-established ideal.

———

There are excellent alternatives to grass. Chamomile and thyme lawns are both fragrant and durable. In the Midwest, wildflower meadows that mimic ancient prairies are replacing the front lawn. In the arid Southwest, native bunchgrasses make a pleasing alternative. In the South, many people are returning to the swept yard, exposing the beautiful native red clay. And the once-despised parterre (patterns of stone and paving that make pictures under shade trees) traditions of southern European immigrants—are being revived.

But if you live where turf grass can thrive without coddling, especially in the eastern United States, growing and maintaining a lawn offers one of gardening's greatest satisfactions. The principal caveat in this endeavor is to avoid vastness. A 30' × 30' lawn is in reality about a million tiny grass plants, so be sure to choose a lawn small enough to care for yourself, without the use of power tools. Lawn care ought to be an invigorating garden chore, not eight hours of drudgery. Planting, fertilizing, mowing, and dethatching—all are operations that a family can manage on its own with fine hand tools.

> *"The grass peeps up and puts forth like small hairs, and finally it is made the sporting greenplot for Ladies and Gentlewomen to recreate their spirits in."*
>
> —*MAISON RUSTIQUE*, 1564

The love of lawns comes from the medieval ideal of the Pleasaunce, a part of the garden where women and men might take their ease on turf seats, listening to the sound of a fountain and enjoying the flowers. Planted with strips of sod brought in from wild meadows and maintained with scythes and tamping tools called beetles, these small grassy areas ultimately led to the immense lawns of the eighteenth-century English countryside.

But only because of the American homeowner did the lawn come to belong to ordinary people. In the late nineteenth-century pattern books that showed middle-class Americans how to create their half-acre of paradise, the draftsmen almost always drew homes with surrounding lawns so that all parts of the architecture could be plainly seen. The eager imitators not only built the houses down to the last little curlicue of scrollwork, but faithfully installed the lawns as well.

Today, with lawns shrinking in size, fine old tools are coming back into general use. The trick is to choose those that not only look the old ones, but work like them as well.

THE LAWN MOWER

Looking rather like a printing press on wheels, the first lawn mower had already been made in 1830 by an Englishman named Edwin Budding. Over the next half-century, dozens and dozens of patents were issued for lawn-cutting machines that resembled everything from paddle-wheel steamers to race cars to Ferris wheels. All that time, the tinker-inventors were trying to come up with a system that would cut cleanly with minimum effort, offer a selection of mowing heights, and ride the terrain without bouncing over holes or scalping tiny hillocks.

By around 1900, the reel mower had been perfected. With the advent of mass production, lawn tools became a must-have overnight sensation and remained so for seven decades. The rotary power mower, which was easier to use but produced a rougher cut, largely replaced the reel mower. Nurserymen vied to create new lawn grass breeds that would survive even in shade. Entomologists struggled to find easier and better ways to kill the numerous pests that gorged themselves on root and blade. An entire industry came into existence almost overnight to accommodate lawn-hungry homeowners.

THE GREEN GRASS OF HOME

Kentucky bluegrass (*Poa pratensis*) isn't from Kentucky; it's originally from Asia Minor and was long naturalized in northern Europe. When it came to New England and Virginia with the English colonists, it quickly spread along rivers and trails into the climates it liked. In fact, it preceded many of the first homesteaders, who were mystified to find grass from the Old Country already awaiting them on their new land.

The Reel Mower

Through it all, the classic reel mower has remained unsurpassed for cutting the lawn. It produces a finer, lovelier cut than the power mower does, and it's by no means onerous to push on lawns kept to a reasonable size. Equally if not more important, it doesn't use gas.

Unlike the power mower, under whose substantial housing spins a single, high-speed rotary blade, the reel mower is made so that gears hidden inside the wheels spin a whorl of between five and eight spiral-shaped blades. Instead of tearing the grass, the reel slices it off between the revolving blades and a fixed blade located at the lower rear of the machine. If your grass is tender a five-blade mower is sufficient; if you tend a lawn planted with a tough variety of grass, however, a mower with six to eight blades is a better option.

When selecting a reel mower, see that the blades are high-carbon steel and the mechanism for adjusting the height of the cut can be adjusted from the T-handle without the use of screwdrivers or other tools. The best models have pneumatic rubber tires that cushion the machine's path on any terrain; their revolving blades are so finely made that they pass within ½,000 of an inch of the cutting blade without making contact, so the machines are almost silent.

Mowing with a reel mower is a study in geometry. You must mow the length of the lawn with the wheel edge slightly overlapping each previously mown strip. When you're done with this lengthwise cut, turn crosswise and mow the lawn again, this time across its width. The result is a very pleasing pattern that leaves the lawn at a uniform height.

Be sure to set the height properly so that the blades do not scalp the grass, revealing the yellow bases of the plants. It's best to keep turf grass at a height of 3". And never cut more than a third of the length of the grass at a time, or use the mower when the lawn is wet.

The wheel edge of a reel mower should slightly overlap each previously cut path of grass. Crosscutting produces a beautiful pattern on the lawn.

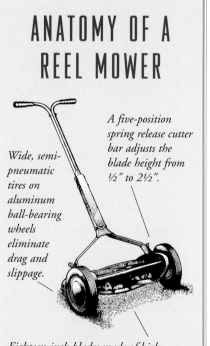

ANATOMY OF A REEL MOWER

Wide, semi-pneumatic tires on aluminum ball-bearing wheels eliminate drag and slippage.

A five-position spring release cutter bar adjusts the blade height from ½" to 2½".

Eighteen-inch blades made of high-carbon steel and tempered for maximum strength constitute the reel.

Lawn Mowers

1. **SILENT-REEL LAWN MOWER:** The best-quality mower available, this finely tuned tool has a hand-honed cutter bar and an independent roller bar that throws grass clippings directly behind the blade. Wide semipneumatic tires surround cast-aluminum wheels for good balance and maneuverability without drag or slippage. Six steel blades, measuring 18", are tempered for durability and cut grass in silence. A five-position, spring-release cutter bar lever adjusts from ½" to 2½" in height. The frame is fashioned from 12-gauge steel coated in rust-resistant enamel. 24" × 14" × 9¼", WEIGHT 40 LBS., HANDLE LENGTH 44".

2. **COMPACT LAWN MOWER:** A smaller version of the Classic Lawn Mower, this agile tool is good for small yards or hard-to-maintain strips of grass, and can be easily stowed away on a wall or in a potting shed. May also be used by kids, with supervision. Constructed of the same high-quality materials, it features 14" blades and 10" wheels. 20" × 14" × 10", WEIGHT 28 LBS., HANDLE LENGTH 27".

1. SILENT-REEL LAWN MOWER

3. CLASSIC LAWN MOWER

2. COMPACT LAWN MOWER

3. **CLASSIC LAWN MOWER:** A good choice for alternative lawns of native grasses, this push mower has five 16" tempered steel blades, 10" treaded rubber tires, cast-iron wheels, and a sturdy steel frame. The cutter bar adjusts from ½" to 1¾" in height. More compact and lighter in weight than the Silent-Reel Lawn Mower. 22" × 13" × 9½", WEIGHT 32 LBS., HANDLE LENGTH 44".

GRASS SHEARS AND EDGERS

Even the best lawn mower can't cut the hairy tufts that hang over the paving like so many unkempt mustaches, nor can it reach places where the lawn butts against a tree or a raised bed. But there is something peculiarly satisfying about using shears and edgers to take care of these untidy growths with a few simple motions.

THE SHEARS

You can make the finest cut of all by getting down on your knees with a pair of hand grass shears. If you're willing, you can choose the wonderful old sheep-shearing shears that some now call "singing shears." Because they're made of a single piece of steel that is bent, hammered, tempered, and honed, they do in fact ring like a tuning fork. Though they close easily, there is just enough resistance to make using them good exercise for the wrist.

Top-handled grass shears that have blades perpendicular to the upright spring-loaded handle are simple to use when you have a lot of cutting to do and your hands are not in good shape. Unfortunately, you must trade the mechanical advantage for slightly less precision in the cut. A standing model that you operate by closing a long handle with both hands is excellent for those who can't bend or sit.

THE EDGERS

Long-handled edgers put less strain on your back if their blades are sharp enough so you don't have to reach down constantly to extract impacted lumps of soil and grass.

The rotating edger, with a cutting blade like a ninja's throwing star, is a particularly good example of a tool that is utterly useless when poorly constructed. It needs truly sharp (and sharpenable) blades as well as a solid, steady-turning rotor ball. When it's working properly, this is the most convenient tool for making clean, straight edges along the drive.

An even finer edge can be achieved with an edging knife, a tool that resembles a pogo stick fitted with a half-moon cutting blade instead of a spring. When you stand on the steel steps built into the blade, it sinks down to make a perfectly straight cut—ideal for edging along a driveway or formal terrace.

ANATOMY OF BORDER SHEARS

Padded rubber grips protect the hands and make the tool easier to wield.

Xylan-coated blades resist rust and dulling.

The tubular fiberglass handles are lightweight.

Lawn Shears

1. **LONG-HANDLED GRASS SHEARS:** This tool trims lawns and grasses with precision, allowing the user to easily cut around rocks and trees without bending down. Horizontal blades are xylan coated to resist rust. The sturdy fiberglass handles are 38" long, with padded rubber grips to absorb impact.
LENGTH 39",
WEIGHT 4.1 LBS.,
BLADE LENGTH 8".

2. **SHEEP-SHEARING SHEARS:** Based on the design of implements used for shearing sheep, these tempered metal shears are a great all-purpose option that works especially well on grass. Simple to use, the blades are ground and polished and will keep a sharp edge when maintained with a sharpening stone. They make a singing sound with each snip.
LENGTH 12½",
WEIGHT 0.65 LBS.,
BLADE LENGTH 6".

3. **HAND SHEARS:** This modern rendition of the traditional grass Scissors Shears features the most up-to-date craftsmanship to ensure seasons of use. Nickel-chromium-plated steel blades are adjustable, allowing the user to cut at three angles with a simple gesture, which reduces tension on the wrist. The blades are squeezed by pressing the padded polypropylene levers vertically—another wrist-saving motion. Rust-resistant spring mechanism keeps levers and blades moving.
LENGTH 13⅜",
WEIGHT 0.7 LBS.,
BLADE LENGTH 5½".

4. **SCISSORS SHEARS:** This tool offers a more traditional choice in professional-quality grass shears. Featuring an action preferred by some gardeners, the blades come together by pressing horizontally on the padded handles, like a hand pruner, while shock-absorbing bumpers cushion each cut. Heavy-duty chromium-steel alloy blades are drop forged and heat treated to withstand years of rugged use. Slightly heavier than the vertical grip Hand Shears.
LENGTH 12",
WEIGHT 1 LB.,
BLADE LENGTH 6".

5. **LONG-HANDLED BORDER SHEARS:** A vertical-action specialty tool specifically designed for trimming lawn and border edges without stooping. Xylan-coated, antirust steel blades have a self-adjusting bolt. The 36" handles have padded rubber grips to absorb impact. LENGTH 36",
WEIGHT 4 LBS.,
BLADE LENGTH 7½".

2. SHEEP-SHEARING SHEARS

5. LONG-HANDLED BORDER SHEARS

1. LONG-HANDLED GRASS SHEARS

3. HAND SHEARS

4. SCISSORS SHEARS

Rakes and Edgers

1. THATCHING RAKE:
This rake has quarter-moon-shaped steel tines that are spaced apart by semicircular "buttons" and bolted together by a single long bolt. An adjustable bracket changes the pitch of the blade to give optimum angle. Hardwood handle. LENGTH 65", WEIGHT 4.25 LBS., HEAD 14½".

2. LONG-HANDLED EDGER:
A long, straight handle gives stand-up comfort and extra leverage in this example of a semicircular edging knife. Features a stamped steel head with rolled tread, riveted to a cast steel socket. LENGTH 53½", WEIGHT 3.5 LBS., BLADE 8⅞".

3. ENGLISH EDGING KNIFE:
This T-handled lawn edger makes straight, even edges and borders. Solid forged steel head and socket with ash T-grip handle. LENGTH 32", WEIGHT 3 LBS., BLADE 8".

4. SOD TAMPER:
This useful tamper comprises a heavy, square, bolstered iron plate on the end of a medium-length hardwood handle. For small sodding jobs or back fills, this tool ensures that there are no large air pockets and that filling is complete. LENGTH 43", WEIGHT 8.5 LBS., HEAD 7¾" SQUARE.

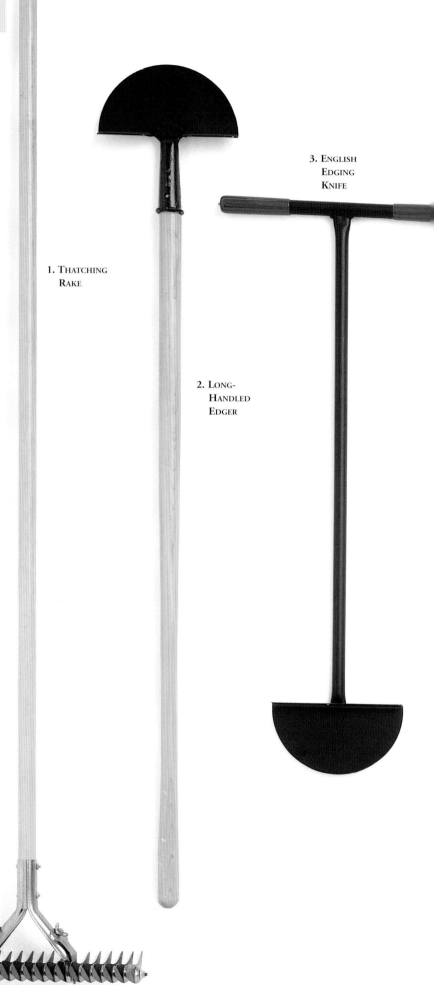

1. THATCHING RAKE

2. LONG-HANDLED EDGER

3. ENGLISH EDGING KNIFE

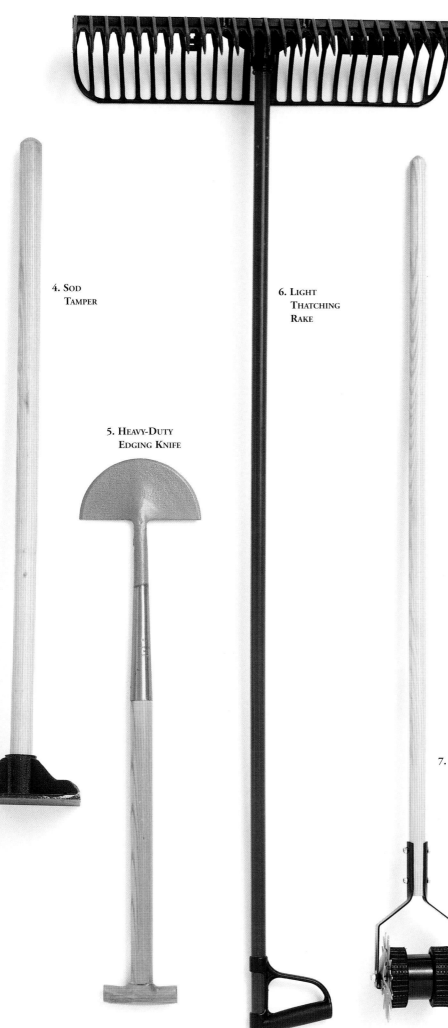

**4. Sod
Tamper**

**5. Heavy-Duty
Edging Knife**

**6. Light
Thatching
Rake**

**7. Rotating
Edger**

5. **Heavy-Duty
Edging Knife:**
This American-made,
all-steel edger is a
heavy-duty model
and should last for
years. Like the other
edging knives, it
must be filed very
sharp to be most
effective. Welded
carbon steel con-
struction.
LENGTH 36½",
WEIGHT 4 LBS.,
BLADE 8½".

6. **Light
Thatching Rake:**
This specialized lawn
rake is made entirely
of tough plastic. The
long handle allows
the tines to just skim
along the surface of
the soil, gathering
leaves and other
materials. The tines
are sharp enough for
light thatching
duties. LENGTH 65",
WEIGHT 3 LBS.,
HEAD 24".

7. **Rotating
Edger:** This rubber-
tired edger is a little
bit like a push rotary
mower, but it cuts at
right angles. It is
used for trimming
the grass at the edges
of lawns—and not
for cutting sod, as
are the other edgers.
LENGTH 56",
WEIGHT 4 LBS.,
CUTTER 5¾" DIA.

STARTING THE LAWN

Putting in a new lawn is like painting a room. There's a lot more to it than meets the eye. You can simply slap on two coats of paint or broadcast a couple of pounds of lawn seed, but in neither case are the results a pleasure to behold.

What makes a lawn desirable is its smooth, thick appearance. Once the ground has been broken with the spade and leveled with the rake, you must spread the seed and the organic fertilizer evenly across the area to be planted. The next step is to assure that each of the tiny seeds makes firm contact with the soil. For a good-size lawn, the best way to achieve this is to force the seeds gently into the broken soil with a roller. A smaller lawn may require only a light raking to press the seeds into the soil surface.

If you're using a roller but can't make it fit into little corners or irregularities along the edge of the planting area, a heavy metal tamper will accomplish the same end.

SPREADERS

Spreaders are effective for seeding or fertilizing a large area. They can disperse materials unevenly, however, so be sure to monitor for adequate coverage.

All spreaders descend from the oval bags and buckets that sowers once carried tied to their waist. The rhythm of sowing was hypnotic: scoop, throw right, scoop, throw left. The secret was to make a spout out of your fingers so the seed spewed out in measured amounts, feathering in the air and falling gently and evenly. A good sower was a valuable person; a poor one, however, left many spots blank or bald.

Mechanical broadcast spreaders imitate the old method, but with much greater reliability. Handheld models employ a crank that causes a disk to whirl as seeds fall onto it at a measured rate from the hopper. Wheeled versions have a greater seed capacity, and a gear attached to the wheels spins the disk, so you're guaranteed an even flow of seeds regardless of how quickly you roll the spreader. In both cases, the seed is flung with great force to the right and to the left. In the most powerful models, the seed may travel as far as 10'.

Whether you choose a handheld or a wheeled spreader, pay particular attention to the mechanism that opens and closes the hopper. This is the part most prone to breakage. Though there is nothing wrong with a plastic spreader, many of the cheaper ones have problems after one or two uses with the hopper mechanism and pot-metal axles. Either look for something sturdy or rent the tool from the local tool shop.

THE BROADCAST SPREADER: When you want to cover a lot of ground fast, a broadcast spreader is your best choice. When you're seeding or fertilizing a large area that grades into woodland, for example, this spreader works very well. Just be certain that there's enough overlap to assure an even coverage, since broadcast spreaders will leave much more material near the machine than at the extremity of the throw arc.

THE DROP SPREADER: Unlike the broadcast spreader, this type of spreader is a precision tool. Dropping measured amounts of seed or fertilizer only on a traveling rectangular path the width of its wheelbase, the drop spreader will give you absolutely even distribution as long as the ground is mostly smooth and level. When you're working on a lawn with relatively straight edges, it's by far the better choice since it will not waste seed or fertilizer by flinging it onto the driveway or patio or into the pool.

ROLLERS

Rollers are fun tools to use. In fact, they're scaled-up versions of the roller toys that toddlers enjoy so much. Made of steel or plastic, rollers may weigh a mere 20–30 lbs. empty, but when filled with water they can weigh in at nearly 300 lbs. Once the fertilizer and the seed are laid down, the roller's job is to make sure the seed is in firm contact with the soil. The only caution to rolling is: don't get one started down a hill.

Once, rollers were commonplace tools for preparing a lawn. On the average lawn today, however, you may need to do no more than lightly rake the seed into the soil. Unless you're putting in a large greensward, there's not too much need for this tool. But a lawn that has developed frost heaves over the winter or little depressions can effectively be smoothed over with a good heavy roller.

TAMPERS

A tamper is a roller minus all the fun. There is no pleasurable action to this heavy square-bottom tool. You just lift and drop it, again and again, until that bumpy corner or depression in the grass is finally leveled or filled.

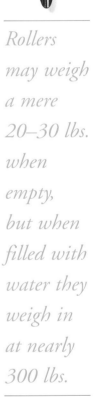

Rollers may weigh a mere 20–30 lbs. when empty, but when filled with water they weigh in at nearly 300 lbs.

Spreaders

1. HOPPER SPREADER

2. DROP SPREADER

3. HAND SPREADER

1. **HOPPER SPREADER:** A self-cleaning, rustproof broadcast spreader for large areas. This standard model features a 50-lb. capacity, a square polypropylene hopper for wide dispersal of seed or fertilizer, a painted steel frame, and a slide shut-off mechanism. Pneumatic tires are mounted to plastic wheels connected by a steel axle. 19¾" × 14¾" × 19½", WEIGHT 12 LBS., HANDLE LENGTH 33".

2. **DROP SPREADER:** Designed to be either pushed or pulled, this large spreader drops fertilizer in wide, even rows. The steel frame is attached to a corrosion-resistant, enamel-coated steel hopper with pneumatic tires and stainless steel axle. The tool has a 24" spreading width with an adjustable flow-control mechanism. 33" × 16" × 15½", WEIGHT 3.1 LBS., HANDLE LENGTH 35".

3. **HAND SPREADER:** A step up from the traditional coffee can, this widely available, plastic hand spreader may be enough for seeding the average-size suburban lawn. A 1-lb. capacity hopper evenly sifts and disperses seed when the bottom hinge is open. 8" × 7" × 8½". WEIGHT 1.4 LBS.

4. LAWN ROLLER:
A tool that has been used since the 18th century for preparing sod for lawn seed, the roller has changed little since its invention. This superior version features a high-grade 24-gallon steel drum filled with water, attached to a sturdy steel handle. Coated enamel surface resists dings and dents and is easily washed off with a hose. May be pushed or pulled. WEIGHT EMPTY 41 LBS., WEIGHT FULL 241 LBS., DRUM 18" DIA.

Lawn Roller

4. LAWN ROLLER

AERATING THE LAWN

To remain healthy, an established lawn needs to get plenty of air and water to its roots. The constant trampling to which lawns are prey both compacts their soil and helps build up a strangling layer of dead lawn stalks called thatch. The latter condition is best taken care of with a sharp thatching rake (see page 228), but hard and compact soils call for aeration to assure that air and water nourish the grass. Of all the soil types, clay is most vulnerable to compaction, but even sandy soils can benefit from one or more of the tools specifically designed for aerating lawns.

Originally used in England to maintain athletic fields, the spiking fork is a short-tined garden fork that serves to aerate the lawn and help water get to grass roots through thick turf. The fork should be inserted into the turf at a 45° angle to a depth of 4–6 inches, and a slight pressure exerted on the handle before the tool is withdrawn. The procedure is then repeated at 1' distances across the breadth of the lawn.

On small lawns, people frequently use a two- or four-tined soil corer. These are tools that you push into the soil to create tunnels between the surface and compacted layers below. The plugs of soil are automatically ejected. For a brief time, your lawn will resemble a green pegboard, but within two weeks it will have responded with thicker, healthier growth.

If you're fond of your roller, you'll be happy to know that some rollers have an aerator attachment—an armor of spikes that creates numerous holes for air and water to enter as the roller is pushed across the lawn.

Other aerators are ideal for impatient gardeners or for those who live in areas affected by drought. These two-tined tools can be attached to the garden hose; when you push the tines into the soil, you turn on the water and open an air-intake valve. The roots are instantly fed.

FOR THE SMALLEST LAWNS

An effective aerating device can be fashioned merely by driving some spikes into the bottom of a board. Just set the board on the grass and walk on it to press the spikes into the soil. Repeat the procedure until you've covered the area that needs attention.

An even simpler method is to walk back and forth across the lawn wearing a pair of wooden sandals with spikes on the bottom.

Aerators

1. **LAWN AERATOR:** This is an essential tool for maintaining a healthy green lawn. A lightweight, tubular steel handle connects to two hollow prongs that pierce the sod 5" deep to allow air and water beneath the roots of choked grass. A hose easily attaches to the comfortable T-handle, padded with rubber grips. This tool may be used in conjunction with the Lawn Corer. LENGTH 36", WEIGHT 3.9 LBS.

2. **SPIKING FORK:** An alternative to the standard Lawn Aerator, this is a top-quality tool. Four thick, square tines are driven into the sod 4½" deep to open up soil to oxygen without damaging beneficial organisms. Forged carbon steel head is attached to an ash handle by solid-socket contruction. More of an investment, but this tool will last a lifetime with proper care. LENGTH: 32½", WEIGHT 3.3 LBS.

3. **LAWN CORER:** This specialty tool helps restore and maintain lawns by creating circulation tunnels between the surface and the layers of compacted soil beneath the grass. Tubular steel handle and foot plate are connected to two tubes with hardened steel edges. When the plate is stepped on, the tubes cut out two sod cores ½" in diameter and 4" deep, creating a passageway for moisture, air, and nutrients. LENGTH 36", WEIGHT 2.6 LBS.

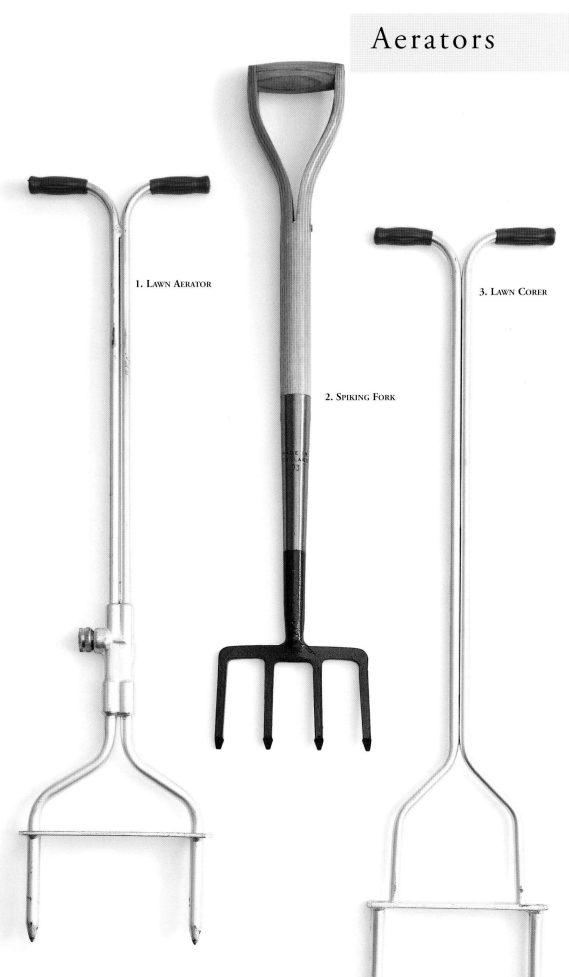

1. LAWN AERATOR

2. SPIKING FORK

3. LAWN CORER

CHAPTER TEN

HOLDING
AND
HAULING

Hardly anything in the garden remains there. Seeds turn straightway into plants. Flowers and fruits come in to the table. Fallen leaves, cut grass, and dried stems go to the compost pile. Stones are exported to the perimeter, and firewood is burned indoors. Not even the soil remains the same; at every moment it's gaining or losing humus, leaching away minerals, and receiving new influxes from erosion, rain, and timely fertilizing.

The garden is a vast living system in which human beings play a crucial part. It's our responsibility to bring into the garden what it cannot supply for itself, and to take away what we require in harvest as well as what has no business there. So containers and carriers—tarps, baskets, pails, bags, seed scoops, bins, wheelbarrows, and garden carts—are essential gardening tools.

They are also the most often neglected. How many times have you tried to convert a Christmas gift basket into a tool basket only to watch it exfoliate all over the shed? Or a painter's dropcloth into a garden tarp, only to discover that the ladder dragged a hole through it last month? When was the last time you struggled with an old wheelbarrow whose tire was flat, wondering why it wouldn't work properly? As simple as carrying and carting tasks may be, they still benefit greatly from appropriately designed and durable tools.

Many excellent traditional models of baskets, bins, and seed scoops are available today. Each different tool carries its own lore and symbolism, adding to its value in the gardener's eye. In fact, the making of baskets is likely the most ancient industrial art of all—predating even the ax.

So much depends
upon

a red wheel
barrow

glazed with rain
water

beside the white
chickens

—WILLIAM CARLOS WILLIAMS

HISTORY OF THE HOLDERS AND HAULERS

There is a horizon of time beyond which we know little, when men and women lived lightly on the earth, building with soft materials that have disappeared with the passage of time. We do not even know exactly when basketry began—or indeed whether it preceded or followed pottery. Different variations are found in every culture. By 4000 B.C., the use of baskets was widespread. In Central America, people developed a whole method of harvesting by beating fruit and nut trees and collecting the falling fruits in baskets. At the same time in Fayum, farmers wove large baskets and buried them in the sand to make granaries that preserved harvested wheat.

So important was basket making to Native Americans that it often formed a central part of their culture. The Potowatomi, for example, told a story that the Moon was where an old woman was weaving a basket; when she finished her task, according to the legend, the world would end.

The quest for the best carrying and storing tools has resulted in baskets and bins that seem as right and natural to the user as gardening itself. A trug like those English countrywomen carried into their cutting gardens two hundred years ago is particularly stunning. Or a deep galvanized bin, corrugated gently like a melon rind, harks back to the woven bins found in Egypt that are more than five thousand years old.

Garden carts, on the other hand, are comparatively recent inventions. The Romans didn't have them. To transport heavy materials like soil or compost, they used ox-drawn carts or slaves who toted large baskets. In other early cultures, a kind of sledge was used, drawn laboriously on runners by draft animals.

The wheelbarrow originated in China around A.D. 200. It's emergence revolutionized the carting of stones, soil, and other heavy elements involved in gardening. With its simple pair of levers attached to a large wheel, it allowed a farmer to transport twice what he had carried before by hand. The Chinese were so happy with this invention that they named it "gliding horse" or "wooden ox," and sometimes even powered it with sails.

The modern garden cart improves on the design of the wheelbarrow. With two wheels, it's not only an efficient lever, but also a stable tool that's less likely to empty itself whimsically when you strike a hidden stone.

So important was basket making to Native Americans that it often formed a central part of their culture.

CHOOSING THE RIGHT
CONTAINERS AND CARRIERS

Every garden container should be as capacious as possible. Nobody wants to take more trips to the mulch pile, the compost heap, or the cutting garden than are absolutely necessary. And nobody likes a bin that won't take a whole big sack of fertilizer, coir, or sand.

Containers must also be easy to fill and to empty. A lid that is hard to remove or a tip bag that keeps folding itself shut is more nuisance than help in the garden. A container that is too heavy to tip without straining your back can be dangerous.

Carrying and containing tools must be slow to spill. However much you want it to empty with ease, the container should not start leaking material on the way to its final destination. A cheap, flat seed scoop will spill seed from the moment it's filled, while a carefully made model will hold the grains securely in place until you tip the handle. A flat wheelbarrow tray piled high with soil looks more like a spreader when you try to push it across the lawn.

Lastly, these tools must be as mobile as possible. This is true for bins (you want them to be light enough to push about in the potting shed even when they're partly filled), but it's much more important for carriers and carts. These must be well balanced for the size of the load they will bear, and light enough so you don't have to strain just to put them in motion.

FRUIT AND
VEGETABLE BASKETS

For every use and in every culture, there are different traditional weaves or styles of baskets, each matched to its preferred materials: the broad, cross-plaited rushes of the typical American picnic basket; the lovely, dovetailed ash slats of the classic Sussex trug; the woven wicker of a wide weeding basket or a deep, strong basket used for laundry; and the upright oak slats of a bushel basket, bound with hoops of willow.

Of course, plastic bags and sacks are everywhere today, and for lightness and strength they're hard to match. But many gardeners don't like their greasy sides to rest against freshly picked fruit and complain about their tendency to close when you want them opened and to open when you want them closed. Though plastic has replaced basketry in the supermarket and even at the fruit stand, there is no reason for it to do so in the garden. After all, the garden is the place where the best economy is what yields most delight.

TRUGS: A flower-picking basket should be shallow like a tray because you don't want to make layers that will crush the blooms. This is why the trug is such a fine tool. It's stable and easy to carry, and it cradles flowers gently. The classic English trug has wooden slats, but in the northeastern United States you can find similar baskets made of plaited rush and equally appropriate for just-picked flowers.

FRUIT-PICKER'S BASKETS: For harvesting apples, pears, plums, or cherries, a handled picker's basket is best: It will not hold more than you can carry, and you can't fill it to a point where fruit on the bottom is subject to bruising. You can still find the old-style picker's baskets that are bound to the harvester's waist, but those with sturdy handles are better for the home harvest. Solid wooden baskets are indeed beautiful (you're more likely to find these in antique shops rather than in garden catalogs), but just as functional are the canvas baskets that can be cleaned, folded, and put away in a corner of the shed until next year's harvest.

WIRE BASKETS: Your basket collection ought to include one that you leave by the kitchen door or at the gate to the vegetable garden. It's the one that you take with you daily when you go out to harvest salad vegetables for the evening meal or a few small squashes or peppers to sauté. This is the one more suited to wire construction than to natural fibers. Slender wire gives the best combination of strength and openness, so the freshly picked produce can breathe. It can also be wetted down repeatedly without rotting, which is a decided advantage since you'll want to wash all your vegetables before you bring them inside. Some people keep a tub of water for this purpose, simply dipping the basket into the tub and shaking it vigorously.

HARVEST BASKETS: Harvest baskets are wonderful for containing the bulky and durable fruits and root vegetables that you harvest all at once. With slats bound in with wooden hoops, bushel baskets are strong enough to hold a hundred pounds of apples or potatoes; moreover, because space is left between the slats, air is allowed to circulate freely, helping to prevent rot by keeping the fruit dry.

After all, the garden is the place where the best economy is what yields most delight.

Harvest Containers

2. BUSHEL BASKETS

3. APPLE BUCKET

1. GALVANIZED BUCKET

7. SAP BUCKET

8. FRENCH MARKET WIRE BASKET

9. BERRY BASKET

1. **GALVANIZED BUCKET:** Reminiscent of the old milk pails used by dairy farmers for centuries, this galvanized steel bucket is a sturdy, multipurpose container.

2. **BUSHEL BASKETS:** This traditional, lightweight wooden basket is used by farmers and seen at produce stands.

3. **APPLE BUCKET:** Primarily used during apple harvests, this wooden bucket is extremely durable.

4. **WIRE BUCKET:** This steel wire bucket was popularized in the Victorian period. It can hold produce or be lined with moss and used to pot up bulbs.

5. **POTAGER BASKET:** Woven of willow, this basket is incredibly strong. Its durability makes it an asset for hauling all types of produce.

6. **FRUIT PICKER'S BASKET:** Intended for use in light harvesting, this utilitarian canvas basket can be held on the arm to transport fruit and vegetables from the garden or orchard.

7. **SAP BUCKET:** Usually constructed of zinc or tin, these buckets are hung on maple trees to collect sap.

8. **FRENCH MARKET WIRE BASKET:** Used to gather fresh vegetables. The open steel wire construction allows for rinsing produce while it's still in the basket.

5. POTAGER BASKET

4. WIRE BUCKET

10. WOODEN TOMATO BASKET

6. FRUIT PICKER'S BASKET

11. ENGLISH TRUG

9. **BERRY BASKET:** Made of various lightweight woods, this basket holds nearly the perfect amount of berries required to make a tart.

10. **WOODEN TOMATO BASKET:** This shallow wooden basket with sturdy handle holds ripe tomatoes without bruising them.

11. **ENGLISH TRUG:** This wooden garden workhorse will last for years and carry everything from vegetables, cut flowers, and herb bouquets to gardener's gloves, hats, and hand tools.

LEAF, WEED, AND SEED CARRIERS

These are the everyday containers that help you relieve the garden and lawn of their debris. For want of good ones, an otherwise pleasant afternoon outdoors can turn sour and difficult. You will need to choose versions scaled to the task at hand and check the workmanship, often the difference between good and poor carriers.

THE ENGLISH TIP BAG

"Tip" is a British colloquialism that refers to any kind of trash or leavings. Hence, the "tip" bag is large, but not so large that you can't lift it when it's full of leaves and sticks. It's made of very tough woven polypropylene, so stick ends will not destroy the bag, and the handles are securely stitched to the body. Best of all, it's made with a bendable hoop of plastic sewn into the top rim, so it stays open while you're trying to fill it.

Store the tip bag in the shed when it's not in use; sunlight can hasten its eventual wear-and-tear.

THE TARP

For carrying away leaves, there is nothing quite like a burlap or canvas tarp. Each fall begins with the great tarp search that in the end yields one of torn plastic, one of paint-stained ripped canvas, and one that is a perfectly intact 1' × 8' length. Better, though, is to reserve a large square tarp for garden hauling only. A 6' or 8' square with firmly hemmed edges will hold as many leaves as you wish to carry. Store this tarp in the garden shed, and don't let it be used for other tasks. Be sure to dry it thoroughly before folding it away for the winter, or come spring you'll have a mildew garden growing in your tarp.

Plastic tarps will do for occasional use, but few are durable. Sticks tear them, and they're hard to grasp at the ends. Polypropylene tarps, made of the same plastic as tip bags, are much more durable, but they always seem to creak or crackle when you fold them and they never seem to remain neatly in place.

THE WEEDING BASKET

There is a basket meant to contain literally anything you might pick in the garden. Witness the weeding basket, Gertrude Jekyll's favorite. Broad, shallow, and oval in shape, it's a perfect container to drag by its edge behind you across the bed. It's also big enough that when you throw a plucked dandelion its way, you're unlikely to miss.

For carrying away leaves, there is nothing quite like a burlap or canvas tarp.

SEED SCOOPS

To transfer fertilizer, seed, lime, or finished compost from a large bin into a carrying bucket, a seed scoop is the best tool. You might simply use a coffee can or your bare hands, but a well-made scoop is such a simple triumph of physics that you may insist upon having one.

There are only two parts to the implement: the handle and the scoop itself. The former should be generous, both long and thick enough to grasp and hold without strain; the latter must look like a tiny barrel that has been cut away at the front and on top. The bottom leading edge should be tapered to make it easier to penetrate piles, and the shape should roll the contents together in the scoop so they hold firm until you spill them out intentionally.

BUCKETS AND BINS

All good carrying tools are thoughtfully constructed. Galvanized buckets and bins shine with the steel that gives them strength. For large metal bins that contain your mixing materials in the potting shed, the body of the receptacle should be lightly corrugated to add holding strength. (A bin full of builder's sand must withstand a couple hundred pounds of pressure.) Smaller galvanized buckets, like old well buckets, have such clean lines that you don't mind the fact that they're heavier than the plastic ones; the weight actually comes in handy when you need to hold a tippy load of stakes or sunflowers.

Galvanized containers have three weak points: the handles, the bottom, and the seams. The handles and the bottom need to be firmly attached to the body of the bucket. The seams where the sheet of bucket metal is joined into a hoop must be smooth and flawlessly galvanized to ward off rust.

Plastic, of course, is impervious to rust and lighter than metal. Some of the finest plastic buckets are nearly as strong as steel. A rubber bucket is not only rustproof but can be thoroughly cleaned in hot or cold water. It's a good bucket for small quantities of seed or soil amendments. A stainless steel bucket is as much a joy to behold as it is to hold. The finest milking pails are made of stainless steel, which can be perfectly cleaned after every use and never succumbs to rust.

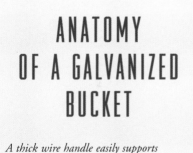

ANATOMY OF A GALVANIZED BUCKET

A thick wire handle easily supports any load.

Double-locked side seams and bottom seam make for a watertight construction.

The heavy-gauge, hot-dipped galvanized steel provides unusual durability.

Carriers

1. SEED SCOOP

1. **SEED SCOOP:** A generous-size scoop is the most efficient way to fill pots with soil or to broadcast seeds and soil amendments over a large area. This particular all-purpose scoop is also handy for transferring bulk material from one vessel to the next. Manufactured in Sweden of stainless steel, it has a thick handle, thin edges, and tumble-home sides to prevent spillage. 4" × 12".

2. **WEEDING BASKET:** A picturesque classic originating in turn-of-the-century England, this wide oval container is highly recommended for collecting weeds or flowers. Woven from lightweight, natural wicker, the flexible basket may be carried in one arm, leaving the other free to weed, pick, or prune. Long lasting and easy to store, it makes weeding more efficient (and almost pleasurable) by providing a large target in which to toss weeds. A broad, low base means the basket won't tip over, while the shallow, spacious tray holds an abundance of vegetation. 24" × 32" × 3".

3. **GALVANIZED BUSHEL BASKETS:** These waterproof and rust-resistant containers have large mouths and drop handles that make them useful for loading and toting a bushel or more of material or liquid. Lighter and more durable than wood or fiber containers, they may be stored outdoors or used in the garden shed as storage receptacles themselves. Fluted sides make an elegant presentation while stiffening the basket tub. Large basket holds 1½ bushels; small basket holds 1 bushel.

3. GALVANIZED BUSHEL BASKETS

2. WEEDING BASKET

4. **TIP BAG:** A British design, these reusable, broad-based, woven polypropylene bags with a plastic band sewn into the rim stand up tall wherever they are placed, eliminating the need to have a helper hold the mouth open when filling with leaves or other refuse. More durable and environmentally responsible than plastic garbage bags, the sturdy handles make these bags easy to carry when full. 30" DIA. × 18".

5. **GALVANIZED BUCKETS:** The less-glamorous cousins of Galvanized Bushel Baskets. Fashioned from galvanized steel in an array of sizes, they are durable and multipurpose. They may aid in transferring liquid or bulk items from one place to another, in scooping, in collecting, or in storing a variety of loose landscaping material. High rims keep liquid from sloshing over the side when carried. These buckets will last for many more years than the plastic variety and are an indispensable and inexpensive tool. Smaller pails have one long handle; larger varieties feature two side handles. Buckets pictured here hold 2 and 4 gallons.

7. COMPOST PAIL

4. TIP BAG

6. **MESH TARP:** This lightweight, polyester-mesh tarp folds up easily and quickly and may be used for a variety of tough hauling tasks, from transferring a lawn's worth of leaves to the compost pile to moving soil amendments from one place to another. Reusable, rot resistant, and easier to maneuver than burlap. 120" × 120".

7. **COMPOST PAIL:** A small, convenient receptacle for collecting kitchen scraps to be toted to the compost heap. Attractive enough to be kept indoors, the lightweight, rust-resistant bucket is fashioned from galvanized steel. Tight-fitting lid keeps odors locked inside and fruit flies out. Longer lasting than plastic and washes up clean. The long handle makes it easy to carry. Holds 1 gallon. 8½" DIA. × 9¾".

5. GALVANIZED BUCKETS

6. MESH TARP

THE HAULERS

The two main hauling devices used by gardeners are the wheel-barrow and the garden cart, each with its individual benefits and drawbacks. In fact, to ask which is the better device is tantamount to comparing a shovel with a spade. The wheelbarrow, like the shovel, is more versatile and therefore ultimately more useful. Yet the cart, like the spade, is beautifully adapted for its purposes. The serious gardener would do well to have both.

THE WHEELBARROW

Operated on the lever principle, with the wheel as the fulcrum, the handles taking the effort, and the load lying in between, the wheel-barrow is a wonder of appropriate technology. Fill it with dirt, sand, stones, compost, or whatever loose matter you want to transport to or from the garden. Lift it by the handles, and the weight presses toward the wheel in front so that the very mass helps you to move the load without undue effort.

The glory of the wheelbarrow, after all, is that you can run it through an area only slightly wider than its tire, then pour out the load to the front, to either side, or in a fan that covers the whole forward area. But that isn't the only purpose it serves. You can also mix soil in its tray—or even concrete if the need should arise. And it makes a sturdy vehicle for carrying your heavy tools back and forth, as well as pots or flats of plants.

The more awkward its load, however, the more difficult the wheelbarrow is to use. Stones, for example, seem eager to throw their weight to one side or the other, unbalancing the single wheel and send-ing the whole thing over on its side.

To keep this from happening, choose a wheelbarrow with a broad pneumatic tire—at least 4" thick. The wider tire lends greater stabil-ity. Also, be sure that the undercarriage is strong and well reinforced. The unreinforced tubular steel in a cheap wheelbarrow is not of suffi-cient gauge to resist the bending forces of a shifting load. A small bow in the support mechanism can be enough to send you and the wheel-barrow sprawling on your side.

A quality wheelbarrow—sometimes called a contractor's wheel-barrow—has a large, deep, high-capacity tray (up to 5 cubic feet). Usually, the tray is made of steel coated with a baked epoxy finish. Both the undercarriage and handles may be made of steel, or it may be a combination of steel undercarriage and ash handles.

The glory of the wheel-barrow is that you can run it through an area only slightly wider than its tire.

The shallow-tray models hold a little more than half the volume of a high-capacity contractor's model. These wheelbarrows will serve for the occasional earth-moving job, but they're not the best tool for anyone with a sizable garden.

THE GARDEN CART

A garden cart has two definite advantages over the wheelbarrow. First, because it has two wheels, it can't tip over as easily as the latter, and it actively helps the gardener balance the load. As a consequence, you can carry much more in a single load—up to 400 lbs. Second, the bottom is flat, allowing you to stack materials like firewood, or potted plants, or bales of hay or lumber.

The garden cart's wheels are typically modeled on bicycle wheels. They have a diameter of better than 2', with pneumatic tires, spokes, and an axle with ball bearings. The very best are like the wheels of a harness driver's sulky: free turning, shock absorbing, and light.

While a cart is excellent where stability is required, it's not so good for loose soil, sand, or other amendments because it's harder to empty. Some models are designed with a front gate that lifts to facilitate pouring; others consist of sturdy plastic bins with lips for pouring their contents. In either case, however, the double wheels make it more difficult to spill materials while directing the flow exactly where you want it to go.

The latest generation of garden carts approach the flexibility of the wheelbarrow. They contain a large removable plastic tray—often made of recycled plastics—that not only is well balanced for pouring but can also be set forward on its lip so that material can be raked, swept, or shoveled right into it. Once removed from the chassis, the tray becomes a mixing trough for fertilizers or even a water bath to clean the day's fresh vegetables.

THE PRESIDENT'S CART

While the two-wheeled garden cart has only recently come into its own, it was the garden vehicle preferred by Thomas Jefferson two centuries ago. Jeffereson reported in his *Farm Book* that a laborer using his prototype "two-wheel barrow" could cart material twice as fast as the same man with a one-wheel barrow.

Haulers

1. **CONTRACTOR'S WHEELBARROW:** A construction-grade wheelbarrow, intended for the heaviest of use. The handles and frame are made from welded steel tubing and the deep, seamless galvanized tub is bolted down for secure and stable load carrying. The 4-ply pneumatic tires ensure easy rolling.
25" × 57½" × 22¼".

2. **KID'S WHEELBARROW:** A miniature wheelbarrow, sized and balanced to keep young gardeners from two to six years old involved. Powder-coated steel basin has curled edges for safety and rolls smoothly on a one-piece plastic tire. With hardwood handles.
16" × 31" × 11".

3. **GALVY WHEELBARROW:** The best version of a ubiquitous design—the classic tripod wheelbarrow. Less-sturdy plastic or enameled-metal versions tend to rust, bend, and break over time, but this solid, galvanized steel model is as strong as a wheelbarrow can be without sacrificing maneuverability. Especially useful for dumping, as the contents of the bin empty fully when tipped, this wheelbarrow correctly balances a sizable load, even when hauling around corners or up and down hills.
24" × 50½" × 24".

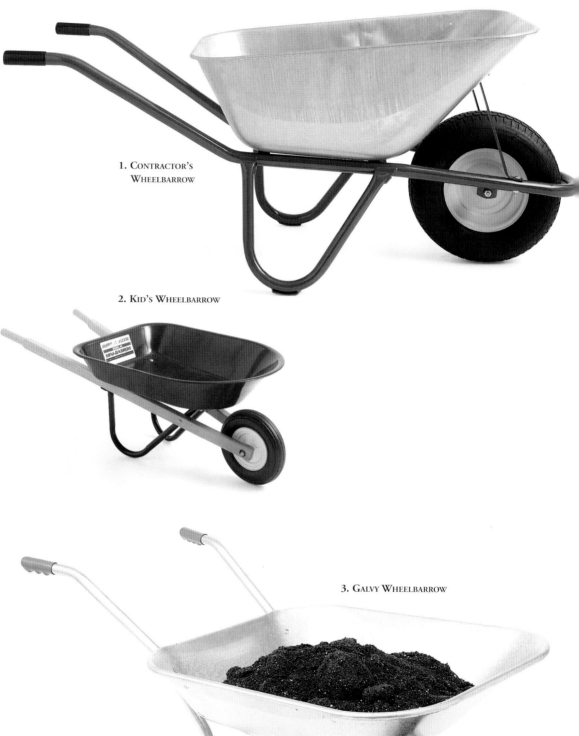

1. CONTRACTOR'S WHEELBARROW

2. KID'S WHEELBARROW

3. GALVY WHEELBARROW

4. **ALL-TERRAIN BIG RED WAGON:** A workhorse on wheels, this ultra-sturdy wagon hauls adult-size loads with ease. With non-tip, twin-axle steering, extra-wide pneumatic tires, steel chassis, and an American hickory bed. Removable side railings 8¼" high.
20" × 39½" × 26".

5. **GARDEN CART:** This cart is the best, but higher priced, option for anyone who needs to haul large, heavy loads (ranging from soil to sheets of plywood) over long but flat distances. When the load is evenly balanced over the two front tires, the weight is moved off the user's arms and is carried by the cart. This makes any load up to 500 pounds easy to push or, more importantly, pull along. In addition, the weight does not have to be balanced side to side, as it does with a standard wheelbarrow. The cart has two pneumatic tires, a steel axle, and ball-bearing wheels that measure 26" in diameter. Constructed of 5-ply, exterior-grade ½" plywood, with a heavy-duty galvanized steel frame and trim, it should last a lifetime with proper use. The front door opens to facilitate loading and unloading while the handle adjusts to the user's height. The cart's flat bottom may also be used as a portable potting surface.
31" × 47" × 16".

4. ALL-TERRAIN BIG RED WAGON

5. GARDEN CART

CHAPTER ELEVEN

RAKING AND
SWEEPING

No matter where you go, people understand what it is to rake and sweep. The tools are so universal that you could pass them from hand to hand through the whole human family without a word of explanation. Whether you're raking clods out of the vegetable garden, sweeping the path, or picking up autumn leaves, you participate in the steady, rhythmic, repetitive task of humanizing the earth. The process says of your yard and garden that here lives a human being whose love of nature is tempered with a love of order.

Raking and sweeping are practices common to all cultures. In a Japanese temple garden, you can watch the sand being raked into swirling patterns. Dirt yards in Georgia are swept clear of dust, leaving the red earth clean and smooth. Fields in Yorkshire are raked over, breaking the clods, making them finer, leveling the ground, and fitting it to receive seed. In Amiens, they sweep the gravel path with a broom of twigs; you can hear a steady *wshhh-wshhh* sound while the afternoon wanes. And on an October morning in Vermont, they rake up the yellow, red, and purple sugar maple leaves that lie lightly on the lawn.

The rake evolved chiefly as an instrument of harvest. In Roman times, a rake might be made with an ash or willow handle, an oak head, and iron or wooden teeth screwed into the head. (This construction made it easy to replace broken teeth.) The ends of the teeth were kept blunt so that the rake would not damage roots or get caught in the stubble.

Another kind of rake, made with longer and slightly recurved teeth, was used by the harvesters for gathering the sheaves and tying them into a bundle. Also used in harvesting was a rake that featured

> *Here by the baring bough*
> *Raking up leaves,*
> *Often I ponder how*
> *Springtime deceives—*
>
> —THOMAS HARDY

closely spaced, recurved teeth to glean stubble for any grain that might have been left.

Finally, around the end of the eighteenth century, there came the drag rake, ancestor of the bowhead rake. Iron A-frame side supports stabilized the head on the handle, turning the rake into an instrument tough enough not only to gather straw, but also to rake and move soil and gravel.

The rake reached its greatest glory in England just before the introduction of mechanized agriculture. Reapers would range over the hay field with their scythes, cutting down the tall stalks. Behind them came rakers, wielding great rakes as large as 4' across, with long flexible willow handles and tough ash tines. The rakes would sweep the hay into windrows, where men would throw it high into the air with forks. Rake again, fork again—the process was repeated over and over until the hay was dry enough to bind into sheaves. At the end of it all, the rakers would move over the field one more time, clearing stray straw and smoothing the surface in preparation for the next year's crop.

THE GARDEN RAKE

Push it, pull it, flip it, and slide the flat edge back and forth over the land. A garden rake is a sculptor's tool. With it, you can take a bumpy or uneven landscape full of peaks, valleys, and big dark clods, and convert it into a fine-textured level bed for vegetables, flowers, or a new lawn.

Look carefully at a rake's construction before you buy it. The best rake heads are forged—without welds—from a single piece of high-carbon steel. The only parts that should be inserted later are the teeth themselves, and only those on flathead rakes. This construction sounds crazy, but if the rake loses one of its teeth, you can easily replace it. On most cheaper rakes, a lost tooth means a gap-toothed rake forever.

There are two basic types of garden rake. Each has its own advantage. On a flathead rake, the head is attached—almost always with a tang and fer-rule—directly to the shaft. The bowhead rake, a descendant of the eighteenth-century drag rake, likewise has its head affixed with tang and ferrule, but the teeth are forged in a metal bow so the head is more stable on the shaft and the tool operates with a slight spring action.

ANATOMY OF A GARDEN RAKE

The smooth ash hardwood handle is a pleasure to grip.

The heavy guage, hot-dipped galvanized steel provides unusual durability.

The spiked steel teeth are inserted through the bridge for added longevity.

THE FLATHEAD RAKE: The flathead rake is best for preparing and leveling a bed and breaking down clods to a fine tilth. Used on its back, the rake drags without hanging up over the soil surface, making a smooth level track. (The bowhead, on the other hand, is the better tool when you have to rake out rocks, pebbles, and other impediments before preparing the bed.)

THE BOWHEAD RAKE: The bowhead is very useful in preparing a wide vegetable garden. Its extra lateral strength makes it invaluable in more difficult or stonier soils. Its average width, 14"–15" is perfect for wide rows. To mark out the row, all you need to do is set a straight line in the garden and draw the rake along the line until you get the desired length. Later, when the row is thick with seedlings, drawing the rake lightly over the row will effectively thin them to the ideal density.

THE GRADING RAKE: The big, wide rakes that you see in the hands of landscapers are called leveling, contractor's, or grading rakes. These rakes serve best for leveling large stretches of ground for a new lawn or driveway. Because they're so wide (the width of typically twice an ordinary rake), they're best made of wood or aluminum, not steel. They should be reinforced with angle braces or willow hoops where the head attaches to the shaft. The teeth are always replaceable and made of wood, nylon, or aluminum. A particularly nice version has wavy aluminum teeth that do a very good job of picking up every large pebble in their path.

THE THATCHING RAKE: This tough metal rake (see pages 228–229) looks more like a device for punishment than for raking. The thatching rake has numerous sharp tines, like so many short knives, that penetrate the sod, digging up the matted thatch that keeps your lawn from growing vigorously.

LAWN AND LEAF RAKES

L awn and leaf rakes are the tools of autumn. Because they can both sweep and drag, they are at least half broom; in fact, when they were first introduced in the nineteenth century, they were called "leaf brooms." At any given moment on a fall weekend, several million Americans can be found leaning on a rake, surveying what they have accomplished and gauging what is left to do. To older people, the "whooshing" sound of the leaf rake is associated intimately with the often lingering smell of burning leaves. To those of us born in more enlightened times, the rake's sound goes with the smell of the compost heap.

The garden rake can be used on the push or pull stroke. The pull stroke is effective for clearing the soil of debris. Flip the head on the push stroke to smooth the soil.

Lawn and leaf rakes may be made of spring-steel, plastic, or bamboo. There are two different patterns. Steel and bamboo rakes are usually fashioned in a slightly arched fan shape. These rakes are used like a sweeping broom, lifting and pushing leaves and debris in a single motion. Plastic lawn rakes have a wide, flat, "boxy" A-frame shape; pulled like a garden hoe, they tend to pick up more debris quickly. Almost all rakes are made in a variety of widths. According to your needs—raking a broad lawn or a narrow swath among the azaleas—you can select one that fits the task. For close-in work, there are hand rakes that can be fitted to a long handle should you be disinclined to bend over.

The plastic and steel models require little maintenance. The bamboo rake can dry out during a winter indoors, so it's best to wash the bamboo head in soapy water at the outset of a season. The tines will never break and you can use the rake the way people have delighted in using it for years: wearing down the tines a little at a time until at last you must buy a new one.

Raking is such a common international pastime that each year inventors create dozens of new models. Most are more clever than they are effective, but a few innovations have stuck because they represent a real advance over the plain old rake.

The Springbok Rake: A Springbok rake (also known as an English steel rake) draws its tines back into a sturdy, broad metal frame. The head is shaped less like a fan and more like your hand. And the pattern provides unusually strong pulling power. The rake is favored not only for removing leaves, but also for aerating lawns and removing light moss and thatch.

The Wizard Rake: A wizard rake has a broad frame, with short, stiff rubber tines. It looks like a rake that has gone bald, but it's remarkably effective. The rubber tines make a clean sweep on the lawn, driveways, and paths. Furthermore, because the short tines remain on the surface, they will not damage shallow-rooted plants.

Raking is such a common international pastime that each year inventors create dozens of new models.

Garden Rakes

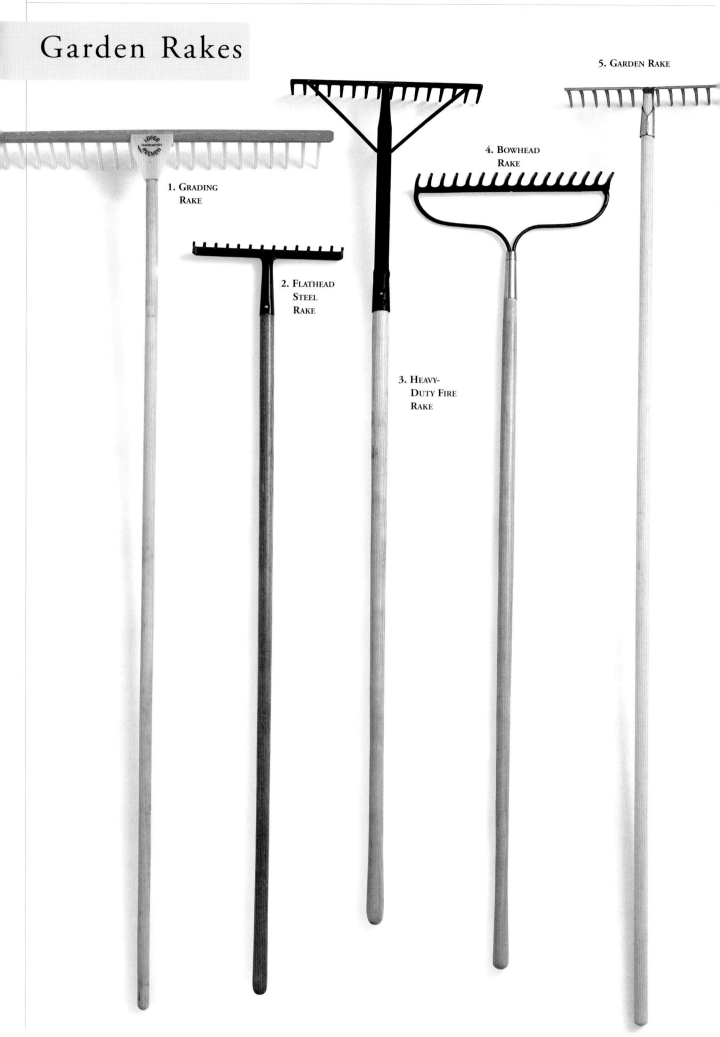

5. GARDEN RAKE

1. GRADING RAKE

2. FLATHEAD STEEL RAKE

4. BOWHEAD RAKE

3. HEAVY-DUTY FIRE RAKE

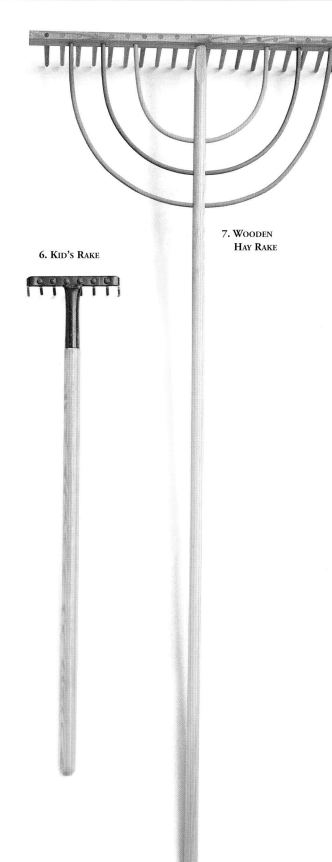

6. KID'S RAKE

7. WOODEN HAY RAKE

1. **GRADING RAKE:** This wide grading rake is a useful tool for spreading and leveling topsoil, smoothing seedbeds, and raking grass clippings and leaves. It features a solid ash handle connected to a broad head with 24 molded-nylon tines. The short, blunt tines gently grade soil without digging into the surface, and the long handle eliminates bending. Light weight means the user can sculpt a bed without straining. LENGTH 72", WEIGHT 2.3 LBS., HEAD 31".

2. **FLATHEAD STEEL RAKE:** This tough drag rake with short, straight steel tines is widely used as a general-purpose garden rake. Suitable for many landscaping tasks, it is ideal for preparing a seedbed—the tines gently rake the topsoil, and the flat back levels the soil over the planted seeds. Solid-socket construction secures the forged steel head to the hardwood handle and is reinforced with a single screw. The 14 tines are bolstered at the base for added strength. LENGTH 61½", WEIGHT 2.7 LBS., HEAD 13".

3. **HEAVY-DUTY FIRE RAKE:** This sturdy, top-quality rake is diagonally braced on either side by steel arms. The extra-long handle and 16" tang, combined with the forged steel head, make it ideal for heavy-duty garden tasks such as tending backyard fires, raking up rocky soil, and grading landscape. LENGTH 70", WEIGHT 5.1 LBS., HEAD 16".

4. **BOWHEAD RAKE:** Another good example of a durable, all-purpose steel garden rake. The bow-shaped supports and tang-and-ferrule joint lend a slightly springy, flexible action to this rake, preferred by many users. Somewhat less sturdy than rakes with diagonal bracing, the Bowhead Rake may be used for the same functions, but some users may find it more comfortable when performing lighter grading, leveling, and garden tasks. One-piece forged steel head with slightly curved tines scrape over topsoil with minimum disturbance. Hardwood handle. LENGTH 65½", WEIGHT 3.7 LBS., HEAD 16½".

5. **GARDEN RAKE:** A light, elegant garden rake, this tool features a zinc-plated steel head with 14 closely set tines that are slightly curved. A minimal steel-collar joint attaches to the polished ash handle, eliminating extra bulk. Garden rakes usually have 14, 15, or 16 tines. LENGTH 73½", WEIGHT 2 LBS., HEAD 13¼".

6. **KID'S RAKE:** An ideal way to get kids to help out with the raking, this junior-size garden rake features 8 bolstered teeth made from enameled steel. The edges are blunt, to minimize injury when raking over small feet, and the polished ash handle won't blister little hands. Solid-socket construction ensures that kids will grow out of the tool before it wears out. Also useful as a lightweight patio or border rake. LENGTH 37½", WEIGHT 2 LBS., HEAD 7".

7. **WOODEN HAY RAKE:** An essential tool for lawn grooming, this lightweight wood-and-aluminum rake is the descendant of the original hay rake used for centuries on farms. The wooden head and closely set wooden tines grab grass clippings, leaves, and thatch from growing plants while the three wooden braces add a pleasing, springy tension to each stroke. All 28 of the tines are replaceable. LENGTH 60", WEIGHT 1.9 LBS., HEAD 27".

Lawn and Leaf Rakes

1. **METAL-TINE RAKE:** This style of fan-shaped lawn rake is widely available in garden supply stores and combines the close-set, flat, flexible tines of the bamboo rake with the durability of metal. A better choice than most metal fan rakes, this example has a stress-distribution bar that prevents tines from twisting or breaking when pressed on. Enamel-coated metal head resists rust. LENGTH 54", WEIGHT 2.5 LBS., HEAD 23½".

2. **SPRINGBOK JR. RAKE:** A narrower version of the spring-steel Springbok Rake, this tool features the same versatility and control but is designed for use in small areas, especially around new plantings, under shrubs, and in hard-to-reach corners. Eight wire teeth will not bend or break over time. LENGTH 48", WEIGHT 2 LBS., HEAD 7¾".

3. **WIZARD RAKE:** A specialty rake of English design, the Wizard Rake collects leaf litter and debris from lawns, soil, and pavement. Thirty-three rubber prongs noiselessly pass over a surface without disturbing shallow root sys-

tems. The wide head covers a large amount of ground in one stroke. Prongs are durable and easy to clean. LENGTH 58", WEIGHT 2.7 LBS., HEAD 20".

4. **BAMBOO RAKE:** A traditional rake used throughout Asia, Europe, and the United States. The tines are set tightly to collect debris, yet they are light and springy to enable the user to rake over uneven or stubby ground. A steel reinforcement bar maintains even tension when pressed down. Bamboo rakes are not appropriate for heavy-duty work or for raking on concrete or pavement. Tines will dry out without consistent use, but may be rehydrated after a long storage by soaking in warm water. With proper care, a bamboo rake will withstand seasons of use. LENGTH 60", WEIGHT 1.4 LBS., HEAD 16".

1. **METAL-TINE RAKE**

2. **SPRINGBOK JR. RAKE**

3. **WIZARD RAKE**

4. **BAMBOO RAKE**

5. SPRINGBOK RAKE

7. HAND RAKE

6. MERLIN RAKE

8. PLASTIC FAN RAKE

5. SPRINGBOK RAKE: The most common form of lawn rake, this spring-steel rake features round, flexible prongs that aerate grass and remove thatch, all the while collecting debris. Solid steel base and reinforcement bar maintain tension on the tines and resist bending. Lightweight wooden handle. LENGTH 56", WEIGHT 2.7 LBS., HEAD 13".

6. MERLIN RAKE: A smaller version of the Wizard Rake, this specialty tool features short, flexible rubber prongs that glide over grass, concrete, and paving without disturbing sensitive, shallow-rooted plants or new grass shoots. The rubber is easy to clean. The smaller head is appropriate for raking around individual plants or amid borders and beds. LENGTH 58", WEIGHT 2.2 LBS., HEAD 9¾".

7. HAND RAKE: A small hand rake is a recommended addition to a basic tool collection. Ideal for raking up debris around individual plants, small beds, or other hard-to-reach areas, this long-lasting enamel-coated steel rake nestles in the palm of the hand and gently gathers leaves without disturbing shallow roots. LENGTH 16", WEIGHT 0.5 LB., HEAD 5".

8. PLASTIC FAN RAKE: A widely available version of the standard fan-shaped lawn rake, this polypropylene version withstands heat and moisture without bending or rusting. Extremely lightweight and versatile, the close-set teeth will clean up leaf litter and clippings, while the solid triangle of plastic helps when lifting or carrying piles of material to the compost heap. Plastic tines have a stiffer action that may be preferred by some. LENGTH 63", WEIGHT 1.7 LBS., HEAD 12".

THE BROOM

T he knowledge of sweeping is likely as old as human settlement. Cro-Magnon people used flexible "fingers" of brushwood to push refuse out of the cave. The very same "fingers"—formalized somewhat by binding sheaves of broomcorn or by crafting wooden tines—have been used for similar purposes ever since.

The tools known as brooms were named for the broom plant, a small wild shrub with butterfly-shaped yellow flowers that belongs to the pea family. (It's interesting to note that the English royal house of Plantagenet got its name from this plant after the dynasty's founder, father of Henry II, took to wearing a sprig of broom—*Planta genista*—in his hair.) The broom plant should not be confused with broomcorn, a kind of sorghum also grown to produce straw for brooms.

The besom broom, a version of an ancient tool, uses heather branches for sweeping. Even if you prefer to use a standard push broom, however, there is no reason to purchase one with artificial bristles. Broomcorn bristles may wear slightly faster than synthetic ones, but they wear at precisely the angle you sweep, which makes them slightly better at picking up.

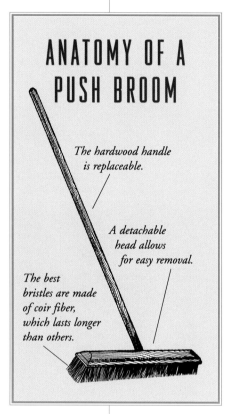

ANATOMY OF A PUSH BROOM

The hardwood handle is replaceable.

A detachable head allows for easy removal.

The best bristles are made of coir fiber, which lasts longer than others.

Brooms are available with bristles of different densities and stiffnesses. The softer, denser ones pick up the smallest litter but may leave behind larger detritus. The stiffer bristles can hold larger debris not only because they don't bend as easily as slender bristles, but also because they spring back with greater force. Choose a softer broom for the patio and other areas near the house. A stiffer one does best in the driveway and street.

Brooms

1. **HEAVY-DUTY PUSH BROOM:** An oversize push broom geared for very coarse sweeping. Blue plastic bristles will withstand years of vigorous outdoor use. A 60" hardwood handle attaches to the 3"-wide hardwood block head by a steel connector and brace.
LENGTH 62",
WEIGHT 5.9 LBS.,
HEAD 24".

2. **STANDARD PUSH BROOM:** This essential implement can be found in any hardware or garden supply store and is useful throughout the garden, garage, and grounds. Detachable hardwood handle screws into a replaceable hardwood head. Bristles are available in a wide variety of materials, depending on the job. This particular example is made with natural coir bristles. Unbeatable for general sweeping, including patios, decks, and paths.
LENGTH 65½",
WEIGHT 2.9 LBS.,
HEAD 18".

3. **BESOM:** The besom is a broom made of twigs. It is likely that the first besom was used long ago when a farmer simply picked a branch from a nearby hedge and used it to sweep up. Ideally suited to outdoor use, this particular version is English and is fashioned from heather twigs bound by vine and metal strapping. The hardwood handle is easier on the palms than the original tree limb, but just as convenient for dusting away cobwebs, moss, and leaf debris.
LENGTH 59",
WEIGHT 2.5 LBS.,
HEAD 14".

3. BESOM

1. HEAVY-DUTY PUSH BROOM

2. STANDARD PUSH BROOM

CHAPTER TWELVE

CLOTHING

AND

PROTECTION

A measure of the difference between garden clothes and ordinary clothes is that "accessories" come first in the garden. First and foremost are the shoes and gloves through which the gardener comes into contact with the living earth. These items create a standard of utility, safety, and beauty by which all others—hats, shirts, pants, skirts, and jackets—are judged. The clothes that a gardener wears are tools, and they have all the attributes of good tools. They are supple, adaptable, durable, comfortable, and readily cleaned.

Wherever people have gardened—except in those cultures where little clothing is ever worn—standard gardening attire has consisted of a short tunic, shift, or shirt, and a pair of loose-fitting breeches. Throughout the medieval world, while a variety of robes and layered patterns served the nobles, the typical farmer's clothing consisted of baggy trousers and a tough pullover tunic held together with a belt. Old woodcuts from tenth-century China and thirteenth-century Europe reveal that the farming class dressed almost alike in clothes that covered the whole body for protection yet were light and loose enough to allow freedom of movement.

The tasks never varied and neither did the clothes. The modern version of the medieval loose-fitting duo began with shirts and jeans, modeled on traditional sailor's attire. The seaman cut his pants out of old sail canvas: a tough cotton cloth that had withstood the gales of the "Roaring Forties," where the wind comes straight around the world, never touching land and making swells a quarter-mile long and a hundred feet deep. Tough and heavy, this same cloth was used for fire hoses and

> "*John had Great Big Waterproof Boots on; John had a Great Big Waterproof Hat; John had a Great Big Waterproof Mackintosh— And that (Said John) Is That.*"
>
> —A.A. MILNE

covering Conestoga wagons, and sailors knew that it was strong enough almost to turn away a knife. The pattern was made plain and ample enough to keep the canvas from biting a man's skin or pinching at the elbows, waist, and knees.

In fact, it was from sailors that Levi Strauss learned how to make the first denim pants. Though he soon switched to a thick-yarned twill, whose blue warp and white filler threads give "blue jeans" their shiny blue sheen, he began the company with canvas he bought from ships disgorging their Gold Rush passengers in San Francisco in 1849. To strengthen the cloth at the highest stress points around the pockets, Strauss used actual brass rivets and reinforced every major sewn joint with bar tacking, running the needle and thread repeatedly back and forth along the stressed section.

Footwear was the only component of gardener's attire that differed noticeably from culture to culture. Where it was cold, boots prevailed. In warmer, rainier lands, wet feet were no problem as long as they didn't get muddy. The Japanese geta, or wooden sandal, elevated the feet a few inches above the mire. The Dutch wooden shoe and its common descendant, the garden clog, served the same purpose.

Footwear was the only component of gardener's attire that differed noticeably from culture to culture.

BOOTS AND SHOES

Nowhere is there more variety of opinion among experienced gardeners than in the choice of footwear for the garden. Part of the preference depends on tradition. English gardeners swear by their slender knee-high wellies, made of lined rubber; indeed, anyone who works in mud in a climate that is not too hot and muggy appreciates how well wellies fit and protect the feet from wetness. But others would not think of coating their feet in something so restrictive, opting instead for an open clog that protects the tender part of the foot yet slides on and off without excessive effort. There are also the all-American Paul Bunyan gardening types who would not be caught dead in anything less sturdy than a pair of steel-toed, ankle-high Redwing boots.

Out of all this strident opinion, there is indeed a proper choice for each gardener, and it should depend on use rather than tradition. To this end, the following factors need to be taken into account: 1) How heavy is your work and how manicured is your garden? 2) How often do you put on and take off your shoes? 3) How hot or cold is your climate? 4) How wet is your climate? Each successive question should narrow your choice until you arrive at the foot covering that's right for you.

*The plea-
sure of
wellies is
that they
fit snugly
because
they draw
tight to
the calf at
the top
without
binding.*

WELLINGTONS AND GARDENER'S BOOTS: Heavy-duty garden boots are hard to lace up and take off several times each day. A better choice for doing heavy-duty, muddy work in a large garden are wellies or other gardener's rubber boots. The soles are reinforced so that you can jump on the spade's tread without bruising your feet. There is a good heel to the boot, so that it will be less liable than sneakers or other flat-soled shoes to slip in the mud. And the absence of a tread pattern in the soles means fewer muddy footprints to be wiped away.

The pleasure of wellies is that they fit snugly because they draw tight to the calf at the top without binding; indeed, you can wade right into a bog without getting your feet wet. In a warmer climate, however, you may prefer a boot about half as high and open at the top to improve air circulation. You have to watch your depth, though, if you pass the boot top in the bog water—you can actually feel as if you're sinking.

LEATHER BOOTS: A gardener who works in woodlands as well as on the lawn and in the vegetable patch will need a different shoe from that of the flower gardener. Lace-up leather boots, with pronounced heels and Vibram-type soles, are best for those who will spend a lot of their time in the rough end of the property. These boots keep out ticks and are impervious to the ends of sharp twigs, barbed wire, and similar hazards. Moreover, the soles are thick enough to keep your feet from getting bruised when you stumble over rocks.

Steel toes are not needed in the garden, except by those who do a great deal of cutting. If you're the manager of the family woodlot, however, they may indeed be the right choice for you.

GARDEN CLOGS: Perhaps the most convenient footwear ever invented for gardening is the garden clog. While this shoe won't do for heavy-duty work and is liable to be sucked down into a swamp without a trace, it's hard to beat for durability and usefulness among the vegetables or flowers. Good clogs are better than sneakers, because their heels keep them from slipping. They are also very easy to put on and take off frequently during the day. (In fact, gardeners may do best to select closed-back rather than open-back models because the latter are *too* easy to get on and off.) They are cleaned effectively and quickly with any garden hose, are almost as cool as going barefoot, and come with liners for increased comfort.

Footwear

1. **WELLINGTONS:** The preeminent choice in water- and mud-proof footwear, these are the classic British Wellingtons. Almost every garden supply store has some rendition of this rubber boot, but the best have a fabric lining, reinforced stress points, and ankle and arch supports. This example also features cleated bottoms, buckled straps, and over-the-calf height.

2. **GARDENER'S BOOTS:** A lower-cut version of the traditional Wellingtons, these boots boast the same quality construction: crack-resistant rubber, fabric lining, and a steel shank that reinforces the boot. In addition, they also feature an extra-strength pad under the instep to help the user when digging.

3. **CLOGS:** Brightly colored plastic clogs kick on and off for fast trips through inclement weather—and won't get lost in foliage. Easy to clean with the hose, they are a simple alternative to more elaborate footwear, but not suited to heavy-duty work.

4. **FRENCH RAIN SHOES:** Originally manufactured for French farmers, these rain shoes are fashioned from easy-to-clean, waterproof PVC rubber. The welted soles give good traction in mud and rain. This shoe style may be preferred by many wearers in the warmer months, as over-the-calf boots can get hot.

1. WELLINGTONS

2. GARDENER'S BOOTS

3. CLOGS

4. FRENCH RAIN SHOES

GLOVES

In the Middle Ages, gardeners didn't wear gloves. Knights did. They wore them to defend their hands, wrists, and arms from a glancing blade and from the chafing of their own armor. Almost always, they wore long gauntlets, and they prized a leather that would withstand terrible punishment yet remain supple and firm so they had fingertip control of their weapon.

The gardener's enemy is armed with nothing more than thorns, or whippy canes, or long taproots, but the gloves that are worn today for protection must still virtually blend with the hands inside them. Gardeners want their hands to feel as much as possible the way they would without gloves, but they also need to guard against pricks and pokes.

ANATOMY OF GARDEN GLOVES

All finger seams are turned out to prevent blisters.

Goatskin will not stiffen after getting wet.

A 4" split-cowhide cuff gives extra protection from branches and thorns.

CHOOSING A PAIR OF GLOVES

Some gardeners spend a lifetime looking for just the right gloves. One pair might be supple enough, but they wear out in a season; another is tough enough to resist rose thorns but almost impossible to close into a fist. And if they finally find a pair of gloves that are both tough and flexible, it turns out that the material hardens on contact with water.

The truth is that no single pair of gloves is suitable for all tasks. Heavy nitrile or a similar rubber-like synthetic is best when you're working in brambles, but a hard day of digging calls for leather gloves. Cloth gloves (either with leather palms or with plastic dots or lines) are less durable than either of the above, but they're light, supremely flexible, and not harmed by water.

USING GLOVES

Treat your gloves as you would your own hands, and they will serve you well. Keep them clean, and should they stiffen up after wetting, work them gradually back to suppleness. At the end of a long day's work, don't leave your gloves stuffed into your jeans or a windbreaker pocket; instead, lay them out in a warm place where they'll be ready for tomorrow.

SURGICAL GLOVES: The least restrictive of gloves—favored by the gardener who needs to go harvest a bouquet or a few tomatoes without getting dirty—are surgical gloves similar to those used by doctors. These gloves are reasonably priced, very supple, and capable of transmitting some of the fine sensations of touch. Regrettably, the smallest rose thorn will destroy them.

CANVAS GLOVES: Canvas gloves are almost as reasonably priced as surgical gloves, and a well-fitting pair is adequate for almost any garden task. The canvas gloves that are made with plastic dots attached to the palm come in handy when you have to grasp a wet tool handle. The trouble with canvas is that it soaks up water readily, so these gloves can be most unpleasant to wear on a cold wet day in spring or fall. Even so, they won't become stiff when wet.

LEATHER GLOVES: If you garden at all seriously, a pair of leather gloves is worth the investment. But what kind of leather is best? All leather gloves feel comfortable when they're worn wet, and all leathers will stiffen to some extent as they dry. No matter what kind of leather you choose, never dry the gloves on a radiator, in front of the fire, or by means of any other direct-heat source. If possible, let them dry naturally until they are merely damp, then put them on again to fit them snugly to your hand.

GO WITH THE GRAIN

TOP GRAIN: The smooth top layer of the hide. (The term has nothing to do with quality.)

SPLIT OR REVERSE GRAIN: The layer of hide that is exposed when a thick hide is split into two or more thinner layers, or the inner side of the hide. It has a rough texture.

A well-made glove of any kind of leather will protect you to some extent from rose or hawthorn pricks, but it may take a second layer of cowhide in the palm to make the gloves relatively thornproof. In any case, the seams of the glove should be double- or triple-stitched. They should also be turned outward or otherwise shielded from direct contact with the palms or fingers, so the gloves don't cause blisters with heavy use.

A good test for the quality of leather gloves is to put them on and flex your hands. The leather should not "bite" anywhere, and it should feel smooth on the hand. Well-made leather gloves have oils added in the tanning process to help keep them supple. A dry, rough feeling often indicates cheap tanning.

Construction also makes a noticeable difference. The usual run of leather gloves are sewn from four pieces—fingers, palm, front, and back—in what is known as the "gun" pattern. The best garden gloves, however, are sewn in the "klute" pattern, where the back of each finger is cut out separately to improve dexterity.

Cowhide gloves. Cowhide is the most common material used for garden gloves, and even if a glove is made of some other leather, a second layer of cowhide may be sewn across the palm for strength. Cowhide is tough: in abrasion tests, it lasts one-third longer than deerskin or goatskin. Furthermore, the grain is often tight and attractive. Its one drawback is that it stiffens after wetting.

Pigskin gloves. Only pigskin is tougher than cowhide. Pigskin tanning was once a primitive process and gloves made from this leather were rough and uncomfortable. Now pigskin gloves are as supple as cowhide. And although they have a somewhat coarser, less pretty grain, they will probably last for as long as you garden, or until you lose them—whichever comes first.

Goatskin and deerskin gloves. Although these leather gloves aren't as strong as cowhide or pigskin, they're more supple and just the thorns of the bramble patch may penetrate them, but the pricks will not tear the leather because the grain is tight and well knit.

Sheepskin gloves. Sheepskin is the weakest leather, but it's also the most comfortable. Sheepskin gloves are excellent for light flower gardening, and their creamy white color gives them an elegant look. The grain structure of sheepskin, however, is such that once the top grain has worn down, the glove is liable to tear. In the old days, cowboys who wanted to keep their roping hand soft enough for the ladies used up sheepskin gloves one after another because the leather secretes lanolin that conditions the hands.

RUBBER GLOVES: If you choose to wear leather, of course, there will always be the thorn that manages to penetrate it. (It's pretty surprising when pruning hawthorns to find that one of those 2" spines has hit the flesh of your palm at just the proper angle to skewer you right through the glove.) Gardeners usually tolerate these small ouches, but if you're working a great deal with thorny plants, you may want to invest in a pair of gardener's rubber gloves.

These are not the gloves that you wear when you do the hand wash. Rather, they are made of good thick rubber or a synthetic rubber on a foundation of comfortable cotton cloth. Rubber gloves are also good for gardening in mud. Like a good pair of clogs, they can simply be hosed off when they need cleaning without fear of the gloves going stiff on you.

Sheepskin gloves are excellent for light flower gardening, and their creamy white color gives them an elegant look.

Gloves

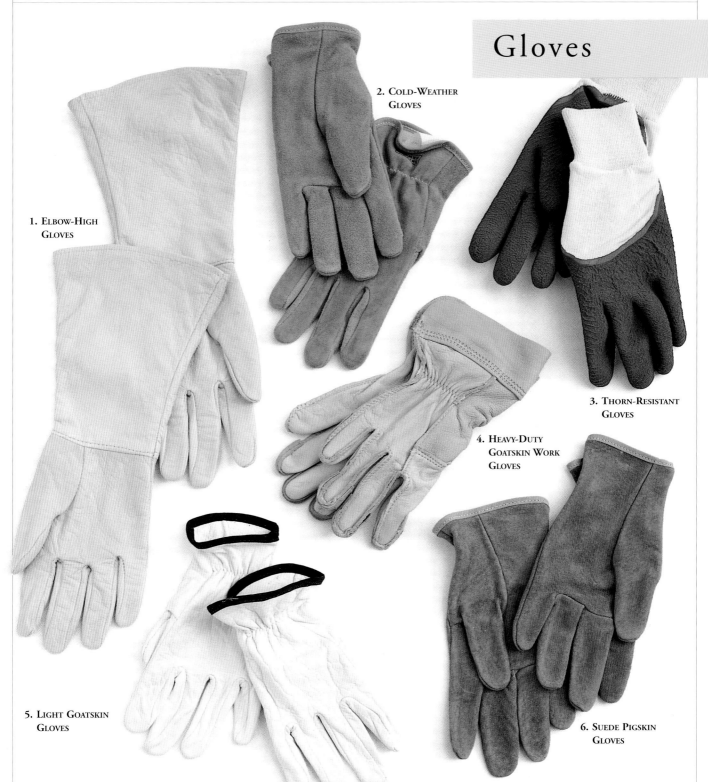

1. ELBOW-HIGH GLOVES

2. COLD-WEATHER GLOVES

3. THORN-RESISTANT GLOVES

4. HEAVY-DUTY GOATSKIN WORK GLOVES

5. LIGHT GOATSKIN GLOVES

6. SUEDE PIGSKIN GLOVES

1. **ELBOW-HIGH GLOVES:** These gloves feature a protective gauntlet designed to shield wrists and arms from thorns and scratches. Medium-weight goatskin resists tears and punctures.

2. **COLD-WEATHER GLOVES:** Fleece- or wool-lined gloves are the best choice in cold weather if the outer skin is puncture-proof. These gloves feature an all-leather exterior with fleece lining for maximum warmth without sacrificing movement or control.

3. **THORN-RESISTANT GLOVES:** Rose gardeners must have a pair of thorn-resistant gloves. They are also useful when weeding or land clearing, and they tolerate wetness. These are made of 100% cotton knit covered with a textured latex surface that resists punctures while maintaining a sure grip.

4. **HEAVY-DUTY GOATSKIN WORK GLOVES:** These gloves are at the top of the line. Crafted from supple but indestructible goatskin, the finger seams are turned outside and all the seams are positioned away from contact points to avoid blisters. The 4" cuff is made of split cowhide to protect wrists.

5. **LIGHT GOATSKIN GLOVES:** Suited to light or moderate tasks, these unlined white gloves feature a goatskin exterior infused with lanolin to guard against chapping and abrasion. The next best thing to wearing no gloves at all.

6. **SUEDE PIGSKIN GLOVES:** An industry standard, these gloves are lightweight but thick enough to stand up to a solid day's work without tearing or puncturing. Suede pigskin adapts to the wearer's hand with use. An affordable, heavy-duty option that may or may not feature a lining.

HATS

A lot of good gardeners confess to having two sets of gardening clothes—one for the front yard and one for out back. The former are a pleasure to see and will look to the occasional passerby like a proper accompaniment to the beauty of the garden. The latter are the grubbiest of the grubby. Only in the backyard will you see ancient torn T-shirts, faded shirts, patched pants—and the hats that go with them.

CHOOSING A HAT

In the backyard, you wear the billed cap that Uncle Fred brought you from the John Deere dealership in his hometown, or a baseball cap so old that it's frayed at the bill. It's a kind of rough-and-ready kick to don a cap with somebody's motto or logo on the front. Even the most style-conscious gardener may buy this same sort of simple cap, with a slightly longer bill to keep off a lower-angled sun, from mail-order catalogs. Some billed caps come with netted backs for working in the garden in high summer.

PANAMA HATS: The front yard is the place for panama hats. Actually made in Ecuador from the young leaves of a plant called jipijapa *(Carludovica palmata),* these hats are the traditional garb of men and women in Latin America who harvest in the hot sun. The great thing about them is they not only look stylish and are woven into numerous different shapes, but they also "breathe" remarkably well so you don't end up with a sweaty, overheated head. If you put on a panama hat with the intention of doing some gardening, however, be sure it's the kind that has a chin strap to hold it on while you're working.

CLOTH AND CANVAS HATS: Cloth hats, depending on their condition, are either front yard or backyard hats. An old Stetson cowboy hat may be worn through by finger pressure on both the front and back of the crown, but still it gives its wearer great pleasure and protection. The rollable soft canvas hats, with 2"–3" brims, come in many colors and, though often used as sun hats by hikers, will work equally well in the garden. The more serious oiled cotton duck hats, like the best cowboy hats, are made for gardeners who don't go indoors when the first raindrops fall. (The best Stetson advertisement shows a picture of a cowboy using his hat to water his horse and, indeed, the hat can serve that purpose.) A good rain hat should be able to withstand a whole day in a Pacific Coast rainstorm—one of those winter blasts when the clouds open up for hours on end.

It's a kind of rough-and-ready kick to don a cap with somebody's motto or logo on the front.

Hats

1. **PANAMA LIFE-GUARD HAT:** This lightweight Panama has a 5" brim. Five eyelets allow air circulation. Cotton cord with chin strap keeps hat on head or around neck.

2. **COTTON HAT:** A classic design topping gardeners throughout the warmer months. Crushable cotton means the hat can be stored in a pocket or bag until needed.

Six eyelets provide air circulation, while the padded brim stays pliable. An affordable, washable option that will keep the user's head cool and shielded from the sun.

3. **CHIN STRAP PANAMA HAT:** Similar to the Panama Lifeguard Hat, this design originated in Ecuador and features a rounded lid, 5" brim, and leather chin strap. Breathable fibers keep the head cool while protecting the face and back of neck from the sun.

4. **RAIN HAT:** Cotton rain hat features a thinner brim and taller lid to protect the wearer from rainfall. Rolls up for easy storage when the sun comes out.

1. PANAMA LIFEGUARD HAT

2. COTTON HAT

3. CHIN STRAP PANAMA HAT

4. RAIN HAT

PANTS AND SHIRTS

The garden can wreak havoc on ordinary clothing. Pants tear at the knees; a shirt catches on a tough twig and its elbow hole gapes. As a result, the gardener who wears the wrong clothes soon comes to resemble a scarecrow. No professional would tolerate such a look of rags and patches, and neither should you. Choose instead good, heavy-weight cotton or linen garden clothes.

CHOOSING PANTS AND SHIRTS

Appropriate garden clothing uses heavyweight or two-ply yarns rein-forced at the stress points for durability. A twill weave, in which each warp thread crosses two or three weft threads, creates a subtle diagonal pattern and increases the lengthwise strength of the cloth. This is a valuable feature considering how often you must stoop, bend, kneel, or even crawl in the garden, stressing the cloth up and down rather than side to side.

Manufacturers once intentionally put sizing, a kind of starch, into their clothes to make them look fulsome and presentable on the shelves. But because many people are sensitive to stiff cloth, there are now finishing treatments that soften the cloth instead. "Prewashed" denim, twill, or canvas has a fine, soft feel to it. In fact, prewashing also involves gentle abrasion. The cloth is put in a hot-water wash together with lava rocks that have been soaked in chlorine, so chemical reactions and mechanical scraping account for much of the softening. A "permanent press" finish on natural fibers likewise softens the cloth, but because formaldehyde is involved, it's a good idea to avoid it. (Formaldehyde is not used for permanent press clothing that is woven of mixed natural and polyester materials.)

A canvas weave, the simplest pattern of one warp to one weft (used since Egyptian times at least), may be slightly weaker, but canvas pants and shirts are scarcely less durable provided they're well rein-forced with bar tacking. Lightweight canvas pants and shirts should feel no stiffer than chambray or broadcloth. Medium- and heavy-weight canvases are less supple but not uncomfortable, and they can withstand serious, constant abuse without tearing or coming apart at the seams.

COTTON: Both twill and canvas weaves, regardless of weight or finishing, are typically made with cotton yarns. Cotton is an excellent fiber because it lasts a long time and is able to "breathe." Cotton fab-ric, for all its apparent inertness, is actually a transformer that wicks

The gardener who wears the wrong clothes soon comes to resemble a scarecrow.

moisture away from the skin, converts it into vapor, and expels it into the air. Most cotton cloth takes up 6% of its own weight in water. Only wool breathes better.

LINEN: Although in theory wool would make fine gardening clothes, it's too expensive to produce in the necessary weights, so the best alternative to cotton is linen. Most people associate linen with vacations in the tropics, but it's an excellent cloth for garden clothes. It breathes just as well as cotton, and because the individual fibers are longer (linen is spun from long flax stems, while cotton is spun from short cotton bolls), it's stronger than cotton in any weave. There are only two drawbacks to linen: first, it's more expensive than cotton, and second, its longer threads tend to wrinkle more easily.

PROTECTING YOUR KNEES

All good garden pants and shirts are cut full so they don't "bite." Just the same, there are places where, no matter how your clothes are cut, the ground is likely to try to bite you. In these cases, you may want additional protection for your knees.

Little kneelers, like small prayer benches, can be toted around the garden to protect your knees. Less cumbersome, however, are the pants that come complete with twin knee pockets, filled with replaceable foam rubber padding. The best of these have a water-resistant layer in the knee pocket to keep your knees from getting soaked. You must try on these pants before you buy them to be sure that the padding falls where your knees do inside the pants.

In addition, for gardeners who need to go rapidly from gardening to other pursuits, there are quick-change versions of the standard work clothes. Gardening chaps and aprons strap quickly over your clothes, protecting slacks or skirts as well as your skin; most are fitted with many deep pockets for tools and other necessaries.

SKIN PROTECTION

No gardener in history has escaped entirely from pests and plants that attack the skin. The best way to deal with insect pests is to use a repellent that contains no more than 50% DEET. If you live in deer-tick country, however, repellent is not enough. It's better to not garden in shorts if you are going to encounter any underbrush, and to keep your pants tucked into your boots. After spending the day outdoors, do a thorough "tick check"—you may catch the little demon in time. Even if it has dug in for a bite, you may still have a couple of hours before it begins to inject the bacteria that cause Lyme disease. If you remove a deer tick that has already bitten, be sure to save the tick and go directly to the doctor.

To keep poison ivy under control after exposure, wash the affected area immediately with mineral spirits or rubbing alcohol. Put clothes through a long hot-cycle wash and double rinse. Wash off shoes thoroughly with water.

Clothing

1. CANVAS WORK SHIRT: A valuable layer of protection against the elements, this work shirt is made from triple-stitched, tightly woven, machine-washable canvas. Good for layering over other clothes or on its own. This particular example is so durable, it should withstand years of steady use.

2. GARDENER'S PANTS: These long gardening pants sport several roomy pockets plus interior knee pockets that hold removable knee pads. Made of sturdy cotton canvas, they are heavier than Farmer's Pants, but their loose fit does not restrict movement. Elasticized waist adjusts for comfort.

3. COTTON BANDANNA: A lightweight, washable bandanna, scarf, or rag is a great item to have on hand, especially when the sun heats up. Wrapped around the head, it helps keep sweat and dirt out of the eyes and is also handy for brow mopping or seed gathering.

4. COTTON T-SHIRT: Lightweight, breathable cotton T-shirts are a practical, affordable gardening essential. Top-quality cotton holds its shape, wicks away moisture, and lasts much longer than cheaper varieties. T-shirts have the added bonus of being recyclable: use them as cleanup rags when they are worn out.

5. DENIM OVERALLS: Long or short, overalls have been the working pants of choice for generations of outdoor workers. Sturdy cotton denim gets better with use and age, while the adjustable straps and lack of waist allow maximum movement and comfort. Deep pockets store supplies and small tools, with an added side loop for hanging a hammer or pruner. This example features the short version, suitable for activities that don't include kneeling.

6. CANVAS VEST: A handy layer that helps when transporting small items and tools to and from the garden. Large armholes and flexible canvas fabric don't restrict movement. This example features four extra-large pouches in front and a two-sided pocket in back.

7. FARMER'S PANTS: Based on a Japanese design, these pants are a durable example of the best in gardening wear. Lightweight cotton canvas keeps the wearer cool and clean, while the deep front pockets and rear pocket tote tools and supplies. Knee pockets have a slot for foam knee pads. The waist adjusts for comfort, and the elasticized cuffs accommodate boots without admitting weeds and burrs. Machine washable.

1. CANVAS WORK SHIRT

2. GARDENER'S PANTS

3. COTTON BANDANNA

4. COTTON T-SHIRT

5. DENIM OVERALLS

8. FLORAL COTTON SMOCK: A washable, lightweight smock protects clothing while the bright print hides dirt and stains between washings. This particular example may be worn like a jacket over several layers for added warmth or thrown over a T-shirt to protect against the sun's rays. Large front pockets are riveted for extra strength. This smock has side slits and back pleats for total freedom.

8. FLORAL COTTON SMOCK

4. COTTON T-SHIRT

6. CANVAS VEST

9. APRON, KNEE PADS, GOGGLES

7. FARMER'S PANTS

9. APRON, KNEE PADS, GOGGLES: An apron is a useful item to have on hand near the potting bench, the vegetable garden, or anywhere a lot of loose dirt or mud abounds. This example features thick, washable cotton, adjustable comfort straps that cross in the back to distribute weight evenly across shoulders, and two large front pockets. Knee pads are essential to protect sensitive knee joints when kneeling down to weed or harvest. These feature thick (½"), dense foam rubber pads covered with fabric shells. The pads attach securely with elastic webbing and adjustable clasps that won't restrict up-and-down movement. Clear plastic goggles are an affordable safety item available at any hardware or garden supply store. Essential when using swinging, chopping, or driving tools, or when pruning heavily, the best goggles fit snugly and wrap around the sides of the head to protect eyes from dangerous peripheral flying objects.

JACKETS AND VESTS

No matter where you live, there comes a time of year when it's too cold to work in shirtsleeves. Even California in the autumn may be in the forties when you're raking leaves. In the Northeast, the days of late autumn, when you are out pruning and turning the soil in the vegetable plot, can be days of frost.

For this reason, it's a good idea to have a coat dedicated to garden work that can serve as the outer layer of your cold-weather clothes. It should be simple, durable, loose-fitting, and easily cleaned—a denim jacket or a barn coat will do. You should be able to fit a sweater or a sweatshirt underneath it, or have a wool lining that zips or buttons into it. Regions of the country each have their own favorite for this time of year. The West favors the short jean jacket; the Midwest, the Carhart; and the Northeast, the Bean barn jacket.

Recently, British and Australian waxed cotton coats have become popular because they are virtually waterproof. Be aware, however, that they pick up dirt very quickly and can't be machine-washed or dry-cleaned. (Rubbing them with a special wax will renew them, though it may not restore the original color.) If you buy one of coats, choose a deeper color like forest green.

The gardener who wants to avoid unnecessary trips to and from the toolshed will opt for a durable cotton vest. These can be found in many different incarnations, but the best have numerous pockets for hand pruners, seeds, twine, or plant labels. Traditionally, a quality vest will have four pockets in front—two small and two large—and one large divided back pocket. Be sure to check that the pockets are reinforced. Some vest pockets are bar-tacked, like denim jeans.

ANATOMY OF A VEST

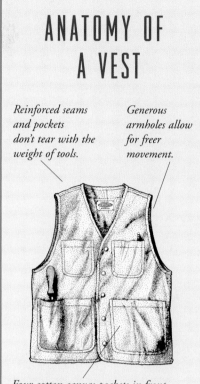

Reinforced seams and pockets don't tear with the weight of tools.

Generous armholes allow for freer movement.

Four cotton canvas pockets in front are deep enough for small tools.

Jackets

1. **DENIM JACKET:** The all-purpose, machine-washable choice for chilly gardening days in spring and fall. Heavy-duty denim fabric stands up to seasons of dirt and wear but is light enough to not restrict movement. The button-up front and long torso keep body warmth in.

2. **OILCLOTH JACKET:** A top-quality, early-season jacket based on a traditional English design. Rain rolls off the waxed oilcloth fabric, while the wool lining keeps the wearer snug even in frosty temperatures. A zippered front with snaps keeps drafts out. This jacket is an investment, but one that only gets better with age.

3. **NYLON RAIN JACKET:** A standard rain jacket with a waterproof nylon shell that has polyurethane backing and taped seams. The cuffs and waist are elasticized to keep out the elements and the front zips up. Drawstring hood lends added warmth and protection. Two large front pockets accommodate gloves, seed packets, and other small supplies.

1. DENIM JACKET

2. OILCLOTH JACKET

3. NYLON RAIN JACKET

Chapter Thirteen

Care and Storage

There comes a day when you know the gardening season is over. Harvest is done—even the last root crops have been pulled up. The hoses and the

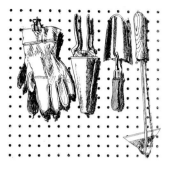

outdoor spigots are drained. All the red and yellow leaves have been raked and put into the compost heap. A hard frost has wilted the impatiens. Your arborist has finished the big autumn pruning and left you with two dozen rounds of maple to split into firewood.

Now is the time to pamper your garden tools, so that next year they will serve you flawlessly. Indeed, after a season's use, some of the tools in your collection can look pretty sorry. The pruners have gone dull. The end of the shovel is notched. There are cakes of mud on everything. And the saw blade is coming loose from its handle. Cleaning and sharpening, therefore, are the last gardening tasks of the year. And once they have been accomplished, each tool can be put safely away in its own place in the garden shed or garage, with no strays left rusting out of sight in a damp corner under a dirty tarp.

I'll trace this garden oer & oer
Meditate on each sweet flower
Thinking of each happy hour

—WALT WHITMAN

FINISHING TOUCHES

First, turn your attention to the tools with long handles. Use an old plastic kitchen spoon, a stiff-bristled brush, or a wooden wedge—called a "woodman"—to scrape off the greater part of the dried muck. Then dip the head of each tool several times into a five-gallon bucket filled with coarse sand that has been lightly impregnated with vegetable oil. The head should come out clean, if not gleaming. If any rust remains, sand it off with a sanding block. (There are great rubberized models of these available.) To finish the head, wipe it down with an oiled rag.

Now look over the saws, pruners, loppers, and trowels. Gently sand away any spots of rust, and lubricate the fulcrums with a drop of oil. Replace any loose or missing screws.

LOOKING SHARP

The next area of maintenance is sharpening. Take out the file handle and screw on a fresh 8" bastard mill flat file. This is a file of medium fineness. It will not remove too much material or put too fine an edge upon the spade and the hoe, but it can work out the dinks and chips and make a good straight bevel. Furthermore, it is fine enough to use in sharpening the ax or the scythe, provided that you finish them with a good Arkansas oilstone or Carborundum whetstone afterward. You might tackle the pruning saws with a round file, but you'll probably be better off sending them to a professional to sharpen. The reel mower, likewise, even though you've cleaned it yourself, will benefit from professional sharpening.

Set each tool to be sharpened into a vise and draw the file firmly across it, keeping to the existing bevel. An ax bevel may be 30° or less; a shovel or a hoe bevel is closer to 45°. If a blade is beveled only on one side, sharpen only that side. Unscrew your loppers and bypass pruners, and be sure to sharpen these, too.

The proper file angle is only half of the sharpening equation: the direction of the stroke is the other part. All sharpening should be done in motions away from your body. Lift the file on the back stroke and reset it on the tool with each successive stroke.

The final step is to spray all the metal toolheads with a penetrating oil and wipe them clean. Take a container of boiled linseed oil and rub down each wooden handle with the oil. (You can buy boiled linseed oil; you no longer have to boil it yourself.) If it's a first-year tool, lightly sand away the factory's varnish coating before you use the rubbing oil.

HANG THEM HIGH

Many people like to hang large tools like shovels, spades, forks, rakes, and hoes by their heads. Sturdy pairs of dowels set into a solid wood backing will serve for all these tools, and if you have more than one rake, just lengthen one pair of dowels to hang both together.

It's a simple system, but it can waste energy and requires attention. You have to swing the heavy head up to put the tool away, and carefully swing it down again to retrieve it without damaging your head. Furthermore, the anonymity of dowels seems to invite disorder.

Before your tools sit idle for the winter, be sure to sharpen and clean them in preparation for spring.

With galvanized steel tool hooks and cam holders, you can hang your major tools head down so that removing them is as effortless as lifting them up. And each tool can have its assigned hook, designated by either a label or an outline of the tool actually painted on the wall.

Hooks work for D-handle tools like spades and forks. Some need to be mounted on pegboard, but others can be screwed straight into the wall. The cam hanger works like the cams on sailboats that are used to secure ropes. Two jaws with blunt teeth close upon the straight handle of the hoe, shovel, or rake, holding it in place.

KEEP THEM TOGETHER

Most gardeners like to make a place on the wall even for small tools like secateurs, pruning saws, clippers, and weeders. However, this may be taking a good thing too far. Since groups of small tools are usually needed all at the same time, it's better to keep them together and ready to move as a unit.

Carpenter's tool bags won't really do for storage. The two-tray models are not at all adapted to the size of garden tools, and the big canvas versions are nothing but glorified sacks. Far better is a bag that comes equipped with enough exterior pockets to hold all of your major small tools, plus a pair of gloves. The most ingenious one of these is a simple apron-like tool carrier that belts securely around any 5-gallon bucket. It has twelve pockets—more than enough for the average gardener—and the interior of the bucket can hold other tools or garden supplies. It's even sold with a plastic lid so you can turn the bucket into a comfortable seat.

Properly stored tools not only last longer but also give a sense of order to the toolshed.

HOSE STORAGE

Part of ensuring the long life of a hose involves properly storing it. Of the range of options available, almost all will lengthen the life of your hose. There is a beautiful terra-cotta pot made specifically for hose storage. Coil your hose into it like a snake charmer's cobra until you're ready to draw it out again. Attractive as it is, the hose pot also illustrates the surprisingly important reasons for coiling a hose: you won't run over it by accident, and sensitive vinyl is kept out of the direct glare of the sun.

Less obtrusive are the hangers and reels that you can suspend from the wall of the tool or potting shed. A simple construction is preferable for such devices. They should be made of sturdy, unbendable steel capable of holding as much hose as necessary. There are hangers available that will hold 250' of hose, or as little as 50'. However, a hose cart or wagon may be a better choice for storing because it can be moved around during the off-season if, for example, you need to get at the snowblower or create more space for a small woodpile.

A TIME TO RENEW

The last rays of the westering sun can glance off the door and make the oiled metal shine dully. Everything is cleaned, oiled, and sharpened. The large tools are carefully hung, and the smaller ones are stowed together in a place where they will remain dry and ready for next year. Neatly coiled, the hose assumes its natural shape. The clean, dry sprinklers hang in a corner. The tarps and bags are stacked. The bins of soil amendments and lime are covered beneath the bench. The stakes and supports have bins of their own, and all remains of ties or string have been removed from them. The tomato cages are clean and folded. Over everything, there is the warm damp smell of oil mixed with the sharp odor of wood smoke.

Somebody has lit a fire at the hearth. The sun has set. The gardening season is over. It's time to go in.

Care and Storage

1. **MAPLE TOOL RACK:** This superior example of a classic tool-hanging rack features 22 removable pegs that adapt to almost any tool imaginable. Easily installed on a wall, the rack is made of hand-sanded premium white and northern hard rock maple. One of the best ways to save space and keep valuable tools clean and dry. LENGTH 46", HEIGHT 2".

2. **METAL TOOL RACK:** Performs the same function as the Maple Tool Rack, but is crafted from heavy-duty steel with a coating of baked black epoxy. Some may prefer this rack's utilitarian look, bi-level design (long-handled tools below, hand tools above), and rot-resistant materials. Upper hooks slide to adjust to spacing needs. Holds up to 11 tools. LENGTH 29½", HEIGHT 12".

3. **TUBULAR HOSE HANGER:** Fashioned from high-tech, chrome-plated tubular steel (the same material used to make bike racks), this hose hanger is tough but extremely lightweight. It will mount on any wall and will hold 150' of ⅝" hose. 11¾" × 8" × 7".

4. **HOSE HANGER:** This sturdy device mounts to any wood, stucco, or masonry wall and is fabricated from solid steel finished in weatherproof polyurethane. It will hold 150' of ⅝" hose and will last longer than the standard hangers found in most hardware stores. 5¾" × 8" × 11".

5. **TOOL CARRIER AND SEAT:** Combining a bucket, carrier, and seat, this handy contraption has a removable, water-resistant nylon apron with deep pockets to tote smaller tools and supplies out to the garden. The 5-gallon plastic bucket has an air-cushioned lid that does double time as a seat. 12" DIA. × 15".

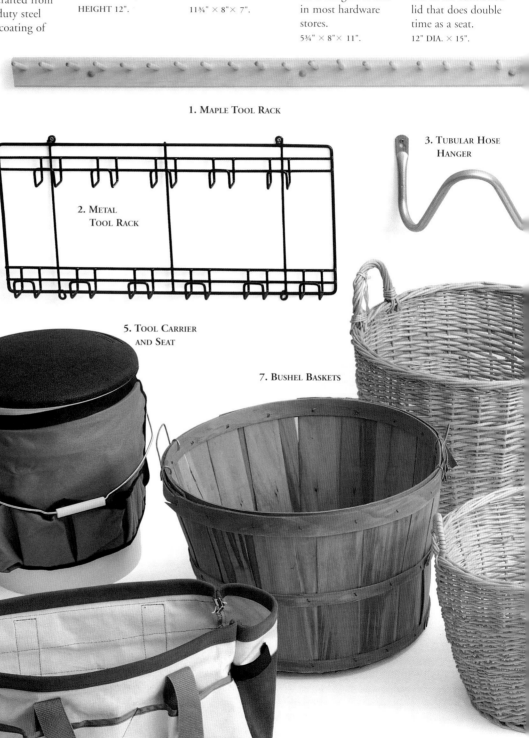

1. MAPLE TOOL RACK

3. TUBULAR HOSE HANGER

2. METAL TOOL RACK

5. TOOL CARRIER AND SEAT

7. BUSHEL BASKETS

6. CANVAS TOTE BAG

6. **CANVAS TOTE BAG:** Large pockets along each side carry weeding, cultivating, and pruning tools, as well as other necessities such as gloves, seed packets, and twine. The bottom is made of stiff oiled leather to prevent the bag from collapsing when it is set down. The canvas handles are reinforced with leather at the maximum point of pressure. The large center compartment will hold an ample harvest. 9" × 16" × 9½".

7. **BUSHEL BASKETS:** See page 242.

8. **COMPOST PAIL:** See page 247.

9. **GALVANIZED BUSHEL BASKET:** See page 246.

10. **GALVANIZED BUCKET:** See page 247.

11. **HOSE POT:** An attractive alternative way to coil and store 25' of ⅝" hose, this pot is made of terracotta and features a hole near the bottom for drainage and easy access to a faucet. This choice may be preferred by patio and rooftop gardeners who need to save space. 14" DIA. × 10".

12. **HOSE GUIDE:** See page 197.

13. **HOLSTER:** A stiff, clip-on leather holster is a necessity for protecting the blades of saws, knives, and hand pruners. Many tools come with their own holsters, but it is always useful to have additional ones on hand. This one holds hand pruners. 3" × 6".

14. **CERAMIC FILE:** A 4" long-lasting, pocket-size ceramic sharpening stone for honing the small blades of hand pruners.

15. **8" FILE:** A long-lasting file sharpener for the larger blades and tines of spades, forks, hoes, and axes, this steel file features an 8" blade that is single cut on one side, double cut on the other.

16. **DIAMOND FLAT FILE:** A small, pointed sharpening tool that is good for the individual teeth of pruning saws. Light and precise, the 4½" blade is diamond-edged for a lifetime of use.

4. HOSE HANGER

9. GALVANIZED BUSHEL BASKET

10. GALVANIZED BUCKET

11. HOSE POT

8. COMPOST PAIL

12. HOSE GUIDE

13. HOLSTER

14. CERAMIC FILE

15. 8" FILE

16. DIAMOND FLAT FILE

Hose Reels

1. **HOSE CART:** An ample, freestanding cart for coiling and storing up to 350' of ⅝" hose. The frame is made of heavy-duty steel that is double-coated with baked enamel to resist rust. The crank is zinc-plated and the whole cart is easily wheeled to its proper place of storage or use. 21" × 40" × 37½".

2. **METAL REEL:** This chrome-plated metal hose reel stores up to 150' of ⅝" hose. It has a swing-out option that allows it to be mounted flush to a wall or pulled out at a right angle. It can also be picked up and moved. Side-winding hand crank allows user to coil and uncoil hose with minimum effort. 18" DIA. × 12".

3. **PLASTIC REEL:** An affordable, compact hose reel made of UV- and rot-resistant polypropylene. Portable or mountable, it stores up to 50' of ⅝" hose. A good choice for lightweight hoses. 14" DIA. × 4".

1. HOSE CART

2. METAL REEL

3. PLASTIC REEL

INDEX